YEMENITE JEWRY

Jewish Literature and Culture

Series Editor, Alvin Rosenfeld

YEMENITE JEWRY

Origins, Culture, and Literature

REUBEN AHRONI

INDIANA UNIVERSITY PRESS • BLOOMINGTON

To my father
who instilled in me a love for learning

Manufactured in the United States of America

Library of Congress Cataloging-in-Publication Data

Ahroni, Reuben.
Yeminite Jewry.

(Jewish literature and culture)
Bibliography: p.
Includes index.
1. Jews—Yemen—History. 2. Judaism—Yemen—History.
3. Yemen—Ethnic relations. I. Title. II. Series.
DS135.Y4A46 1985 953'.32004924 84-48649
ISBN 0-253-36807-3
1 2 3 4 5 89 88 87 86

CONTENTS

PREFACE ix

Introduction 1
1. Encounter with Yemenite Jews in Palestine 1
2. Yemen and Its People 8
3. The Social Structure of the People of Yemen 12
4. Yemenite Jewry: Social Structure 15

I Antiquity of Jewish Settlement in Arabia 20
1. Scarcity of Historical Records 20
2. Early Jewish Settlement of Yemen 24
3. Biblical Evidence of Early Jewish Settlement in Arabia 27
4. Extra-Biblical References to Jewish Settlement in Arabia: Nabonidus' Inscriptions 34

II Post-Biblical and Pre-Islamic Times 38
1. Early Historical Sources 38
2. Mass Judaization in the Kingdom of Ḥimyar 42
3. Judaization of Ḥimyar 43
4. Dhū Nuwās 44
5. Conclusions 47

III Yemenite Jewry in the Early and High Medieval Ages 49
1. Muḥammad and the Jews: Dhimmat al-Nabī 49
2. The Founding of the Zaydī State in Yemen 53
3. Al-Hādī's Attitude toward Non-Muslims 54
4. Natan'el Ibn Fayyūmī 56
5. The Geniza Documents 67
6. Traditions, Customs, and Religious Writings 72

IV Jewish Literary Creativity in Yemen in the Thirteenth and Fourteenth Centuries 78
1. The Rasūlid Period 78
2. The Ottoman Occupation of Yemen 82
3. Rabbi Zecharia al-Ḍahrī (ca. 1516–ca. 1581) 83
4. The Expulsion of the Turks from Yemen 87
5. Rabbi Shalom Shabazi (1619–after 1679) 89

V The Impact of the Sabbatean Movement on the Jews of Yemen 100
1. General Background 100
2. Jewish Reaction to the Messianic Call of Sabbatai Ṣevi 102
3. The Reaction of the Imam 104
4. The ᶜAtarot (Headgear) Edict 111
5. The Earlocks Edict 112
6. The Latrines or Scrapers Edict 114
7. The Orphans Edict 117

VI The Exile of the Yemenite Jews to Mauzaᶜ (1679) 121
1. The Cause of the Exile 121
2. Demolition of Synagogues and Expulsion 125
3. The Annulment of the Decree 131
4. The Effects of the Exile 132
5. Jewish Reaction to Galut Mauzaᶜ 133

VII Yemenite Jewry in the Eighteenth and Nineteenth Centuries 136
1. Carsten Niebuhr 136
2. Rabbi Shalom ᶜIrāqī 137
3. Rabbi Yeḥıa Ṣāliḥ 139
4. The Decline of the Qāsimī State 141
5. The British Occupation of Aden (1839) 144
6. Messianic Expectations: The Two Shukr Kuḥeils 145
7. The Second Ottoman Occupation (1872–1914) 148
8. Yosef ᶜAbdallāh: A Yemenite Pseudo-Messiah 152
9. Endeavors for Reform: The *Dor-Deᶜah* 154
10. The End of the Ottoman Occupation 156

Epilogue In the Land of Israel 159

NOTES 170
BIBLIOGRAPHY 204
INDEX 221

ILLUSTRATIONS

Yemenite Jews carrying Torah Scrolls with them on their way to Israel 2
Old manuscripts were often used for the bindings of books 23
Yemenite Jews with earlocks 113

MAP

Yemen 9

PREFACE

The significance of this study lies in the fact that such a comprehensive treatment of the origins, culture and literary creativity of Yemenite Jewry has not been made heretofore. This fact is, however, not at all suprising. The field of Yemenite studies, in itself, has so far been scarcely cultivated. A great deal of the material is still in unpublished manuscripts in the possession of public institutions and private collectors. Moreover, the period stretching from antiquity to the end of the sixteenth century is extremely deficient in source material and is, therefore, very difficult to explore.

The present work is not intended to be an exhaustive treatment of Yemenite Jewry. The topic is vast and complex and could easily fill several volumes. Considerations of space have forced me to limit the scope of my study mainly to the presentation of an accessible prologue to salient aspects of the history, culture, and literature of the Jews of Yemen. Thus many areas have been accorded only a cursory treatment. Despite its limitations, this work does, however, offer a background that no single study has so far provided.

As reflected in the Bibliography, I have gone through a vast number of works—biblical, post-biblical, classical, historical writings, rabbinic writings, Islamic writings (Qur'ān, Ḥadīth, historical works), and Genizah material—in order to glean every shred of information pertaining to the topic of my study. I have used in particular the extant Yemenite writings, Jewish and Muslim, in order to delineate some main features of Yemenite Jewry during the period under discussion.

To my best knowledge, all available and accessible primary sources relating to my work were utilized. A certain amount of material in these pages had to be drawn from secondary sources, in order to present a coherent synthesis of previous scholarship and ultimately as comprehensive a picture as possible of this unique community.

The uniqueness of Yemenite Jewry is underscored not only by the fact that it was one of the oldest of the Jewish communities in the Diaspora but also by its relative physical and spiritual isolation in a country which has been described by Ameen Riḥani as being "in itself a quarantine—people quarantined by religion." The story of its survival as the only non-Muslim minority in the midst of an extremely sectarian and fanatic Muslim regime is in itself a precious document of human history.

It should be noted that with the almost wholesale departure of Yemenite Jewry to Israel, which assumed the dimensions of a mass exodus after 1948, an end was brought to its pulsating life. Moreover, the rapid integration of the Yemenite Jews into the Jewish social pattern of Israel precipitates the loss of its distinctiveness. This fact makes investigation of this community all the more imperative. Needless to say, this work may be viewed as a pioneering attempt to bring a somewhat coherent picture of this unique community into the purview of the English reader. With very few exceptions, the subject in English literature is simply blank.

By and large Yemen and Yemenite Jewry are still the research-domain of a relatively few scholars. Among the most prominent scholars who greatly contributed to this field are S. D. Goitein, Yehuda Ratzaby, Yosef Kafiḥ, and Yosef Tobi. It is due to the activities of these and other scholars that Yemenite Jewry, to which comparatively little attention has been paid before, has come to be an object of scholarly interest. My indebtedness to them throughout the entire book is evident. My thoughts on a number of problems related to this study have been stimulated by my conversations with my colleague Michael Zwettler, who has given of his time and erudition most generously. Thanks are also due to Frederic Cadora, my Department's Chairman, for his constant encouragement, to Ben Fireman and Stafford Noble for their contribution to the polishing of this study from the linguistic standpoint, and to LaNell Corley and Jeanne Jaros who typed the manuscript with great care and precision, and above all to my wife who lavished upon me boundless love and understanding.

In the material sense, the writing of this book has been made possible by generous grants from The Ohio State University's Melton Center for Jewish Studies, College of Humanities, Graduate School, and Middle East Studies Center. My thanks are extended to all.

For the transliteration of Arabic and Hebrew names and terms I have generally followed the Library of Congress system for romanization. The transliteration of Hebrew, however, is provided with minimal diacritical marks. Translations from the Hebrew, Arabic, and other languages, unless otherwise stated, are by the author.

The Ohio State University — Reuben Ahroni
Columbus, Ohio

YEMENITE JEWRY

INTRODUCTION

1. Encounter With Yemenite Jews in Palestine

One of the most dramatic episodes in modern history is the wholesale transplantation of Yemenite Jewry, probably the oldest of the Jewish communities, to Israel. In a gigantic operation known as On Eagles' Wings (very often referred to as Operation Magic Carpet),[1] which began in 1949, about fifty thousand Yemenite Jews were flown to Israel. The newly born Jewish state was then experiencing the fantastic phenomenon of the ingathering of the exiles from many countries in the world. This massive influx of immigrants came with different languages, cultures, clothing, complexions, and folklore. Nevertheless, the uniqueness of the Yemenite immigrants was the most pronounced and the most fascinating. For hundreds of years, the Jews of Yemen had remained relatively intact and had existed with unbroken continuity in that same region, almost totally secluded from the rest of the world, veiled in mystery and myth. As a result of this isolation, it had developed specific cultural traits and peculiarities distinct from other Jewish communities. The *Palestine Post,* welcoming the first arrivals of the Yemenites with an editorial which highlighted the exotic nature of this historical saga, exclaimed in exultation that "no tale out of the Arabian Nights is so romantic and picturesque, so adventurous and exciting as the story of this homecoming of a whole community."[2]

The Yemenites, most of whom had never seen an airplane before, associated this "miraculous" operation with the biblical verse, "I bore you on eagles' wings" (Exod. 19:4). They viewed themselves as a severed part of Israel, and as Jeremiah (31:16–17) had prophesied, they were now "returning to their own habitations." Indeed, as Shlomo Barer, who had accompanied them on their way from Aden to Israel, aptly indicated, the Yemenite Jews belonged for all practical purposes to biblical times, moving in the agitated whirlpool of their unfamiliar, modern environment "in a state of almost apocalyptic frenzy." They created an interesting sight indeed since they

Yemenite Jews carrying Torah Scrolls with them on their way to Israel.
(From the collection of Nissim B. Gamlieli, Ramlah, Israel)

arrived with almost no possessions. Some of their elders clung to holy parchments or scrolls. It is no wonder that this colorful, exotic, religious people with their dangling earlocks were viewed by one of the American captains of the airlift as "prophets stepping out of the Bible."[3]

The drama of the "homecoming" of these Yemenites was heightened by the marked contrasts between their long-established, primitive ways of life and the highly developed civilization and technology of the new environment into which they were suddenly thrust. Thus, they scarcely knew how to use many of the things that they found in their new homeland, causing the Israeli newspapers at that time to note that in the reception camps these Yemenites at first slept *under* the beds provided for them, "for they do not understand the purpose of a bed." They wrapped the bed sheets around their shoulders as shawls; they did not know how to use the modern toilets; and they stared in amazement, bewilderment, and consternation at the moving traffic and the "magic" of technology around them. Indeed, as it has vividly been expressed, the planes that carried them to Israel spanned "not only a thousand miles but also a thousand years."[4]

Some of the many fascinating and intriguing stories which circulated with respect to the Yemenites were true, while others belonged to the realm of myth. Many of the exotic customs related by Jacob Saphir, who visited Yemen in 1859, were recalled when the Yemenites stepped off the planes.[5] For example, Saphir wrote that because polygamy was prevalent among the Yemenite Jews, it was customary for the Yemenite men to have two or three wives. Saphir also reported that it was usual for a Yemenite Jewish girl to be betrothed to her would-be husband while she was still very young, even before the age of puberty, "lest someone else acquire her." Her father, continued Saphir, received her marriage money, as well as her bill of divorce, in accordance with the Jewish halakhic law. Her bridegroom would wait for her until she reached the age of puberty, and then the marriage would be consummated. Thus, concluded Saphir, it was not unusual to see a twelve-year-old Yemenite girl who was already a mother.[6]

Some explanations, however, need to be made with regard to the previous description of the Yemenites and the reaction to them. To most of the post-1948 Israelis who, like the Yemenites themselves, comprised a motley group of new immigrants from diverse parts of the world, these Yemenites seemed like visitors from another planet. This was particularly true of those European Jews, survivors of the Holocaust, who had never seen an Oriental Jew before their arrival in Israel, much less a Yemenite Jew. But for those Israeli veterans, particularly the *ḥaluṣim,* "pioneers," of the first *ʿaliyyot,* "immigrations," the Yemenites were not unfamiliar. Throughout the centuries Yemenites had come to Israel either in very small groups or as individuals. The most famous group was that of the year 1881, preceding the noted arrival of the *Bilu* group from Russia.[7] These small groups of Yemenite immigrants were, however, much less fortunate than the airborne ones who arrived in Israel after 1948. The Yemenite families who emigrated to Israel in 1881 had literally traveled on foot to Ḥudaida or to the port of Aden, where they embarked on ships which carried them to Palestine. Hundreds of years of oppression, as well as occasional famine and tribulations in Yemen, had left their imprint upon the physical condition of the Yemenite Jews. These debilitating effects were exacerbated by the long, arduous, and perilous journey through the Yemenite desert. Those who survived this trip arrived in Palestine with emaciated bodies and depleted energies.

Their pitiful and decrepit appearance contrasted sharply with the image of the Yemenite Jews which had been created by Jewish travelers throughout the centuries. It had long been believed that the Arabian Peninsula, including Yemen, was the domain of the ten lost tribes. Jewish explorers, like Eldad the Danite (ca. 880), Benjamin of

Tudela (1165–1173), and Obadiah da Bertinora (1487–1490), had fed the imagination of world Jewry with colorful reports about the existence of wild and bellicose Jews in Arabia and elsewhere who enjoyed absolute freedom from the yoke of the Gentiles.[8] The Arabian Jews were depicted as being awesome in their ferocity, treading the land with their horses, dashing their enemies to pieces. Obadiah, for example, spoke about a Jewish tribe, descendants of Rechab, who were "of gigantic stature, one of whom can chase a thousand Arabs." The Arabs, according to Obadiah, had called this people El-Arabes, that is, children of the Almighty (*Shaddai*). The Arabs assert, Obadiah went on to say, "that one of these people is able to bear the burden of a camel in one hand, while in the other he holds the sword with which he fights."[9] Elsewhere, Obadiah claimed that he was told by some Jews from Aden, whom he had met in Jerusalem, about the existence in the Arabian desert of other Jewish tribes, descendants of Jacob. The Sambation River, which "throws up stones and sand and rests only on the Sabbath," surrounded their lands like a thread. No one, therefore, could cross over it.[10]

In all likelihood, these and other embroidered legends were intended to console and inspire the Jews in exile, as well as to refute Christian contentions that with the destruction of the Second Temple the scepter had departed from Judah. These legends did have, however, a far-reaching impact upon the Jews, for they fostered a strong belief in the continuing existence of these "lost" tribes. Messengers were sent by the Jewish communities in Palestine to Arabia and Ethiopia with a unique mission: to find the ten tribes. This search was motivated by the belief that the discovery of these tribes would expedite the process of redemption. Thus the intensive and persistent quest for these tribes had a pronounced messianic implication.[11]

But the physical features of the first waves of Yemenite Jews were totally incompatible with this romantic literary image. It is little wonder that they were looked upon by the Ashkenazi Jews with utter disappointment. How do the Yemenite Jews account for their downfall from a prominent and influential position, as they claimed, to a most debased social status? How could these formerly prosperous masters, who had been in total command of their fortunes, have sunk to their abject contemporary circumstances, those of a humiliated community, subject to the mercy and whim of others? An intriguing story current among the Yemenite Jews attributes their social deterioration to an unhappy incident that supposedly occurred between their forefathers and Ezra the Scribe in 538 B.C.E.[12] To judge from the extant Yemenite Jewish writings, this episode was first recorded by the Yemenite Rabbi Shelomo ʿAdani.[13] In the introduction to his book *Melekhet Shelomo,* which is an exegesis on the Mishna, ᶜAdani wrote:

> It has also been transmitted to us that we are [the descendants] of that group whom Ezra called upon to return [to Jerusalem] at the building of the Second Temple, but they refused. Then Ezra cursed them, condemning them to an everlasting life of misery. Indeed, as a result of [those] sins, we have been afflicted with both spiritual and material poverty.[14]

The incident is related with various embellishments. The version recorded by Rabbi Yeḥia Ṣāliḥ provides us with the reason that lay behind the rejection of Ezra's call.[15] The Yemenite Jews, wrote Rabbi Ṣāliḥ, were then convinced of the futility of their return, for they foresaw that the Second Temple too would be destroyed and that Israel would again go into exile. Thus, according to Rabbi Ṣāliḥ, the Yemenite Jews viewed Ezra's initiative as premature, since the final salvation was still far removed in time; "why should we then," they reasoned, "suffer afflictions once again? It is better for us to stay where we are now and worship God. . . ."[16]

A third version, that of Saphir, introduces two additional elements into the story: (a) Ezra himself came to Yemen to plead with the Jews to return with him to Jerusalem, and (b) An angry exchange of curses took place between Ezra and the Jews of Yemen as a result of their refusal to heed his call. Ezra laid a disastrous curse upon them and the Yemenites retaliated with one of their own, condemning him to be buried outside the boundaries of the land of Israel. Both of these curses, so Saphir's version goes on to say, did materialize: the Jews of Yemen were deprived of repose and everlasting peace, and Ezra was buried in the wilderness of Baṣra. It is because of this curse, continues Saphir's version, that moments of peace and prosperity are rare and ephemeral among the Yemenite Jewish community. Saphir's story concludes with the following note: "To this day [the Yemenite Jews] hate him [Ezra] and refrain from naming their sons after him."[17]

The contention regarding the hostility that the Jews of Yemen supposedly harbored against Ezra is picked up by B. Lewin who claimed to have found a possible corroboration of this claim in a document discovered in the Cairo Geniza. In a letter of an unnamed Babylonian Gaon addressed to the Jews of Yemen, the sender, contended Lewin, refrains from using the usual benedictory formula which invokes the blessing of biblical personalities, since this formula includes Ezra. Thus, in his correspondence with Yemen, the sender used a special language: "We decree that you may be blessed by the *Yeshiva* [Talmudic college] and by all the houses of the prophets and of the righteous in Babylon." This vagueness, surmised Lewin, may be attributed to the sensitivity of the sender to the feelings of the Yemenite Jews' resentment toward Ezra.[18]

A salient element which recurs in all the versions of this story is the feeling of guilt which prevailed among the Yemenite Jews and their perception of their misery as a retributive punishment from God for their forefathers' rejection of Ezra's invocation to return and participate in the building of the Second Temple. Indeed, the acknowledgment of guilt, בעוונותינו, "because of our transgressions," referring to this and other acts of rebellion and sinfulness against God throughout the generations, pervades all the Yemenite writings.

In all the vast writings of Yemenite Jewry, as well as in the many interviews that I have conducted, not even the slightest grudge against Ezra has been discerned. All the expressions of wrath and of agony made by the Yemenite Jews have been directed strictly against themselves. While the majority of the Yemenite Jews strongly believed the Ezra story as evidenced by Saphir and the interviews, the attitude of Yemenite scholars and rabbis now living in Israel ranges from cautious skepticism regarding its authenticity to outright dismissal of it as a purely legendary tale, devoid of even a shred of historical basis.[19] Thus, it has been contended that other Jewish communities, particularly the nobles and the wealthy among Babylonian Jewry, refused to heed Ezra's call. Why, skeptics asked, would Ezra then single out the Yemenite Jews for such a severe curse?[20]

The alleged hatred of the Yemenite Jews for Ezra, stressed Kafiḥ, is totally groundless. If anything, they hold him in high esteem and even refer to him in their prayers as "Ezra our Lord."[21] How do the Yemenites, then, account for the scarcity of the name Ezra among them? The Yemenite Jews, they claim, chose their names from a very limited pool of names. This pool, they say, excluded not only the name Ezra but also other very prominent biblical names such as Daniel, Nehemiah, and Malachi. This explanation indeed finds corroboration in Saphir, who observed that "there is hardly any Jewish family in Yemen in which names such as Yeḥia, Saᶜid, ᶜAwaḍ, Yosef, Harun, Musa, Dahood, Salim, Suleiman are not to be found."[22]

Several factors account for the decline of Yemenite Jews and for their pitiful conditions. Their social degradation, explained Ratzaby, is certainly not the outcome of Ezra's alleged curse; rather, it stems from the extremely primitive and underdeveloped life in Yemen in general, and from the constant rooting out of the Jews from significant economic posts in particular.[23] Indeed, the recorded history of the Jews of Yemen, which focused mainly upon occasional outbreaks of violence, the pervasive atmosphere of hostility, and the contempt cultivated by religious fanaticism, clearly confirms Ratzaby's view.

These conditions must have had a debilitating effect upon the Yemenite Jews, causing them to dwindle into insignificance and destitution. Yeshaᶜyahu believed that the Ezra story stemmed from a non-Yemenite origin. It is very likely, Yeshaᶜyahu suggested, that Rabbi Shelomo ᶜAdani heard the story from his rabbis in Safed and Jerusalem, regarding the adversities of other Jewish communities. Rabbi ᶜAdani might have thought that the story was best suited for his persecuted brethren in Yemen, and might have, therefore, attributed it to them.[24]

The skeptical attitude of these scholars with respect to the alleged exchange of bitter recriminations and curses is fully justified. The fact is, as noted by various scholars, that the alleged Ezra incident is not unique to the Jews of Yemen. The story, in its main features, particularly the rejection of Ezra's summons, appears in the traditions of several other Jewish communities, such as those of Persia, Spain, and Worms, to name but a few. Thus, the author of *Sefer She'erit Yisra'el* recorded a strikingly similar tradition, which he claimed was current among the Jews of Spain. Like that of the Yemenite Jews, this tradition states that "Jews lived in Spain already in the times of King Solomon," and that Jews settled there "because they found the cities there as good as those of the Land of Israel." However, as this tradition goes on to say,

> In the time of the Second Temple, the Jews did not want to return to Jerusalem together with Ezra. The final salvation, they said, has not yet arrived, as evidenced by the missing ark, lack of prophecy and other things missing in the Second Temple. But when the Lord restores the fortunes of Zion and gathers all the dispersed exiles from the four corners of the earth, then and only then they shall return.[25]

The prevalence of this story in the traditions of various Jewish communities is, however, not surprising in view of the need of the Chosen People to justify their debased position among the nations of the world. It is no wonder that an enticing story like that of Ezra, whose main element, the failure of some Jewish communities to heed his call for their return to Zion, was invoked as one of the many attempts to vindicate the abject status of the Jews. The failure to respond favorably to Ezra's call was presented in midrashic and medieval literatures as an unforgivable act of neglect by the Jewish people of a great opportunity for ultimate salvation. Thus, the story with its midrashic and allegorical embellishment was utilized by Yehuda Halevi, who viewed this rejection of Ezra's call as the sin which prevented the fulfillment of the divine promise of salvation at the time of the Second Temple. Halevi admonished, with a remorseful tone, that divine providence

> . . . was ready to restore everything as it had been at first, if they had all willingly consented to return. But only a part was ready to do so, whilst the majority and the aristocracy remained in Babylon, preferring dependence and slavery, and unwilling to leave their houses and their affairs. An allusion to them might be found in the enigmatic words of Solomon . . . , "It is the voice of my beloved that knocketh" means God's call to return. . . . The words, "I have put off my coat," refer to the people's slothfulness in consenting to return. The sentence: "My beloved stretches forth his hand through the opening" may be interpreted as the urgent call of Ezra, Nehemiah, and the Prophets, until a portion of the people grudgingly responded to their invitation. In accordance with their mean mind they did not receive full measure. . . . Were we prepared to meet the God of our forefathers with a pure mind, we should find the same salvation as our fathers did in Egypt.[26]

2. Yemen and Its People: General Background

The mystery which envelops the origins and early history of Yemenite Jewry is, to a large extent, a function of the obscurity which characterizes Yemen itself. Until the middle of this century, the country was secluded from the rest of the world, unscathed by foreign infiltration. Because of the Zaydī imams' persistent policy of isolation, the country was almost a *terra incognita* to outsiders. Because of the great risk to their lives, very few explorers ventured to penetrate deep into the land, and many of those who did so failed to return from this venture. The first and most detailed account of Yemen comes to us from Carsten Niebuhr, who was one of the members of the Danish Middle East Expedition which visited Yemen in 1762–1763.[27] Niebuhr, "the Father of Arabian exploration," was, however, the only survivor of this expedition.[28]

Yemen (now called The Yemen Arab Republic) is the most fertile part of Arabia and the most populated. Its many virtues were well known to the geographers of antiquity. The Greeks referred to this part of the world, situated in the southwestern corner of the Arabian Peninsula, as *Eudaimon Arabia;* the Romans called it *Arabia Felix;* and to its Muslims it was *al-Yaman as-saᶜīda,* all of which mean "Fortunate Arabia." The people of Yemen themselves, proud of what they consider to be a divinely favored country, associate the name Yemen with the Arabic root Y M N, meaning "prosperous" or "blessed."[29]

Neither the area nor the population of Yemen has ever been precisely determined. Its eastern frontiers, which merge with the wilderness known as ar-Rubᶜ al-Khālī, "The Empty Quarter," are still not marked. Saudi Arabia's claim for exclusive sovereignty over this

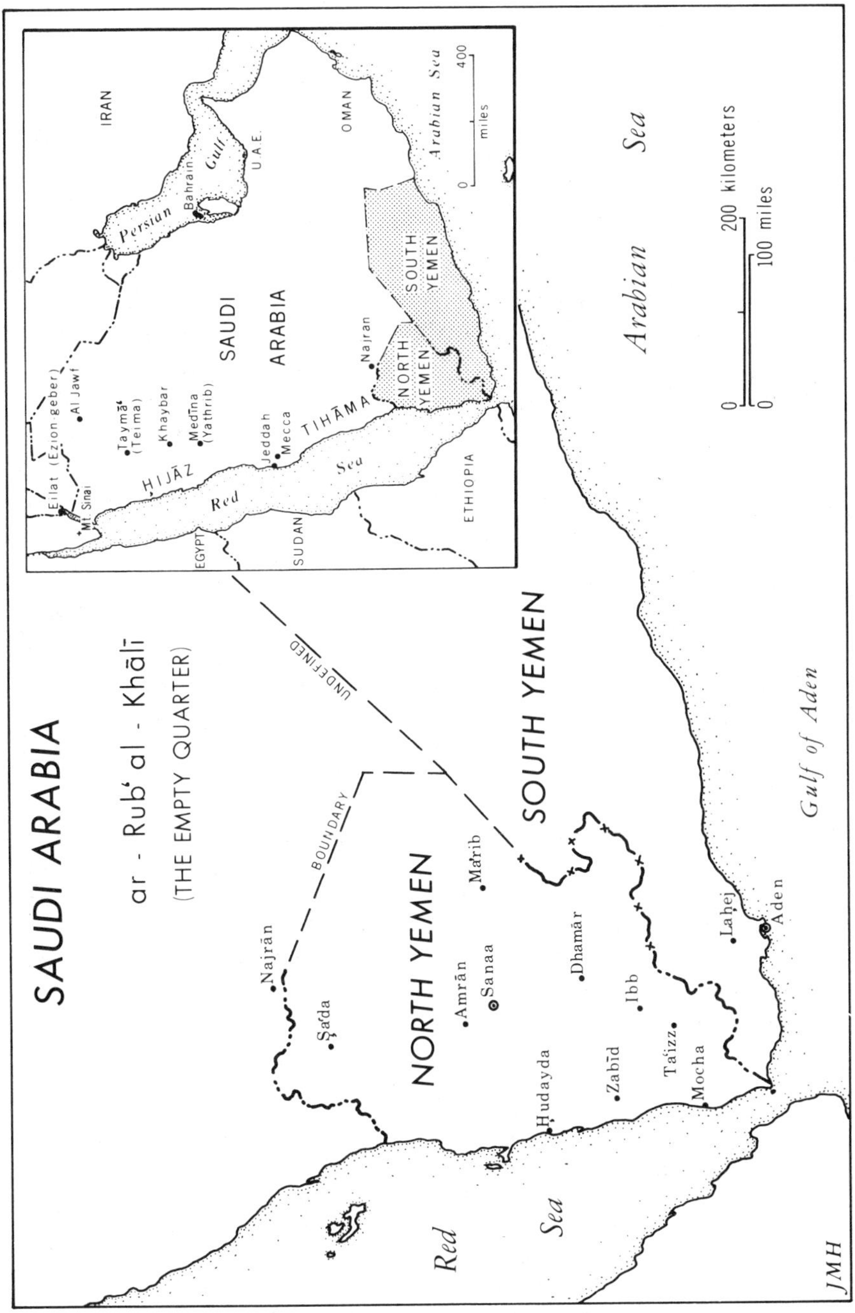
SAUDI ARABIA
ar - Rub' al - Khālī
(THE EMPTY QUARTER)
UNDEFINED
BOUNDARY
NORTH YEMEN
SOUTH YEMEN
Najrān
Ṣa'da
Amrān
Sanaa
Ma'rib
Dhamār
Ibb
Ta'izz
Zabīd
Mocha
Hudayda
Laḥej
Aden
Red Sea
Gulf of Aden
Arabian Sea
0 200 kilometers
0 100 miles
JMH
IRAN
Persian Gulf
Bahrain
U.A.E.
OMAN
Arabian Sea
0 400 miles
SAUDI ARABIA
SOUTH YEMEN
NORTH YEMEN
Najran
TIHĀMA
HIJĀZ
Jeddah
Mecca
Medīna (Yathrib)
Khaybar
Taymā' (Teima)
Al Jawf
Eilat (Ezion-geber)
Mt. Sinai
Red Sea
EGYPT
SUDAN
ETHIOPIA

Yemen

desert has been a perennial source of conflict between her and Yemen. No census of population was ever taken in Yemen. Thus, the various estimates with respect to both the area and population of Yemen tend to be highly discrepant. The former ranges from 46,000 square miles to 77,200 square miles, and the latter from 3½ millions to Imam Yaḥia's (1911–1968) claim of 8 millions.[30]

Yemen is characterized by a remarkable diversity of geographical features, varying from low strips of lands to highland ranges surmounted by several major peaks and eminences. While the coastal strip, known as the Tihāma, which stretches eastward along the Red Sea, is mainly an expanse of arid, sandy lands endowed with only a sparse vegetation, the mountainous interior highlands, which run through the center of the country, are extremely fertile. This region is characterized by a very rugged topography: canyon-like jagged valleys and plateaus crowned with high mountains about 5,000–11,000 feet above sea level. These valleys are interwoven by terraces, which were built in antiquity and are carefully maintained. Every inch of land in this area is extensively cultivated and yields rich crops of fruits and vegetables. The bulk of the country's population, nearly three-quarters of it, lives in this mountainous region, which is in contrast not only to the arid level strip of Tihāma, but also the general desert character of the Arabian peninsula.[31]

Despite the innumerable wadis which crisscross the mountainous region of Yemen, there are no perennial rivers. Thus the country is totally dependent upon rainfall. Any marked scarcity of rain in the agricultural regions entails a general famine. Indeed, famine has scourged Yemen repeatedly throughout history: Food would be sold at exorbitant prices, many sheep and cattle would die of hunger and thirst, whole villages would be deserted, and the streets would be littered with corpses. References to these devastating famines are numerous in Muslim Yemenite chronicles.[32] However, since the Jews were far more vulnerable to such scourges, the themes of hunger and mass starvation are more frequently addressed in their writings. Thus, for example, the Yemenite Jewish chronicler, Saᶜīd Ṣaᶜdī provided a cogent depiction of the famine in Yemen in 1723–1724:

> The year began with its famine, famine of consternation, famine of drought, famine which wiped out all that remained of our resources, famine which caused the destruction of houses to sell their wood and stones, famine which caused people to flee to exile because of their inability to support their wives and children, famine which caused neglect of study of the Torah and of prayer. Because of its severity, synagogues were shut down on weekdays as well as on the Sabbaths and festivals. School children roamed in the public squares, through the streets, to the houses of Muslims to beg for food. Fam-

> ine was decreed in Heaven and extinction followed . . . and the human carcasses of men were scattered in the streets and in the public squares, lying as dung upon an open field and like sheaves behind the harvester, and none was there to gather them.[33] Many, too many, were the slain of the Lord,[34] consumed by famine. They were of all sorts: There were those whose skin shrivelled upon their bones;[35] and those whose skin swelled and became [as transparent] as glass because of hunger; those whose legs were dried; . . . those whose mind became confused; . . . those who ate stalks [of plants]; those who ate mats used for packing dates; there were non-Jews who drank the blood of slaughtered animals, those who gathered insects in the dunghills for food. . . . Even the gentiles were in great distress, but not so much as to compare with the distress of Israel; for if cedars [gentiles] caught fire, what will the moss on the wall [Jews] do? . . .[36]

Another scourge which frequently hits the land of Yemen is that of locusts, which eat up all fruit and vegetation. A plague of this kind, which hit Ṣaʿda and its environs in 1045–1046, was described as follows: "they [the locusts] made their way into the houses and shops unless doors and windows were kept shut. Near the town, a sick man was smothered and eaten by them and a girl suffered the same fate."[37]

Because of the extreme scarcity of food which resulted from the various natural scourges, coupled with the constant afflictions caused by anarchy, frequent internecine wars, tribal disputes, and so forth, the locust constituted in Yemen a source of food. "*Al-Jāwe*ʿ," says a revealing Yemenite proverb, "*ya'kul makhāwe*ʿ" (The hungry eat even the legs of the locust). The chronicler Shalom Koraḥ gives poignant expression to this phenomenon. Addressing Yemen, he says: "On the table of your ministers and high officials, the locust is served as a delicacy."[38] While the locust is considered as strictly *kosher* by the Jewish law, and Maimonides even counts eight kinds of *kosher* locust, the Yemenite Jews are, to the best of my knowledge, the only Jewish community which consumed locust as a part of its diet. The locust is indeed considered a delicacy by the Jews of Yemen. A Yemenite Jew quoted to me the proverb, "*Jarāda ʿalā mishfarī aḥsan min barbarī*" (A locust in my mouth is better than a fattened lamb). The significant role which the locust played in the Yemenite Jewish diet is aptly described as follows:

> It has been a tradition in all the regions of Yemen since ancient times that the famous locusts which rise in great swarms . . . are a clean and pure kind of grasshopper. . . . When a swarm of them is seen, all welcome them with joy. . . . At evening time they watch from the roofs to detect their place of encampment. Even if the locusts

camp at a walking distance of one hour or more, they would still rise before dawn while the locusts are frozen from the cold and would go out of town, men, women and children, each carrying a sack in his hand, and they would gather all the locusts that they could carry. Whoever has a donkey would fill many sacks and would load them on his donkey. All would enter the city happy and gay like one who finds a great spoil.

In every house there are two or three stoves whose openings are directed upward. They would heat them until the straw is consumed. They would then rake the fire, empty the sacks into them, and block the mouth of the stove till the locusts are well roasted. After that they would take them out, sprinkle salt water on them. . . . For the rich the locusts are served for dessert; for the less rich they constitute the main part of their meal, and for the poor—their entire meal.[39]

3. The Social Structure of the People of Yemen

Although virtually all the people of Yemen are Muslims (the Jews being the only non-Muslim community), they nevertheless formed a composite and variegated society. The Muslim population is divided into two traditional Islamic sects: the Sunnī (represented by the Shāfiᶜīs) and the Shīᶜa (represented by the Zaydīs and the Ismāᶜīlīs). The Shāfiᶜīs are orthodox Muslims belonging to one of the four orthodox schools (*madhhabs*) of Sunnī Islam. This school of Muslim jurisprudence is named after Imām Muḥammad ibn Idrīs ash-Shāfiᶜī (767–820). Despite the lack of a census of the Yemenite population, there is a general agreement that the Shāfiᶜīs constitute at least 45 percent of the general population, concentrated mainly in the Tihāma and the southern regions of Yemen.

The Zaydīs, on the other hand, are a Shīᶜite sect in Islam, followers of the Imām Zayd, son of ᶜAlī Zayn al-ᶜAbdīn, the fourth Shīᶜite imām.[40] The Zaydīs occupy the highlands of the center and north of Yemen as well as the eastern desert regions. Most prominent among the Zaydīs are the Sayyid (*sāda*), who claim descent from the family of the Prophet Muḥammad through his two grandsons Ḥasan and Ḥusayn (sons of ᶜAlī), from his daughter Fāṭima.[41] Because of this claim, they are held in very high esteem (*iḥtirām*) in Yemen. Their hands and knees are kissed, and their blessing (*baraka*) was once sought. The Sayyids constituted the aristocracy of Islam and were an extremely privileged class in Yemen.[42] They served as government functionaries and administered the affairs of the state. They supervised the collection of taxes and served as justices in the courts. Thus, the Sayyids, by virtue of both their official capacities and noble descent, were very influential in Yemen. They were given to vainglory and ostentation. They were distinguished by the green band which they wore around the turban. Ameen Riḥani, who visited Yemen in the beginning of this century, described them as

> . . . those who wear more than one robe and have a tongue for high-falutin speech. Aye, the Saiyeds, creatures of pomp and vainglory, with their voluminous sleeves, flowing mantles, heavy turbans—sitting on high cushions and chewing *ghat* and offering their hands to be kissed—riding on caparisoned mules with servants walking on either side of them and servants before them. . . . [43]

Both the Zaydī and Shāfiʿī Islamic sects in Yemen, which are sharply divided by religious and geopolitical factors, are punctuated socially by a pronounced tribal diversity. This feature of tribal heterogeneity, characteristic of the whole Arabian Peninsula, is "as ancient as society itself."[44] The autonomy of each tribe is zealously guarded, and, as Gamal-Eddine aptly observed, each tribe formed in a sense a small nation with its own names, areas, grazing grounds, market-fairs, clients, and alliances.[45] The tribes are guided by their own conventions and unwritten codes of conduct (*ʿurf*), a very elaborate system transmitted from generation to generation.

An important factor in this code of conduct is the quality which the tribesmen refer to as *sharaf* (honor). A tribesman without *sharaf* is termed as *nāqiṣ* (deficient). Any dishonorable conduct on the part of a tribesman—such as killing a woman or a person of inferior status or allowing any other person to hurt or murder a man or woman placed under his protection—would be considered an extremely shameful act. The only way to wash away such a damaging disgrace (*ʿayb*) is by spilling blood, in order to rectify the injustice committed, or by restitution in money.[46]

It is for this reason that the Jews of Yemen felt much more secure under the protection of the tribes than among the townsfolk. The Yemenite Jewish writings relate numerous instances of bloody intertribal conflicts on account of a molested or killed Jew. For example, the chronicler Ḥayyim Ḥabshush related that a Jew who lived under the protection of Ibn Maʿsar was molested and robbed. Responding to the victimized Jew's plea for justice, Ibn Maʿsar immediately mobilized five hundred of his tribesmen and attacked the tribe from which the robbers came. In the fierce battle that ensued, two of Ibn Maʿsar's men were killed, but the Jew's merchandise was returned in full.[47]

Prominent among the numerous tribes in Yemen were those of Ḥāshid and Bakīl in the north and the Zaranīq in the Tihāma (in the area between Ḥudaida and Zabīd). Because of the significant role that Ḥāshid and Bakīl played in the political and military domains of the imamate, they were referred to as *al-janāḥāni,* "the two wings" of the imām's kingdom. These two confederations of Zaydī tribes were noted for their military might and their zeal for independence. Even the Ottomans, who ruled Yemen for a long time (1548–1629 and 1872–1918), could not bring these tribes under their domination. Very often the fate of the imām was determined by these tribes whose loyalty and support, which were never to be taken for granted, were crucial for an imām's effective reign over areas of his domain.

The known history of Yemen is that of a perennial round of intertribal and factional conflicts. Many of the tribes, like the Zaranīq, were lawless and predatory. These belligerent tribes enfeebled the central authority, and undermined any attempts at social and structural cohesiveness in the country. The weaker the ruler, the stronger was the tribal restlessness and rebelliousness. The tribal and factional lawlessness precipitated the actual fragmentation of the country into several petty states, which were chronically at war with each other, thus draining each other's physical and economic strength. Much of the central authority's effective rule depended upon the acumen of the imām or the actual ruler as he made his way through the treacherous complexities of this tribal anarchy, seeking to manipulate the tribes by means of alliances and counteralliances. Very often the central ruler used one tribe as a rod to discipline another. Thus the intertribal anarchy along with the above-mentioned natural scourges (famine, locust, etc.) sapped the strength of the country, aggravated the economic stagnation, and virtually assured the persistence of social backwardness in this part of the world. As late as 1922, the Arab-American Ameen Riḥani recorded a Yemenite's complaint with respect to the quarrelsome attitude of the Yemenites and their ever-readiness to rush to arms:

> Our people are still primitive—barbarians still. They live in fear, and doubt, and suspicion. . . . They are like the brutes, ever suspicious of approach, ever ready to leap. And here in Al-Yaman, they are always fighting against each other. You have seen them—they are all armed. They fight, the people of Al-Yaman, on the slightest provocation. . . . That is the way of the people of Al-Yaman. We tolerate no trespassing—not the slightest usurpation of our rights. If a quarrel between two families in this village, for instance, results in a fight, and they start shooting from their houses at each other, the inhabitants will immediately take sides with one or the other party and begin firing their guns. After the battle, they ask what it is about. That is the way of the people of Al-Yaman. They will fight—it is their nature—on the slightest provocation. They will fight even against their kinsmen, to defend their rights or to maintain the pledge of an ally. My brother was killed by his son. If this is our way with our own people, what would it be with the foreigner?[48]

Ingrams confirmed Riḥani's account in his own observations regarding the tribesmen of Yemen. He described them as "brave soldiers, loving poetry and given to eloquence." However, he adds, that they are fragmented and quarrelsome. "In no other region in Arabia," Ingrams concluded, "do the people display such exaggerated individualism and conservative nature as these hardy mountaineers."[49]

As we have seen, Yemen's internal social structure was molded by ancient traditions, which allowed a very low degree of social mobility. Membership in a tribe or a social class, writes Stookey, "was by ascription: A Yemeni was born a Sayyid, a Shāfiʿī, a peasant, a craftsman, an Arḥabī, etc., and that was his life-long identity."[50]

The Zaydīs, by their extreme abhorrence of outside influence and their constant and unrelenting vigilance against foreign infiltration, managed to keep the traditional social structure of the country intact without any meaningful alterations. This attitude of hate and suspicion toward foreigners is given expression in numerous Yemenite proverbs. One of these proverbs, "*ma yajī' min al-mashriq illā dhī yaḥraq,*" in essence says that a foreigner only causes heartburn. Riḥani observed the deep-rooted hate among the Zaydīs toward outsiders: The Zaydīs, he wrote, "are by nature very secretive—and suspicious. They would question the rise of the sun, and whisper of it to you, if it were not a daily occurrence."[51] This zeal for self-imposed segregation secured Yemen's isolation from the rest of the world, and preserved it untouched by the winds of change. This fact accounts in the main for its cultural, economic, and industrial backwardness, which was also so characteristic of the Jews of Yemen.

4. Yemenite Jewry: Social Structure

Outside the fold of this rigidly stratified, encapsulated, caste-like Islamic society, the Jews of Yemen stood at the very bottom of the social ladder.

Four important factors characterized the Jews of Yemen: (a) Since the disappearance of the once very powerful Christian communities in South Arabia, particularly that of Najrān, the Jews were virtually the only non-Muslim community in Yemen. Thus the term *dhimmī* (a protected person) in Yemen was identical with "a Jew." (b) The Jews constituted a relatively small community in Yemen. On the eve of their mass transfer to Israel, following the establishment of the state of Israel, their number did not exceed sixty thousand. (c) They were widely dispersed throughout the country. About 80 percent of the Yemenite Jews lived in villages or small towns. Many of the Jewish hamlets were comprised of a few isolated individuals, or a few extended families. Thus, the concept of the traditional Jewish community with its vital religious and communal institutions and social manifestations could hardly be applied to Yemen. Jewish life and activity revolved almost exclusively around the synagogues and there was very little in the way of a meaningful social life beyond the context of the religious frameworks. (d) Despite its relative smallness, Yemenite Jewry did not constitute a uniform community. A wide range of differences existed between its various sections, particularly between the Jews of the south and those of the north. These differences included customs, physiognomy, vernaculars, socioeconomic structure, and living style.

The broad fragmentation of Yemenite Jewry within a vast area comprised mainly rugged mountainous regions—which, until the rise of Imām Yaḥia (1914–1948), were governed, or rather misgoverned, by rulers or sultans generally hostile to each other—was not conducive to the development of a Jewish spiritual center. To be sure, the Jewish community of Sanaa, the capital of Yemen, did play a major role, at least in the past few centuries, in providing spiritual and religious guidance and leadership. Thus, Shalom Shabazi, the most celebrated Yemenite poet of the seventeenth century, lavished praise upon the Jewish community of Sanaa in several of his poems. A verse from one of his poems reads:

> O you who thirst for wisdom and knowledge,
> Go thee to Sanaa, the place of utmost happiness;
> Its sages will guide you in all respects.[52]

Sanaa's capacity to serve as an effective cohesive spiritual center was, however, often diminished by the frequent political upheavals, which in many cases had a devastating impact upon Sanaa the capital in general, and upon its defenseless and extremely vulnerable Jewish community in particular. The Yemenite Jewish writings (poems, chronicles, etc.) are replete with depictions of such disastrous events, which wrought havoc upon Sanaa's Jewish community. The relatively preeminent spiritual role that this community played waxed and waned with the volatile political circumstances. Favorable conditions, concomitant with the emergence of strong and charismatic Jewish personalities such as Rabbi Shalom ʿIrāqī and Rabbi Yeḥia Ṣāliḥ in the eighteenth century, greatly contributed to the enhancement of the reputation Sanaa's Jewish community and hence of its influence and authority upon the majority of the disjointed, tiny Yemenite Jewish communities.

Generally speaking, the Jews of Yemen were, compared to other Jewish communities who lived within the fold of Islam, subjected to far more humiliating and severe *dhimmī* regulations. Indeed, the poetry and the chronicles written by Yemenite Jews read like scrolls of agony and are dominated by the note of "lamentations, moaning and woe." Rabbi Shalom Shabazi complained about the great misery inflicted upon the Jews of Yemen by the Ishmaelite "savage,"[53]

> Who ridicules my faith,
> And despises my Law,
> And deprived me of my glory.[54]

Shabazi described the life of the Jews of Yemen as a catalogue of disasters and misfortunes. "*Wakam atgarra*ᶜ *'alajbān*" (O, how deeply I gulp of the disasters), he cries in one of his poems.[55] Such despondent chords are struck in all of the extant Yemenite writings, prior and subsequent to those of Shabazi. Indeed, in a lament which purports to sum up the experience of Yemenite Jewry throughout the centuries of its existence in Yemen, Rabbi Shalom Koraḥ wrote (in the twentieth century):

> Yemen, Yemen, a land of gloom and deep darkness . . . you are not to be called a land of the living; but it is more appropriate to call you a land of dread. . . . Your rivers are rivers of distress, and your streams are streams of anxiety. Let it not come unto you, all you that pass by. Behold and see if there exists any pain like the pain of the Yemenite Jews. . . . Woe unto you, Yemen, for you have darkened by light. . . . You have made the sons who are more beautiful than gold despicable and ugly.[56]

He who is acquainted with the life and history of the Jews of Yemen certainly recognizes the authenticity of the bitter cry evinced by its literature. One, however, should be wary of sweeping generalizations and oversimplifications. The fortunes of the Jews of Yemen varied widely over time and regions. Motivated to a large extent by penitential and didactic purposes, Yemenite poets and chroniclers reacted mainly to disastrous events that befell the Jews of Sanaa and other urban areas. Many features of Jewish existence, particularly in the widely scattered villages and townlets of rural Yemen, do not find adequate expression in these writings. Furthermore, it is quite reasonable to attribute much of the hyperbolic depiction of life in Yemen to the employment of metaphors, literary conventions, and embellishments borrowed from the wide stock of biblical and post-biblical Jewish laments. Thus, while the core of feelings expressed in Yemenite Jewish writings is indeed genuine, the almost exclusive and selective preoccupation with urban misfortunes and their hyperbolic presentation tend to obscure the rather intricate contours of the reality of Jewish life in Yemen, its vitality and diversity.

Fortunately, the folklore and folktales of Yemenite Jewry provide us with very valuable insights into the complexity of life in this rural community. Compared to the dark and despondent picture presented by Yemenite Jewish poetry and chronicles, what emerges from folktales is far more sober and balanced. The folktales reflect the Yemenite Jews, particularly those of the rural areas of Yemen, as leading a relatively normal life, well-adapted to the humiliating conditions imposed upon them. They present the relationship between Muslims and Jews as relatively congenial, even symbiotic. The protection bestowed upon Jews by tribal chiefs, local sheikhs or potentates, though at times frail and inconsistent, enabled Jewish life to be relatively secure. The Arab tribes considered the murder of Jews as most shameful and degrading, and a murderer of Jews was in many cases severely punished by the tribal or local patrons. The folktales depict the itinerant Jewish craftsman peacefully traversing wide areas, crossing tribal borders in the pursuit of his livelihood. Indeed, the frequent scourges, the successive wars, the famines due to recurrent droughts, and the epidemics which were so characteristic of Yemen, all served to prompt the high mobility of Yemenite Jews within the confines of the land of Yemen. Ironically, the inferior *dhimmī* status of the Jews in Yemen provided them with some circumstantial advantages. As long as the Jew managed to live outside the field of political contentions and to maintain a low and humble profile, he was generally safe. In Yemen, which was plagued by intermittent wars, hostilities, and bloodsheds, this relative security was indeed a tangible advantage.

As a rule, *dhimmīs* were tolerated and protected by Islam as long as they adhered rigidly to the limitations imposed upon them. This, however, did not prevent Jews from occasionally becoming targets of Muslim hostility, particularly in times of political upheavals. Yemenite Jewry was no exception.

Yemen is considered by many Arab authorities as the most "Arabic" of all Arab countries. This country, wrote Gamal-Eddine "provides an extremely interesting example of an original and 'unspoilt' Muslim community in that there has been very little foreign infiltration."[57] By the same token, his statement may well be applied to the Jews of Yemen, whom Saphir rightly characterized as "the most authentic Jews in the world"[58] While this unique Jewish community did not generate scholars and writers of universal renown, its very antiquity and isolation enabled it to preserve ancient customs and traditions in a relatively unadulterated form. Yemenite Jewry, says S. Lieberman, has preserved an archive of documents and literary works which would have otherwise been lost.[59] Little wonder that the influence of the Yemenite Jews on the developing Israeli culture is very discernible.

The web of popular legends spun around this unique Jewish community, so utterly different from all other Jewish communities, causes one to ask: Who are these Yemenites? What is their origin? The claim has been made that the Yemenite Jews are not of pure Jewish extraction and that they are mainly descendants of indigenous Arabs who embraced Judaism in pre-Islamic times, culminating in the Ḥimyarite kingdom and Dhū Nuwās.[60] The Yemenite Jews strongly reject this allegation and trace their origins back to biblical times. One of the main objectives of this study is, therefore, to attempt to shed light on some aspects of the origin, history, culture, and literature of the Jews of Yemen. The fact that the reliable historical sources pertaining to this topic are very few in number makes our endeavor extremely difficult. It is, nevertheless, worthwhile.

I

ANTIQUITY OF JEWISH SETTLEMENT IN SOUTHERN ARABIA

1. Scarcity of Historical Records

The early origins of the Arabs are still veiled in the mist of antiquity. The little we know about their early years is derived chiefly from the Assyrian records, classical writers, and numerous inscriptions. The earliest reference in recorded history to the Arabians occurs in an inscription of the Assyrian Shalmaneser III with reference to the battle of Qarqar (853 B.C.E.). Referring to this victory over the Aramean king of Damascus and his allies, Shalmaneser says:

> I destroyed, tore down and burned Karkara, his royal residence. He brought along to help him 1,200 chariots, 1,200 cavalrymen, 20,000 foot soldiers of Adad-'idri (i.e., Hadadezer) of Damascus (*Imerisu*), 700 chariots, 700 cavalrymen, 10,000 foot soldiers of Irhuleni from Hamath, 2,000 chariots, 10,000 foot-soldiers of Ahab, the Israelite, . . . 1,000 camel-(rider)s of Gindibu', from Arabia. . . . [1]

Far more obscure is our knowledge regarding the beginnings of Jewish settlement in the Arabian peninsula, and especially in the land of Yemen. Credible historical records pertaining to the origins of the Jews of Yemen are not available. It is small wonder, then, that this topic has been an enticing field for conjecture. The few chronicles written by the Yemenite Jews themselves cover only the past few hundred years, and even then they do not provide a systematic presentation of the events that befell them in Yemen. The records that do exist are replete with gaps and lacunae.

The scantiness of the historical materials that attempt to shed light on Yemenite Jewish history may be best illustrated by a cursory glance at the chronicles written in the nineteenth century by the Yemenite Ḥayyim Ḥabshush, which were given the presumptuous title *History of the Jews in Yemen*.[2] These chronicles consist almost exclusively of a record of disastrous calamities which befell the Jews of Yemen: persecutions, expulsions, oppressive edicts, and messianic movements. Ḥabshush began his chronicles with a brief note regarding an injunction to purge the allegedly sacred land of Yemen of all the non-Muslim religious minorities, particularly Jews and Christians, issued in the year 890 C.E. by Imām al-Hādī Yaḥia.[3] As a result of this injunction, the Christians were indeed totally eliminated from Yemen. Ḥabshush stresses that many of the Jews preferred martyrdom; others saved their lives by converting to Islam. He admits that he had no explanation for the phenomenon of the Jewish survival as the only non-Muslim religious minority in Yemen; "Visions from beyond the mists of that period," says Ḥabshush, "were not revealed to me."[4]

Ḥabshush's chronicles, which are characteristic of other Yemenite historical records, do not consist of a systematic exposition of the recent history of Yemenite Jewry. They are, rather, in the nature of snapshots of selected events that he passes before us in a fragmented procession. His sources, he claimed, consist of memoirs and notes recorded by Yemenite writers in colophons and in the flyleaves of the bindings of manuscripts, Yemenite Muslim chronicles, and oral traditions. Because of these and other limitations, his chronicles, like others originating from the Jews of Yemen, provide us with only an isolated, incoherent, and incomplete treatment of the recent history of the Jews of Yemen. For example, Ḥabshush jumped from the year 890 C.E. to 1495 and then to the year 1568 in his disjointed narration of Yemenite Jewish history. Our knowledge of medieval Yemenite Jewry is equally sparse, and the historical legacy of its antecedents is enveloped in myth and legend.

Several factors account for the scarcity of historical records written by Yemenite Jews. One may be associated with the high cost and sparseness of writing materials and the total lack of printing facilities. As late as the beginning of the twentieth century, Ameen Riḥani noted that paper was a very rare commodity in Yemen and that the thriftiness of the Yemenites in the use of writing materials in the Imamdom "reaches the sublime." He remarked that

> Seldom one sees an envelope, seldom a full sheet of stationery—the scrap is the rule, and very rare is the exception. . . . Books, coupons, petitions, documents of every sort, they have all been cut to scraps to be used in every department of the Government. . . . A messenger brings you "a cigarette," which you find is from the Imam, and in his own hand. After reading it, you tear off the blank portion, and write your reply upon it.[5]

The scarcity of writing facilities in Yemen undoubtedly accounts for the marvelous ability of the Yemenite Jews to read a book sideways or upside down and from all possible corners. This ability was developed as a result of the necessity of the Yemenite Jewish children to study the Hebrew Scriptures and other sacred writings seated around one single copy of a book.

The scarcity of writing materials may also account for the selective attitude which the Yemenite Jews had developed toward their own writings. Manuscripts which had practical value were copied and preserved. Some were used as flyleaves and for the binding of sacred books, while others were discarded and subsequently sank into oblivion.[6] Thus, for example, only fragments of the work of Rabbi Yeḥia Ṣāliḥ (1715–1805), who is known to have written a history of the Jews of Yemen, are extant.[7]

The chief reason for the scarcity of Jewish historical records, however, seems to be rooted in the negative Yemenite attitude toward secular writings as a whole, including historical records. Although secular writings were composed in Yemen in medieval times under the influence of the Spanish Hebrew literature, indulgence in this kind of writing was later viewed, particularly since Shabazi's time, as a preoccupation with "vanity and idle talk." This is indeed the expressed view of Rabbi Saᶜīd ben Shelomo Ṣaᶜdī, who wrote *Dofi ha-Zeman* (Faults of the Times).[8] This chronicle, which relates the disastrous events that befell the Yemenite Jews in the years 1717–1726, is the oldest extant Yemenite Jewish record.[9] In the course of his writings Rabbi Ṣaᶜdī repeatedly apologized for his indulgence in such a "vain" undertaking, which he labeled as a waste of both time and money.[10] He deemed it necessary to record these events, as he repeatedly stressed, not for the sake of history, but for purely moral and didactic purposes: to awaken the slumbering soul from its foolish sleep and to "save souls" of future generations. Their moral and religious deficiencies, claimed Ṣaᶜdī, had unleashed the wrath of heaven. Indeed, this concern is the focal point of his diary. He viewed the calamities that befell the Jews of Yemen as just punishment for their sins:

> Because of the multitude of our transgressions God refrained from dwelling in the midst of His camp [Israel]. He shut the door so that our prayer may not pass through, and His anger did not abate from the congregation of Israel until he uprooted them and removed Israel from being queen. It is so because our backslidings are many.[11]

Rabbi Ṣaᶜdī saw that it was essential for him to write a diary describing the calamities so that "if God turns from the fierceness of His wrath, and things calm down," his record will serve as a warning and admonition "lest His people turn back to folly." This is the only motivation for his writing venture, Rabbi Ṣaᶜdī assured us, enforcing

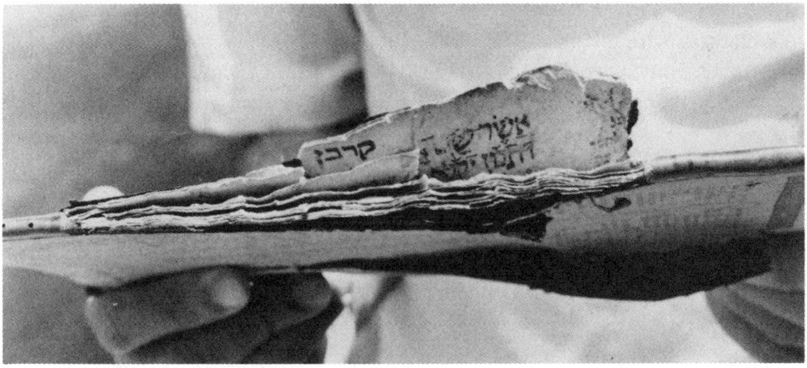

Old manuscripts were often used for the bindings of books. Leaves were glued one upon another to form a thick cover. By a careful separation of such flyleaves, Yemenite scholars have managed to discover many valuable manuscripts. (*From the collection of Yehuda Levi Nahum, Holon, Israel*)

his claim by an oath: "I swear by God Who is all-knowing, Who searches the heart and examines the kidneys, that my only intention is that we may remember and not forget. . . ."[12] Reading the diary of Rabbi Ṣaᶜdī, one indeed gets the impression that the descriptions of the events were not meant to be ends in themselves, for they are interspersed with lengthy discourses of admonition and invocations for repentance.

Whatever may have been Ṣaᶜdī's motives for writing his chronicles, the end result is that he left us some very valuable historical records, the only historical sources that shed light on the life of Yemenite Jewry during that turbulent period. Thus, these records give us a glimpse of a small chapter of Yemenite history about which we had been almost totally ignorant. These are also the oldest extant records ever written by a Yemenite Jew who had lived through the events.[13]

It is safe to assume that Yemenite Jews of older times, impelled by considerations similar to those of Rabbi Ṣaᶜdī, may have indulged in recording the events of their time and of their past generations. These records, however, must have been destroyed particularly during the course of persecutions and the many calamities that befell the Jews of Yemen. From the few extant Yemenite Jewish records and laments, we learn that edicts issued by various Yemenite rulers brought about not only the demolition of synagogues and houses, but also the subsequent destruction of Jewish writings. This is particularly true of the destruction of synagogues prior to the expulsion of the Jews of Yemen to the remote region of Mauzaᶜ in 1679.[14] Extant Jewish documents relate that some Jewish writings were torn and trampled upon by the mob, while others were burned; still others were abandoned by the Jews who could not carry them into exile.

2. Early Jewish Settlement of Yemen

As stated earlier, authentic accounts regarding the antiquity of Jewish settlement in the Arabian peninsula are not available. Various traditions concerning the Yemenite Jews' origin do exist, however. It should be noted that the scant knowledge about Yemenite Jewry prior to Maimonides's times (1135–1204) does not come to us from the Jews of Yemen themselves, but from an accumulation of fragmentary and sparse external sources.[15] Many of these emanate from Arab sources which are relatively rich in material concerning pre-Islamic Jews and Judaism. According to one Arabic version, the Jewish settlement in Arabia began in the time of Moses, who sent a battalion there for the purpose of exterminating the Amalekites in the land of Ḥijāz.[16] The Israelite soldiers, however, did not fulfill the command fully: Out of pity they spared the life of one of the sons of

King Arqam and led him captive to Moses (in Syria!) to decide what to do with him. But Moses, so the story goes, died before their arrival, and their brethren, enraged by their disobedience, expelled them from their midst. The ostracized Jewish soldiers returned to Yathrib (now Medīna) and settled there. According to another story, King David himself settled in Khaybar for seven years following the revolt of some tribes against him headed by Ish-Busht, who was, this tradition says, the son of David.[17] Still another story relates that a group of Israelites settled in Khaybar and other oases in the Arabian peninsula in anticipation of the coming of the prophet Muḥammad, whom they believed would come at the end of time.[18]

Various traditions concerning the early settlement of Jews in Arabia are current among the Yemenite Jews themselves. These traditions, they claim, are very ancient, transmitted orally from one generation to the other. One of these traditions traces their settlement back to the times when the tribes of Israel wandered in the wilderness following the Exodus. According to this tradition, a number of the wandering Israelites rebelled against Moses, turned southward to Yemen, and settled there. It is from the descendants of these Jewish settlers that the Queen of Sheba learned about the unsurpassed wisdom of Solomon. Another tradition holds that the first Jewish settlers came to Arabia during the time of Solomon, following the visit of the Queen of Sheba to Jerusalem, and accompanied her returning entourage.

The most prevailing tradition, however, relates that the earliest Jewish immigration to Yemen took place forty-two years before the destruction of the First Temple (587 B.C.E.). This immigration, so it is claimed, was prompted by Jeremiah's proclamation: "He who remains in this city [Jerusalem] shall die by the sword, by the famine and the pestilence; but he who goes forth to the Chaldeans shall live" (Jer. 38:2). As a result of this prophecy of doom, seventy-five thousand courageous men from the nobles of the tribe of Judah, who firmly believed Jeremiah's prophecy of impending national catastrophe, left Jerusalem accompanied by priests, Levites, and slaves. This multitude, carrying their possessions with them, crossed the Jordan River and went into the desert in search of a place of refuge, thus tracing backward the route of their entry into Canaan. They traveled for eleven days in the desert and arrived in the land of Edom. From there they turned south until they arrived in Yemen. Tradition has it that they saw the land was as good, fertile, and broad as the garden of the Lord, even as the land of Israel; there was no lack of anything. Even the four kinds of plants (palm, citron, myrtle, and willow) that were needed for the ritual of the Feast of Tabernacles grew there.[19] The tradition goes on to say that these early settlers appointed a king from their midst, built a stronghold on Mount Nuqūm (east of Sanaa) and developed into a mighty and prosperous kingdom.[20]

The Yemenite Jews, as can be judged from the many who have been interviewed personally, strongly believe this tradition.[21] Indeed, this alleged antiquity finds a strong echo in a prayer that the Yemenites recite on the eve of the Ninth of Av (a fast in memory of the destruction of the Temple). In this dirge the Yemenites proclaim the number of years that have elapsed since the destruction of both Temples in this manner:

> Because of our transgressions and the transgressions of our fathers, we count the years since the destruction of the House of Our God and the dispersion of the People of God from our sacred Land. Today [the number of years is specified] of woe have passed since the destruction of the Second Temple which our Lord Ezra built. And since the destruction of the First Temple and the dispersion of our people, we the exiles have been living here in the land of our oppressors [the number of years is specified].[22]

This lament, however, can be traced back only to Yemenite *tiklals* of the last three or four centuries, and it is not found in earlier ones. According to Rabbi Yosef Kafiḥ, it is possible that this custom was established on the basis of a very ancient tradition which was orally transmitted from generation to generation, but which was recorded only in recent times, lest it go into oblivion.[23] Indeed, the Yemenite writer Mahalal hāᶜAdani provided us with a vivid depiction of the solemn atmosphere which prevails among the Jews of Yemen during the period of *ben-ha-Meṣarim,* the three weeks between the seventeenth of Tammuz (when the walls of Jerusalem were breached) and the Ninth of Av (the destruction of the Temple). During this period, joy withers away from the community, melancholy and gloom spread over them; every individual feels grief-stricken and lives parsimoniously on coarse meals. On the Ninth of Av the Yemenite Jew wraps himself in sackcloth. In the course of his description, hāᶜAdani remarked:

> In most of the communities of the Diaspora, the true character of the Ninth of Av has been forgotten. But, the Jews of Yemen, who are deprived of even a semblance of freedom, are the ones who preserved this legacy from generation to generation until this very day. Every year, when the cantor declares before the congregation [in the synagogue] the approaching fast of the seventeenth of Tammuz, every member feels a tremor in his heart. The image of the impending Ninth of Av is stirred in his mind. From the fast of Tammuz onward, until the tenth of Av, every Yemenite Jew manages his life circumspectly . . . new business deals are postponed, and none utters a word concerning betrothal and wedding needs. A kind of heart-break affects every Jew, a kind of humility, submission and willing acceptance of [God's] judgment.[24]

It is noteworthy that the Jews of Sanaa, as observed by Saphir, held themselves aloof from the Jews who lived in the villages, whom they viewed as the descendants of slaves and of the proselytes who their forefathers brought with them from Jerusalem. They also claimed that until very recently records of their pedigrees, extending back to the noble families of Judah, were extant. These records of their genealogies, they contend, were destroyed by Rabbi Shalom ᶜIrāqī for the following reason: Rabbi ᶜIrāqī (died in 1765), who came from Egypt to settle in Yemen, was very wealthy and played a prominent role in the affairs of the Jews of Yemen. He served as the minister of finance for the Imām of Yemen, as well as the leader and pillar of Yemenite Jewry. Despite his wealth and greatness, the Yemenite Jewish noble families of Sanaa, so the story goes, refused to allow his son to marry one of their daughters because he failed to provide them with evidence that he was of an ancient and noble extraction. Rabbi ᶜIrāqī responded by asking them to provide him with their own records of nobility. When they did so, he took all these records and burned them, saying that all the children of Israel were nobles and no distinction whatsoever should be made between them. Saphir went on to say that the pedigrees of one family, that of Rabbi Ṣāliḥ, did survive and was preserved in a secure place outside the Jewish quarter. A prominent rabbi promised to show him this pedigree, but "the turbulent time" did not allow for that.[25]

The long-persisting Yemenite Jewish traditions which laid claim to a history of thousands of years are certainly not to be construed as authentic historical records. These traditions differ widely in their accounts as to the precise date of the establishment of the first Jewish settlement in Yemen. The Yemenites' claim to antiquity, however, is not to be dismissed as sheer fantasy. Even given the lack of historical data, there is nothing to make the Yemenite suppositions and traditions impossible. In fact, the very existence of these many traditions would lend support to the contention that there were Jewish communities in southern Arabia at the very least as far back as the destruction of the First Temple. These traditions, together with cumulative evidence which has been culled from various sources, would also lend support to these suppositions.[26]

3. Biblical Evidence of Early Jewish Settlements in Arabia

Any attempt to trace the antiquity of Jewish settlement in Arabia must begin with the Hebrew Scriptures which are replete with accounts of diversified contacts between Israel and its southern neighbor, the Arabian peninsula. These ties were manifold and encompassed the broad spectrum of interrelations which were then customary among tribal neighbors: social and commercial, peaceful and belligerent. This was particularly true of those Hebrew tribes (Reuben, Gad, and half of the tribe of Manasseh) whose territories bordered the desert.[27] It should be remembered that in biblical times caravans traversed the vast expanses of the peninsula along a tapestry of commercial routes. From ancient inscriptions (Egyptian, Assyrian, and Babylonian) as well as from ancient authorities such as Herodotus we learn that a variety of spices (frankincense, myrrh, cassia, cinnamon, etc.) as well as gold were exported from Arabia to other countries.[28] These included the land of Israel as evidenced by various biblical references.[29]

The many inscriptions contemporaneous with biblical times (Assyrian, Babylonian, Egyptian, etc.) attest to the unique commercial and strategic role of the Arabian peninsula, by virtue of its geographical position and the control of the Arab tribes over the commercial routes leading from the Persian Gulf to Syria and from Syria to Egypt and southern Arabia. The struggle among the powers of that time for the control of these and other important highways that go through the peninsula naturally influenced the course of history during the last two millennia B.C.E. and the classical period. It should be borne in mind that the Arabian peninsula is a huge territory many times larger than the combined area of the regions inhabited then by the Babylonians, Assyrians, Phoenicians, and Hebrews and would have easily accommodated the many interactions among all these peoples.[30]

It is commonly agreed that the economy of southern Arabia depended largely on exports of luxury commodities, chiefly gold, frankincense, and myrrh. The last two commodities were indeed the life blood of the economy of the southern Arabian states, which monopolized their distribution in the then-known world markets. It is significant that these two commodities were of vital importance in the world of antiquity and were widely used in various phases of religious rites and rituals. The Egyptians needed these aromatic substances for the embalming of the dead. In Babylon they were used in the funeral rites and in the ritual of the temples. According to Herodotus, the Arabians supplied Persia in the time of Darius with "a thousand talents' weight of frankincense yearly."[31] Frankincense was used in Israel as an offering of incense to produce a fragrance.[32] Mixed with other spices, flowing myrrh was used as fragrant oil for adornment and anointment. Among the many other uses of myrrh and frankincense in antiquity is the manufacture of cosmetics and perfume for personal use. Solomon is said to have scented his chambers with these substances, and the beloved would come out of the wilderness "like pillars of smoke, perfumed with myrrh and frankincense."[33]

One should, however, keep in mind that all we can safely adduce from biblical accounts of the trade between Israel and Arabia is that from time immemorial, such ties existed between these two neighboring regions. The Bible does not, however, furnish us with even a shred of genuine, conclusive evidence as to the existence of Jewish settlements in the Arabian peninsula during biblical times, although the many allusions and intimations to this effect may point in that direction. We should, therefore, be very skeptical of "definite" theories, such as that advanced by Dozy, which try to build superstructures upon obscure biblical verses and references.[34] Thus, scholars have rightly rejected the ingenious theory of Dozy, which he based on a statement in I Chron. 4:38–43 relating to the incursion of Simeon into Gedor and Mount Seir. Dozy contended that portions of these immigrants pushed southward, especially during the reign of Hezekiah, and formed the nucleus of the colonies founded many years later in the Ḥijāz.[35] Biblical scholars have rightly pointed out the ambiguity of this passage, which refers to two or more exploits, none of which correlates clearly with the other. Moreover, the Hebrew text does not provide us with a clear indication as to the precise data of the text under discussion or the raid of the Simeonites. Whether these incursions of the Simeonites took place in Hezekiah's time or not is quite uncertain. No definite conclusion can be reached as to the scene of the raid or the location. It is widely agreed that Gedor is a possible corruption of Gerar. If this emended reading is correct—and considering the locality of Simeon it is most likely so—the movement would then have been toward Philistia.[36]

The Book of Kings, however, provides us with a vivid and most intriguing account of the relations between Israel and the kingdom of Sheba as early as the tenth century B.C.E.[37] According to this account, the Queen of Sheba (her name is not provided), having heard of the glory and fame of Solomon (ca. 960–930 B.C.E.), came to Jerusalem *le-Nassoto be-Ḥidot* "to test him with hard questions" (I Kings 10:1). This account goes on to say that the Queen visited Jerusalem with "a very great retinue, with camels bearing spices, and very much gold, and precious stones" (I Kings 10:2). What exactly transpired at this visit is difficult to ascertain from the biblical source.

The story has frequently been dismissed as sheer fantasy, a figment of the imagination of an oriental storyteller, and a reflection of a later tendency to enhance the glory of Solomon and magnify his person to superhuman dimensions. It has been contended that it is inconceivable that the Queen of Sheba's visit would have been made after such an exceptionally long and arduous journey (1,500 miles) just for the sole purpose of paying homage to Solomon and satisfying her curiosity regarding his intellectual attributes.[38] Moreover, scholars have found it difficult to correlate the nameless queen and the biblical account of her visit with the known historical data regarding the tenth century B.C.E. kingdom of Sheba.

Recent explorations and excavations in Yemen have brought to light a veritable treasury of inscriptions which, together with accounts of classical historians and geographers, reveal a pageant of highly developed civilizations which flourished in the southern regions of the Arabian peninsula. We know mainly of four kingdoms in southern Arabia—those of the Sabaeans, Mineans, Hadramautians, and Qatabanians. There is, however, a wide range of disagreement among scholars regarding the chronology of these kingdoms and the precise dates of each of them. It is generally agreed that these four kingdoms should not be viewed in terms of a lineal succession, for there were periods when two or more of these states existed side by side, and there was considerable overlapping and shifting of power among them.[39]

It is widely held that the Sabaean kingdom was the most prominent of the four. Yet the numerous inscriptions discovered in southern Arabia, which have provided us with significant information regarding the monarchic system of the time, mention several kings, but they never mention a queen in the royal line.[40] In contrast, Assyrian cuneiform inscriptions from the sixth and eighth centuries B.C.E. provide definite references to the Sabaeans and mention quite a number of queens of the land of Aribi. Thus, the Annals of Tiglat Pileser IV (745–726 B.C.E.) relate that in the year 738 Zabibe, the queen of the Aribi land, sent him tribute.[41] However, we have no knowledge about the precise location of the tribes under her rule. In 732 B.C.E. Tiglat Pileser IV engaged in war with Samsi, another queen of Aribi, and subdued her.[42] Unfortunately, these inscriptions, which are usually brief and fragmentary, constantly refer to northern Arabians but seldom mention southern Arabians. This, together with the fact that the Sabaeans are mentioned in the Hebrew Scriptures in connection with tribes such as Dedan (Gen. 25:3) and Tema (Job 6:9), led some scholars to suggest a northern origin for the Queen of Sheba.[43] This queen, contended N. Groom, "was not a queen from south Arabia, as is popularly supposed, but the head of a tribe of Sabaeans of north Arabia who engaged in commerce with Tyre through Israelite territory."[44]

Such conclusions seem to be overly hasty, however, particularly in view of the fact that we are still in the dark regarding many facets of the southern Arabian civilization prior to the sixth or seventh century B.C.E. True, the whole issue regarding the identity and personality of the nameless Queen of Sheba is enveloped in obscurity, but so is our knowledge of the origins of the highly developed civilization that existed in southern Arabia. The fact that the hitherto available historical data do not attest to the existence of such a queen in those regions does not necessarily mean that the entire biblical account of the Queen's visit is a sheer fabrication. Numerous other biblical stories which were held by some skeptics as legendary have been confirmed by archaeological research into the civilizations that existed in biblical times.[45] These studies are far from being exhaustive, and much has yet to be explored. For example, Marib, the capital city of Sheba (in eastern Yemen), has not as yet "been excavated in sufficient depth to reach levels dating from her time, the tenth century B.C."[46] The absence of authentic historical data, however, should not necessarily preclude our examining the historicity of this biblical story.

Indeed, many reputable scholars of the Bible and of biblical archaeology caution against dismissing the story of the Queen of Sheba's visit to Solomon as being a product of the creative oriental imagination. In his commentary on the Book of Kings, John Gray remarked that the story of Solomon and the Queen of Sheba "may well rest on a historical basis" and "was probably a historical incident."[47] John Bright wrote in a similar vein, stressing that the visit of the queen to Jerusalem is "by no means to be dismissed as legendary." The story, he added, is "intelligible" in the light of Solomon's interest in overland trade with the south.[48] A study of the archaeology of the Solomonic age drew Pritchard to a similar conclusion: "The general picture of the international climate in the times of Solomon given in the biblical account is in accord with what we have come to learn about the ancient Near Eastern world of the tenth century B.C." Pritchard also remarked that the biblical accounts of the relations between King Solomon and King Hiram of Tyre "are highly credible," and that the tradition which credits Hiram's workmen with fashioning the Temple of Yahweh should be respected as "historically accurate."[49] Such a conclusion was also reached by William F. Albright, who himself participated in archaeological work in southern Arabia. Referring to the biblical account of the Queen of Sheba, Albright wrote: "In the light of numerous striking archaeological confirmations of episodes and references in the biblical story of Solomon, it does seem hazardous to treat this particular episode as though it were legendary."[50]

It is noteworthy that the story of the Queen of Sheba's visit comes as a sequel to the mention of Solomon's navy of ships in Eziongeber, his cooperation with King Hiram of Tyre, and the reference to his mercantile exploits.[51] One may safely assume that the Queen's visit was prompted by her desire to reach an agreement with King Solomon which would avoid rivalry and a conflict of interests between the two kingdoms. It seems obvious that the Queen would have wanted diplomatic relations with Solomon, given the geographical setting of Solomon's kingdom along the principal trade routes of antiquity and that Solomon had gained control over them. These major arteries, such as the King's Highway in eastern Palestine, served as caravan routes by which frankincense, myrrh, and other Sabaean commodities were distributed to potential markets.[52] Thus, Montgomery remarked that in antiquity

> the Peninsula and its northern extension of the Syrian Desert were crisscrossed by great avenues of commerce, extending northwards from the Yemen to the head of the Red Sea on the one hand and to Mesopotamia on the other; and by great routes traversing the desert east and west, connecting the ancient civilizations of Egypt and the Mediterranean with those of Mesopotamia and the Persian Gulf. . . .[53]

Indeed, Isaiah (60:6) speaks about "the caravans of camels" which would cover the Land of Israel, "all coming from Sheba, carrying with them gold and frankincense." Ezekiel (27:22–23) also refers to the "traffickers of Sheba" trading with "the best of all kinds of spices, and with all precious stones and gold." In his judgment of doom against Tyre, Sidon, and the regions of Philistia, Joel (4:8) declares that the sons and daughters of these nations shall be sold to the people of Judah, who in turn "shall sell them to the Sabaeans, to a nation far off." One of the main objectives of the Queen's visit would, therefore, have been to secure the safety of the caravan routes. These and other factors might have necessitated the royal visit of the Queen, a visit which may be construed as being both a commercial and a diplomatic mission. It would have been for the purpose of securing the success of this mission that the Queen lavished upon Solomon a treasure of gifts, "a hundred and twenty talents of gold, and of spices very great store, and precious stones" (I Kings 10:10). Indeed, the account goes on to stress that "there came no more such abundance of spices as these which the queen of Sheba gave to King Solomon."[54]

Comparison of 1 Kings 10:10 to 2 Chronicles 17:11 is very illuminating. It is related there that the Arabians brought Jehoshaphat a tribute of flocks, "seven hundred thousand, and seven hundred rams, and seven thousand and seven hundred he-goats." One wonders what prompted these Arabians to lavish such gifts upon the king of Judah. A plausible explanation is provided in I Kings 22:49, where it is stated that Jehoshaphat (King of Judah, 873–849 B.C.E.) "made ships of Tarshish to go to Ophir." Jehoshaphat, like Solomon before him, controlled the harbor of Eilat and most probably the trade route leading therefrom. It is, then, highly likely that the gifts he received were given as tribute by those tribes passing along the route in the trade caravans.[55]

As stated previously, the biblical account of the Queen of Sheba's visit to Solomon gives the impression that the visit was prompted by her desire to verify for herself the widespread rumors regarding Solomon's vast wisdom. It seems that the account's almost exclusive focus on this aspect of Solomon's wisdom has effectively suppressed the main objective of the visit, thereby investing the story with legendary flavor. It should be stressed, however, that this element of the story in itself is not devoid of truth. As scholars have noted, mental gymnastics, practical sagacity, and the recounting of riddles (*ḥidot*) were and still are an integral part of cultural conversations among many peoples, and diplomatic encounters involved a great deal of this apparently irrelevant intellectual gamesmanship.[56] Such a contest of wits was held, according to Josephus, between King Solomon and King Hiram of Tyre.[57] Stripped of its legendary and dramatic overtones, the story accords in the main with the many-sided and cumulatively overwhelming evidence provided by the biblical account with respect to Solomon, in that it projects an image of a wise and powerful monarch. This also seems to be the conclusion of Scott, the well-known explorer of Yemen. "The South Arabian Jewish colonies," he remarked, "may have originated in the commercial and naval enterprises of Solomon and his ally Hiram, King of Tyre, early in the 10th century B.C."[58]

There would seem to be no evidence in the biblical accounts of Solomon to support the Yemenite Jewish tradition which traces early Jewish settlement in Arabia all the way back to the times of Solomon. Moreover, the current state of scholarship cannot provide such evidence. Nevertheless, the manifold amicable and commercial relations that Solomon is said to have enjoyed with neighboring states, his maritime exploits, and the high culture which is known to have flourished in southern Arabia as evidenced by archaeological excavations, as well as other accounts of his exploits, are all sufficient to make plausible the claim of the penetration of the Hebrews into Arabia. The reign of Solomon would seem to provide a propitious setting for the establishment of Hebrew colonies (particularly for commercial purposes) in Arabia. Thus, it does seem hazardous, to borrow Albright's expression, to dismiss the Yemenite tradition as totally legendary. It should be noted, however, that the picture which emerges from the diverse Yemenite Jewish traditions regarding their ancient origins would seem to indicate that the establishment of Jewish settlements in Arabia was not the result of a single incursion in a specific period, but of successive waves of immigrations, which reached their climax in the catastrophe of 587 B.C.E., the destruction of the First Temple. The historical annals relating to Nabonidus' invasion of Teima provides us with more tangible evidence of one such incursion.

4. Extra-Biblical References to Jewish Settlement in Arabia: Nabonidus' Inscriptions

The discovery of the numerous Assyrian cuneiform inscriptions[59] which are contemporaneous with the reign of the Chaldean king Nabonidus (555–539 B.C.E.) puts us on relatively firm ground regarding the establishment of colonies in the land of Aribi. From these inscriptions we learn that, for reasons which have not thus far been conclusively determined, Nabonidus, the last king of Babylon, transferred his royal residence to the oasis of Teima in the vicinity of the Arabian region of Ḥijāz and established it as his capital for ten years.

Teima (תימא) is mentioned in several biblical contexts as an important trading station: Isaiah (21:13–15) refers to the destruction that threatens the caravans of the Dedanim and admonishes the inhabitants of Teima to bring water to the thirsty and bread to the fleeing. Jeremiah (25:23–24) foretells the ruin that threatens Dedan, Teima, and Buz as well as all the shaven heads and all the kings of Arabia and the *ʿErev* who would live in the desert.[60] Job (6:19–20) describes the vain search of the caravans of Teima and the trading expeditions of Sheba for the rainwater in the valleys. Genesis 25:3 traces Sheba and Dedan to Abraham and Keturah.[61] Thus, in biblical times Teima already served as a junction of commercial routes. From there commercial tracks proceeded in three principal directions: to Egypt, Syria, and Babylonia.

What prompted Nabonidus to "set his face" toward the remote city in the midst of the West land has not yet been conclusively determined. Various theories have been propounded to explain Nabonidus's motive for his departure to Teima. The theories range from the assertion that he had political and territorial ambitions to the claim that he moved because of purely personal considerations. Dougherty suggested that Nabonidus was prompted by political reasons, such as his wish to consolidate and extend the western part of his kingdom, in order to establish sovereignty over the West land and "to make Arabia the center from which his influence radiated."[62] Gadd, on the other hand, believed that inscription H_2 provides a more plausible motive: opposition to Nabonidus' religious program.

The king, contended Gadd, "withdrew before a mutiny of his subjects dwelling in the great cities of Babylonia, led by their priests."[63] Other explanations voiced by scholars emphasize his quest for commercial and trading advantages, and the appeal of the healthful climate of Teima. While it is true that hints and references in the inscriptions could be adduced in support of each of these conjectures, no conclusively solid motive has been furnished by any of the relevant inscriptions.[64]

Whatever prompted Nabonidus' incursion into Arabia, it was by no means a peaceful march. There are strong indications that he invaded Teima and subdued it by means of the overwhelming military force which accompanied him. It is clearly stated in one of the inscriptions that Nabonidus "killed in battle the prince of Tema, slaughtered the flocks of those who dwell in the city (as well as) in the countryside."[65]

This dramatic historical event is of utmost importance for our discussion regarding the antiquity of the Jewish settlement in Arabia since it raises the strong possibility, cogently argued by Torrey, that the new Arabian colonies established by Nabonidus must have included large numbers of Jews who settled with Nabonidus in Teima and Ḥijāz. This section of Teima as the official residence of the Babylonian king, contended Torrey, would undoubtedly have made this already important center of commercial routes and its vicinity an attractive place for potential settlers who were in quest of new commercial advantages.[66] Ample incentives of this sort must have been bestowed by virtue of the prestige invested in them by the very presence of the Babylonian emperor there. Indeed, the Harran inscriptions discovered by D. S. Rice in 1956 lend support to this view. In the Harran inscription H_2, Nabonidus clearly refers to the prosperity which the colonists who accompanied him enjoyed, saying,

> In plenty and wealth and abundance my people in the distant tract
> I spread abroad, and in prosperity I took the road. . . .[67]

A statement to this effect is also provided by the "Verse Account of Nabonidus" saying with regard to Nabonidus and Teima:

> He made the town beautiful, built (there) [his palace]
> Like the palace in Su.an.an (Babylon), he (also) built [walls]
> (For) the fortifications of the town [. . .].
> He surrounded the town with sentinels [. . .].[68]

These newly opened vistas of opportunities must have been most attractive to many of those Jews who had recently survived the national catastrophe of 587 B.C.E., which brought about the devastation of their homeland, the uprooting of its Jewish inhabitants, and their dispersion to foreign lands. It is very reasonable to assume, then, that Nabonidus' incursion into Arabia triggered the arrival of waves of Jewish immigrants to northern Arabia. There is nothing intrinsically wrong with Torrey's assumption that the Jewish settlements in the Ḥijāz, known to us later at the time of Muḥammad (seventh century C.E.), "were established at this early date," under the impulse of Nabonidus' dramatic transfer of his residence to Teima and its vicinity.[69]

Further corroboration of the settlement of Teima by Nabonidus and of the later establishment of Jewish colonies in the Ḥijāz is provided in the evidence given by the Assyrian inscription H_2, which, when combined with information from later centuries, "may lead us to infer, with some confidence, that Jews . . . were strongly represented among these soldiers and settlers in Arabia." Moreover, inscription H_2 mentions besides Teima, such places as Pa-dak-ku, Hi-ib-ra-a, Ia-at-ri-bu, which Gadd identified with Fadak, Khaybar, and Yathrib (Medīna), respectively. These cities were later known to have strong Jewish communities in pre-Islamic times as well as in the time of Muḥammad. With the appearance of inscription H_2, concluded Gadd, "at least a presumptive occasion is found for a widespread Jewish occupation of the northern Ḥijāz. . . . Short of actually naming the Jews, its implication could scarcely be stronger."[70]

Further support of this position comes to us from one of the Dead Sea Scrolls, where a fragment of the "Prayer of Nabonidus" has been discovered. In this prayer the king related that he was inflicted with plague from the sole of his foot to the crown of his head. The king stated that a Jewish diviner saved his life by advising him to worship God and to abandon the idols.[71] True, the manuscript originates from a late period (first century B.C., according to the translator), and its content, particularly that relating to Nabonidus' conversion to Judaism, sounds rather fictitious. However, as Gadd correctly asserted, this fragment is "one more testimony to the particular interest felt by the Jews in this dramatic episode of the years-long exile of a mighty king amid the distant wastes, and one more reason for believing that the Jews had a special part of their own in that episode."[72]

The diverse Yemenite Jewish traditions regarding their antecedents, although differing widely in tracing the precise date of their earliest settlement, are by no means mutually exclusive, but rather complementary. The history of the Jews of Yemen is as manifold as it is complex, and one should be cautious not to attribute certain features to a single cause or event. What emerges, however, from the divergent traditions and suppositions regarding the origins of Yemenite Jewry is a picture of incessant infiltration of Israelites into the Arabian peninsula. Two kinds of factors seem to have precipitated this immigration of Jews to that region in ancient times. One would have resulted from the establishment of trade, giving rise to social and tribal relations between neighboring countries, which would have brought about a gradual increase in the number of Jews in Arabia. This is evidenced by the various biblical and extra-biblical references. The other more decisive factor would have been the disasters which triggered massive Jewish migrations to northern and southern Arabia. One may reasonably assume that Israelite migration into the Arabian peninsula assumed vast dimensions with the destruction of the First Temple (587 B.C.E.) and then increased with the shifting conditions of the subsequent centuries. The various traditions, whether oral or written, regarding the antiquity of Yemenite Jewry should not, therefore, be viewed as conflicting accounts but rather as reflections of the early influx of Jews into southern Arabia and the continuous augmentation of those already existing settlements.

II

POST-BIBLICAL AND PRE-ISLAMIC TIMES

1. Early Historical Sources

Our investigations of the origins and antiquity of the Jews of Arabia in general and those of Yemen in particular seem to have yielded strong indications of Jewish penetration into Arabia, whether the Jews were pursuing mercantile opportunities or seeking refuge in times of adversity and national catastrophes. The latter, which occurred frequently in the biblical history of the Jewish people, might have triggered successive waves of Jewish immigrants into Arabia. Although this inquiry did not produce any conclusive historical evidence regarding the existence of Jewish settlements in Yemen (or Arabia in general) during the biblical period, there is reason to believe these communities did exist. Islamic literature yields several references to the presence of Jews in southern Arabia in pre-Islamic times, and recent archaeological finds indicate that bodies of Jews had been transported from Ḥimyar to be buried in Israel (see below). These sources provide evidence that communities existed in southern Arabia as early as the third and fourth centuries B.C.E. The lack of evidence which could conclusively support the contention that Jewish settlements existed in ancient Arabia is not at all surprising, especially since our knowledge of Arabia in biblical and even in pre-Islamic times is very sparse. We are thus left in the dark regarding many facets of the development of the peoples in Arabia and the major events that had transpired in that region. Some fifty years ago Philip Hitti expressed his concern about our continued abysmal ignorance of Arabia in the following terms:

> Here is a country that is about one-fourth the area of Europe, one-third the size of the United States of America, yet what is known about it is out of all proportion to what is unknown. We are beginning to know more, comparatively speaking, about the Arctic and Antarctic regions than we do about most of Arabia.[1]

If this statement can be made about our lack of knowledge about modern Arabia, what can we say about ancient Arabia? Its history is enveloped in the mists of antiquity which have hitherto been almost impenetrable. In light of this lack of conclusive historical evidence, all we can seem to do is devise theories, suppositions, and hypotheses. Although some of these may be considered insubstantial because they are not supported by credible historical sources, they do seem somewhat plausible given the amount of evidence that can be drawn from early narrative accounts, ancient literary sources, and recent archaeological finds. Close reading and careful evaluation of these sources uncover references to the early Jewish settlement of northern and southern Arabia. It remains uncertain, however, whether the bulk of the Jewish communities constituted Jewish immigrants from the exiles of Israel or Arabs who were converted to Judaism.

The earliest credible historical evidence of the penetration and probable settlement of Jews in Arabia comes to us from the first century B.C.E. In his book, *Antiquities of the Jews,* Josephus reported that Herod "sent five hundred chosen men out of the guards of his body as auxiliaries to Caesar, whom Aelius Gallus led to the Red Sea and who were of great service to him there."[2] Josephus' report, while extremely vague and lacking in details regarding the objective, exact location, and outcome of this expedition, is generally agreed to refer to the ill-fated expedition sent in 25–24 B.C.E. by Augustus to Arabia Felix and commanded by Aelius Gallus, the prefect of Egypt. The main objectives of this venture, according to various other sources, were to conquer South Arabia, to get hold of the treasures that allegedly existed there, and to gain control of the incense and spice trade.[3]

The significance of Josephus' report is that it not only provides us with the first reliable historical evidence of Jewish penetration into Arabia, but also indicates that this auxiliary Jewish contingent was "of great service to him [Aelius Gallus] there." What was the task of these five hundred Jewish soldiers and what "great service" did they render to the Roman expedition? Baron contended that it is unlikely that this small Jewish contingent was meant to augment Roman manpower, but rather "to facilitate the expedition through its knowledge of the roads and its contacts with the local population."[4] If this understanding of the role of this Jewish unit is correct, then Josephus' statement would seem to presuppose the presence of extensive and well-established Jewish settlements in Arabia at the time of Gallus' expedition. It is a matter of history that long before the advent of Muḥammad many Jewish oases flourished in Arabia as well as prosperous and vigorous Jewish tribes, such as the Banū

Naḍīr, Banū Qurayẓa, and Banū Qaynuqā'.[5] That these Arabian Jews were so deeply rooted and so well-established in their local environment attests to a long period of development, perhaps covering centuries.

The view that the Jewish auxiliary contingent sent by Herod might have been charged with the task of contacting Arabian Jews and seeking their support for the Roman forces is certainly not farfetched. Such a role would be commensurate in its principle with that of the Nabatean auxiliary contingent which, we are told, formed a part of that expedition. According to Strabo, Syllaeus, the commissary of the Nabateans, was expected to guide the Roman forces through Arabia. However, Strabo complained that Syllaeus had deceived the Romans and treacherously guided them along trackless and circuitous routes. The results of this expedition, as related by Strabo, were disastrous to the Roman army: It was consumed by disease, famine, and the arduous journey.[6] Although the sources do not provide us with any information regarding the fate of the Jewish contingent, it may be assumed with a high degree of probability that survivors of this unit may have settled in Arabia, either augmenting the already existing Jewish settlements or establishing new ones.

Another source of early historical evidence of Jewish presence in southern Arabia comes to us from Philostorgius, the fourth century ecclesiastical historian. Philostorgius relates that in 356 C.E. the Byzantine emperor Constantine sent a Christian mission to southern Arabia headed by Theophilus Indus. The purpose of this mission was to spread the Christian faith among the people of southern Arabia and subsequently to bring them under the influence of the Byzantine empire. Theophilus complained, so Philostorgius reported, that the considerable number of Jews whom he had found in Southern Arabia proved to be a stumbling block to his missionary endeavor.[7]

The presence of Jews in southern Arabia as early as the third century C.E. is further attested by the archaeological finds in the central cemetery of Bet-Sheʿarim, an ancient city on the southern slopes of Lower Galilee.[8] Excavations in 1936 at this site, which was used as a necropolis until the fourth century C.E., revealed, among other things, a series of graves containing Ḥimyarite wooden, stone, and leaden sarcophagi, which contained the bodies of Jews from Ḥimyar. The Ḥimyarite origin of the coffins is identified by the Greek inscription on the wall which reads:

⁶ Ομηριτῶν
(of the people of Ḥimyar)

The Jewish identity of the buried bodies is clearly borne out by the drawings on the walls of characteristically Jewish ritual articles, such as a *menorah* with seven branches, a *shofar* (ram's horn), and an incense bowl. In another chamber a Ḥimyarite monogram was found. It reads, "Menahem the Ḥimyarite Qawl" (in classical Arabic: *Qayl*), the head of a South Arabian tribe.[9] A Greek inscription discovered in the same chamber reads: *Menae presbyteros,* "Menahem, the elder of the community."[10] The inscription, together with the fact that the bodies were in coffins from Ḥimyar, leads to the conclusion that these were Jewish dead who had been transported from Ḥimyar to Israel for interment.

Some scholars, however, do not view this testimony as being compatible with our knowledge of the travel conditions that existed at that time. Ḥimyar, as Hirschberg pointed out, is very far from Bet-Sheᶜarim (sixty or seventy days by camel caravans) and the journey itself is arduous. It is argued, therefore, that bodies would not have been carried from Ḥimyar for interment in Israel. Hirschberg suggested that these coffins originated not in Ḥimyar proper but from a Jewish community in one of the Ḥimyarite commercial colonies or stations in northern Arabia, the Gulf of Eilat, or Transjordan. Hirschberg accounted for the Greek inscriptions as evidence of the assimilation of the Hellenistic culture in that environment.[11]

Although Hirschberg's views hold some degree of credibility, they fail to consider an important aspect of Jewish culture and religion. The custom of carrying the bodies of prominent Jews from various parts of the Diaspora for interment in the Land of Israel, particularly in Bet-Sheᶜarim, had long been practiced by the Jews. Talmudic literature contains references to this practice,[12] which attested to the wish to maintain strong ties with the Holy Land; it is deeply rooted in religious convictions that are prevalent to this day. It is not surprising, therefore, that the bodies of prominent Jews from southern Arabia (Ḥimyar) would have been carried for burial in the Land of Israel, regardless of the distance from their native land. A prime example of the observance of this custom is provided by the biblical account of Joseph, who had made the Israelites solemnly swear that when the time of their salvation came, they would carry his bones from Egypt to the Promised Land, a promise that, we are told, Moses completely fulfilled (Exod. 13:19). Evidence of the ancient practice of returning Jewish dead to be buried in Israel, coupled with the inscriptions found in Bet-Sheᶜarim, unmistakably testifies that the bodies in the Ḥimyarite coffins originated from Ḥimyar itself. If Hirschberg's argument regarding the origin of the coffins is correct, it would only attest, as he himself maintained, the presence of a strong Jewish community in Ḥimyar proper from which the Ḥimyarite colonies are claimed to have originated.[13]

2. Mass Judaization in the Kingdom of Ḥimyar

Much has been written about the Judaized kingdom of Ḥimyar, the last of the independent kingdoms that flourished in southern Arabia in pre-Islamic times and particularly about the time of Dhū Nuwās, the last of the kings of Ḥimyar (ruled ca. 517–525 C.E.).[14] Although this topic would appear to be outside the scope of this study, examining the issue of the Jewish presence or conversion in Ḥimyar is indeed related to our inquiry into the origins of the Yemenite Jews. Sociologists have long stressed that the distinctive features of the Yemenite Jews defied their classification within the parameters of the existing Jewish groups. Arthur Ruppin, the author of the voluminous study, *The Sociology of the Jews,* suggested that the Jews of Yemen were not of pure Jewish extraction, but rather descendants of those Ḥimyarite and Arabian tribes that had embraced the Jewish faith.[15] Such a view, which has been voiced by various scholars, demands exploration and close scrutiny.[16]

Despite the immense labor that has been expended on exploring the topic of the Judaization of Ḥimyar, we are still uncertain as to its precise historical setting, motivation, extent, and religious impact.[17] We should remember, however, that our information regarding the history of southern Arabia comes to us mainly from ancient Arab literary sources, which are indeed very copious.[18] The problem is, however, their quality. The authors of Muslim traditions were centuries removed from the events that they depicted. It is widely held that much of the material that these writings impart is spurious; some has been modified to make it compatible with certain contemporaneous attitudes and tendencies of Islam; some has come down to us after having undergone the process of selection, editorial work, and embellishment by Muslim transmitters. Because of these and other pitfalls, few scholars would vouch for the historicity of these sources.[19] Regardless of the limitations of these ancient sources, they nevertheless provide some pieces of evidence to support the contention that southern Arabia had Jewish communities as early as the third and fourth centuries C.E. The problem remains one of conclusively identifying the source of these communities. Based on evidence from ancient texts and artifacts, the conclusion is drawn that Yemen's Jewish settlements were populated not by Judaized Ḥimyarites but by Jews from the tribes of Israel who had migrated to Yemen. It is this strong presence of Jews in

Yemen that accounts for the considerable influence that the Jewish faith had on the Ḥimyarites.

3. Judaization of Ḥimyar

The extant literature relating to the kingdom of Ḥimyar gives rise to confusing accounts regarding the time and particulars of the Judaization of the Ḥimyarites. Arabic sources imply that Dhū Nuwās was the last of a series of kings who embraced the Jewish faith. According to Ibn Isḥāq, as related by Ibn Hishām, Ṭabarī, and others, the conversion of the Ḥimyarites occurred during the reign of the Tubbaᶜ Abū Kārib Asᶜad (ca. 385–420 C.E.). It should be remembered that these traditions were written centuries after the alleged event and that they vary in details. The gist is as follows:

> When King Abū Kārib went to the East, he passed through Medīna and left his son among the people there. But the people of Medīna killed his son, and the bereaved king decided to destroy the city and kill its inhabitants. The city was saved, however, by two Jewish sages from the tribe of Qurayẓa, who approached the king and implored him not to carry out his evil scheme. They told him that this city [Medīna] was destined to serve as a refuge to a prophet from the people of Quraysh in Mecca. As a result of this, the king commanded that the seige be lifted from Medīna and he returned to Ḥimyar with his army. Influenced by the two Jewish rabbis who accompanied him, the king converted to Judaism, and ordered his people to do so. But when his people refused to abandon their faith, he suggested that the matter be settled by divine judgment, a suggestion which they accepted. There was a fire in Yemen which consumed the wicked who drew close to it, but spared the innocent. It was decided that both sides, the idolators and the two Jewish sages, approach this fire. When the idolators drew close to the fire, they were consumed, together with the idols which they carried in their hands. In contrast, the two Jewish sages, who approached the fire with the Torah scrolls wrapped over their necks, were not scathed. The Ḥimyarite multitudes saw in this the triumph of Judaism and they converted *en masse.*[20]

In contrast, the contemporaneous sources give us the impression that this phenomenon of Judaization was a solitary episode triggered not by Abū Kārib but by Dhū Nuwās, the last of the Ḥimyarite kings of the Tubbaᶜ dynasty. Whether Abū Kārib Asᶜad or Dhū Nuwās and their people were, in fact, converted to Judaism remains a point of controversy. However, there is enough evidence to support the claim that the Ḥimyarites were heavily influenced by the Jewish religion. The nature, extent, and implications of this influence remain to be examined.

4. Dhū Nuwās

The historical episode relating to Yūsuf Ash'ar Dhū Nuwās (ruled ca. 517–525 C.E.) is perhaps the most famous and most illuminated in the history of pre-Islamic Arabia in general and the kingdom of Ḥimyar in particular.[21] While our knowledge of the events in pre-Islamic Arabia is derived chiefly from epigraphic material, scanty historical notes, and embellished traditions, those pertaining to the reign of Dhū Nuwās come to us from contemporaneous literary sources—Syriac, Greek, and Ethiopian.[22]

These ecclesiastical sources, as copious as they are, still are not without serious limitations. They tend to focus mainly on one single event in the life and reign of Dhū Nuwās, namely, the persecutions to which this king subjected the Christians of his kingdom, particularly those of Najrān. Thus, we are left with uncertainties regarding many facets of this intriguingly small but important chapter of history. We know very little about Dhū Nuwās's genealogy and the motivation for both his own Judaization and that of the multitudes of his people. Moreover, the very personality of this king is greatly obscured. What is known about Dhū Nuwās and his conversion to Judaism is further complicated by the "startling revelation" that Shahid claimed to have adduced from Simeon's *Letter G.* Shahid maintained that "Yusef must have become a Christian at some time. . . ."[23] Such a statement only indicates the extent of our ignorance regarding many aspects of the life of Dhū Nuwās. Needless to say, both his royal family lineage and the circumstances of his death are tainted with legend.

Words of caution have been voiced by scholars regarding the accuracy and hence the credibility of these accounts because they emanate chiefly from Christian ecclesiastical sources. While the persecution of the Christians by Dhū Nuwās is essentially historical, its depiction is widely believed to be manifestly tendentious and overly charged with religious and polemical overtones. Scholars generally agree that the description of the large-scale, anti-Christian atrocities allegedly perpetrated by Dhū Nuwās are exaggerated and colored with fabulous details.[24] Moreover, the depiction of Dhū Nuwās as a blood-thirsty butcher motivated by fanatically anti-Christian feelings, as evidenced by the many "anathemas and execrations" heaped on him in these writings, is far from being balanced.[25] It has been noted that the general portrayal of the events by the Christian sources is to a large extent divorced from the international political background, namely, the rivalry between the Roman and the Persian empires for influence in southern Arabia.[26] Christianity, remarked R. Bell, was then used by Rome as a tool for domination, and its adoption "meant an extension of the influence of Rome."[27] To reach this goal of extending its political influence over southern Arabia, Byzantium sought to arrange the collaboration of Christian Abyssinia against Ḥimyar.

The political ambitions of Abyssinia at the expense of Ḥimyar and its attempts to subjugate the latter are matters of historical truth which had been demonstrated even before the accession of Dhū Nuwās. Indeed, it was Abyssinia which ultimately put an end to Ḥimyar's political independence by means of its occupation forces (ca. 525 C.E.). Viewed within the context of the general political situation of the first half of the sixth century, the contention that the persecution of the Christians by Dhū Nuwās was impelled by fanatical religious feelings, as the Christian-ecclesiastical sources lead us to believe, loses much of its strength. Modern scholarship tends to shift the emphasis away from this long-held assertion. The suppression of the Christians of Ḥimyar is no longer viewed as an event of local character, but rather as an integral part of the larger framework of a nationalist uprising against Christian Abyssinia, which posed a threat to Ḥimyar's independence and national integrity. Hitti might be right in contending that Dhū Nuwās associated the Christians of his kingdom with the "hated rule of the Christian Abyssinians."[28] O'Leary went even further, claiming that Arethas, whose martyrdom is the most famous story in the annals of the persecution of the Christians by Dhū Nuwās, was probably "an agent of the Abyssinian government, or in alliance with it."[29]

Most assuredly, history is manifold in its issues; dogmatic formulas and narrow interpretations unjustifiably suppress the multiplicity of considerations that might have been substantive factors in a given issue. This is particularly true of our dealings with certain chapters in history, for example, that of Dhū Nuwās, the sources of which have been aptly characterized as "exiguous, conflicting, of various orders, written from different points of view."[30] Nevertheless, it seems safe to conclude that political considerations played, at least, a major role in the unfortunate episode of the Najrān persecution. Religious antagonism might have contributed to the intensity of the onslaught.

The question remains: Were Dhū Nuwās and the multitude of his people converted to Judaism? If so, what prompted that Judaization? What motives lay behind it? Was it dictated by intense religious convictions? Unfortunately, the extant sources do not provide us with any credible information regarding this event, and the contemporaneous Jewish sources do not reflect any knowledge of Dhū Nuwās's conversion to Judaism.[31] An event of such gravity, namely, the establishment of a Jewish kingdom with a Jewish king, should have made a strong imprint in Jewish writings. Yet the astonishing fact is that Jewish tradition is silent with respect to it. This silence is all the more perplexing in view of the strong ties which, according to Simeon of Beth Arsham, were maintained between Dhū Nuwās and the *ḥakhamim* (Jewish sages) of Tiberia.[32] The latter, claimed Simeon, used to "send priests of theirs year by year and season by season to stir up commotion against the Christian people of the Ḥimyarites."[33] This testimony, although plausible, is not corroborated in any other credible source.

The Yemenite Jewish scholar, Rabbi Yosef Kafiḥ, goes so far as to dismiss the whole story of mass conversion among the Ḥimyarites, calling it totally fictitious. All that the Ḥimyarites received from the Jews, said Rabbi Kafiḥ, was ". . . the faith in one God, the God of Heaven and Earth; they did not study the Torah, nor maintain the Jewish precepts; they did not keep the Sabbath and did not put on phylacteries; they did not take a *lulav,* and did not fix a *mezuzah.*"[34]

Arab tradition, however, speaks of the legendary story of the conversion of Dhū Nuwās in a way that is reminiscent of the one relating the Judaization of the Ḥimyarite king Abū Kārib Asᶜad and his people. The story, as told by Muṭahhar al-Maqdīsī, claims that the Jews of Yemen approached King Dhū Nuwās and urged him to abandon the vain worship of fire. To prove the futility of the king's faith and the efficacy of theirs, they performed a miracle by which they extinguished the fire by the mere reading of the Torah. This miracle prompted Dhū Nuwās to embrace Judaism. The story goes on to say that the Ḥimyarite king also decreed that all his people were required to accept the Jewish faith, and he executed those who refused to do so.[35]

Our knowledge regarding the profundity of the Ḥimyarites' conversion in terms of commitment to Jewish laws and customs is rather scanty. It has been suggested that if the Ḥimyarites adopted Judaism, they did so mainly because of utilitarian considerations, "for the refutation of Christian propaganda," or as Baron put it, "to erect through Judaism a dam against Christianity."[36] Christianity, we are reminded, posed a serious danger to the independence of Ḥimyar; this was not the case with Judaism, which was then devoid of political power. Therefore, Dhū Nuwās's conversion seems plausible. Goitein's opinion reflected a similar conclusion in his remarks about the Ethiopians who

> accepted Christianity and became subordinate to Byzantium. A strong Christian propaganda was prevalent also in Yemen. But the Ḥimyarites wanted to preserve their independence. Since Monotheism was "in the air" and it was impossible to avoid it, the Ḥimyarites accepted a form of Judaism that befitted them.[37]

The previous references seem to indicate that the Ḥimyarites' Judaization would have been, if anything, very superficial, primarily impelled either by political and pratical considerations or, as Arab tradition has it, by the threat of death. This impression of superficiality is notably illustrated in the fifth and sixth century monotheistic inscriptions which were discovered in Ḥimyar. Some of these inscriptions, erected by the kings of Ḥimyar, include phrases "suggesting vestiges of the ancient Israelitic popular religion."[38] For example, the expression "the *Raḥmān*" (the Merciful One) figures in several of these inscriptions. One of these even contains the phrase, "The *Raḥmān* who is in the heavens, and Israel and their God, the lord of Judah." The same inscription mentions the name Meir which, as scholars have noted, is a typically Jewish name.[39] There is nothing in these inscriptions or in any of the extant sources which attests to the adoption of the laws and precepts of Judaism. As Margoliouth aptly indicated, the epigraphic evidence "shows no trace of Biblical phraseology, or other trace of the Jewish system."[40] The inscriptions on the monuments, however, may reflect the strong influence that Judaism had exerted on the Arabians in general and the Ḥimyarites in particular. It is this influence that might have prompted the Ḥimyarites to discard paganism for monotheism and to adopt some ideas and practices of Judaism, if not Judaism itself.

The superficial adherence of the Ḥimyarites to Judaism may account for the silence of the Jewish sources with respect to this episode. It would seem that the Judaized Ḥimyarites would never have been considered as perfect Jews by the Jewish authorities, who were known to be very strict in matters of conversion. A similar attitude seems to have been displayed by Jewish tradition toward the Khazars.[41] The lack of interest of the Jewish authorities in the Judaized Khazars "was due at least partly to their imperfect adherence to Judaism," and their continued retention of pagan ways and customs.[42] Both Jewish kingdoms, the Ḥimyarite and the Khazar, with superficial commitments to Judaism, were short-lived and disappeared from the historical scene.[43]

5. Conclusions

Because of the inconclusive evidence regarding the conversion to Judaism by Dhū Nuwās and his people, the suggestion that the Jews of Yemen were descendants of the Judaized Arabians of Ḥimyar appears, therefore, to have very little to recommend its acceptance. The strong influence that Judaism had on the Ḥimyarites only indicates the presence of those Jewish communities in Yemen that had been populated by the descendants of Jewish exiles, and not by Judaized Arabs. Literary sources and archaeological finds, as pointed out above, clearly corroborate the existence of these Jewish communities in Yemen. It should be admitted, though, that throughout history, especially during the classical period, Judaism exercised a powerful attraction to some of the gentiles. This fact is also true of the Arabians. It is very likely that the Judaization of southern Arabia led in some cases to a complete acceptance of Judaism with its laws, customs, and practices, as was the case in other regions of the world. These converts to Judaism were most probably integrated within the existing Jewish communities. Thus, it seems safe to conclude that Yemenite Jewry is essentially of a pure Jewish extraction, an integral part of the dispersed tribes of Israel who had found refuge in Yemen during different periods.

Whatever the true nature of the southern Arabian Judaization might have been, it evidently did not strike deep roots. It is therefore not astonishing that when Muḥammad gave the call to embrace Islam, the southern Arabians exhibited little resistance and eventually responded positively to the Prophet's invitation. According to al-Masᶜūdī, ᶜAlī ibn Abī Ṭālib managed in one day to induce the Yemenite confederation of Hamdān to accept Islam at his hands. Other Yemenite tribes followed suit. While their "Jewishness" had never been profound, it seems to have nevertheless contributed to the preparation of the spiritual soil for the acceptance of Islam.

The occupation of southern Arabia by the Abyssinian forces precipitated a further decline of the once rich and developed civilization which flourished in that region from the first to second centuries of this era. The deterioration of the economy of southern Arabia began mainly with the introduction of the Graeco-Roman shipping fleets which competed with the traditional caravan routes of commerce and eventually supplanted them.[44] Moreover, the expansion of Christianity significantly diminished the demand for the once highly valued south-Arabian export commodities, myrrh and frankincense. Thus, this small part of the world which was once designated as *Arabia Felix* gradually lost its position as a center of commerce.[45]

The rivalry between the Roman-Byzantine and Persian-Sassanian empires, which made the Arabian peninsula, particularly Ḥimyar, one of their battlegrounds, caused a further deterioration of agricultural lands and of the complex system of irrigation which once existed there. Indeed, as Montgomery aptly remarked, "The remains of really stupendous waterworks of antiquity still survive to apprise us of the reason for ancient glories."[46]

III

YEMENITE JEWRY IN THE EARLY AND HIGH MEDIEVAL AGES

1. Muḥammad and the Jews: Dhimmat al-Nabī

It is most unfortunate that the chronicles which we have regarding the Jews of Arabia during the sixth and seventh centuries owe their existence to major clashes between Jews and non-Jews in the peninsula. The persecution of the Christians by Dhū Nuwās provided us with the Christian ecclesiastical chronicles relating to that particular event. The bitter clash which Muḥammad had with the Jews of the Ḥijāz prompted its recording by Arab historians. Although these writings emanate exclusively from non-Jewish sources and are understandably one-sided and narrow in their scope, they nevertheless provide us with very valuable glimpses into small chapters in the history of the Jews on the Arabian peninsula.

Arab historians provide us with detailed accounts of the wars between Muḥammad and the Jews. Fierce battles culminated in the ruthless destruction of the once strong Jewish communities in the Ḥijāz. These included the most prominent Jewish tribes: Qurayẓa, Banū Naḍīr, and Qaynuqā'. Regarding Qurayẓa, it is reported that Muḥammad "killed their men, and distributed their women, children and properties among the Muslims."[1] The Jews of Medīna, Banū Qaynuqā', and Banū Naḍīr were expelled from the Ḥijāz. Moreover, Khaybar, then a very prosperous Jewish settlement, was raided and plundered by Muḥammad and his followers in 628 A.D. A pact contracted between Muḥammad and the impoverished Jewish survivors of Khaybar allowed the Jews to cultivate their land, but they were required to hand over one-half of the produce to the Muslims.[2] Similar treaties were imposed upon the Jewish colonies of Faddak, Wādī-l-Qura, and Teima, reducing the Jews to the status of land-serfs.

During the reign of Caliph ᶜUmar ibn al-Khaṭṭāb (634–644) the status of the surviving north-Arabian Jews took a turn for the worse. Arab sources report that Caliph ᶜUmar decreed the total expulsion of all the remaining Jews in northern Arabia. This disastrous decree was based on a will attributed to Muḥammad that allegedly stated, "Two religions cannot exist together in Arabia."[3] Caliph ᶜUmar also made use of a *Ḥadīth* reported by Abū Huraira, according to which Muḥammad had addressed an assembly of Jews saying, "accept Islam (and) you will be safe."[4] When the Jews failed to respond positively to Muḥammad's offer, he proclaimed, "You should know that the earth belongs to Allāh and His Apostle, and I wish that I should expel you from this land. Those of you who have any property with them should sell it."[5] According to another *Ḥadīth,* ᶜUmar himself heard the messenger of Allāh say, "I will expel the Jews and Christians from the Arabian peninsula and will not leave any but Muslims."[6] Acting on these alleged proclamations, Caliph ᶜUmar drove the remaining Jews from northern Arabia.

Some Muslim scholars are of the opinion that this harsh edict expelling Jews and Christians was prompted by the view that Arabia was the spiritual center of Islam. The presence of Christians and Jews in its midst was seen as detrimental to the attempt to create a pure and ideal Islamic society there. Therefore, non-Muslims were ordered to shift to Islamic territories outside the bounds of Arabia. Furthermore, it has been claimed that military considerations were behind this expulsion. Non-Muslims were not supposed to occupy the strategic points between the Ḥijāz and Abyssinia. Thus, the Christians were expelled from Najrān and the Jews from the Ḥijāz.[7] The Arab historians also report that many of the Jews and the Christians converted to Islam, while others emigrated to various adjacent regions.

It must be stressed that a sharp distinction should be drawn between the Jews of southern Arabia and those of northern Arabia. The development of both differ widely in many respects, particularly in the social and economic realms. However, while our knowledge of the relations between these Jewish communities is very scanty, there are, nevertheless, strong indications of interactions between them. Mention has been made earlier of the Judaization of the Ḥimyarite king Abū Kārib Asᶜad and multitudes of his people. This conversion was, according to Arab traditions, prompted by the strong influence that Jews from Yathrib (Medīna) had over him. Moreover, we are told that the decline of international commerce in the fourth and fifth centuries brought about a deterioration in the economy of south Arabia and subsequent neglect of agriculture and of irrigation of lands. This decline, so it is related, caused waves of immigration from Ḥimyar toward the north, which included tribes such as the ᶜAws and the Khazraj, who settled in the vicinity of Yathrib (Medīna).[8] It is most likely that among these wanderers were Jews who might have settled among their brethren in the north. It is also quite reasonable to assume that, with the expulsion of the Jews from the Ḥijāz by Muḥammad and later on by ᶜUmar, some of the expatriated Jews sought refuge among their brethren in Yemen, thus augmenting the already existing Jewish communities there.

With the elimination of the Jews of northern Arabia and the suppression of the Jews of Yemen by Islam, the surviving Jews of the Arabian peninsula were no longer of major concern to the Arab historians. Because of this lack of interest on the part of the Arab chroniclers in the affairs of the Arabian Jews, Yemenite Jewry lapsed again into obscurity. It should be noted that the sweeping expansion of Islam far beyond the borders of Arabia brought about a decline in the practical and cultural importance of the whole peninsula, which found itself on the fringes of the vast Muslim empire. It is little wonder, then, that the focus of the Arab writers had shifted to the newly established Islamic centers of power outside the peninsula.[9] Thus, with the reduction in significance of the whole peninsula, and particularly that of Yemen, Yemenite Jewry virtually sank into oblivion.

The survival of the Jews of southern Arabia (now Yemen) in contradistinction to the total disappearance of those of the northern part (the Ḥijāz) may be attributed to the less harsh attitude of Muḥammad toward them. While the Jews of Medīna, Khaybar, and other settlements in the north were wiped out, those of the south were spared. Moreover, the additional measures taken by Caliph ᶜUmar ibn al-Khaṭṭāb (634–644) to expel the remaining Jews from the Ḥijāz did not affect the Jews of Yemen.

The survival of the Yemenite Jews is all the more astonishing in view of the total elimination of the once very strong Christian communities of southern Arabia, particularly that of Najrān. Muslim sources do not elaborate on the particular reasons for sparing the Jews of Yemen. All that they relate is that Muḥammad ordered his messenger Muᶜādh ibn-Jabal, who was about to leave Medīna for Yemen, to see to it that لا يفتن يهودي عن يهوديته (no Jew be enticed to leave Judaism).[10] The Yemenite Jews, however, provide a very intriguing explanation for this enigmatic phenomenon of their survival. They attribute it to the vital service that they claim to have provided Muḥammad during his wars with his enemies. The nature of this service and its subsequent reward are recorded in a Writ of Protection (*Dhimmat al-Nabī*) which, they contend, was given to them by Muḥammad himself.[11] The Writ states that the Children of Israel fought valiantly on the side of Muḥammad against his enemies, the heathens. The Writ lavishes praise upon the Jews, who in their utmost devotion to the cause of Muḥammad desecrated their Sabbath[12] and raided the territory of the unbelievers, "killing 7000 knights, 7000 riders, and 7000 infantrymen." According to this document, the Jews even pledged their lives for Muḥammad, proclaiming, "O Prophet of Allāh, we shall redeem you with our lives and possessions." The prophet, continues the document, was so gratified that he responded, "O men of the Children of Israel, by Allāh, I shall reward you for this. . . . I shall grant you my protection, my covenant, my oath, and my witness for as long as I live and as long as my community shall live after me, until they see my face on the Day of Resurrection." Subsequently, he issued this Writ of Protection which recognizes the valiant role played by the Jews in helping him to overcome his enemies, grants the Children of Israel certain privileges (enumerated in the document) in addition to the free exercise of their religion, admonishes his followers strictly to honor this covenant, and imposes a curse upon violators. The document states that Muḥammad dictated these privileges to ᶜAli ibn Abī Ṭālib and concludes with the signature of ten prominent witnesses who were among those close to Muḥammad.

Generally speaking, the Jews of Yemen sincerely believed in the authenticity of this document. At any rate, they presented it as such before Yemenite Muslim authorities and influential local Muslim personalities, and they did not miss an opportunity to use it as a basis for admonishing their Muslim persecutors and exposing them as ungrateful violators of a sacred covenant signed by the Prophet himself. Thus, the Yemenite Jewish writer, Nissim B. Gamli'eli, who now lives in Israel, related that whenever a prominent Muslim visited his father's house in Yemen, his father "would not let him leave before he read to him the "Writ of Protection" . . . from the beginning to the end. This he did with great enthusiasm, as if rebuking all concerned and admonishing them to treat the Jews in accordance with what is stated in the document."[13] The Jews of Yemen used to argue for the authenticity of this Writ with such vigor that many Muslims believed that it had indeed emanated from the Prophet, and they felt both embarrassment and remorse regarding their mistreatment of the Jews. Gamli'eli described the reaction of his father's Muslim audience in the following words: "I also remember that those prominent Muslims listened to the Writ with open mouths and bowed heads. They stood before my father as reprimanded students, ashamed of their ignorance in history. . . . "[14] Gamli'eli went on to say that he never saw a Muslim who dared to doubt the genuineness of this document.

The picture emanating from this document is certainly a tendentious one, and the scholars who have examined it agree that it is an outright fabrication created by the Yemenite Jews for their own defense, in order to extract from the Muslims a more favorable attitude toward them.[15] This forgery is, however, not at all surprising in view of the occasionally fanatical outbursts on the part of Muslim mobs and rulers, which impaired both their safety and their long-established privileges. Such falsifications were indeed prevalent among the *dhimmīs* (non-Muslim minorities) throughout the vast Muslim empire, to prove that special agreements had been concluded in the past assuring certain privileges. A salient example of such falsification, as noted by Gottheil, is the document which is claimed to have been granted by Muḥammad to the monks of Mt. Sinai.[16] Like that of the Yemenite Jews, this one is claimed to have been dictated by Muḥammad to ᶜAlī ibn Abī Ṭālib and witnessed by an array of men from Muḥammad's entourage.[17]

Thus, our knowledge with regard to the state of affairs of Yemenite Jewry during the advent and early centuries of Islam is indeed very scanty. This, it should be stressed, is also true of much of the history of Yemen itself during the reign of the four Caliphs of Islam and then the Umayyads. Chapters in the history of this relatively insignificant Muslim province, which was situated on the fringes of the vast Muslim empire, were ignored by Muslim historians, except when they intersected with crucial events in the Caliphate.

2. The Founding of the Zaydī State in Yemen

It should be added that with the establishment of Baghdad as the capital of the ᶜAbbāsid empire by Abū al-ᶜAbbās, al-Saffāḥ, the "Blood Shedder" (750–754), the founder of the ᶜAbbāsid Caliphate, Yemen found itself to be a province even more remote from the center of the empire, without effective supervision. The governors appointed by the Abbāsid Caliphs encountered difficulties in maintaining law and order in Yemen. Intertribal hostilities and intermittent revolts against the rulers fragmented the country and reduced it to anarchy, which was aggravated by occasional droughts and subsequent famines.[18]

As a result of the prevailing anarchy, two clans in Ṣaᶜda (the Futaimī clan of Khawlān and the ᶜUkail of Rabīᶜa) petitioned Yaḥia ibn Ḥusain ibn Qāsim al-Rāssī, a highly prominent member of a clan of ᶜAlids, to come from Medīna, where he was born in 854, and help restore peace and order among them. Al-Rāssī responded positively to their appeal. His coming to Yemen in 893 marks the introduction of Zaydism into that country.

The details concerning the life of Yaḥia, prior to his departure for Yemen at the age of 35, are very scanty. Not so are the ample anecdotes created by his biographers, spinning around him a web of popular legends. He is portrayed as a man of unusual physical strength, vivacity of spirit and vigor, as well as a religious savant of exceptional intellect and learning, excelling in particular in the domains of the sacred sciences. He pursued an ascetic mode of life (*zuhd*). His family held him in high esteem and expected great things of him. They addressed him with the title of "imām." According to his biographers, Yaḥia's coming was foreseen by tradition and confirmed by celestial signs. Deliverance, according to traditions, will come from the direction of Yemen, and Yaḥia will fill the earth with justice and pave the way to salvation. Through him Allāh will bring forth solace to the hearts of the Muslims.[19] According to al-ᶜAlawī,[20] Yaḥia's departure for Yemen was motivated by a strong conviction that he was divinely ordained to do so. He sincerely believed that it would be sinful for him to ignore the call of Allāh and His revelation to Muḥammad. Soon after his coming to Yemen, Yaḥia assumed the name of Yaḥya al-Hādī 'ilā-l-Ḥaqq al-Mubīn (Guide to the Manifest Right). He was strictly devoted to the enforcement of what he viewed as the true faith of Islam, and he demanded uncompromising allegiance to himself as the spiritual leader divinely designated to guide his community to salvation and prosperity. He exhorted the people of Yemen, using the sword if necessary, to follow the Qur'ān, fulfill to the letter the ordinances of the Prophet and to strictly adhere to the ritual of Islam and its espoused values and code of behavior. His rigidity in this respect brought him in constant conflict with insurgent subjects and "heretical" neighbors. Thus his fourteen-year reign was "one of constant warfare to restore discipline over rebellious and sinful subjects. . . ."[21]

Al-Hādī is credited as the establisher of the Zaydī imamate in Yemen and the founder of the Rāssid dynasty, which ruled Yemen with varying degrees of success until 1962, when the republican coup forced Muḥammad al-Badr, the last Zaydī imām, to flee the country. The annals of Zaydī Yemen crown al-Hādī with the laudatory epithet, "Imām al-Yaman, the reviver of the divine precepts and ordinances."[22]

3. Al-Hādī's Attitude Toward Non-Muslims

The only reference to al-Hādī in Yemenite Jewish chronicles is that of Ḥabshush which depicted al-Hādī as an extremely fanatical Muslim, intolerant of non-Muslim religions. According to Ḥabshush, al-

Hādī sought to cleanse the land of Yemen of all abominations. He decreed, among other things, to exterminate all non-Muslims and to spare only those who converted to Islam. Ḥabshush went on to say that many Jews accepted martyrdom rather than abjure their faith. Others, however, succumbed to al-Hādī's demand and embraced Islam. Ḥabshush stressed, though with sarcastic overtones, that the decree of this "great and mighty king" was not prompted by sheer cruelty, but by a profound piety and concern for the non-Muslims, who were condemned to live an ignominious life in this world and doomed to hell in the other. Ḥabshush viewed the survival of the Jews of Yemen despite this decree as a miracle.[23]

Unfortunately, Ḥabshush, who wrote his chronicles sparingly and intermittently on scraps of paper, did not reveal his sources of information. Thus, his story with respect to al-Hādī's decree of forced conversion remains so far uncorroborated by other sources. Al-ᶜAlawī, author of the bibliographical work *Sīrat al-Hādī,* does, however, inform us of an attempt made by al-Hādī to force the *dhimmīs* to sell their lands to Muslims. Al-ᶜAlawī related that al-Hādī was greatly disturbed when he learned that the *dhimmīs* in his newly acquired territory of Najrān owned a considerable amount of property and vast lands, much of which they acquired from impoverished Muslims. This state of affairs was viewed by al-Hādī as detrimental to the imamate and to the cause of Islam that he championed. It was detrimental because the *dhimmīs* were exempt from paying the *zakāt* (almsgiving) and the *'aᶜshar* (tithes) that were imposed by the Prophet Muḥammad exclusively upon Muslims for the enhancement of their virtues and for their purification. Thus, al-Hādī was distressed by the fact that an extensive property within his realm did not generate revenues for the state. To rectify this disability—so al-ᶜAlawī wrote—al-Hādī decreed that all lands and property purchased by *dhimmīs* from Muslims be sold back to Muslims. The decree allowed, however, the non-Muslims to keep those lands acquired by them during the *jāhiliyya* (pre-Islamic times). Al-ᶜAlawī went on to say that the *dhimmīs* of Najrān strongly protested against this decree, which they viewed as a flagrant violation of their long-established rights. Al-Hādī's response was very cautious: He assembled the leaders of the *dhimmīs* and concluded with them a *Ṣulḥ* (accord) acceptable to both sides. The accord provided the *dhimmīs* with the choice of keeping all their lands and property and even purchase more, but imposed upon them taxes similar, but not identical, to those applicable to Muslims. They had to pay *tusᶜ* (one-ninth) of their harvest if it was produced by natural irrigation, and half-*tusᶜ* (one-eighteenth) of that produced by artificial methods. These taxes were in addition to the usual *jizya* imposed upon all non-Muslims living in Muslim territories.[24]

As we can see, al-ᶜAlawī's presentation of the relations between al-Hādī and the *dhimmīs* is a far cry from that of Ḥabshush, although Ḥabshush might be referring to a later period in the reign of al-Hādī. Unfortunately, al-ᶜAlawī's reference to the *dhimmīs* is vague and it is difficult, if not impossible, to determine if and to what extent the Jews were involved in al-Hādī's accord with "*Ahl-al-dhimma.*" The accord refers mainly to the *dhimmīs* of Najrân, which was then the last stronghold of the Christians in Arabia, after their expulsion by ᶜUmar. In any case, we are still left in the dark with respect to the political and social conditions of the Jews in Yemen during a very crucial period in the history of Yemen, the establishment of the Zaydī imamate.

4. Natan'el Ibn Fayyūmī

The first half of the twelfth century, however, provides us with a significant Yemenite Jewish work, *Bustān al-ᶜUqūl* (Garden of the Intellects).[25] This book—so far the oldest Yemenite Jewish work known to us—was composed by the Yemenite Natan'el ibn Fayyūmī, the father of Rabbi Jacob ibn Fayyūmī to whom Maimonides addressed his *Epistle to Yemen* (ca. 1172).

The thrust of this composition is ethical, philosophical, and theological. *Bustān al-ᶜUqūl* is modeled after Bahya ibn Paquda's book, *Kitāb al-Hidāya 'ilā Farā'iḍ al-Qulūb,* known in Hebrew by the name of *Ḥovot ha-Levavot* (Duties of the Hearts).[26] Ibn Fayyūmī's work, like that of his predecessors, Ibn Paquda and several other medieval Jewish philosophers in Spain (e.g., Ibn Gabirol, Yehuda Halevi), bears the marks of influence of the Muslim sect known as *Ikhwān al-Ṣafā'* (The Sincere Brothers), which was famous for its numerous *rasā'il* (Epistles).[27]

Bustān al-ᶜUqūl consists of seven chapters. Of particular interest, is the sixth chapter, which has a strong religious-polemical thrust directed against Muslim anti-Jewish religious contentions. The significance of this chapter is underscored by the fact that the quantity of Jewish polemical works against Islam is extremely scant when compared to that leveled against Christianity. "It is remarkable," wrote Perlman, "that Jews wrote against Christianity in Christian lands, despite their harsh social climate, but refrained from writing against Islam in Islamic lands with their more favorable social clime."[28] This phenomenon, however, may find its explanation in the fact that Jews generally deemed it impractical and even futile to embark upon polemical discussions with Muslims. This is mainly because Islam's attitude toward the Hebrew Scriptures differs radically from that of

Christianity. For the Christian churches—despite their insistence upon interpreting portions of the Hebrew Scriptures in terms of conceptions drawn from the doctrinal system of the New Testament, and in light of the Christocentric philosophy of history—the validity, sanctity, and authenticity of the Hebrew Scriptures were beyond challenge. The Christian churches recognize the divine origin of these scriptures in their entirety and considered them an integral part of the Bible. Both Jews and Christians used, each side in its own way, the Hebrew Scriptures extensively as an authoritative source to validate and corroborate their contentions in their religious disputations. The antagonism between them is essentially that of controversial exegeses of the same common tradition.[29]

Radically different is the attitude of Islam toward the Hebrew Scriptures: These do not form an integral part of Islam's holy writings. Islam ascribes holiness and authority solely to the Qur'ān, which it claims is a divine revelation, the perfect expression of the divine will, the last and eternal word of God.[30] Moreover, Islam contends that it is an all-comprehensive religion which includes all the religions of the world, and Muslims speak of their Qur'ān as the combination and compendium of all sacred scriptures. Hence, according to Islam's contention, the Qur'ānic revelation "abrogates all that is antiquated in previous revelations and renders the remainder superfluous by superseding it."[31]

Muḥammad is spoken of in the Qur'ān (33:40) as *khātam al-nabīyīn,* "the seal of the prophets," the last in the succession of prophets that began with Adam. He is claimed to be the apex of prophethood, the main and ultimate channel whereby the will of God was revealed to mankind.[32]

To be sure, biblical material, especially from the Pentateuch, is prevalent in the Qur'ān, woven into its structural core. However, Muḥammad adduced this material mainly for the purpose of corroborating the truth of his message. In a manner similar to that of the Midrash, Muḥammad freely reproduced biblical events and episodes with an admixture of homiletic lore to serve the exigencies of his times and mission. Thus, in his study of the origins of the biblical material reproduced in the Qur'ān, Obermann remarked:

> [Whenever] a given Biblical passage or incident may be found to underlie the text of the Koran at a variety of places . . . we may find it reproduced by Mohammed in different manners, given different implications, or even cast in renderings mutually exclusive . . . it is rarely that Mohammed's adaptation reflects a faithful and accurate conception of the particular matter. In the majority of instances, on the contrary, the Old Testament material appears more or less considerably distorted when recurring as a revelation to Mohammed in

> the Koran. Indeed, the distortion may be found to be so far advanced as to make it impossible for us to identify the precise scriptural data that might have served as a basis for the given koranic revelation.[33]

This lack of a common ground on which Jewish-Muslim religious disputations could be based is further augmented by the Muslims' accusation that the Jews had corrupted the text of the Torah. The origin of this accusation is in the Qur'ān itself, which contends that the Jews twisted and distorted their biblical texts for their own interest, resulting in complete ignorance and misunderstanding of its true message.[34] The main purpose of this contention was to advance the persistent claim that the Jews had deliberately tampered with the text of their scriptures, purging them of all the passages alluding to the advent of Muḥammad. This allegation of "forgery" does not, however, prevent Muslims from interpreting some biblical verses as annunciations of Muḥammad and Islam. Thus we learn, from Maimonides's *Epistle to Yemen,*[35] that the Yemenite Rabbi Jacob ibn Fayyūmī (to whom the Epistle was addressed) complained to him that a certain "transgressor" was inciting the Jews in Yemen to believe that several verses in the Hebrew Scriptures allude to Muḥammad. Basing his assertions on the equivalence of the numerical value (*gematria*) of the words במאד מאד (Gen. 27:20) with the value of (MHMD), that transgressor contended that these words and other references presage the coming of Muḥammad.[36] In his *Epistle,* Maimonides categorically refuted these arguments and declared them to be manifestly fallacious. "These arguments," he asserted, "have been rehearsed so often that they have become nauseating. It is not enough to declare that they are altogether feeble; nay, to cite as proofs these verses is ridiculous and absurd in the extreme."[37]

Another reason that may account for the scantiness of Jewish-Muslim polemics is the fact that Judaism is essentially far more akin to Islam than to Christianity. Like Judaism, Islam holds to a strict and uncompromising monotheism, to the doctrine of the oneness and indivisibility of God. The notion of the *tawḥīd* (Divine Unity), which is the cornerstone of Islam, is contained and briefly summed up in the most repeated Islamic saying: *lā 'ilāha 'illā-llāhu* (there is no deity other than God).

The Christian doctrine of the Trinity is categorically denounced by Islam. To impute to Allāh companionship, partnership, or plurality is regarded by Islam as a heinous crime.[38] This Islamic concept of the Divine Unity was commended by medieval Jewish theologians and scholars. Maimonides explicitly stated that "the Muslims ascribe to God a perfect unity, a unity in which there is no stumbling block."[39] Moreover, Islam, like Judaism, is opposed to other basic Christian doctrines, such as incarnation, icon worship, transubstantiation, and the messianic role of Jesus.[40] Because of these similarities, the Jewish polemicists found it much more difficult to combat Islam's basic religious contentions than to combat those of Christianity. For although the Jews could challenge the Christian doctrines, particularly the Trinity and Incarnation, and dismiss them (as they always did) as being logically impossible, self-contradictory, and incompatible with the intellect,[41] such rational refutations could hardly be applied to Islam.

It should be stressed that with the almost total elimination of the Jews from the Ḥijāz and all northern Arabia by Muḥammad (in the seventh century C.E.), Judaism no longer posed a threat to Islam. The Jewish element was a peripheral one for Islam and religious disputations with the Jews lost their incentive and significance. To be sure, few Muslim anti-Jewish polemical treatises were composed. These, however, were mostly written by Jewish and Christian converts to Islam who sought to expose the falseness of their former religions in order to prove their zeal for their newly acquired faith. These works in turn spurred Jewish counterattacks. Except for the very few anti-Islamic polemical treatises composed by Jews, the Jewish responses against Islam are generally sparingly interspersed within the framework of diverse collections of literary writings, such as poetry, letters and chronicles, homiletics, liturgy, and in exegeses and commentaries on the Hebrew Scriptures. Stinging allusions and indirections also play an important role in Jewish polemics against Islam. All in all, however, anti-Islamic polemical works are remarkably rare compared with those leveled against Christianity, which felt a strong theological need to undermine Judaism in order to sustain its own claim to legitimacy.[42]

The attitude of Jews in general and of the Yemenite Jews in particular was extremely unfavorable with respect to interreligious disputations. Besides being far from friendly contests of wit and wisdom, these disputations were never held in consonance with the spirit of equality. They were invariably initiated by non-Jews, and Jews were coerced into participation in them. In dealing with such religious confrontations, one should recognize the disparate roles of the Jewish and non-Jewish participants. The ruling power and the social and economic welfare of the Jewish minority rested in the hands of the latter, which enabled them to act aggressively and insolently. By contrast, the Jews were strictly confined to a defensive and apologetic posture. Such "contests" were often accompanied by ridicule, vituperation, and vilification—the ultimate goal of which was to undermine the Jewish Law and customs.

In Yemen, Jewish involvement in polemics directed against Islam was a traumatic experience and a risky venture that could jeopardize the life of the Jewish polemicist. And indeed in most cases the Yemenite Jews deemed it both useless and unwise to refute the slanderous attacks of their revilers or to dispute their contentions. This was so because, "if the Jew says that he [Muḥammad] is not a true prophet, there is but one law for him: to be put to death, unless he redeems his soul by conversion. And if he says that he is a true prophet, he should then, in the light of his confession, embrace Islam and follow his [Muḥammad's] teachings."[43]

What then prompted Ibn Fayyūmī's religious polemics against Islam? Unfortunately, his extensive work *Bustān al-ᶜUqūl* says nothing specific about the Jews of Yemen, much less their internal life and conditions. Information regarding Ibn Fayyūmī's period (twelfth century) may, however, be culled from various Muslim and Jewish sources. One of the important Muslim sources is Ibn Hātim al-Hamdānī's *Kitāb al-Simṭ,* which provides us with significant glimpses of Yemen during the period of the Ayyūbid and early Rasūlid reign.[44] From this and other sources we learn that Yemen, prior to the Ayyūbid conquest, was almost in a state of political, social, and economic chaos. By the year 1164–1165, ᶜAbd al-Nabī Mahdī conquered Zabīd and the southern area of Tihāma and rapidly advanced northward and throughout the whole of Yemen. This Mahdī is depicted in the Muslim chronicles as an evil character whose reign was characterized by terror and brutality. The northern part of Yemen did not fare any better. Internecine wars lacerated the whole region. In 1150, the Zaydī imām al-Mutawakkil Aḥmad ibn Sulaymān marched against his rival Sulṭān Hātim. He conquered Najrān, al-Jawf, and al-Zāhir. The state of chaos in Yemen during this period is aptly expressed by a traditional Yemenite verse relating to that period:

wa-tafarraqu firāqan fa-kullu qabīlatin
fīhā amīru 'l-mu'minīna wa-minbaru[45]

No wonder that the Sulaymānī leader, Qāsim ibn Ghānim, appealed for help to the Ayyūbids. In 1173, Turanshah ibn Ayyūb (Saladin's brother) embarked from Egypt to Yemen with a large army, conquered the southern part of Yemen and stood at the gates of Sanaa. With Turanshah's conquest begins the Ayyūbid's reign in Yemen, which lasted fifty-six years (1173–1229).[46]

While the extant Arab sources provide us with a very valuable historical picture of the political and social state of Yemen prior to the Ayyūbid conquest, they are totally silent with respect to the Jews of Yemen. It would not, however, be farfetched to assume that the chaotic conditions precipitated by the various internecine wars must have had devastating effects on the Jews of Yemen. Such conditions usually placed the Jews, who would find themselves caught between the warring parties, in a very vulnerable position. Political and social instabilities in Yemen usually triggered persecution of the Jews, which in many cases caused Jews to convert to Islam, having been induced by the social and economic advantages conferred by the adherence to the ruling religion.

Indeed Maimonides' *Epistle to Yemen* (ca. 1172), our only source for the internal conditions of the Jews of Yemen in the period preceding the Ayyūbid conquest, strongly points to such a state of affairs. This *Epistle,* which has a strong anti-Muslim polemical thrust, reveals a very distressing period in the life of Yemenite Jewry. From this *Epistle* we gather that the rise of a Jewish false messiah and the painful frustration that followed caused immense confusion in the hearts of the Jews of Yemen; uncertainty befell them, and their beliefs were weakened, causing many to drift away from their faith. Maimonides' *Epistle* was, therefore, aimed at sustaining the Yemenite Jews in this period of adversity and at rekindling and fortifying their faith in the supremacy of Israel and the Torah. "Ours," stressed Maimonides, "is the true and authentic Divine religion, revealed to us through Moses, the master of the former as well as the latter prophets."[47] One may safely assume that such a sweeping belief in a false messiah must have been spurred by the chaotic political conditions in Yemen at that particular period.

Maimonides encouraged his Yemenite brethren to bear their suffering with patience, forbearance, and an unflinching faith in their imminent salvation. He reminded them that the suffering of the Jews is an atonement for the "vast number of sins" which they have committed. Because of the continuous defiance of God, Maimonides exhorted,

> He hurled us in the midst of this people, the Arabs, who have persecuted us severely, and passed baneful and discriminatory legislation against us, as Scripture has forewarned us. . . . Although we were dishonored by them beyond human endurance, and had to put up with their fabrications, yet we behaved like him who is depicted by the inspired writer, "But I am as a deaf man, I hear not, and I am as a dumb man that openeth not his mouth" (Ps. 38:14). Similarly our sages instructed us to bear the prevarications and preposterousness of Ishmael in silence. They found a cryptic allusion for this attitude in the names of his sons "Mishma, Dumah, and Massa"[48] (Gen. 25:14), which was interpreted to mean, "Listen, be silent, and endure". . . . We have acquiesced, both old and young, to inure ourselves to humiliation, as Isaiah instructed us, "I gave my back to the smiters, and my cheeks to them that plucked off the hair."[49]

It seems to me safe to conclude that Ibn Fayyūmī's polemical work was motivated by these dire events to which Maimonides later on referred in his *Epistle.* Ibn Fayyūmī, in the sixth chapter of *Bustān al-ᶜUqūl,* strove to respond seriously to diverse Muslim anti-Jewish polemical allegations, invoking the authority of both the Hebrew Scriptures and the Qur'ān for the substantiation of its refutations. In this most salient Yemenite polemical work, Ibn Fayyūmī reflected many of the basic motifs and fundamental issues which repeatedly occur in the wider stream of Jewish polemics. In essence, he responded to those traditional charges that the Muslims generally leveled against Judaism, reproducing in the main the same polemical arguments of his predecessors such as Saᶜadia Gaon[50] and Rabbi Yehuda Halevi.[51]

Like other Jewish polemicists, Ibn Fayyūmī strove to combat Muslims' attacks on the Jewish religion and to refute their contentions of preeminence over Judaism.[52] In his endeavor to thwart the Muslims' persistent attempts to proselytize the Jews by, among other things, the force of persuasion, he enumerated the virtues of Israel with the purpose of supplying his brethren with desperately needed words of comfort and inspiration, and of keeping alive the messianic ideal and the hope of redemption. His counterpolemic sprang, mainly, out of the overriding necessity to guide the disheartened Yemenite Jews through the confusing spiritual labyrinth of life, to uplift their souls and to infuse them with pride, confidence, and vitality.

While Ibn Fayyūmī categorically refuted the Muslim anti-Jewish polemical onslaughts, he explicitly refrained from using the inflammatory language of accusation. The tenor of his writing is subdued, calm, and dispassionate. He generally exercised great prudence and circumspection in the spirit of the rabbinic dictum, "Ye sages be heedful in your words" (Avot 1:11). As a rule, he gives a subtle expression to his controversial ideas using apologetic and defensive language. In accordance with the train of thought of other Jewish polemicists, he asserted that the debased status of the Jews constitutes no reflection on their special relationship with God. It is true that the suffering of the Jews, the destruction of the Temple, and the exile from the land of Israel, in contrast to the flourishing of Christianity and Islam, might be construed as an element of God's visible rejection of the Jewish nation. However, this suffering should not lead anyone to conclude that God had forsaken Israel and condemned them to perdition. On the contrary, their suffering is due to their being God's Chosen People. Like a father who chastises his son, God chastised Israel in order to purge them of their sins. In a manner reminiscent of Yehuda Halevi, Maimonides, and others, Ibn Fayyūmī wrote:

> But we recognize full well that the Creator has imposed greater responsibilities upon us than upon others, and that He deals with us more severely than with them. Our punishment He determines, theirs not. In this manner God shows His love for us, by this means does he ennoble us. . . . Since He regards us as pre-eminent, He holds us to strict account in this present fleeting life. . . . He hastens to chastise us that He may purify us from our sins, just as the intelligent and affectionate father promptly administers bitter medicine to his son against the boy's will, in order to purge his body of deleterious waste. The father certainly knows better than the boy what is for his good. It is therefore incumbent upon us to accept His chastisement cheerfully, that ours may be the reward. He imposes severe penalties upon us in order to make our portion beautiful, for it is written, "Whomsoever the Lord loveth he chastiseth" (Prov. 3:12).

Ibn Fayyūmī repeatedly stressed that the Hebrew Scriptures are replete with pledges of salvation and of Israel's perpetuity. The very survival of the Jewish people, despite unceasing persecution, is unassailable proof of God's vigilance for them throughout history. Because of the weight of their sins, their redemption was delayed and the coming of the Messiah thwarted. But ultimately the messianic era would dawn, and all the promised marvels would come to pass; the Temple would be rebuilt, resplendent with God's glory. Unfortunately, the world did not, and does not, understand this, and hence, is derisive toward Israel.[53]

One of the major Islamic polemical claims is that the Jews had falsified and distorted the text of the Torah (*taḥrīf*) to such an extent that the present Hebrew Scriptures no longer represent the original divine revelations. Thus, Ibn Ḥazm (994–1064) in his *Kitāb al-Fiṣāl* advanced the argument that the history of the Hebrews, which was replete with calamities, invasions, and internecine wars, was not conducive to the preservation of the Hebrew Scriptures in their entirety.[54] Moreover, Ibn Ḥazm continued, with the devastation of Jerusalem and the destruction of the Sanctuary, the Scriptures went up in flames. What the Jews have today, Ibn Ḥazm claimed, is the result of Ezra's attempt to reconstruct the Torah from what was preserved in the memories of individual Jews. In this endeavor, the original divine revelation was tampered with, resulting in an admixture of true passages and forged passages, a totally distorted and unreliable text. The *taḥrīf* allegation is also voiced by Samau'al al-Maghribī (ca. 1125–1175), who wrote, "When the political independence of a nation is coming to an end through foreign domination and occupation of its land, the true record of its past is obliterated, and the vestiges of its antiquity are blotted out and difficult to trace."[55] This allegation is categorically repudiated by Ibn Fayyūmī. The Torah, argued Ibn

Fayyūmī, has been preserved intact and unadulterated. Nothing was added to it and nothing was diminished therefrom. "How can we change His tradition and His religion which Moses brought down?" asked Ibn Fayyūmī. He then continued:

> Our pious forefathers witnessed no change in God's tradition and religion received from Moses His messenger. Following in their footsteps we have made choice of it, and emulating their laudable qualities we cling fast to the Torah and to the performance of its duties and precepts, for its exchange or alteration is forbidden.[56]

Ibn Fayyūmī also addressed himself to the Islamic polemical claim that the Torah was nullified and abrogated by the Qur'ān. This theological notion of abrogation (*naskh*) was strongly voiced, among other things, by Ibn Ḥazm and Samau'al, who contended that the Hebrew Scriptures themselves reveal numerous cases of *naskh*. Earlier divine revelations or commandments, they argued, were later on superseded or supplemented by others. Thus—Ibn Ḥazm pointed out—Jacob's marriage to two sisters (Leah and Rachel) is in contradiction to the law of Moses in Leviticus 18:18; God's determination to consume the Israelites following their worship of the Golden Calf (Exod. 32) was repealed as a result of a fervent intercession by Moses.[57] In this manner, claimed these Islamic theologians, the Qur'ānic revelation abrogates and supersedes all that is antiquated in all the previous revelations, including that of the Hebrew Scriptures. Like other Jewish theologians, Ibn Fayyūmī strongly defended the notion of the utter integrity of the Hebrew Scriptures. Pointing a finger to the Muslim polemical theologians, he argued:

> And if they say, "Lo, our Book abrogates your Book, just as your Book abrogates the Book of Abraham," we reply, "That is not true. On the contrary, we uphold the religion of our father Abraham, and especially circumcision which God made incumbent upon him. . . . And God made incumbent upon them [Israel] what He had made incumbent upon Abraham, but to those duties he added what the times required. But He did not annul the Law of Abraham. . . . "[58]

In the course of his treatment of this problem, Ibn Fayyūmī affirmed:

> . . . when we argue with non-Jewish disputants in regard to the nullification of our Law, we give them a silencing reply "What do you say about the Law received by Moses al-Kalīm?[59] What distinguishes it, ignorance or wisdom?" They must perforce answer not "ignorance" but "wisdom." This answer suffices, for wisdom is never altered, changed, abrogated or replaced by something else. God forbid that He should give a command at the hands of a prophet with signs, proofs, miracles and extraordinary manifestations in the heavens, and then should set about to abrogate and annul it.[60]

Ibn Fayyūmī totally refrained from outright attacks on Muḥammad or the Qur'ān. On the contrary, he quoted extensively from both the Hebrew Scriptures and the Qur'ān in order to prove to the Muslim orthodoxy that their attitude toward the Jews and the Torah is not in keeping with the true teachings of their prophet. To achieve this, he capitalized on Muḥammad's occasional utterances of praise about the Jews and the Torah. Ibn Fayyūmī contended that Muḥammad himself recognized that "God favored us, that he made us superior to all other men."[61] The Muslims' assertion concerning the abrogation of the Torah, argued Ibn Fayyūmī, is in contradiction to the Qur'ān itself.[62]

Ibn Fayyūmī advanced the theory which presupposes a progressive unfolding of the human moral nature, a theory propounded by several medieval Jewish thinkers. According to this notion, the non-Jewish faiths, particularly Christianity and Islam, fulfill an essential role in refining human nature and promoting the moral advancement of the world. The conquest of idolatry and paganism by such religions is, according to these Jewish thinkers, a step forward in the progressive march toward cosmic perfection and the attainment of a purer idea of God, which will culminate in the appearance of the Messiah. Thus, the hand of Providence is evident in the spread of Christianity and Islam.[63]

While Ibn Fayyūmī subscribed to this notion and generally followed the polemical trail blazed by other medieval Jewish thinkers, there is, in his polemical approach to Islam, at least one essential departure, which Abraham Halkin found to be disturbing and labeled as "deviations from the Jewish tradition."[64] Ibn Fayyūmī conceded that Muḥammad was indeed a prophet and a messenger of God, although his mission as prophet was confined solely to his fellow Arabs: "Had He sent a prophet to us," contended Ibn Fayyūmī (basing his contention on Qur'ān 14:4), "he would surely have been of our language. . . . " God, stressed Ibn Fayyūmī, exercises his will in human history, and

> He sends prophets in every age and period, that they might urge the creatures to serve Him and do the good, and that they might be a road-guide to righteousness. . . . It is incumbent, then, upon every people to be led aright by what has been communicated to them through revelation and to emulate their prophets, their leaders and their regents.[65]

Ibn Fayyūmī's extensive quotation from the Qur'ān, complained Halkin, although meant to defend the contention that the Torah cannot be altered or abrogated, is nevertheless based on the assumption that the Qur'ān is also a divine revelation and that Muḥammad is a prophet commissioned by God.[66] A Jewish attitude such as this toward Muḥammad and the Qur'ān, remarked Halkin, has unintentionally contributed to confusion, uncertainty, and weakening of faith among the Yemenite Jews, a situation about which Jacob ibn Fayyūmī (the son of Nathan'el ibn Fayyūmī) grieved in his correspondence with Maimonides, and to which Maimonides referred in his *Epistle to Yemen.*[67]

In his introduction to *Bustān al-ᶜUqūl (Gan ha-Sekhalim),* Rabbi Kafiḥ responded to Halkin's criticism of Ibn Fayyūmī, contending that these so-called "deviations from the Jewish tradition" are no more than a mere tongue-in-cheek acquiescence, dictated by the specific condition of the Jews in Yemen who were socially oppressed and constantly subjected to religious persecution. The Yemenite Muslims, contended Kafiḥ, used to harass the Jews with polemical questions concerning Muḥammad and the Qur'ān, forcing them either to acknowledge Muḥammad as God's messenger and consequently embrace Islam, or to label him a false prophet and thereby incur the death penalty. Ibn Fayyūmī's intention was, therefore, to provide his brethren with a way out of this predicament, by acknowledging Muḥammad as a true prophet, and yet confining the validity of his message to his own people and to other idol-worshiping nations who were not yet accorded divine scriptures.[68]

It should be noted that the notion of Muḥammad as a true prophet of God, dispatched solely to the Arabs, was not promulgated by Ibn Fayyūmī. It was voiced at least four centuries before him by some isolated Jewish sects.[69] Such an elevation of Muḥammad to the rank of a prophet of God made it possible for a Jew or a Christian to recite the Muslim's *shahāda,* "There is no God but God and Muḥammad is the messenger of God," without adhering to Islam.

This uniquely abject and precarious status of the Yemenite Jews also produced the bizarre "Writ of Protection," which surpasses all previous bounds in its endorsement of Muḥammad as a prophet of God. One version of this Writ claims that the Jews, in their utter devotion to the cause of Muḥammad, desecrated their own Sabbath by fighting valiantly on his side against his enemies, the heathen. Another version of the Writ depicts Moses praying for the prophet Muḥammad, the "most beloved of the prophets," and enjoining the Children of Israel to help Muḥammad against his enemies, the unbelievers.[70] It should be pointed out, however, that all the versions of this Writ of Protection stress the distinction between Judaism and Islam and call for the utter safeguarding of the integrity of the Jewish religion and its secure coexistence with that of Islam in mutual respect.

It seems clear that the Yemenite Jewish "concessions" to Islam, including those of Ibn Fayyūmī, do not stem from ideological or theological convictions. Such documents or statements emanating from the Jews of Yemen should not be taken at their face value; they should rather be evaluated with strict reference to their social, cultural, and historical matrix, and within the context of Yemenite Jewish writings as a whole. In this light, such "deviations" emerge as mere lip service, conditioned by the desperate need of Yemenite Jewry to steer between the horns of the dilemma articulated above by Rabbi Kafiḥ.

5. The Geniza Documents

With the discovery of the unique and invaluable collection of the Cairo Geniza documents, our knowledge of the parallel communications between the Jews of Yemen, particularly those of Aden, and other Jewish communities has been significantly enhanced.[71] Letters and fragments of letters, dating from the tenth through the thirteenth centuries, furnish us with a glimpse of the relations between the Jews in Yemen and the Gaonic academies of Babylonia. From such a collection, edited by Lewin,[72] we learn, for example, that the Yemenite Jews not only maintained strong ties with the Jewish centers in Babylon, but even supported them financially. Significant in this respect is a letter dated 1133 C.E. sent by a Jew in Aden, Jacob bin Sālim, to the Fusṭāṭ Dayyan Nathan Hakkohen bin Solomon. The former acknowledged the receipt of the latter's letter and apologized for his inability to induce the Jewish community of Aden to "give generously" to the recipient of the letter, whom the sender considered a "great scholar" worthy of support. Jacob's failure to help, he wrote, is due to strained relations between him and his community in Aden, which had prompted him to move away from the city.[73]

In 1962 Goitein edited other documents from the Cairo Geniza which attest to substantial contributions sent by the Jews of Yemen to Babylon, Palestine, and Egypt for the maintenance of *yeshivot* ("Jewish academies") and schools there. These documents, Goitein concluded, indicate the strong allegiance of the Yemenite Jews to the Jewish schools of higher learning, as well as their economic capacity. This fact, added Goitein, explains why so many precious Hebrew manuscripts found their way to Yemen and were preserved there.[74] Indeed, Maimonides, in his *Epistle to Yemen,* lavished praise upon the generosity of the Yemenite Jews:

> Just as plants bear testimony to the existence of real roots, and waters are evidence for the excellence of springs, so has a firm shoot

> developed from the roots of truth and righteousness, and a huge river has gushed forth from the spring of mercy in the land of Yemen, to water therewith all gardens and to make the flowers blossom. It flows gently on to satisfy the needs of the weary and thirsty in the arid places; wayfarers and folks from the isles of the sea satisfy their needs with it. Consequently it was proclaimed from Spain to Babylonia, from one end of heaven to the other; "Ho, ye every one that thirsteth come for water." (Isaiah 55:1) Men of business and traffic unanimously declare to all inquirers that they have found in the land of Yemen a beautiful and delightful plantation, and a rich pasture with faithful shepherds wherein every lean one shall wax fat. They strengthen the indigent with bread and greet the opulent hospitably and generously. . . . Their hands are stretched out to every passer-by, and their homes are wide open to every traveler.[75]

The greatest value of the Geniza treasures, as they relate to the Jews of Yemen, is that they attest to a multifaceted relationship, particularly commercial and cultural, between the Jews of Aden and other Jewish communities far beyond the borders of Yemen. As early as the tenth century Aden served as an emporium of extensive trade between the countries bordering the Mediterranean and Persia, Africa, and the Far East (especially India). The status of Aden as a port of call, particularly on the far-eastern trade route, was greatly enhanced by the supremacy that the Red Sea route had gained over that of the Persian Gulf.[76] The reference to Aden as "the eye of al-Yemen," underscores its role as a conduit through which Yemen maintained relations, commercial and cultural, with the outside world.[77] Aden, in turn, by virtue of its position as a prominent center of wide-ranging mercantile activities which lasted until the sixteenth century, served as an important vehicle by which external influences were brought to bear upon the Jews of Yemen. This unique position of Aden immensely influenced the spiritual and cultural development of the Jews of Aden, and through them of those of Yemen. Thus Aden was highly conducive to a mutual social and cultural influence.

The information that the Cairo Geniza furnishes us regarding the commercial and cultural role of Aden is of a variegated nature. From some Geniza documents we learn that the Jews of Aden and heads of *yeshivot* (Jewish academies) in Egypt corresponded regarding religious, legal, and theological issues as early as two generations before Maimonides.[78] Furthermore, communications between the various Jewish communities were not confined to mere correspondence but extended far beyond that to direct and personal contact. Jewish traders, for instance, from Spain, Egypt, Sicily, and elsewhere would, in the course of their long journey to and from India, spend some time in Aden. Geniza documents, for example, reveal that a Jew by the name of Abraham bin Yiju (or Yaju), born in Tunisia at the beginning of the twelfth century, spent in the course of his commercial and industrial exploits at least seventeen years in India and three years in Yemen.[79] A fragment of a Geniza letter written by a Jew in India to his business correspondent in Cairo underscores the commercial role that Aden played as a port of exchange. The fragment reads: "He makes journeys from Malabar to Ceylon but his goods are the whole year in Aden. . . . I have not voyaged to Aden this year."[80]

One remarkable outcome of the bond that developed between the diverse Jewish communities in the course of their mercantile enterprises and exploits is the emigration of Jews from one country to another. From Geniza documents emerges a picture of intensive movement of Jews around the Mediterranean region and far beyond its boundaries. Thus, it is strongly believed that the origin of the prominent Jewish family of Ḥasan (Japheth) bin Bundar and his son Madmun, the superintendent of the port of Aden and head of the Jews of Yemen, was Iran. This origin is indicated, as Goitein pointed out, by the family name Bundar.[81]

Some of the more important factors that had contributed to the intensity of international mobility of Jews during the High Middle Ages, other than mercantile incentives, were the search for better occupational opportunities on the part of artisans and skilled workers, the pursuit of knowledge by wandering scholars (and the urge to spread knowledge), personal considerations (such as marital or family disputes), and the lure of adventure for enterprising young men. Above all, streams of migrations were prompted by troubles and misfortunes that befell the Jews in their native countries. Some Geniza records reveal lists of people, most of them foreigners, who because of their dire necessity were recipients of charity from the Jewish community of Old Cairo.[82] Among the multitude of Jews who emigrated to Egypt for various reasons were Jews from Yemen. "It is perhaps noteworthy," remarked Goitein, "that the names of the Yemenites [Jews from South Arabia] occur exclusively in the lists of contributors to public collections, never in those of receivers of alms." The implication of this, inferred Goitein, is that these Yemenites came to Egypt, "not as refugees, but as merchants, craftsmen, or scholars."[83]

Evidently, within this context of the movement of Jews from one country to the other, some Jews chose to emigrate to Yemen, prompted by mercantile or personal considerations. This emigration to Yemen was undoubtedly intensified in times when fanatic outbursts of anti-Jewish feelings in Muslim countries brought about rigorous and intolerable religious persecution.[84] Judging from the status of the Jews of Aden, it is reasonable to assume that conditions in Yemen in medieval times were generally and relatively favorable for the Jews, giving rise to the immigration of Jews to that country.

It should be noted, however, that the extant documents do not provide us with any evidence of waves or even streams of Jews moving to Yemen, but rather of sporadic movements of individuals or small groups. This occasional immigration, although only a trickle, became over the course of time a considerable increment to the Yemenite Jewish communities. It is noteworthy that among these Jewish immigrants to Yemen were the families of prominent personalities such as Jacob Natan'el Fayyūmī, the recipient of Maimonides' *Epistle to Yemen,* and the previously mentioned Ḥasan (Japheth) bin Bundar, the head of the Jews of Yemen and the superintendent of the port of Aden.[85] The foreign origin of these and many other Yemenite Jews is clearly borne out by their non-Yemenite names.[86] Indeed, a succinct comment by the Yemenite Jewish writer ᶜAmram Koraḥ attests to this continuous influx of Jewish immigrants to Yemen.[87] In his commentary on a poem written by Shabazi,[88] Koraḥ made the following statement: "Though our tradition holds that we are of the exiles of the First Temple, do not believe that we are purely from them. We are also of those of Halah and Habor,[89] the remnants of the ten tribes; [we are] also from Babylon and Egypt who came here [searching] for livelihood."[90]

The extant material pertaining to the Jews of Yemen, including the relevant documents from the Geniza published to date, testify to the strong and multifaceted relations that had existed between the Jewish communities in Yemen and other Jewish communities, particularly those of the Mediterranean region, during the Early and High Middle Ages. The knowledge that we cull from these documents, though scattered, haphazard, and disjointed, is nevertheless most valuable. The accounts are significant, not only because of their historical nature, but also because they are our main source of information regarding Yemenite Jewry during medieval times. Without these flashes of light, our knowledge of Yemen's Jewish community during this period would have been infinitesimal.

It should be stressed, however, that this information, though ample, is very narrow in its scope. Its main focus is on the Jewish community in Aden, saying very little about the relations of other Yemenite Jewish communities with their co-religionists abroad. This fact is quite understandable in view of the privileged status that medieval Aden entertained as a prominent commercial center for trade and commerce. Moreover, the available information is limited mainly to the diverse relations that the Yemenite Jews (especially those of Aden) had with other Jewish communities and furnishes very little knowledge regarding the internal affairs of Yemenite Jewry. Thus, except for the few glimpses provided by Ibn Fayyūmī's *Bustān al-ʿUqūl,* and Maimonides' *Epistle,* we are left knowing almost nothing of the inner structure of the Jewish communities in Yemen, their relations with the Muslim authorities of Yemen, and their sociopolitical and economic development.

As we have seen, the references in the Arab sources to the Jews of Yemen are very scanty and the above-mentioned "Writ of Protection" is a sheer fabrication. The Geniza documents provide glimpses of the relations between Jews in Yemen and other Jewish communities, but they say almost nothing about the internal affairs of the Yemenite Jews. It seems safe to conclude that, with regard to the historical events that befell the Jews of Yemen from the rise of Islam until the beginning of the seventeenth century, we know mainly of two major events that befell the Jews of Yemen in the twelfth century. The first event is related in Maimonides' *Epistle to Yemen,* which so far is the most (and perhaps the only) significant source relating to the Jews of Yemen that has emanated from the Early and High Middle Ages; the other is provided by two Geniza documents relating to the Jews of Aden.[91]

From these two Geniza documents we learn that the Ayyūbid ruler of Yemen, al-Mālik al-Muʿizz Ismāʿīl (reigned 1197–1202) tried to impose forced conversion upon the Jews of Aden. This monarch, who is depicted in Arab historical sources as an eccentric and megalomaniac ruler,[92] threatened to execute all Jews who would not yield to his decree. From a letter written in August 1198, we learn that "On Friday, the third, the bell (of the market-crier) was rung: 'Community of Jews, all of you, anyone who will be late in appearing in the audience hall after noon, will be killed.' " The letter goes on to say that as a result of this decree "all apostatized. Some of the very religious, who defected from Islam, were beheaded."[93] From another letter, written by Madmun bin David, the head of the Jewish community of Aden, we learn, however, that with the death (more precisely, the murder) of this ruler of Yemen, relief was brought to the Jews of Aden, and they were allowed to return to their faith. This letter alludes to the intercession of Maimonides and other prominent Jews in Egypt on behalf of the Jews of Aden.[94]

Beside these two events, which are both related to Maimonides, nothing *significant* is known about the internal life of the Jews of Yemen during that long period. It should be stressed, however, that this statement regarding our abysmal knowledge of the Jews of Yemen during Islamic and medieval times is true only with respect to our current knowledge of Yemenite Jewry of that period. The traditions, customs, and religious writings preserved by the Jews of Yemen, as well as the references of Geniza documents to this community, give us every indication that Yemenite Jewry was not as isolated from other Jewish communities as has been widely held. The little evidence that we have clearly points out that a spiritual and cultural intercourse was maintained by the Jews of Yemen and the spiritual centers of Judaism in Palestine, Babylonia, Egypt, and later on in Spain. While there is every indication that the study of Jewish lore was well cultivated in Yemen and that the Yemenite Jews received spiritual guidance from the Jewish religious academies abroad, the extent of this contact is still difficult to ascertain.

6. Traditions, Customs, and Religious Writings

The Jews of Yemen were most probably familiar with the liturgical poetry composed during the *piyyuṭ* period (between the fifth and tenth centuries C.E.) in Palestine by the celebrated Jewish poets of that period: Yosse ben Yosse,[95] Yanai, Elᶜazar Hakkalir, and others. Several poems of this literary genre from this particular period are extant because they were copied and preserved by Yemenite Jews. It should be noted further that Yemenite Jewry has furnished us with the only known copies of the liturgical poems (*piyyuṭim*) composed by Saᶜadia Gaon and other Babylonian poets. Furthermore, poems were composed in Yemen under the influence of the Babylonian *piyyuṭ*. A particularly well-known form of this liturgical poetry is the *maranot,* which consist mainly of short hymns writen in Aramaic.[96]

Manuscripts of fragments of the Talmud which were discovered among the Yemenite writings clearly show, with respect to various details, distinct differences between the version preserved in Yemen and the other prevalent versions known to us. With the discovery of these fragments the erroneous claim voiced by various scholars that the Jews of Yemen were completely ignorant of the Talmud and of the works of the Gaonim were proved to be totally fallacious.[97] Moreover, it is widely held today that the extant fragments of the Talmud which have been preserved by the Yemenites might reflect, if not the original Babylonian version of the Talmud, then what is most probably the closest of all the extant versions to the original. It is evident from the fragments that the Yemenites have preserved a more condensed and more lucid version of the Talmud. Thus, the Talmudic scholar Rabbi Mordechai Hakkohen, who published one of these fragments, commented, "Without entering in depth into the question whether this is indeed the original version of the Babylonian Talmud or not, it should be recognized that every page of the Yemenite [version] of the Talmud is of great importance for the elucidation of the versions."[98]

Yet one wonders how to square this evidence of Yemenite familiarity with the Talmud with the testimony of such a careful and reliable person as Jacob Saphir, who visited Yemen in 1859 and had the following to say about the Yemenites: "Most of the Jews in this land [Yemen] are not devoid of Torah. But very few of them study the Talmud and Rabbinic literature. Only one out of a thousand has some familiarity with the Talmud, because it is not available in the land."[99] Yemenite scholars have furnished a plausible explanation for this apparent discrepancy, saying that Saphir's observations do indeed reflect the situation that prevailed in Yemen over the last few centuries, but they do not hold true for earlier times.[100] The devastating persecutions and tribulations that befell the Jews of Yemen, particularly since the seventeenth century, brought about the narrowing of their intellectual horizon and subsequently their spiritual decline. Symptomatic of these misfortunes was a corresponding decline in talmudic study. These precarious conditions did not allow for indulgence in hairsplitting dialectics (*pilpul*) such as those of the Talmud. The circumstances, therefore, forced the Jews of Yemen to steer away from sophisticated writings and strained logical argumentation and to stick to the essentials of the Torah.[101]

This decline in the study of the Talmud was undoubtedly accelerated by the supremacy that Maimonides's work *Mishne Torah* gained in Yemen, as in many other countries, over all the rabbinic writings, and particularly over the Talmud. The heightened prestige of his work, which constitutes a codification of the Jewish law in a logical sequence and in a readily accessible form, is easily understood when one considers the tremendous impact that Maimonides's personality had on the Jews of Yemen. The "great Eagle," as Maimonides is often called, won the hearts of the Yemenite Jews by his well-known *Epistle to Yemen* (1172). Since then, Yemenite Jewry has viewed him as the crown and glory of Israel. Except for Saᶜadia Gaon (882–942),[102] no other personality has exerted such a tremendous influence on the Jews of Yemen in so many spheres, including that of the prayer rites.[103] Yemenite rabbis and leaders corresponded with him. They showered unstinting praise upon him and sought his guidance in theological and practical issues. Some insight into the high esteem of the Yemenite Jews for Maimonides may be gained from the testimony of Nahmanides, who said that the Yemenites who accepted Maimonides as the greatest religious authority used to mention his name in every *qaddish* בחייכון וביומיכון ובחיי דרבנא משה בן מימון (In your lifetime and during your days, and within the life of rabbi

Moses ben Maimon.)[104] The extraordinary reverence of the Yemenites for Maimonides was also witnessed by Saphir, who wrote:

> They [the Yemenite Jews] say that before Maimonides they used to rule only in accordance with the Talmud and following their own traditions. But after Maimonides sent them his well-known *Epistle to Yemen* and his book *Mishne Torah,* some of their sages went to Egypt to test him; when they recognized how great was his fame, wisdom, and piety, they accepted him as a teacher and spiritual guide for themselves and their offspring. . . ."[105]

It should be added that both the introduction of the Qabbalah to Yemen in the sixteenth century and the extensive indulgence of the Yemenite Jews in mystical speculation also contributed to the decline of the Yemenites' preoccupation with talmudic discussions.

A further evidence of the ties that Yemenite Jewry maintained with Babylonia is provided by the Hebrew inscription which was discovered in 1970 by Walter W. Müller in the mosque of the Yemenite village, Bait al-Ḥāḍir.[106] This inscription contains the most complete list of the priestly courses extant. Its main significance, said Urbach, resides in the fact that it provides the earliest evidence of the ancient custom among the Jews of the diaspora of inscribing the names of the priestly courses in public places. This custom, remarked Urbach, is indicative of a desire on the part of priestly families to preserve their family pedigree.[107] But the fact that some readings in this inscription reflect the Babylonian version confirms the close attachment of Yemenite Jewry to Babylonia.

Another indication of the strong relations that the Jews of Yemen maintained with the Babylonian Jewish academies is the retention of the Babylonian superlinear system of punctuation in Yemen. It is noteworthy that the Yemenite Jewish communities are the only ones which preserved this system of punctuation in their biblical texts. Indeed, as early as the first half of the tenth century C.E., al-Qirqisānī, the well-known Karaite historian, stated that the Babylonian version of the Bible was in use in Yamāma, Baḥrain, and Yemen.[108] Moreover, the Yemenite pronunciation of the Hebrew text of both the Bible and the Talmud, which is totally different from that of the *Sephardi* (of Spanish stock) and *Ashkenazi* (Central or Eastern European) Jews, is indeed unique in this respect. The Hebrew pronunciation of the Jews of Yemen, remarked Neubauer, "is very minute and accurate according to the tonic accents." These Yemenites, concludes Neubauer, possibly "retain the old tradition of reciting Biblical passages."[109] This distinctive pronunciation could be viewed as indicative of continued interaction between the Yemenites and the Babylonian Jewish academies.

Such interaction is also evidenced by the fact that the Yemenite Jews were the only Jewish community which unceasingly adhered to the system of dating events in accordance with the "era of the contracts" (Seleucid). Thus, for example, the dating of epitaphs in the old cemetery in Aden by means of this system certainly points to the Yemenite ties with the Babylonian schools. Indeed, the Yemenites adhered to this ancient system of dating until the 1950s when they were transported en masse to Israel.[110]

The bond which existed between the Jews of Yemen and the Babylonian Jewish spiritual centers is further evidenced by the fact that some customs of the Yemenite prayer rites go back (even after Maimonides) to the pervasive influence of the prayer book of Rabbi Saᶜadia Gaon (882–942). The Yemenite Jews, as Saphir and others have noted, strongly adhere to Saᶜadia's Arabic translation of the Hebrew Scriptures, as well as to his Arabic commentary, known as *Tafsīr.* The Yemenites, added Saphir, were so enamored with Saᶜadia Gaon and his biblical work that they sincerely believed that either he was one of them (a Yemenite) or he must have spent some time in their midst. Saphir raised the possibility, which has so far not been substantiated, that Saᶜadia might indeed have lived in Yemen following his dispute with Ben-Zakkai, since he was very much revered by the Yemenites.[111] While Saphir's assumption is no more than speculation, it, together with other considerations previously set forth, does clearly indicate that Yemenite Jewry did not live in total isolation from the rest of the Jewish communities, as has been widely assumed, but were rather an integral part of the larger body of the Jewish people and contributed spiritually and financially to the development of the Jewish academies in Palestine, Babylon, and later in Egypt. As a result of these strong ties, every significant composition from the Gaonic period and even earlier times reached the Jews of Yemen.[112] This fact is made abundantly clear by the testimony of Maimonides, who in his famous *Epistle to Yemen* had this to say about the Jews of Yemen: "They continually study the Law of Moses, walk in the way of R. Ashi, pursue justice, repair the breach, uphold the principles of the Torah, bring back the stray people of God by encouraging words, observe the religious ceremonies punctiliously in their communities. . . . "[113]

Reports regarding the Jews of Yemen come to us from the celebrated twelfth-century Jewish traveler Benjamin of Tudela. Benjamin, who traveled from Spain as far eastward as Baghdad, provides us with vivid reports about the existence of large Jewish communities in "the land of Saba, which is called the land El-Yemen."[114] Unfortunately, Benjamin's reports are desperately confused, at times even contradictory. They betray a total ignorance of the geography of Arabia. Benjamin confused the Jews of Yemen with the purportedly surviving Jews of northern Arabia. For example, Benjamin wrote that in the land of El-Yemen

> dwell the Jews called Kheibar, the men of Teima. And Teima is their seat of government where R. Hanan the Nasi rules over them. . . . The Jews own many large fortified cities. The yoke of the Gentiles is not upon them. They go forth to pillage and to capture booty from distant lands in conjunction with the Arabs, their neighbours and allies. . . . [115]

Benjamin goes on to say that these Jews are ruled by two brothers, Salmon the Nasi and Hanan the Nasi, "who are of the seed of David." Benjamin stresses the strong bond that he claims existed between these Arabian Jews and their kinsmen in Baghdad. He reports that the authority wielded by the Baghdad Exilarch, Daniel the son of Hisdai, extended from Baghdad "over all the communities of Shinar, Persia, Khurasan and Sheba which is El-Yemen."[116]

Despite the overall trustworthiness of Benjamin's reports of Jewish communities in the regions that he himself visited, his accounts regarding the Jews of Arabia should be approached with great caution. Because of the obvious vagueness of Benjamin's data concerning places east of the Persian Gulf, modern scholars do not believe that he ever set foot in regions east of Baghdad. Baron, however, argued that this vagueness may well be attributed to the fact that "the further away from the main centers of Jewish learning he [Benjamin] moved, the less precise was the information supplied to him by local leaders, who themselves neither possessed nor evinced great curiosity in such exact data."[117] Be that as it may, one may safely infer from the extremely fanciful reports provided by Benjamin regarding the Jews of Arabia that he himself had never visited that area. This fact is markedly evident in his description of the Jews of Aden. "These Jews," wrote Benjamin,

> are not under the yoke of the Gentiles, but possess cities and castles on the summits of the mountains, from which they make descents into the plains country called Lybia, which is a Christian Empire. . . . The Jews take spoil and booty and retreat to the mountains, and no man can prevail against them.[118]

It should be noted, however, that Benjamin's account regarding the Jews of Arabia, notwithstanding their wild exaggeration and high degree of embellishment, should not be dismissed as totally legendary. His reports attest to the presence of strong and flourishing Jewish communities in Yemen and to a continuous social, cultural, and spiritual intercourse between them and other Jewish communities. The paucity of data on the Jews of Arabia during Benjamin's period makes these accounts, when stripped of their legendary ingredients, significant. A critical evaluation of these reports in light of the more authentic information furnished by the Cairo Geniza documents provides a more balanced and plausible picture of the Jews of Yemen, during pre-Ayyūbid and Ayyūbid periods.

IV

JEWISH LITERARY CREATIVITY IN YEMEN IN THE THIRTEENTH AND FOURTEENTH CENTURIES

1. The Rasūlid Period

The Ayyūbid reign of Yemen (1173–1229) was followed by that of the Rasūlids (1229–ca. 1454). The Rasūlid period is marked by an extensive literary creativity on the part of Yemenite Jewry. The Rasūlid reign in Yemen was established by Nūr al-Dīn ᶜUmar, following the departure of the last Ayyūbid ruler al-Masᶜūd Yūsuf, who was summoned in 1229 by his father, al-Kāmil, the Ayyūbid ruler of Egypt, to govern Syria.[1] Nūr al-Dīn, who first ruled on behalf of the Ayyūbids, soon proclaimed himself the ruler of Yemen and assumed the title al-Manṣūr. The Zaydī imamate continued to exist, with fluctuating fortunes, in the northern part of Yemen alongside that of the Sunnī Rasūlids who, during most of their reign, governed the greater part of Yemen. These two states, which generally coexisted with mutual hostility, were marked by a sharp contrast in their respective levels of political, social, and economic development. The Zaydī imāms were more concerned with propagating and enforcing the Zaydī doctrines and norms of conduct than they were with the economic development of their realm. Moreover, the imamate was plagued by political and social instability due to the rise of various claimants to the throne, a fact which plunged the state into intertribal armed conflicts. Thus, accession to the throne had to be accomplished by force. Consequently, these internecine hostilities debilitated the imamate and had disastrous effects upon its economy. As a result of these and other factors, the imamate, with its varying fortunes and boundaries, was characterized by economic stagnation and isolation from international trade routes. Such was the state of affairs of the Zaydī state until the Ottoman occupation in 1538.

The economic and social conditions in the Rasūlid state were diametrically opposed to those of its rival in the north. The Rasūlid reign, which lasted more than two centuries, was marked by a far greater degree of political stability and economic development, thereby promoting agricultural reforms and a substantial surplus in production for export. Moreover, as a result of the decline of the ᶜAbbāsid caliphate in Baghdad, the east-west trade shifted back from the Persian Gulf to the Red Sea. This shift greatly enhanced the revival of the southern Arabian ports, particularly that of Aden, which served as centers of wide-ranging mercantile activities.[2]

Unfortunately, we are ill-informed concerning the social and religious conditions of the Jews of Yemen in general, and of those ruled by the Zaydī imamate in particular, during the Rasūlid eras, as indeed we are with respect to the preceding periods. The Muslim chronicles, whose treatment of Yemenite history is in itself sporadic and generally confined in its attention to those events only insofar as they impinge upon wider Islamic affairs, seldom refer to the Jews of Yemen. Moreover, Jewish chronicles emanating from this period are not available. Despite this dearth of information with respect to the social conditions of the Jews of Yemen, the wealth of poetic, midrashic, and other literary material which has come to us from this period clearly shows that the Rasūlid reign was an era of remarkable Jewish literary creativity—poetic and midrashic.

The sources of Yemenite Hebrew poetry, to be sure, are ancient and do in fact go back to Jewish Babylonian and Eretz Israelite poetry, which was exclusively liturgical and sacred.[3] However, once Yemenite literature came in contact with the Jewish culture of Spain, it radically modified its forms and incorporated various aspects of the spirit and character of the Spanish Hebrew literature, which in itself had been enormously influenced by that of Arabic. Indeed, the remarkable revival of medieval Hebrew literature would have been inconceivable without the striking impact of medieval Arabic language and literature upon Hebrew in Spain. The latter adopted Arabic prosodic and thematic conventions, among them the laws of rhythm, ornamental devices, patterns of sound, and especially the Arabic quantitative metrics with their versifications, sophistication, and artistic variations.[4] As Goitein remarked, the Spanish Hebrew poet drew "full measure from a civilization which was closely akin to his own. . . ."[5] Spain, in turn, served as a center of imitation for other Jewish communities, including those of Yemen. Thus Yemenite Hebrew literature developed and flourished to a great extent under the profound influence of the Spanish school of Hebrew literature.[6]

The earliest traces of the Spanish influence on Yemenite literature may be discerned in the poetry of Rabbi Daniel be-Rabbi Fayyūmī, who lived in the first half of the twelfth century. The extant poems of Fayyūmī, the earliest Yemenite Jewish poet known to us by name, revolved mainly around the themes of the *yamim nora'im* (Days of Awe).[7] But the first Hebrew poem with a classical Arabic structure that has reached us from Yemen is *ᶜAl ha-Sheḥiṭa* (On Ritual Slaughter), composed in 1308 by Rabbi Zecharia ben Seᶜadia, who lived in Aden.[8] The poem shows in its form and structure (though not in its content) a clearly Spanish influence.

From the Spanish masters, the Yemenite poets freely and abundantly borrowed expressions, figures of speech, and verses (particularly opening or leading verses) and incorporated them into their own poems. Most indicative, however, of the strong influence that Spanish Hebrew poetry exerted upon Yemenite poets is the poetic genre of the *jawāb* (answer, reply) in which a poet could take a whole poem composed by one of the Spanish masters of Hebrew verse and build upon it or interweave in it verses of his own. He could literally copy the opening line, echo the theme and adopt the rhyme and the meter of a celebrated poem. Thus, through an exercise of ingenuity, a new poem would emerge. This appropriation of Spanish verses or of entire poems, which was so prevalent in Yemen, attests to the enormous attraction that the Spanish Hebrew school had in Yemen. The fact that numerous poems were composed in Yemen as *jawāb* to Yehuda Halevi's poems, particularly to his *Yaᶜavor ᶜAlai Reṣonkha,* indicates the strong influence that his poetry exerted upon the Yemenite counterpart.[9]

The most prominent of the known Yemenite Jewish poets during the Rasūlid period is Abraham ben Ḥalfon, who collected his poems in a *diwān* (anthology of poems) of his own. Rabbi Zecharia al-Ḍahrī, who lived in the sixteenth century, mentioned a book by Abraham ben Ḥalfon.[10] The reference is most probably to this *diwān,* a part of which was published by Yisra'el Davidson.[11] While the precise years of ben Ḥalfon cannot be definitely ascertained, the available evidence dates his work to no later than the first part of the fifteenth century.

The literary and spiritual contribution of Yemenite Jewry lies mainly in the realm of *midrashim,* and its greatest gift to Judaism in this respect is the compendium *Midrash ha-Gadol,* compiled by Rabbi David ben ᶜAmram ha-ᶜAdani (thirteenth century).[12] In this composition, Rabbi ᶜAdani collected all the fruits of the literary creativity of the Jewish sages up to his own time: Babylonian, Jerusalemite, Gaonic, halakhic, and homiletic *midrashim,* and others. Rabbi ᶜAdani's work was not motivated by a mere concern for anthology, but by the desire to collect all the existing *midrashim* in one single compilation relevantly attached to biblical verses. His goal, therefore, was similar to that which Maimonides sought to achieve in his halakhic work *Mishne Torah,* namely to facilitate the study of the *midrashim* by eliminating the need to consult the numerous and diverse midrashic compilations and those interspersed in the voluminous *talmudim.* Like Maimonides, Rabbi ᶜAdani does not provide references to his sources.[13]

Midrash ha-Gadol is structured in accordance with the fifty-four weekly Portions of the Torah. Each Portion is preceded by a poem, which serves as a midrashic introduction to it. One poem serves as an introduction to the whole book, and another one is added to the Portion of *Ḥuqqat* (Num. 19–21), thus dividing it into two. Each poem concludes with a prayer for Israel's redemption and for the ingathering of the exiles. The influence of the Spanish School of Hebrew verse is readily discernible, particularly in the rhyming techniques employed in these poems.[14]

The importance of this compilation of rabbinic scholarship is underscored by the fact that it saved for us extensive portions of lost ancient midrashic works, such as *Mekhilta de-Rabbi Shimeᶜon bar-Yoḥai, Sifre Zuṭa, Mekhilta for Deuteronomy, Devarim Rabbah* of the Spanish sages, *Midrash of the Thirty-Two Principles,* and many others.

The literary creativity of Yemenite Jewry during the Rasūlid era in Yemen was extensive and diverse. It comprised, in addition to the many commentaries on the Hebrew Scriptures, numerous philosophical and theological studies and commentaries on the works of Maimonides. Thus, for example, in 1392, Rabbi Netan'el ben Yeshaᶜya wrote *Nūr al-ẓalām,* a midrashic-philosophical work on the Torah.[15] A prolific writer of this period (fifteenth century) was Rabbi Zacharia ben Shelomo ha-Rofe, who had written numerous books, twelve of which are extant.[16] His works, which addressed a wide range of subjects and were written in Hebrew, Aramaic, and Arabic, include commentaries on Maimonides's books: *Mishne Torah, Sefer ha-Miṣvot,* and *More Nevukhim.* Mention should also be made of the works of Rabbi Ḥoṭer ben Shelomo (ca. mid-fifteenth century). Prominent among his compositions are: *A Commentary of the Thirteen Principles of Maimonides* and *Sirāj al-ᶜUqūl,* a commentary on the Torah.[17] The former commentary contains, as David Blumenthal pointed out, several sections of theological interest, including two proofs for the existence of God, a "proof" for the eternity of matter, two Ṣūfī poems, selections from the *Shiᶜur Qomah,* quotations from *Rasā'il Ikhwān al-Ṣafā',* and several unknown *midrashim.*[18]

2. The Ottoman Occupation of Yemen (1538–1635)

The short period following the Rasūlid reign and prior to the Ottoman occupation of Yemen, which began in 1538, was marked by the wide expansion of the Zaydī imamate, which also managed to assert its authority over the southern part of Yemen. However, disunity among the Zaydīs and continual internecine warfare plunged the country back into a pitiful disarray and disintegration. The collapse of the imām's authority over parts of Yemen and the failure of the Yemenite leaders to pursue common objectives made the country vulnerable to foreign invasion.

The advent of the Portuguese in the Mediterranean region at the beginning of the sixteenth century and their hostile activity against Arab shipping in the Indian Ocean, the Gulf of Aden, and the Red Sea dealt a mortal blow to international commerce. The Portuguese incursion obstructed maritime communications and set in motion a wave of hostilities which included the Mameluke attempt to invade Yemen in 1514 and the Ottoman naval ventures against the Portuguese. In 1517 the Ottoman Turks occupied Egypt, and in 1538 they occupied Aden and, soon afterwards, the major part of Yemen. These and other factors proved disastrous for many commercial centers along the sea routes and brought about a precipitous decline of the port of Aden, which had prior to this period served as a prominent international commercial center. As late as August 1538, Aden had been described as a strongly fortified city. Its port was praised as "large, with good anchorage being safe in all winds." The city, it was added, was "provided with provisions, wood, and every other necessity from other places, and has abundance of Jews."[19] The grave erosion in the status of Aden as a commercial center, however, caused the emigration of many of its inhabitants to other commercial centers.[20]

In 1608, Middleton found Aden "hopeless for trade purposes." In 1609 the British captain reported that his ship, *The Ascension,* succeeded in reaching Aden, "only to find that it was a place of garrison rather than trade."[21]

The decline of Aden as an international emporium brought about a subsequent eclipse of its role as the "eye of Yemen." The once flourishing Jewish community experienced a gradual shrinkage of its numbers and found itself reduced to the status of a small, impoverished, and insignificant community. The contact of the Yemenite Jews with the outside world was drastically severed, and Yemenite Jewry sank into total isolation, cut off from contact not only with the outside world, but also from the mainstreams of Jewish culture.

3. Rabbi Zecharia al-Ḍahrī (ca. 1516–ca. 1581)

Rabbi Zecharia al-Ḍahrī, one of the most gifted of all Yemenite Jewish writers, and certainly the most versatile, was born during the turbulent period in Yemen prior to the Ottoman conquest of the country.[22] The exact dates of his birth and death cannot be determined. However, extrapolating from the various dates of events that he provides in his works, one can reasonably trace his date of birth to ca. 1516 and that of his death to ca. 1581.

Al-Ḍahrī was a prolific writer. His numerous works include secular and religious poems, philosophical and midrashic commentaries on the Torah, and compilations regarding ritual laws of *Sheḥiṭa* (slaughter of animals).[23] His *magnum opus,* however, is his *Sefer ha-Musar,* the composition of which he began in prison, in the year 1568.[24] The author claimed that he had written this work for a strictly didactic purpose, "so that he who reads it . . . may draw a lesson from the tribulations and suffering that befell us, on account of our transgressions and sins, that he may be moved to humble himself [before God] like a slave before his Master. . . . perhaps this will provide a balm for our wounds, a tree of life that bears fruit." It is for this reason, said al-Ḍahrī, that he called his book *Sefer ha-Musar.*[25]

However, it should be noted that, while *sefer ha-Musar* does indeed contain passages and poems of penitence and reproof, its main thrust is rather *secular,* a fact which renders it unique in the body of what are otherwise predominantly religious writings emanating from the Jews of Yemen. The book consists of forty-five chapters written in the style of the *maqāma* (rhymed-prose), a literary genre which the celebrated Muslim writer al-Ḥarīrī (1054–1122) raised to its highest pinnacle.[26] While the influence of al-Ḥarīrī upon al-Ḍahrī is clearly discernible, that of al-Ḥarīrī's Hebrew disciple, al-Ḥarīzī (1170–1235), the master of Hebrew rhymed-prose, is far more pronounced.[27] Indeed in the introduction to his book, al-Ḍahrī acknowledged his indebtedness to al-Ḥarīzī, "who preceded me with his book (*Taḥkemoni*) . . . which he himself had learnt from the Ishmaelite, al-Ḥarīrī, the master of the exquisite verse."[28]

Like his predecessor and master, al-Ḍahrī's *maqāmāt* consist of rhymed-parables, folklore, description of travels and adventures, and the like. His writings, as characteristic of the *maqāma,* abound with literary tricks, conceits, and artifices which display an astonishing facility in the creative manipulation of the language. Each chapter has as its framework the author's extensive travels in various parts of the world. Al-Ḍahrī, according to his own testimony, was possessed of a wanderlust and an adventurous nature, and his curiosity and his restless impulses carried him through many countries. His itinerary includes Egypt, Syria, Iraq, Turkey, Eretz Israel, Persia, and India.

The chief protagonist of his book is the wanderer, Avner ben-Ḥeleq, who is accompanied by his admirer, Mordekhai ha-Ṣidoni. The latter relates the adventures of Avner, his hero. Avner emerges from Mordekhai's descriptions as a multifaceted character: On the one hand, he is depicted as a daring, quick-tongued, roguish, and wily hero who is given to committing acts of folly. Moreover, in the execution of his astute and crafty schemes, he manages to extricate himself from various dangerous predicaments. But on the other hand, he is also portrayed as "the master of verse and magnificent parables," whose words are sweet and pleasing to the ear.[29]

Al-Ḍahrī's *Sefer ha-Musar* is a valuable firsthand source of information regarding the conditions of the Jews in Yemen during part of the sixteenth century. The picture which emerges from the numerous references to the Jews of Yemen is that of an extremely persecuted community. He related that in 1568, the ruler of Yemen decreed the mass incarceration of Jews, scattering them in prisons throughout the country, and imposed hard labor upon them.[30] The author, who was one of the prisoners, lamented in one of his poems that the Yemenite ruler "has drenched the hills and the mountains with my tears." He further complained that this ruler has no compassion for the children and the old, "Fathers and sons were put in fetters." Al-Ḍahrī also related that the prisoners were struck by famine and subsequent plagues, which resulted in the deaths of many of them. The victims, he mourned, were

> Dispersed in the west of Yemen,
> cast out to the heat [by day] and to the frost [by night];
> And these precious ones, O, how they longed for a morsel of bread!
> They perished in the valleys,
> And were not brought to burial.[31]

This period of tribulations, noted al-Ḍahrī, ended in 1573.[32]

Al-Ḍahrī did not mention the name of the ruler who ordered the persecution of the Jews; he referred to him only by the nickname *Ḥigger* (lame). Nor did he provide any details with respect to the reasons which triggered the wrath of the Yemenite ruler against the Jews. The reference, however, is undoubtedly to Muṭahhar, the eldest son of Imām Sharaf al-Dīn. According to Muslim chroniclers, Muṭahhar was lame and misshapen, a fact which gave him the nickname *al-'Aʿraj* (the lame). Al-Nahrawālī related that because of his deformity, Muṭahhar was considered by Zaydī law and custom to be unfit for the imamate. He went on to say that Sharaf al-Dīn declared his younger son ᶜAlī as his successor to the throne, an act which greatly antagonized Muṭahhar, "the eldest, smartest, and most cunning of his brothers." Al-Nahrawālī furthermore said that Muṭahhar responded by declaring war against both his father and brother, inviting Uwais Pasha, the commander of the Ottoman forces of Zabīd, to invade the imām's territory. Prompted by this invitation as well as by the woeful disarray of the country caused by the continuous internecine wars, Uwais Pasha immediately responded by taking control of the southern regions of Yemen, including Taᶜizz. He then marched northward, captured Sanaa and advanced as far north as Ṣaᶜda. But the Turkish forces, which were later led by Uzdumur Pasha, moved against Muṭahhar himself. In 1543 Muṭahhar was forced to conclude a truce with the Turks by which he recognized the Ottoman's sovereignty.[33]

The ninety years of Ottoman rule over Yemen was one of the most unfortunate chapters in the history of this country. The Turkish governors, who followed one another in rapid succession, were greedy and extremely corrupt. The coinage (dinar) was progressively debased, and citizens were robbed and despoiled.[34] The increasing unrest triggered local revolts throughout the country. The growing disenchantment with Turkish rule was disastrously exploited by Muṭahhar, who managed to foment a country-wide revolt against the Ottoman occupation. As a result of two years of fierce battles (1565–1567), the Ottomans were forced to retreat to Zabīd, their former foothold. Thus, Muṭahhar managed to liberate his country from Ottoman occupation. Muṭahhar's victory over the Turks, however, did not last long. In 1569 Sinan Pasha set out by land and sea with an expedition from Suez to Arabia. He marched through Tihāma, occupied Taᶜizz, and moved northward to Sanaa and Dhamar. Muṭahhar's call for *jihād* (holy war) against the Turks did not prevent the latter from sweeping the country. In 1570 the sovereignty of the Porte was restored. Muṭahhar died in 1572.

Al-Ḍahrī's references to waves of persecutions against the Jews of Yemen should be understood within the context of this extremely turbulent period in Yemen. To judge from a pattern which is recurrent in Yemen's history, internecine wars generally exposed the Jews (particularly those of Sanaa, who were most vulnerable) to the situation of being crushed between the hammer and the anvil, each disputant demanding their undivided loyalty. This predicament was greatly aggravated by the Ottoman invasion of the country and by the incessant local revolts against foreign occupation. Moreover, the Jews, as repeatedly expressed in Yemenite Jewish writing, generally felt far more secure under Ottoman rule and therefore preferred the Turks over the imāms and other local rulers. The mass imprisonment of the Jews in 1568, which was ordered by the victorious Muṭahhar, may well be conceived within the context of reprisals against suspected collaborators with the Ottomans. Indeed, local victories against the Turks triggered mass persecution against the Jews.

The insight into sixteenth-century Yemenite Jewry that al-Ḍahrī's *Sefer ha-Musar* provides, though limited in scope, is nevertheless extremely valuable, considering the paucity of data that we have regarding the Jews of Yemen during this particular period. Of no less interest, however, are the many glimpses that this work affords us of the various Jewish communities in the several countries that the author visited. His detailed references to the Jews of Safed, the center of the Qabbalah, and to the Jews of Tiberia and Damascus are very illuminating.[35] Al-Ḍahrī, to judge from his writings, was greatly enamored with the Qabbalah, which he viewed as a source of eternal light, "God's treasured possession for His Chosen People." He stressed the sanctity of the Zohar and called upon everyone to study the secrets of this glorious book, "from which even the sun draws its light," for those who fathom its mysteries will "climb the mountains" of enlightenment. The Zohar, al-Ḍarhī stressed, is the source of life *par excellence,* and he who meditates upon it will never hunger or thirst for spring-water; his soul will repudiate all sweets. Al-Ḍahrī spoke with great reverence of Rabbi Shimeon bar-Yoḥai, to whom the Zohar is traditionally attributed, and he lavished praise upon the teachers of the Qabbalah.[36]

Al-Ḍahrī's encounter with the teachings of the Qabbalah had a far-reaching effect upon Yemenite Jewry. When he returned to Yemen, al-Ḍahrī propagated the teachings of the Qaballah among his Yemenite brethren; since then the Qabbalah and the Zohar had an ever-increasing grip upon the spiritual life of this Jewish community. The influence of this new and esoteric realm reached its climax in the writings of Rabbi Shalom Shabazi, the greatest of all Yemenite writers.

Al-Ḍahrī's *Sefer ha-Musar* is also indicative of the author's great familiarity with medieval Arabic and Hebrew poetry. The influence of Yehuda Halevi, Abraham ibn Ezra, and Shelomo ibn Gabriol, the masters of medieval Hebrew verse, is strongly felt in his book. Al-Ḍahrī wrote several poems as *jawāb* (response) to those of Yehuda Halevi.[37]

Al-Ḍahrī's works show an extraordinary command of the resources of biblical and post-biblical Hebrew. He evinced great skill in bending the language to his will and purpose. Familiar fragments of verses are dextrously juggled by him and transformed into settings which are astonishing in their pervasive allusiveness and ostentatious verbal display. His *Sefer ha-Musar* exhibits a diversity of themes, most of which were intended for entertainment or instruction by entertainment. His writings display a gay enjoyment of life and the passionate ecstasy of love along with a plaintive pensiveness and religious exhortation.

If we were to judge him by the richness of his language and by the artistic variations, intelligent observations, creative power, and literary value manifest in his works, then al-Ḍahrī undoubtedly should have been considered the greatest writer Yemenite Jewry ever produced. *Sefer ha-Musar* however, was never widely accepted among the Jews of Yemen; it was viewed as a foreign element, an exceptional phenomenon of secular literature in the midst of what were predominantly sacred writings. Very few copies of this book were made and eventually it almost sank into oblivion, until it was rediscovered in 1894 by Brody, who published a part from its introduction and the last chapter.[38]

4. The Expulsion of the Turks from Yemen

In 1598 Qāsim ibn Muḥammad, the founder of the Qāsimī dynasty and direct descendant of Yaḥia al-Hādī, proclaimed himself imām and assumed the title al-Manṣūr Billāh (Victorious by the Grace of God).[39] He declared *jihād* (holy war) against the Turks and managed to unite major tribes behind his cause. After a vigorous struggle with fluctuating results, the Turks were forced to conclude a truce recognizing the authority of the Zaydī imām over the territories which he already controlled. In 1626, Imām al-Mu'ayyad, Qāsim's son, resumed his military campaign against the Turks and besieged the Ottoman forces in Sanaa, Zabīd, and Mocha. In 1635 the Ottomans in Yemen were defeated and Ḥaidar Pasha, the Ottoman governor, surrendered. Thus the Ottoman occupation of Yemen came to an end, only to be reestablished more firmly in 1848.[40]

The years of revolt against the Ottomans by al-Qāsim and his sons find relatively ample reflection in Yemenite Jewish writings, chronicles, and poetry.[41] These writings provide us not only with valuable insights into the conditions of the Jews during this short period, but also with numerous details concerning the revolt and its generally dire consequences. In many respects, the Jewish sources concerning this crucial period are richer than those of the Muslims. The Jewish writings focus in particular on the immense suffering that this ferocious war inflicted upon the Yemenite population in general and upon the Jews in particular. They provide us with information regarding the tribes and personalities involved, numbers of casualties, and the dates and details of major events relating to these hostilities; they speak of the scarcity of food during this dire period and even quote the outrageous prices of wheat, barley, and millet which prevailed then.

Generally speaking, the Jews of Yemen had good reason to be more favorably disposed toward Ottoman rule than toward that of the Zaydis. While the former was, as a rule, tolerant and equitable toward the Jews, the latter viewed the Jews as inferiors and imposed numerous humiliating measures upon them. Indeed, Yemenite Jewish writings generally lavish praises upon the Ottomans and express bitterness and contempt toward the Zaydīs. But totally different is their attitude with respect to Fadlī Pasha, one of the Ottoman rulers in Yemen. Fadli Pasha seems to have succeeded in arousing the wrath not only of the Muslims but of the Jews as well. Rabbi Shalom Shabazi depicted him in his work *Ḥemdat Yamim* as a wicked and ignominious governor who inflicted immense suffering upon the Jews. He referred to him by the abusive term *Sarḥi* ("stinky," "transgressor," as against his name, *Faḍlī,* which means "gracious," "kind"). According to Shabazi, Fadlī Pasha tried to impose forced conversion upon the Jews of Yemen. As a result of his decree,

> many Jews deserted the sacred faith and embraced the profane one. Many, however, preferred martyrdom. All this happened in the days of Sarḥi the governor [namely, Faḍlī Pasha], may his bones be ground to powder, and may the name of the wicked rot.[42] And the fine flour was separated from the waste. And they took hold of my father, of blessed memory, together with other Jews and they flogged them and afflicted them until their clothes were sullied with blood. They kept them in jail for twelve months, chained with iron fetters.

Shabazi went on to say that the Jews were saved by Imām al-Qāsim, to whom he referred by the laudatory term *Yefet* ("beautiful," "lovely"). This "righteous Ishmaelite," said Shabazi, "emerged from the east and eradicated the seed of Esau from Yemen."[43]

Indeed, according to a Muslim Yemenite chronicle, Jews rendered help to al-Qāsim in his crusade against the Turks. Armed with slings, they fought for him; others gave money.[44]

These wars and revolts caused immense suffering and extensive damage to the local inhabitants, particularly to the Jews of Yemen. The most affected, however, was the Jewish community of Sanaa, the capital of Yemen. It was always the maxim that the ruler who holds Sanaa holds the kingdom. Most of the fierce battles, therefore, raged around Sanaa. The city would often come under siege for a considerable time, causing hunger to be a frequent and familiar guest there. Along with the two scourges of sword and famine, a third would often follow—drought, which would greatly intensify the misery of the people.

In such turbulent years (and these were many), the Jews suffered the most. In predominantly agricultural Yemen, the Muslims could feed on past crops stored in granaries. The Jews, who were mainly craftsmen and thus totally dependent on Muslims for their livelihood, found themselves in such times without work and consequently helpless in the face of drought and famine. The tribulations of the Jews, especially those of Sanaa, during the siege of this city by al-Qāsim find expression in three laments written by Saᶜid Darin, who was then one of the prominent rabbis of Sanaa.[45] The poet poured out his heart at the devastation that the war had wrought upon the inhabitants of Sanaa, in particular the Jews, and at the subsequent famine in which many perished. The lofty houses, he complained, were demolished, and their sustaining beams were burned:

> My flesh stiffened for fear of the enemy;
> Upon my bones my skin shrivelled,
> My visage was no longer recognized
> Because God summoned the famine. . . . [46]

In another poem, written in Arabic with Hebrew characters, Darin bewailed the fate of Sanaa. This city of glorious kings, which was "the abode of tranquility, repose, blessing, hope, and utmost health, and a center of friendly gatherings," this lovely Sanaa "is now in ruins, a desolation, a snare for the wretched ones who remained in it."

5. Rabbi Shalom Shabazi (1619–after 1679)

The seventeenth century provided us with the most celebrated of all Yemenite Jewish personalities and writers, Rabbi Shalom Shabazi. Shabazi, the only saint which Yemenite Jewry ever produced, left us a literary legacy which consists of a large corpus of poems and an extensive midrashic commentary on the Pentateuch.[48]

The birth, life, and death of Shabazi (popularly known in Yemen by the name "Abbo Sholem") are shrouded in a thick veil of mystery. Legend is inextricably mixed with fact in all that is told of him.[49] His birth was associated with a celestial phenomenon, which he related as follows:

> Our sages of blessed memory said that in the days to come a star would rise from the east, and that it would have a tail. This [they

> said] is the star of the Messiah. Why does it have a tail? To designate the scepter of kingdom, for Scriptures say, "The scepter shall not depart from Judah."[50] [This star] would stay for 15 days; but if it stays for more time, this will be good for Israel. From then on you should expect the coming of the Messiah. Such indeed was the case in 1619. . . . [51] Our fathers of blessed memory told us that in that year two stars rose from the East with tails like a stick. One star remained 15 days, and the other 40 days. They used to say that these were the stars of the Messiah. . . . But now we are already in the year 1646 and we are still waiting for the coming of the Messiah. Perhaps he will appear in the year 80 like Moses, as Scriptures say, "And Moses was eighty years old when he stood before Pharaoh. . . . "[52] Our sages said that on the same day in which the stars rose, the Messiah was born. May God gather our exiles, Amen.[53]

The significant role that astrology played in medieval societies (Jewish, Christian, and Muslim) is too well known to need lengthy treatment. Suffice it to say that personal affairs and terrestrial events were believed to be predestined or influenced by the configuration and movement of the celestial bodies. Although astrology has lost much of the luster and the "splendid scientific pomp" that it had been accorded in ancient times and the Middle Ages, it has not lost its grip on the people of Yemen, Muslims and Jews alike. "The irony of fate," remarked C. A. Nallino, is that today in Yemen, "it is no less personages than the Kadis (judges) who practice the profession of astrologers."[54] Much attention is paid in Yemen to astral and other natural phenomena. These include comets, meteors, unusual winds and storms, thunder and lightning, clouds, earthquakes, and eclipses. They are considered to be indicators (*dalāʾil*) of future events and, as such, are meticulously recorded. Thus, al-Nahrawālī related that a religious judge (*qāḍī*) by the name of Aḥmad al-Yāfiʿī, had incessantly told the people of Yemen that if a simultaneous eclipse of the sun and the moon occurs in the month of Ramaḍān, the Ottoman regime in Yemen would perish. Al-Nahrawālī added that such a coincidence occured in the Ramaḍān of 974 A.H. (1567 A.D.).[55] Indeed, these and other celestial signs gave great impetus to Muṭahhar's ferocious and successful revolt against the Turks in Yemen (1565–1567).

Shabazi claimed that he was born in 1619, the year which witnessed the bizarre appearance of the two "messianic" stars.[56] The question as to whether Shabazi saw himself in the role of one of the messiahs cannot be conclusively determined. But the fact that he resorted again to the event of the appearance of the two comets indicates that he was obsessed with this phenomenon, which stirred in him and in Yemenite Jewry great messianic expectation. In his poem, which begins with the words "*Ḥadal Lekha Dal,*"[57] Shabazi wrote,

> The year of salvation is hidden in intricate calculations,
> Yet hinted at in Jubilee[58] and in Daniel.
> It is concealed and sealed by divine decree,
> Not to be revealed to all seekers.
> But a tender star has already come forth,
> Shaped like a rod, bearing God's grace.
> In the year 1619 there rose, on a swift cloud,
> The two stars of redemption:
> First that of Ephraim and then that of Yinnon,[59]
> The two kings of Israel.
> Repent, so that my Beloved may come
> To build the City (Jerusalem) and its walls.

Despite Shabazi's immense literary output, much of his personal life remains obscure. From his writings, we learn that he was born in one of the villages around Taᶜizz. He wandered from one Jewish community to another, and he spent some years in Sanaa among the Jewish sages, whom he mentioned with great reverence. From two poems which were dedicated to Yemenite rulers, we may infer that Shabazi was a prominent figure in Yemenite Jewry, possibly a spiritual leader recognized by the authorities. One of his poems bears the superscription: "Composed on the day in which the sage [Shabazi] visited the Sayyid Ḥasān, on the day in which he [Sayyid Ḥasān] ascended the throne."[60] It seems safe to assume that Shabazi came to pay tribute to the new ruler on behalf of the Jewish communities in Yemen. Shabazi dedicated another poem to Ṣafī al-Dīn Aḥmad ibn al-Ḥasān who, according to al-Wāsiᶜī, died in 1681.[61] Ironically, this imām, who was known by the name "al-Mahdī" ("the rightly guided one") and upon whom Shabazi lavished praise, was the one who later expelled the Jews of Yemen to Mauzaᶜ.[62] Shabazi's literary work is dominated by religious and national themes. References to his personal life would, as a general rule, be injected into his work only insofar as they merged with or reflected the national or communal experience. These personal details, however, are scanty. The precise date of Shabazi's death has not so far been conclusively determined. All we know is that he must have died after 1679, the year in which the major part of the Jews of Yemen was exiled to Mauzaᶜ. Shabazi had personally experienced this most fateful event in the history of Yemenite Jewry; he lived through it and lamented it.

With Shabazi, Yemenite Jewish poetry attained its highest pinnacle. Its descent thereafter was quick and precipitous. Some of his poems were written in Hebrew, others in Arabic, and still others in Aramaic. In many of his poems, stanzas in Hebrew and Arabic would alternate, often intermixed with Aramaic. Indeed, Shabazi was able to wield these three Semitic languages with equal facility and dexterity.

The thematic and prosodic influence which the Spanish school of Hebrew verse exerted upon Yemenite Hebrew poetry prior to Shabazi is less discernible in his own works. To be sure, Shabazi continued to express his ideas and feelings by means of the stylistic conventions which were established by the Spanish school. Indeed, many of his verses echo various celebrated passages of the Spanish masters of Hebrew verse (Shlomo Ibn Gabirol, Yehuda Halevi, Abraham Ibn Ezra, and others). Although a thematic comparison between Shabazi's poetry and that of his Spanish Jewish predecessors would be extremely revealing, such an endeavor in this context would take us far afield. A few examples would suffice to illustrate this point. Expressing his yearnings for Zion, Shabazi wrote,

> The Love for Hadassah is bound in my heart,
> But, deep in Exile, my feet are sinking.
> If only I were able, I would go up and become as one
> With the gates of Zion, the glorious ones.
> Morning and evening the Princess I do recall.
> My heart, my very being throbs with desire . . . [63]
> My heart is in Yemen, yet my soul took flight,
> Thirsting for the Fair Land like a hind.[64]

Shabazi's verses clearly echo the popular poems of Rabbi Yehuda Halevi, especially these most celebrated verses:

> My heart is in the east, and I in the uttermost west—
> How can I find savour in food? How shall it be sweet to me?
> How shall I render my vows and my bonds, while yet
> Zion lieth beneath the fetters of Edom, and I in Arab chains?[65]

Both poets expressed a burning, fervent longing for Zion in terms of a tragic dichotomy between body and soul, a chasm which rendered their lives intolerable. However, differences in style are readily discernible. One is stunned by Halevi's consummate creative mastery in the manipulation and exploitation of Hebrew vocabulary, his command of sound quality, his elegant idioms and metaphors, his bold comparisons and his surprisingly subtle association and juxtaposition of terms with completely divergent semantic ranges, for example, when he described Zion as lying beneath *Ḥevel 'Edom* (the fetters of Edom), while he himself is in *Khevel ʿArav* (in Arab chains).

Shabazi's poetry does not display the ostentatious rhetorical acrobatics which are so characteristic of the Spanish Hebrew verse. His verse is generally devoid of the exaggerated and elaborate outward ornamentation which might be seen as a mere exercise in poetic ingenuity. His poetry is, rather, characterized by an ease of rhyme and rhythm in a linguistic simplicity which draws primarily on biblical and post-biblical Hebrew sources, while at the same time being replete with hints, secrets, and esoteric implications, in the manner of the Zoharistic Qabbalah. It should be noted that the influence of Qabbalah, which was already discernible in the poetry of the sixteenth-century poet al-Ḍahrī, is strongly manifest in that of Shabazi. Many of his verses are enveloped in a cloud of mystical terms which, at times, baffles penetration. Indeed, in one of his poems (written in Arabic with Hebrew characters), Shabazi characterized his poetry in the following terms:

> In symbols, I have expressed my thoughts
> For those who are of profound knowledge.
> I have set the name of God around me;
> He surely knows my heart and its secrets.[66]

Kabbalism, esotericism, allegory, theosophy, and cosmology are all abundantly represented in Shabazi's poetry.

The themes and tone of Shabazi's lyrics are predominantly religious and nationalistic. The suffering of the exile (*galut*) and the great expectations for redemption (*ge'ullah*) ring throughout his poems. In this poetry, almost entirely dedicated to sacred themes, there is very little place for poems of love and descriptions of landscapes. Markedly absent in Shabazi's lyrics are the themes of lascivious eroticism, jest, and conviviality that are known in Spanish Hebrew verses as *Shire Shaᶜashuᶜim.* These literary genres were manifestly alien to the spirit of Shabazi and his Yemenite followers. "I have not wasted my verse on amorous themes," boasted Shabazi in one of his poems.[67]

Several factors converged in shaping Shabazi's negative attitude toward secular erotic imagery and the gay themes of *joie de vivre* and conviviality. Foremost among these factors was the social status of the Yemenite Jews, which was dramatically different from that of their brethren in other Muslim countries. Although other Muslim states did not display a uniform attitude toward the Jews, the general picture is that the Jews enjoyed a broad religious and social tolerance, which varied over time and from region to region. Certain humiliating restrictions and discriminatory laws were decreed for non-Muslim minorities, but these were neither rigidly nor consistently enforced, nor did they endanger the relatively secure life that the Jews led.[68]

This picture was entirely different in Yemen, a sectarian Muslim state that was dominated by the Shīᶜites who inhabited its central regions. The Shīᶜites in Yemen, who regarded themselves as the bearers of the doctrine of Zayd ibn ᶜAlī, are characterized by a very rigid legalistic attitude toward religion; hence, in Yemen all the religious restrictions and other oppressive measures were fully applied and rigorously enforced. As a result, the Yemenite Jewish poets seldom had the opportunity, so amply enjoyed by their brethren in Spain, to drink from the joyous fountain of life. Unlike Moses ibn Ezra, they could not celebrate the grace and splendor of fields and flowery meadows, nor the enchantment of feminine beauty. None could proclaim, like Yehuda Halevi, "The days dance their merry cycle for me."[69]

Another significant factor was the rigid religiosity of Shabazi himself, who strongly believed that the Hebrew verse should be employed only for sacred purposes. This attitude was probably inspired and strengthened by the attitude of Moses Maimonides, who viewed the Hebrew language as a sacred and exalted tongue. Hebrew, admonished Maimonides, should only be utilized for such noble purposes as the prose and poetic expression of thoughts which tended "to bestir the soul to virtues," and it should never be debased by writings "arousing the power of lust, praising it, and causing the soul to rejoice in it." Maimonides contended that "the Torah prohibited making the words of prophecy into forms of song dealing with vices and unseemly matters," because these stimulated a base attitude.[70]

It should also be noted that the general atmosphere of Yemen, among both Muslims and Jews, was extremely religious and not conducive to the composition of erotic and sensuous poems. This, together with the fact that Shabazi's period was charged with strong messianic expectations, contributed to the poet's aversion to secular and amorous themes.

But passionate chords of love and joy were vibrantly sounded, however, within the context of Shabazi's sacred poetry. In a manner characteristic of the Qabbalah and mysticism, Shabazi used the images, motifs, and language of secular love poetry to describe the ecstasy of divine love. His poems were nevertheless fully religious in content. They are to a great extent expressive of the yearning for salvation. They made use of conventional themes that were prevalent in the earlier erotic love poetry to express a passionate desire for the spiritual and the sublime. The main recurring themes are: the abandoned lover beseeching his mate to return; the radiant light—sun, moon, stars—associated with the beloved; the beloved as a healer and nurturer. Thus, the need for being detached from the abject conditions of the material world and finding salvation in God, the Torah, the Messiah, and so forth, finds its sublimation in these poems of love.

To express the bond between Israel, the Torah, and the Messiah, he incorporated erotic and sensuous language in eulogistic poems of friendship, styled in the manner of the ancient Arabic ode, the *qaṣīda,* which for a long time was the literary medium of Arabic poetry, and it was an influential poetic mode in medieval Spanish Hebrew literature as well.[71] This genre, in which panegyric was a central theme, would characteristically begin with the *nasīb* or erotic prelude and then shift abruptly and skillfully to the subject proper of the poem: the enumeration of the great virtues of a noble, a patron, or a friend.[72]

For the Jews in general and for those in Yemen in particular, the Torah was the greatest treasure on earth. It contained the promise of hope and redemption. It shaped their moral conduct and had a great impact on their spiritual and practical lives, on their character and outlook. It expressed their deepest thoughts and loftiest aspirations. The prophecies of salvation contained in it carried them through the deluges of history. The Torah, it was believed, contains much latent matter relating to the future, and this has to be deciphered. Jews, therefore, dedicated a great deal of their time to its study. It was for them a source of inspiration and fascination and the ever-favorite topic of homiletic exegesis and elaboration.

To the mystic, the Torah has always been a means of communion with God, the gracious and compassionate Father in Heaven. It provides the rungs by which the mind can ascend to the Divine. It is a Jacob's ladder, a link between heaven and earth, providing a sweet sense of divine accessibility.

The Torah fanned the sparks of hope of the Yemenite Jews and served as the source of their invincible faith and unfaltering trust in God. It is, then, little wonder that the most beautiful poems of love and praise for the Torah were composed in Yemen, several of them by Shabazi.[73]

Along with the Torah, the Messiah was the object of Shabazi's affections. His poems addressed to the Messiah are an outpouring of yearning for the Beloved, awaiting his imminent arrival, singing His glory. At times they are full of joyous expressions, and at other times, they are fraught with plaintive tones, demanding His immediate appearance. In a language evoking the universal theme of unrequited love, Shabazi complained of being forsaken by his lover, and he gave expression to the agony which arises from the forlorn state of separation from the Beloved. He recalled the idyllic relations of old and begged his Beloved to return promptly to His "comely habitation." This tension between agony and passion is articulated in several of Shabazi's poems.

The erotic images in Shabazi's poetry, the Yemenite Rabbis contended, are not to be taken literally; though couched in secular language, they are nevertheless fully religious in context and should be understood in the spirit of the Song of Songs. It is to be interpreted allegorically as an expression of the eternal and sacred bond between the Congregation of Israel and its Divine Beloved. In his introduction to *Ḥafeṣ Ḥayyim,* Rabbi Yehuda Jasafan warned us not to be puzzled by the sensual descriptions in Shabazi's poetry:

> . . . Because all of them [the poems] are heavenly secrets. They are like a ladder set up on the earth with its top reaching to the Heavens. And if you find in his poetry praises in terms of bodily attributes, such as of a hand, or a foot or other part of the body, drive and go forward and don't let the corporeality detain you, because he refers to the Most High, heavenly secrets. . . . [74]

Shabazi himself claimed that his poetry is replete with hints and esoteric implications, and he urged his readers to penetrate its deep symbolic meaning:

> Fathom, O holy congregation, the composed poems;
> Bridegroom and bride are joined under a canopy.[75]

In another poem, Shabazi wrote,

> I yearn for my Beloved, because He is my allotted share and portion. . . .
> He will cause my sun to rise, and he will restore the bereaved City;
> Then my head will be uplifted, my soul will be graciously redeemed.[76]

It is no wonder that Yemenite Jewry regards Shabazi's poetry as among the most sacred writings, "holy of holies," as Rabbi Yeḥia Alesech put it.[77] The Yemenites treated these poems like Scripture; they meticulously interpreted and commented upon them, searching for esoteric messages and religious symbolism. Goitein was not indulging in hyperbole when he wrote, "There is hardly a Yemenite house without one or several books of songs, which became as ubiquitous indeed as Bibles and prayer-books."[78]

A salient component of Shabazi's poetry is the *ge'ulla,* "redemption," theme. Although the Yemenite Jews were despised and ridiculed in this world, there was never any doubt in their hearts that they were the Chosen People of God. Following Jewish classical tradition, Shabazi emphasized the catastrophic aspect of the redemption, namely the frightful afflictions that the Yemenite Jews were undergoing were truly the "birth pangs" of the Messiah, and that the woes and horrors that they were experiencing were the "footsteps" of the Messiah. All these travails would soon culminate in a transcendent glory, and a new era of bliss would dawn upon Israel, in which the divine light would shine upon them in all its radiance. This certitude of faith became a living reality for them; it suffused their whole lives, and they based all their hopes on it.

The *ge'ulla* poems are dominated by verses of joyous expectation. One can surely hear in them the wingbeats of the approaching redemption verified and intensified by the poet's creative imaginations. The *ge'ulla* itself is described in great detail, by means of glaring images and extravagant formulations which have been endowed with the dimensions of myth. These descriptions are fed by the deepest wells of Jewish tradition, and they are permeated with biblical, talmudic, midrashic, and qabbalistic associations. All these are molded into a pattern befitting the Yemenite purpose and spirit, fusing together the various strata of the Hebrew language.

The new Exodus from Yemen has been presented as being in the same pattern as the old Exodus from Egypt, which for all Jews "was and is unique in its record of alternating affliction and salvation."[79] The story of the bondage in Egypt embodies the idea of election manifested by God's direct intervention, accompanied by miracles and by the making of the Covenant. That is why all Jews, and especially Yemenite Jews, exulted in it and found spiritual nourishment from it. They awaited the renewal of the historical acts of salvation and the revival of the glorious past, and they saw themselves standing on the threshold of the long-awaited new age. The sustaining effect of the past greatness is well epitomized in Lamentations 3:21–24: "This I recall to my mind, therefore have I hope. . . . The Lord is my portion, said my soul, therefore will I hope in Him."

Israel's redemption, proclaimed Shabazi, will also be a Day of Judgment for the Gentiles (namely, the Arab persecutors), in which the downtrodden Yemenite Jews will settle their bitter account with the torturers, who will be confounded and stricken with terror. The carnage which will be wrought upon Israel's enemies is graphically presented. The chief perpetrator of this carnage will be Seraia, who, according to the Zohar, will come with Messiah ben-Ephraim and will exterminate all the enemies of Israel with his mighty sword.[80] Shabazi encouraged Seraia:

> Seraia, gird your sword
> And destroy the troops of your enemy!
> Be strong and be not perplexed.[81]

Seraia, together with the Yemenite Jews, especially the tribe of Dan (which, according to Yemenite tradition, dwells in the northern regions of Yemen), will move against the enemies in a campaign whose battles are orchestrated by a premeditated plan.[82]

The theme of vengeance, an integral part of the messianic expectation, is marked by jubilation. It must be borne in mind, however, that the apparently jubilant tone at the imagined sight of the enemies' destruction, as well as the concentrated use of images of carnage and death, betray a deep anger and distress on the part of the poet. Evidently, Shabazi was enveloped in bitterness and harbored an implacable hatred for his persecutors, who filled Yemenite Jewish history with so many black chapters of misery and frightful devastations.

It is noteworthy that, in spite of their wretchedness and misery, the Yemenite Jews were not plunged into despondency. Although the melody of deep national sorrow echoes strongly in Shabazi's poetry, he did not let its sorrowful mood dominate it. The biblical injunction, "Worship the Lord with gladness, come before Him with joyful songs" (Ps. 100:2), sets the tone for many of his poems. It is a tone of the enthusiastic affirmation of life.

Shabazi's poetry appealed strongly to the hearts of his brethren in Yemen. On the one hand, it rendered into verse the cries and agonies of a wounded people, and on the other hand, it expressed with mighty chords their burning hope for salvation. His jubilant and exuberant references to the imminent arrival of the Messiah fanned the sparks of hope amid the ashes of despair. His soul-stirring poems evoke spontaneous emotions of happiness and joy, and elicit a profusion of powerful feelings. Many of his poems are chanted by the Yemenites on various occasions, accompanied by dances and rhythmical movements. Rabbi Koraḥ aptly characterizes this poetry as a blending of supplications and praise to the Creator, ethics and faith, joy and rejoicing. It strives to elicit a smile from oppressed mouths. He adds that the Yemenite attitude toward Shabazi's poetry is like the study of the Torah. "The congregation is forbidden to desecrate poetry with any conversation. They strain to hear the poems. One moment they are overjoyed, the next they shed a tear. . . . Scenes of heavenly spheres are revealed to them, and it is impossible to graphically depict this."[83]

Shabazi is certainly the most luminous figure and most gifted poet ever to have arisen among Yemenite Jewry. With him, Hebrew poetry in Yemen reached its highest bloom. Shabazi exercised a deep and lasting influence on the Yemenite Jewish poets who followed in his footsteps. With his death, however, the decline of Yemenite Hebrew poetry was quick and precipitous. To borrow al-Ḥarīzī's apt characterization of Rabbi Shlomo ibn Gabirol, Shabazi "spread such a fragrance of song as was never produced by any poet either before or after him. The poets who succeeded him strove to learn from his poems, but were not able to reach even the dust of his feet as regards the power of his figures and the force of his words."[84]

He is believed to be a man of God, a saint (the only saint produced by Yemenite Jewry) capable of performing miracles from his grave. His grave was constantly frequented by Yemenite Jews (even Muslims) from all parts of Yemen, particularly by the sick, who would risk their lives traversing vast distances in order to pray at his shrine for their healings. Close to his grave there is a cave with a spring of water. Following the prayers, the visitors would wait by the spring with great anticipation for a responsive sign from the saint. Whatever came forth from the gushing spring, such as a leaf or grass, would be taken, preserved in a leather case, and worn as an amulet. Such amulets were believed to be potent charms to ward off evil and to heal the sick, and they were moreover thought to be greatly efficacious in eliminating personal, marital, and other difficulties.

The Yemenites refrained from visiting Shabazi's shrine on the day of the Sabbath. They strongly believed that every Friday before sunset, Shabazi disappears from his grave. By means of a miraculous abridgment of journey (*qefiṣat derekh*), he would spend the Sabbath in the Land of Israel, alternately in Jerusalem, Safed, Tiberia, and Hebron, and would return every Saturday night.

Shabazi was buried in Taᶜizz. His grave is referred to as "*al-Ziyāra* [the shrine] of Mori Salim al-Shabazi." Hugh Scott described Shabazi's shrine as follows:

> Immediately east of the city, towards the lowermost spurs of Jebel Sabir, a track led to a patch of green crops, rank hedges, *qat* gardens and large shady mango trees. Returning by a path over stony euphorbia-covered ridges, we passed the tomb of a Jewish saint, Weli Shebazi. The actual grave, a whitewashed oblong with a little arch on top at one end, was surrounded by a rough stone wall, with a small low one-roomed stone building opening into the enclosure. There was a narrow upright recess in the end of the tomb, near the ground, beneath the little arch. This grave with a Hebrew inscription was a place to which pious Jews resorted. Some weeping women, crouching against the grave, and a man kneeling and reading were too engrossed to notice us passing by.[85]

Yemenite Jewry did not sanctify its personalities; rather, it adhered to the rabbinic dictate, "The righteous need no monuments; their teachings are their memorial." Shabazi was the only exception. The Jews of Yemen have surrounded him with a garland of highest reverence and glory. So great was the unrivaled magnetic hold that he had upon them, that they virtually "canonized" him. Legend has surrounded his death with a halo. He is believed to have died on the Sabbath eve, and that, near death, he had dug his own grave, prepared his shroud, and bathed himself. His students and the congregation in his town wanted to bury him on Saturday evening.[86] One of his students, however, urged them to bury him immediately and not to delay his burial. While they were engaged in the discussion, the sun suddenly blazed. The congregation immediately hastened to bury the sage, because for his sake the sun stood still, so as not to allow the disgraceful exposure of his body until Saturday evening.[87]

V

THE IMPACT OF THE SABBATEAN MOVEMENT ON THE JEWS OF YEMEN

1. General Background

It is a matter of history that Islam has imposed upon non-Muslims, Jews and Christians alike, certain humiliating restrictions, aimed at perpetuating by legal means the alleged inferiority of non-believers and ensuring their social isolation. The ultimate purpose of the various laws and ordinances promulgated by Muslim states was to reduce the non-believers to a state of deep degradation as a means of demonstrating the superiority of Islam. The general tenor of the discriminatory measures employed by Muslim states against non-Muslims was thought to be in accordance with various Qur'ānic homilies and utterances which enjoin the Muslims to humble the non-believers and turn them into lowly tribute payers. Thus, the *jizya* (poll tax), was imposed upon non-believers.[1]

The notorious pact ascribed to ᶜUmar specifies the conditions by which non-Muslim minorities living under Muslim rule would be granted protection and religious freedom.[2] In this pact the *dhimmīs* (non-Muslims) obligated themselves, among other things, to refrain from building new houses of worship (churches or synagogues), holding public religious ceremonies, converting anyone to their religion, displaying signs or symbols of their religion in Muslims' thoroughfares or marketplaces, raising their voices when reciting the service in their temples, building homes higher than those of Muslims, and wielding authority over Muslims. The Pact of ᶜUmar also included the prohibition of non-Muslims from any attempt to resemble the Muslims in their dress and their manner of appearance. These prohibitions laid the basis later for the various distinctive signs (*ghiyār*), imposed upon non-Muslims for the purpose of stigmatizing the non-believers and drawing a sharp distinction between them and the Muslims.

The degree of enforcement of these regulations in the vast and rapidly growing Muslim empire varied widely with time and region. In some cases these restrictions were not only rigorously applied, but also given a local twist for the worst. Thus, in 850 C.E. Caliph al-Mutawakkil decreed that non-believers wear yellow tailasans (a kind of mantle). He further ordered that if a *dhimmī* put on a turban, it should be a yellow one.[3] In a few cases, after outbursts of popular feelings, severely restrictive laws were enacted, subject to the ingenuity of the Muslim theologians and jurists and the zeal or whim of the Muslim rulers. The Fāṭimid Caliph al-Ḥākim (996–1021), for example, decreed that Jews and Christians wear black robes in public. He also insisted that the *ghiyār* regulations should be extended to the baths, ordering the naked Christians to wear large and heavy crosses, and the Jews to wear bells. Moreover, he decreed that the Jews, when in public, display a wooden image of a calf, "in pleasing allusion to a discreditable episode in their early history."[4] Al-Ḥākim, it is reported, ordered non-Muslim women to wear shoes of different colors, such as one red and one black.[5] He is also said to have demolished a number of Christian churches, including that of the Holy Sepulchre.[6] A more fanatical attitude was displayed by the Almohad ruler Abū Yūsuf Yaᶜqūb (1184–1198), who imposed the rules of *ghiyār* even on Jewish converts to Islam. For example, he ordered them to wear blue garments and forbade them to put on turbans; instead, they had to wear ugly and very long veils.[7]

Needless to say, in the vast and complex medieval Muslim empire, one should expect a diversity of attitudes toward non-Muslim minorities rather than a single uniform policy. It should be borne in mind, however, that, despite the occasional outbreaks of fanaticism, Islam was generally tolerant toward the non-Muslim minorities. Although the humiliating measures promulgated against *ahl al-dhimma* were never rescinded, they were generally disregarded, or at least not rigidly enforced, and their degree of enforcement varied with time and locality. In practice, the Muslim rulers' policy was usually determined by practical considerations and by the force of circumstances, rather than by the provisions of the law. Thus it is safe to conclude that, despite the occasional spasms of intolerance, Jews and Christians in Muslim countries enjoyed a broad religious and social freedom. The restrictions did not endanger the relatively secure life that they led.[8]

Dramatically opposed to this somewhat placid picture was the situation in Yemen, where the Jews were virtually the only non-Muslim minority.[9] Yemen was a sectarian Muslim state, ruled by Zaydīs. This offshoot of the Shīᶜite sect displayed an intransigent fanaticism and intolerance toward non-Muslim religions, and even toward other

Muslim sects. The Zaydīs were notorious for their rigid legalistic attitude with respect to religious matters.[10] Thus, all the religious restrictions which were enacted in other Muslim countries against non-Muslim minorities were in Yemen fully applied and rigorously enforced upon the Jews generally. The fanatically religious Yemenite Muslims interpreted the Qur'ānic injunction (9:29) to humble the *dhimmīs* in its most literal sense. In accordance with their rigid interpretation, they relegated the Jews to a markedly abject status. The Zaydīs in Yemen felt an extreme antipathy toward non-Muslims. They considered them to be so impure that their mere touch could taint a Muslim. One of the Zaydī laws states that any dish touched by a non-Muslim becomes unclean and must be smashed. As a result, a traveling Jewish craftsman in Yemen would constantly carry with him a cup fastened to his bag of tools.[11] This austerely pious Zaydī attitude found expression in oppressive measures with a virulent local twist intended to stigmatize and disgrace the Jews. Indeed, some of these measures were unique to Yemen.

Because of the paucity of our knowledge regarding the social conditions of the Jews of Yemen prior to the sixteenth and seventeenth centuries, no precise dates can be provided for the enactment of the various anti-Jewish edicts in Yemen. The picture which emerges, however, from the fragments of Yemenite Jewish chronicles is that the stringent enforcement of many of these humiliating injunctions was provoked by the reaction of the Yemenite Jews to the messianic call of Sabbatai Ṣevi (1626–1676), which triggered the largest and most pervasive messianic outburst in Jewish history. In 1665, Sabbatai Ṣevi, sparked by the "prophetic" support of Nathan of Gaza, declared himself the Messiah. His call stirred frenzied enthusiasm and outbreaks of mass ecstatic behavior among many Jewish communities, particularly those of Aleppo, Smyrna, Egypt, Constantinople, Gaza, Hebron, and Safed.[12] Ṣevi's "great" tidings even penetrated the walls of the relatively isolated Yemenites.

2. Jewish Reaction to the Messianic Call of Sabbatai Ṣevi

Mention has already been made of the two comets which appeared in 1619 and which were believed to proclaim the coming of the Messiah. Shabazi, who provided us with an account of this celestial phenomenon, complained, "But now we are already in the year 1646 and we are still waiting for the coming of the Messiah." He did, however, end his report with a positive tone. The Messiah, he said, will perhaps "appear in the year 80 [1680] like Moses . . . who was eighty years old when he stood before Pharaoh."[13] Thus, Sabbatai

Ṣevi arose and acted in a period of great messianic expectations by the Jews of Yemen, who strongly believed that salvation was around the corner. No wonder that when the "great tidings" of Sabbatai Ṣevi came to Yemen, they stirred the hearts of the Yemenite Jews with jubilation. Indeed, the Yemenite chronicler Ḥabshush bitterly complains that Sabbatai Ṣevi

> set fire in my bones from lands afar. He, may his name be obliterated, slashed open my kidney from beyond the rivers of Ethiopia, from Alexandria of Egypt. Like a magnet he attracted me with his deceit. The tidings of this instigator winged their way like an eagle from Egypt and settled on the face of all the land of Yemen. My poor brethren went about and gathered rumors . . . in order to revive through them their broken spirit . . . .[14]

Yemenite poets welcomed these reports of imminent salvation with excitement and exhilaration. Thus, for example, Rabbi Shalom Shabazi, the greatest of the Yemenite Jewish poets who lived at that period, wrote a poem which, according to several scholars, joyfully greets the advent of Sabbatai Ṣevi.[15] Here are the last four verses of this poem:

> From the uttermost part of the earth we heard songs,
> the upright Ṣevi in East and West.[16]
> The righteous always walk with integrity,
> they are innocent of sin and guilt.
> They bear good tidings, all are sincere, and
> for them my soul yearns in Yemen.
> Send us, O beloved, the balm of Gilead,
> we shall rejoice in Zion—man and maid alike.[17]

In these verses "*ṣevi ṣaddiq*" (the upright Ṣevi) most likely refers to Sabbatai Ṣevi. This can be inferred not only from the intrinsic evidence of the text of the poem itself, but also from the fact that Shabazi himself lived during the period of Sabbatai Ṣevi, who captured the hearts of the Jewish communities all over the world.

The belief of the Yemenite Jews in Sabbatai Ṣevi as the Messiah finds strong expression in a Yemenite apocalyptic work, entitled *Ge Ḥizzayon,* characterized by Gershom Scholem as "A Sabbatian Apocalypse From Yemen."[18] A passage of this Yemenite apocalypse reads:

> Even though this is a time of distress, it is the day in which the light of Ṣevi's face shines forth. . . . Lo, this is Jehovah, we have hoped in Him, this is our God, we have hoped in Him.[19] And this is the name with which he will be called, "Jehovah is our righteousness" (*Adonai ṣidqenu*).[20] This is my Lord and I shall extol him, and he will increase in greatness until he becomes exceedingly great, and his fame will

> spread throughout all the countries. And he will be revealed and concealed, rising from one scale to the other in the scales of the seven *sefirot* (spheres) from greatness to kingdom.[21]

As scholars have pointed out, Jewish response to the Sabbatian movement was marked by a combination of exuberant rejoicing and acts of penance and mortification.[22] Such was also the reaction of Jews of Yemen as described by Rabbi Seᶜadia Halevi in his chronicle, dated 1667.[23] Rabbi Halevi related that these messianic glad tidings captivated the hearts of both the Jewish masses of Yemen and their rabbis. The latter even issued a decree which

> limited the eating of meat, and said that Israel should eat only roasted meat. They also prohibited the drinking of wine, [not even] on Passover Eve. They decreed that the women should shave their hair; that men should not indulge in marital intercourse; that they should eat food unseasoned, without salt, and on dust and ashes; . . . that they should wear woolen black clothes and pray with covered faces.[24]

3. The Reaction of the Imam

Halevi's chronicle went on to relate the disastrous impact of this event upon the Yemenite Jews and the violent waves of persecutions that it triggered. Jewish leaders and rabbis were tortured; Jewish houses, lands, and possessions were confiscated by the imām of Yemen. The intolerable afflictions and the famine which followed caused a conversion of about five hundred Jews to Islam.[25]

A dirge intoned by the Yemenite Shelomo ben Ḥoṭer al-ᶜUzairi, who was an eyewitness to these events, reflects both the devastating famine that afflicted Yemen in general and the tribulations of the Jews of Yemen in 1669. The lament was discovered by Ratzaby in a colophon and published by him in 1958.[26] This poetical work does not set forth the events in specific terms but focuses on communicating the mood of bereavement and distress which the government's "harsh edicts" created among the Jews of Yemen. Employing Biblical verses and idioms related to tragic events, the poet began with descriptions of the famine that afflicted the Yemenites.

> On the month of Tammuz 1669
> Wrath has gone forth from the Lord,[27]
> And every high official was brought low . . . .
> And every soul was afflicted because of the famine,
> And the Angel of Death unsheathed his sword
> And smitten multitudes of people.

Men, women and children wandered from town to town,
Scattered in the streets and squares.
He cut them down in his fierce anger.[28]

The poet then related the immense suffering that was brought upon the Jews of Yemen as a result of both the famine and the religious persecution. The poem is dominated by a mood of agony and bitterness, and a harsh cry for vengeance bursts forth from its verses:

And the wicked government has gone through Israel
Trod upon her and tore her into pieces.[29]
They have besieged and enveloped us[30] with harsh edicts.
The remnant of Israel, he scorned and reviled by every *zed.*[31]
We ask from the Lord of the Universe, who never grows weary,
Let Him hasten to avenge our enemies and cut down the thickets of the forest with an axe.[32]
Let Him send upon them devastation, annihilation, fury, and great wrath.
Let Him make Jerusalem a cup of poison to all peoples [round about].[33]
Let Him cause darkness upon them, and let their feet stumble on the twilight mountains.[34]

The poem, like many other Yemenite Jewish poems, ends with a prayer for the immediate coming of the true Messiah and for the ingathering of the exiles in Jerusalem:

May the coming of our Messiah draw near,
So that he may gather the exiles of Israel.
And fulfill, "They shall bring you sons in their bosom,
and your daughters shall be carried on shoulders.[35]
I am the Lord, in its time I shall hasten it,
The least one shall become a clan.[36]
Blessed be he who waits and comes to the thousand three hundred and thirty-five [days].[37]

A more detailed and coherent account of these very fateful events in the history of the Yemenite Jews is furnished by Rabbi Ḥayyim Ḥabshush.[38] Ḥabshush's account, although written hundreds of years after the event, is claimed to be based upon older sources.[39] Unfortunately, many of these sources are no longer extant, or are at least not yet discovered. Scholars, however, tend to lend credence to Ḥabshush's reports, which are indeed corroborated by other reliable data. The recently discovered chronicle of Seᶜadia Halevi and the dirge of Shelomo, which coincide in many details with that of Ḥabshush, confirm in many respects the reliability of the latter. It should be noted, however, that Ḥabshush's account differs in style and approach from that of Seᶜadia Halevi. Halevi provided us with a description of the event which has the marks of an eyewitness account.

His style is factual and succinct, revealing the immediacy of its author's experience. Ḥabshush's account was written from a perspective of a chronicle far removed in time from the event. The presence of folkloristic embellishments in his narration of the events is quite discernible.

Apart from the apparent stylistic adornments, Ḥabshush's presentation of the Yemenite authorities is colored with a strong feeling of antipathy. It is marked by a humorous twist and is replete with bitter irony, even sarcasm. Moreover, anti-Muslim polemical overtones are readily discernible in his narration. His approach clearly betrays a strong conviction of the superiority of the Jewish faith, a characteristic of the Yemenite Jews. Nevertheless, Ḥabshush's records, though written after the event, are of great historical value, because of their unique contributions to our meager knowledge of certain events in Yemen and the motivation behind them.

Ḥabshush related that the Jewish jubilation at the reports of the advent of the "messiah" kindled the wrath of the imām of Yemen al-Mahdī Ismāᶜīl, who reacted by setting his armies against the Jews of Yemen in their habitations, plundering all their possessions.[40] He then decreed that all the leaders and elders of the Jews of Yemen be assembled in iron fetters before him in the city of Suda.[41] Ḥabshush then said that the imām attempted to induce these downtrodden and heartbroken Jews to convert to Islam. Addressing them in an arrogant manner and with harsh language, the Yemenite ruler said,

> O you filthy, despicable and indolent people! I know the wickedness and evil which you have harbored in your heart against us since the day you came to our land. You think evil of our kingdom and our prophet. You are anxiously awaiting the time of our visitation and downfall, with the advent of your false-messiah, Ḥimar ᶜAzīr, of whom your ancestors spoke.[42] You have sinned in the times of Moses your prophet, until your God was furious against you and He dispersed your fathers from His land and scattered them in all the countries until this very day. Yet you did not hearken to the Lord of your prophets, nor did you obey Him. You also dealt deceitfully with our prophet Muḥammad, the seal of the prophets, and you betrayed him.[43] Your God sent against you confusion, frustration, failure and dread, and you became cowardly in your land of habitation. And [God] will no more look upon you, nor deliver you. Your prophet has already proclaimed against you: "The virgin of Judah is fallen; she shall no more rise."[44] Do you think that your kingdom will be reestablished, so that you may dominate all the world and corrupt it as your fathers did? It is better for you to hearken to our words and to believe in our prophet, not to deny him, so that we may become one nation. [If you don't obey] you shall risk your lives, and you shall descend to the terrible fire of Hell, the place where the Jews and all

> the rebels and unbelievers in our prophet and his teaching go. But [if you obey] you shall be worthy of dwelling in the land, enjoying life full of pleasure, peace and tranquility. Moreover, you shall inherit a good portion in paradise, where you shall delight in abundance of marvelous orchards, streams of honey and buttermilk, with the beautiful maidens[45] and the exalted ones. And you shall also be abundantly satisfied with the good kept in store for the believers in His prophet and his teachings. Here is then my truthful and good advice to you. My counsel to you does not come from hatred but rather from love and compassion. Perhaps God will plant in your heart the wisdom to cast away the yoke of Satan, together with his evil, which leads you astray and deprives you of the two worlds. Then you will be worthy of the good of which I have spoken, and far more. But if you do not hearken to us, you shall be consumed by the sharp sword, becuase it is the mouth of Muḥammad that spoke so.[46] Clearly, you are bent on mischief.[47]

The episode as depicted by Ḥabshush sounds very familiar. Similar instances of attempts to impose forced conversion by the ruling religion upon Jews, whether by Islam or Christianity, could be adduced from the entire stretch of Jewish history. Such endeavors were frequent in Yemen.[48] These pressures included the tempting promises of earthly as well as heavenly rewards, reinforced by threats and intimidation. The history of the Jews of Yemen, as reflected in the fragmentary accounts written by the Yemenites themselves, looks like a parchment full, within and without, of "lamentations, mourning, and woe" (Ezek. 2:10). Ḥabshush's account, it is true, is not that of an "eye witness" to that specific event. However, in his depiction of a remote episode, he seems to have drawn from a religious milieu that was not essentially different from that of his forefathers. Thus, although allowance must be made for the polemical and satirical context, Ḥabshush's account has many aspects that fit harmoniously into the continuum of Yemenite Jewish history; it may be construed as a composite depiction, reflective of a recurrent pattern.

Ḥabshush went on to relate that the persecuted and famished rabbis and Jewish nobles stood before the king trembling from fear, their knees knocking. They refused, however, to succumb to the king's temptation and their tenacious adherence to their faith was not weakened. Their "insolent" reaction aroused the wrath of the imām's vizier, who now took it upon himself to convince the Jewish elders of the superiority of Islam, saying,

> Hear that your soul may live. Convert and do not reject the plea of our king, for your obstinancy and impudence will be avenged sevenfold. You are surely aware of what the Muslims in the times of ᶜAlī,[49]

> the Commander of the Faithful, have done to the heretics who were then in the land: they fought them to their utter destruction, although they were mightier and wealthier than he [ᶜAlī]. For God has delivered them into the hands of the Believers with utmost ease, and they smote them as a reed is shaken in the water.[50] All this was thanks to the Prophet, may God bless him, and there was not one man killed from among the Believers. [Tell me]: Where are the Gods of Halah and Habor who were Jews like you?[51] Where are the gods of the northern region who embraced Christianity? Where are the gods of Egypt? Where are the gods of Sheba who worshipped idols and graven images? Did they save their lives [those of their adherents] from the Muslims? Who among the other gods has saved his people from their [the Muslim's] hands? Therefore, do not persist in your folly, nor let the Evil Will and Satan entice you. Observe and recognize that your God is our God; that He is the God of gods and Lord of lords, God of the Heavens and of Earth; that there is no God but God and Muḥammed is His messenger.[52] We do not have any pleasure in the death of the wicked, but rather that he may turn from his ways so that he may live.[53] If you do not [obey], I swear by God and by the Prophet that you shall be condemned to die.[54]

The Jewish elders and nobles, continued Ḥabshush, responded with a categorical rejection of the pleas of both the imām and his vizier. In a manner reminiscent of the well-known Jewish polemical arguments against Islam,[55] their spokesman said,

> Precious in the sight of the Lord is the death of His saints.[56] Know, my lord, O King, that we cannot bear false witness to what we have neither been forewarned about nor seen. But our Torah says, "The Lord our God will raise up for you a prophet like me [Moses] from your midst, from among your brethren, him you shall heed." Furthermore, [our Torah] commands us, "You shall not listen to the words of that prophet."[57] But this prophet, about which you spoke, is not from among us, nor from among our brethren nor from our midst. He who comes to abolish even one commandment of those of the Torah, we do not hearken to him. We are forever strong in our faith. As for your prophet, he came for the purpose of directing you in the right path of God's worship, because your ancestors were previously idol worshipers,[58] as is evident from the battles of ᶜAlī aginst the unbelievers. But the Jews fought on his [Muḥummad's] side[59] and lived within his boundaries, and he did not harm them nor force conversion upon them, but only imposed a poll tax; and they dwelled safely in his land.[60]

The infuriated monarch, Ḥabshush related, responded by inflicting severe punishment upon the Jewish nobles. He exposed them for three days naked to the hot sun and ordered his soldiers to torture them. Seeing that such afflictions would not change their minds, he ordered them exiled to Kamran, "bound by fetters on their necks and accompanied by brutal soldiers." They were kept there for one year. However, the intercession of some prominent Muslim officials on their behalf brought about their release, and those who survived the calamity were allowed to return to their habitations "naked and barefooted, hungry and sick."[61]

The seemingly unwarranted furious reaction of the authorities in Yemen to the Jewish messianic frenzy are best understood when viewed within the context of the general social and religious atmosphere that prevailed in Yemen. It should be noted that a chief goal of the messianic idea is the dissolution of the existing regime and its replacement by the reign of the Messiah who would inaugurate an era of utmost bliss and justice. Because of this innate characteristic, messianic movements were rightly viewed by rulers, Muslim and Christian alike, as a threat to their authority, or at least a bothersome and disruptive element within the community. And the rulers of Yemen were especially sensitive to messianic uprisings. This land, Ḥabshush remarked, "often conceives and gives birth to messiahs. When one falls down, another rises. And when the foolish believers become poor, others replace them in fulfilling the needs of the messiahs with their money and property."[62] Ḥabshush's statement, to judge from its context, seems to bemoan the situation that existed among the Jewish communities in Yemen. To some extent, however, it is true of the Muslims as well.

The messianic idea is not limited to Judaism and Christianity; it is also deeply rooted, in various recensions, in the traditions of Islam, Sunnī and Shīᶜite alike. These traditions, which reach us through a chain of transmitters, supposedly on the authority of the Prophet Muḥammad, speak of an eschatological personage, referred to as al-Mahdī (the divinely guided one), who will appear toward the end of time, restore the true faith of Islam, and fill the corrupt world with righteousness and justice.

The traditions with respect to the Mahdī are numerous and they greatly vary in details. Some of these traditions are considered as sound and authoritative, others as "weak" and disputed.[63] In general, the traditions agree that the idea of a future coming of al-Mahdī was proclaimed by Muḥammad. "The world will not be destroyed," promised the Prophet, "until the Arabs shall be ruled by a man from my family, whose name shall tally with my name."[64] They also generally agree with respect to the essential role of this future personage, which is to restore justice to the world and to root out oppression and crime. Islam will be exalted.

Some of the traditions provide details which are strongly reminiscent of the Judeo-Christian messianic concept. The pertinent details may be summarized as follows:

> The hour of the coming of the Mahdī will not arise before the earth is filled with injustice, crime and transgression. With his advent, the earth will sprout forth for him its blessing and will cast out the treasure of its interiors. There will be piles of money. The cattle will be safe from wild animals, and the sheep will go with the wolf.[65]

While the idea of the Mahdī is deeply rooted in the tradition of Sunnī Islam and is very popular among its masses, to the Shīᶜite it is an essential creed, an article of faith. The Twelvers give the epithet al-Mahdī to Muḥammad ibn al-Ḥasān al-ᶜAskarī, the twelfth of their imāms. They believe that this imām has been withdrawn by God from the eyes of man and that he is now in a state of concealment (*makhtūm*). This Mahdī, to whom they refer as *al-Muntaẓar* (the expected one), will come forth at the end of time and will fill the earth with justice. The doctrines of *ghaiba* (concealment) and *rajᶜa* (return) are, therefore, central to the Shīᶜites. The extremists among the Shīᶜites (the *ghulāt*) assert the divinity of the imām. They consider him, in a manner similar to that of Christianity, to be the incarnation of God.[66]

It should be stressed that the *Zaydīya,* as a subsect of Shīᶜite Islam, do not share the belief in the Hidden Imām. Nevertheless, the belief in its various forms has a strong grip upon the masses in Yemen, be they Zaydīs, Ismāᶜīlīs, or Sunnīs. This faith in a divinely ordained deliverer becomes more acute in times of trials and tribulations, and these were not rare in Yemen, a land which was continually subjected to the horrors of civil strive, droughts, and famines.

Several cases of claimants to the title of Mahdī in Yemen are reported by Yemenite Muslim chroniclers. According to Wāsiᶜī, such an impostor rose in 290 A.H., claiming that he was the awaited deliverer. He was followed by a multitude of adherents. This "Mahdī," reports Wāsiᶜī, wrought carnage among the inhabitants and violated the forbidden laws. For example, he permitted his companions to drink wine and to have sexual intercourse between brothers and sisters and other acts of debauchery. This impostor used to begin his letters with "From the one who stretches the land and levels it out, and shakes the mountains and firmly establishes them, ᶜAlī ibn Faḍl, to. . . ."[67] Another case, reported by al-Jarāfī, concerns a certain Ṣūfī mystic by the name of Saᶜīd al-'Ansī, who in 1841 arose against the imām and arrogated to himself the title of "the awaited Mahdī."[68]

These "messianic movements" caused a lot of bloodshed and threatened the authority of the rulers. It should be noted that the activity of the Jewish messiahs were not strictly confined to the Jews;

they also swept the hearts of many Muslim followers. Thus, for example, the Jewish false Messiah from Ḥaḍramawt (1495), so we are told, managed to raise a multitudinous army and shake the land of Yemen and its inhabitants.[69] It is little wonder that such movements were cruelly suppressed by the imāms.

The ruthlessness of the imām's reaction to the Yemenite Jews' exuberantly joyous response to the call of Sabbatai Ṣevi also found expression in the public execution of the Yemenite Jewish leader (*nagid*), Rabbi Suleimān al-Gamāl.[70] It should be noted that execution of Jews in Yemen was a very rare phenomenon. The Yemenite Muslims considered it a grave sin to shed the blood of a *dhimmī*. This unusual decapitation of a Jew only underscores the utmost gravity with which the imāms viewed messianic uprisings.

4. The *ᶜAtarot* (Headgear) Edict

The historical event of Sabbatai Ṣevi triggered humiliating enactments against the Jews of Yemen.[71] Rabbi Seᶜadia Halevi related that one of these ordinances was the "*ᶜAtarot* decree."[72] Issued in 1667,[73] this decree prohibited the Jews from wearing a "headgear" (Arabic: *ᶜamāma*). This edict, the avowed aim of which was to disgrace the Jews and deprive them of any respectable appearance, affected them not only socially but also religiously. It forced the Jews to walk bareheaded. Attempts to have this disability removed failed. Only after persistent entreaties and intercessions, on their behalf did the imām consent to modify the regulations and allow the Jews to cover their heads with shabby clothes.[74]

Reverberations of this decree are heard in one of Shabazi's poems in which he admonished God to pour His wrath on his persecutors:

> Let Him pour His fury on the crooked Savage . . .
> Who ridicules my Faith
> And despises my Law
> And removed my *ᶜatara* [headgear].[75]

In another poem written in Arabic, Hebrew, and Aramaic, Shabazi contemplated the tragic aspect of Jewish life resulting from the decrees and their subsequent persecution, and he gave expression to his sense of outrage and humiliation:

> And I became distressed in Yemen/Without glory and crown
> Oh, how deeply do I gulp of the disasters!
> And the House of Faith is desolate
> And the Savage inflicts grief
> And destroys synagogues.[76]

5. The Earlocks Edict

The Yemenite chronicler, Rabbi ᶜAmram Koraḥ related that the ᶜAtarot (headgear) decree was followed by another one, which made Jewish males grow earlocks in order to enforce the outward distinction (*ghiyār*) between Jews and Muslims. The Jews of Yemen, said Rabbi Koraḥ, were greatly appalled by this stigmatizing decree, and they looked upon these sidelocks as "two snakes upon their cheeks." The Jews, the Rabbi added, were forbidden to conceal their earlocks, and it was incumbent upon every Muslim in Yemen to see to it that no Jew violated the decree. Should a Jew hide his sidelocks under a wrap, he would be beaten by any passing Muslim who detected this violation. Rabbi Koraḥ also remarked that whenever a male Jew willy-nilly embraced Islam, the Muslims would first shave his earlocks in order to relieve him of this disgracing symbol.[77]

Rabbi Koraḥ's explanation of the genesis of the curly earlocks, which were so characteristic of Yemenite Jews until their massive transportation to Israel in the 1950s, however, raises some difficulties. It is well known that the Jews of Yemen did not look at these earlocks as a stigma, but viewed them as one of their most revered religious observances. As Rabbi Koraḥ himself pointed out, the Yemenite Jews used to glory in these earlocks, "they comb them and anoint them with oil. . . . They boast of their length and curly form. The common Jews take solemn oaths while holding them as holy objects." Rabbi Koraḥ, however, had no difficulty with this phenomenon. This apparent discrepancy, he claimed, only underscores the remarkable ability of the Jews of Yemen to adapt to their environment and to transform curses into blessing. Thus, the earlocks which were viewed as a stigma by the early generations in Yemen were looked upon by later generations, who were oblivious of their origins, as signs of glory and distinction.[78]

But if these earlocks indeed originated in a malevolent Yemenite decree, how does one square that with the fact that growing earlocks by Jewish males had been prevalent among other orthodox Jewish communities in Europe and other parts of the world long before the rise of Sabbatai Ṣevi? Thus, in his commentary of the fifteenth-century book *Sefer Sheveṭ Yehuda,* Shoḥaṭ related that among the many maleficent edicts that King Don Juan the son of Don Enrique of Spain (1406–1454) imposed upon the Jews of his country was the growing of their hair and their earlocks.[79]

Moreover, the growing of earlocks was presented by the seventeenth-century historian Paul Rycaut as an old and neglected Jewish religious custom, which was adopted by the Sabbatian Jews (Believers in Sabbatai Ṣevi as the Messiah). Rycaut related that a Jew at

Yemenite Jews with earlocks
(From the collection of Nissim B. Gamlieli, Ramlah, Israel)

Constantinople claimed to have met Elijah the Prophet in the street "habited like a Turk," and that Elijah

> injoyned [*sic*] the observation of many neglected Ceremonies, . . . This apparition of *Elias* being published, and as soon believed, every one began to obey the Vision, by fringing their garments; and for their heads, though always shaved according to the Turkish and Eastern fashion, and that the suffering hair to grow, to men not accustomed was heavy and incommodious for their health and heads; yet to begin again to renew, as far as was possible, the ancient Ceremonies, every one nourished a Lock of hair on each side, which was visible beneath their Caps, which soon after began to become a sign of distinction between the Believers and the Koparims [heretics], a name of dishonour . . . given to those who confessed not *Sabatai* to be the Messiah.[80]

Rycaut's account finds corroboration in Gershom Scholem, who remarked that as a result of the alleged admonition of the prophet Elijah, "the believers also introduced new customs, that is, they insisted on the strict observance of certain ancient practices that had fallen into neglect." Scholem also remarked that this custom of letting sidelocks grow at the corners of the head "was well-established in German and Polish Jewry" and "was introduced as a Sabbatian innovation." Scholem also noted that the origin of the custom to grow long sidelocks is not definitely known. This characteristic Yemenite and Ashkenazi feature, added Scholem, "was known since the late Middle Ages."[81]

It follows from the cumulative evidence that the custom of growing long earlocks was an ancient one, reintroduced by the Sabbatians and later on by the kabbalistic circles. Indeed, the historical association of the Yemenite adoption of this custom with the rise of Sabbatai Ṣevi is very intriguing. It should be noted that the Yemenite Jews referred to the earlocks by the name of *simonim*[82] "marks," "signs," which might accord with the above-mentioned need of the Sabbatians for distinguishing marks. Whether the Yemenite Jews adopted this custom willingly or were forced to do so by the government, which might have known of this custom and used it as an additional tool for *ghiyār* (distinction between Muslims and Jews), is difficult to ascertain.

The social stigmas and disabilities which were imposed upon the Jews of Yemen, triggered (or may have been reintroduced with more stringency) by their enthusiastic faith in Sabbatai Ṣevi as the Messiah of Israel, were ultimately accepted with a spirit of resignation. The Yemenite Jews learned how to cope with the various degrading restrictions. On the one hand, they adhered to them punctiliously; on the other hand, they tried to keep a low profile, never conspicuous in their public life.[83] Yemenite Jews, remarked Goitein, men and women alike,

> always were clothed like beggars (and some of the older generation cling to this habit even in Israel). . . . The Jews avoid any appearance of affluence. In times of anarchy or in regions beyond the reach of the central government, Jewish property, even houses, were taken away from them under the pretext that they presented a picture of wealth incompatible with the state assigned to the Jews by God.[84]

Indeed, in his Passover epistle to the Jews of Yemen, the celebrated Yemenite Rabbi and leader Mahriṣ, enjoined his brethren to refrain from appearing in public places. "Should a Jewish woman feel it necessary to go out of her house," advised Mahriṣ, "she should then refrain from wearing beautiful clothes, lest she arouse the envy of her adversaries . . . ."[85]

6. The Latrines or Scrapers Edict

The various anti-Jewish measures, which were aimed at the total degradation and social isolation of the Jews of Yemen, reached their climax with an edict that the Yemenite Jews refer to as *gezerat ha-Meqamṣim,* "The Latrines or Scrapers Edict." This decree, which

Koraḥ characterized as being "the most abominable of all the evil edicts,"[86] imposed upon the Jews of Yemen, rabbis and laymen alike, the task of cleansing the country's public sewers and latrines from human excrements. It also made it incumbent upon Jews to rid the markets, courtyards, Muslim quarters, and other public areas of the stench and carcasses of dogs, horses, camels, and other animals.[87]

According to Ḥabshush, the decree was issued in 1646 by the imām of Yemen[88] at the advice of Judge Muḥammad al-Sahūlī. Until then, all the work of cleansing the latrines and public places, including those of the Jews, was done by Muslims. Judge al-Sahūlī, related Ḥabshush, contended that

> it is not proper for us [Muslims] to allow people of our faith to clean the country from human excretion, all the more so the latrines of Jews. [This task] is a shame and disgrace to all Muslims. Let us then impose this contemptible task on those whom we greatly detest. If it is good before the Imam, we shall assemble all the jurists and formulate [a decree] against the Jews, who are most hostile to us [to Muslims]. You shall then approve it with your seal, making it incumbent upon the Jews to cleanse the country and the public latrines from all excrement and loathsome materials. With these [excrements] they will heat the public baths. They shall also remove the carcasses of dogs, donkeys, horses, and camels. [By doing so] we eliminate this disgrace from our midst . . . .[89]

Ḥabshush went on to say that Sahūlī's advice "found favor in the eyes of the imām and his ministers," and a decree to that effect was issued by the Yemenite ruler. The Jewish leaders, added Ḥabshush, having failed to bring about the rescission of this edict or the mitigation of its severity, hired people from their midst, particularly the poor and the needy so that they may fulfill this task.[90]

The earliest reference to this edict in Yemenite Jewish writings is in an epistle sent ca. 1679 from the Jews of Ḍuran to the Jews of Ḥebron. In this epistle, which relates mainly to the exile of the Jews of Yemen to Mauzaᶜ (1679), the writer bitterly complained that even a whole book would not be sufficient to contain the "one hundred and one" tribulations that befell Yemenite Jewry. He, however, singled out one "disgracing edict" which was imposed upon the Jews. "They have decreed," moaned the writer of the epistles, "to remove all their [Muslims'] carcasses . . . amid scorn and derision."[91]

The following verses taken from a seventeenth-century Yemenite Jewish poem allude to this and other edicts:

> They sold me and afflicted me with all sorts of tortures,
> The sons of Esau and his multitudes accompanied by other nations.
> And Ishmael made his yoke heavy and shackled my jaws

And he subdued and imprisoned and bound with fetters. . . .
The violence of ᶜAlwan and also Javan consumed me and crushed me,
And he bit and darkened my eyes with his decrees.
With unceasing afflictions and restrictions he torments me. . . .
They ravaged me, they seized me cruelly like a bear bereaved of its young.[92]

It should be noted that degrading tasks of this nature, imposed by Muslim rulers on non-Muslim minorities, were not unique to Yemen. Such humiliating vocations were imposed upon *dhimmīs* (Jews and Christians) at various times in several Muslim countries. Thus, we learn from a letter written by Abū ᶜAbdallāh Muḥammad ibn Yaḥia ibn Faḍlān to Caliph al-Nāṣir (ruled 1180–1225) that "in Bukhāra, all the cleaners of the latrines and the sewerages are from the *dhimmīs*."[93] It should be stressed that such fanatic manifestations were rare and of a transient nature.

In contrast to other Muslim countries, however, this edict vigorously persisted in Yemen until the 1950s. Thus, in his letter to Earl Russell, the British Foreign Minister, J. M. Montefiore drew attention to "atrocities of a most fearful description" that were inflicted upon the Jews of Yemen, "the poor defenseless creatures." In the course of this letter, Montefiore referred to the "Latrines Edict," saying, "aged and honourable members of the community are compelled to collect the excrements of dogs from the streets, amid the jeers and insults of the Mahomedans."[94]

In his *Arabian Peak and Desert,* Riḥani related that the Yemenites used to heat their *ḥammāms* (baths), not with charcoal or wood but with the dung of human beings. This dung, continued Riḥani, is gathered and prepared for fuels by Jews. Riḥani commented on the plight of the Jews of Yemen as follows:

The Jew of Al-Yaman, who still pays a tribute as in the days of the Prophet Muḥammad, is held in deep contempt by the Muslem, especially the Zaidi, but he is an industrious and ingenious member of the community. I have seen objects of art in filigreed silver and gold, which only he can make, and which are beautiful. But more about him later.

The rubber was delighted in telling how his bath is heated by the Yahuda, and I was disgusted. I could not even get him to change the subject, or to use only his hand upon me. At last he held both his tongue and hand in peace, and I went back to the reclining room, eager for a nap. But as soon as I lay down—O Muḥammad! O Yahuda! I have seen in the vapour room cockroaches as big as a mouse, but they could run; and anything, of the things that creep, that can run or even perform visibly the act of locomotion, I dread not so much as that which quietly, slowly, stealthily attaches itself to you, and makes you feel, when you see it upon your sleeve, worse than a leper. And there it was on the cushion—a big fat white louse! I left the coffee, the *madaah,* the incense on the tray, and dressing quickly, I walked out of the place feeling like Diogenes when he came out of public bath in Athens.[95]

7. The Orphans Edict

The oppressive measures aimed at perpetuating the social degradation and isolation of the Jews were, as we have seen, most extensive and most vigorous in Yemen. Yet despite these restrictions, the Yemenite Jews seemed to have succeeded in adapting themselves to their fragile and barely tolerated status of a minority amid a fanatical sectarian Islamic environment. By accepting these humiliating measures as a decree from Heaven, they managed to carve a life, albeit precarious, in coexistence with the ruling Muslims. Although their constant affliction affected them physically and socially, it never broke their spirit. Their unshakable faith in the Torah and in the ultimate redemption, which was incessantly and emphatically stressed by their spiritual leaders, sustained them and alleviated their suffering. Their spiritual leaders and poets managed to draw a sharp dichotomy between the physical and the spiritual, the gloomy present and the awaited future. They continually impressed upon the minds of their brethren the idea that they were still the chosen people of God. They also stressed the spiritual superiority of the persecuted over their persecutors. This note is clearly sounded in many of their poems. Thus, Shabazi drew the line between the oppressor and the oppressed:

> His days [the oppressor's] are like a walking shadow
> And his misfortune is hastening
> But My people are in hands of their Guardian
> Splendid and magnificent.[96]

In another poem, Shabazi proclaimed with pride: "How good is my root, the planted crest of a cedar."[97] And the poet Yosef ben Israel reminded his persecutors of his people's noble descent and distinctive spiritual status:

> Do not touch me, because I am of holy and priestly heritage. . .
> And destined for the King's court.[98]

Although the Yemenite Jews adhered almost punctiliously and with a spirit of equanimity and resignation to these degrading social laws, their attitude toward the decree that is known in their annals as *gezerat ha-Yetomim* (The Orphans Edict), was totally different. This decree imposed forced conversion to Islam on all *dhimmīs* (protected persons), male and female alike, who had not attained puberty before their fathers had died.[99]

Like other anti-Jewish decrees in Yemen, it is difficult to ascertain the precise date of the enactment of the orphans' edict. It seems that Shabazi provided us with the earliest allusion to it. In one of his poems he lamented:

> Look, the Savage's violence dispersed me
> He took away my precious one.
> From synagogues he rushed me
> I have trodden alone.
> To embrace his faith he counselled me
> Because he scorned my tenacity.
> How can I forsake the Oneness of my Rock and Creator
> Who guards my path
> . . . And abandon the Object of my praise?[100]

In another poem, Shabazi bemoaned the fact that the Yemenite rulers are "seeking to blend faiths / Snatching my child-orphans."[101]

One wonders about the source and justification for this unusual edict. This ordinance is in absolute contrast to the sacred law of Islam, which expressly prohibits coercion in religious matters. It is also a flagrant infringement upon the right of the *dhimmīs* as it was set forth in the Qur'ān and the Pact of ᶜUmar. Indeed, as the Yemenite chronicler Ḥabshush complained, the Zaydī regime in Yemen imposed upon the Jews "Statutes that are not good and which were not commanded, and which did not come to the mind of their lawgiver.[102]

In the search for possible parallels to this decree in the vast Muslim empire, the well-known Ottoman law *devshirme* readily comes to mind. This law entailed a periodical levying of Christian boys as tribute. After being converted to Islam, these children were trained for various governmental purposes, and especially for the Janissary corps, which formed the heart of the Ottoman military system.[103] However, this law is different in many essential respects from that of Yemen. Its origin, as commonly held, is in the application of the ordinary Muslim law of *ghanīmah* (booty) to human captives. Thus, this ancient law makes the Ottoman Sultan entitled to one-fifth of the spoil and human captives as *penjik.* The prisoners were utilized mainly for the establishment of a New Force (*Yenicheri*).[104]

The *devshirme,* namely, the periodical and selective conscription of Christian children, seems to be a later development of the law of *ghanīmah.* It should be stressed that the frequency of the levy's occurrence is uncertain, with estimates ranging from an annual basis to once every five years. In many cases it was imposed on an ad hoc basis to meet the Janissaries' needs.[105] Moreover, reports regarding the age limits and the numbers of the conscripted vary greatly (ages ranged from as low as eight years old to as high as twenty).[106] The *devshirme* in itself rested, as Lybyer pointed out, "on a unique and almost unparalleled idea; then, it involved an extraordinary disregard of human affection and of the generally acknowledged right of parents to bring up their children in their own law and religion." The levying of Christian boys as tribute, continued Lybyer, "has always elicited a great amount of moral indignation, as representing an extreme of oppression, heartlessness and cruelty." However, although the departure of these children was indeed heartbreaking for their parents, in the long run it was highly advantageous. Many parents, remarked Lybyer, were glad to have their sons selected, because this enabled them to "escape from grinding poverty . . . and enter upon the possibility of a great career." Some parents, Lybyer went on to say, "came to regard the process as a privilege rather than a burden."[107]

The Yemenite orphans decree, however, was totally different in its origins, extent, and impact from that of the *devshirme.* It affected only Jewish orphans of minor age, males and females alike.[108] Its sole motivation was religious—the conversion of these Jewish children to Islam. There is a great deal of uncertainty as to its origin and justification. Most probably it stems from the obscure and disputed concept of *fiṭra* which occurs in Qur'ān 30:30 and is elaborated upon in a *ḥadīth* reported by various Muslim authorities. According to this *ḥadīth,* Muḥammad stated that every one is born according to the *fiṭra* (to his true nature, namely, a Muslim) and he remains such so long as he does not express himself with his tongue. It is his parents who make him a Jew, a Christian, or a Magian.[109]

Muslim theologians differ widely as to the interpretation and practical implications of this saying. Some understand it in the figurative sense, recognizing that the legal religion of the infant is automatically that of his parents. Others interpret the expression "born according to the *fiṭra*" as meaning to have been created in a healthy condition, with the potential ability to choose the right religion when the time should come.[110]

In Yemen, however, this *ḥadīth* was understood in its narrow and literal sense, namely, as making it incumbent upon Muslim authorities "to spread the wings of Muḥammad who is the 'Father of all Orphans' on Jewish orphans of minor age."[111] This practice of forcibly taking away non-Muslim orphans is a flagrant deviation from the practice followed by the majority of Muslims. Such extreme deviations, it should be noted, were isolated phenomena manifested mainly in sectarian movements in Islam. Thus, for example, Joseph ibn ᶜAqnin related that the Almohades (twelfth century) imposed forced conversion on all non-Muslims and put to the sword those who refused to do so. Almohades, continued Ibn ᶜAqnin, who was himself an eyewitness to their horrors, took away the Jewish children (including those of converted parents) and handed them over to Muslim guardians. Ibn ᶜAqnin also remarked that the Almohades operated on the principle of the *ḥadīth* quoted above.[112]

The effect of this edict on the Jews of Yemen was devastating. Unlike the laws of *ghiyār* and other degrading measures which affected their social status, this one affected their religious convictions and posed a threat to their very existence as Jews. Because of the constant decimation of Jewish families by famine, disease, and other calamities, widows were often left with several children of minor age. These were all torn from their mothers and converted to Islam.

It should be noted that the Orphans Edict was operative in Yemen until the 1950s, when all of Yemenite Jewry was transported to Israel. Since no birth records were kept by the imāms, a government official would be sent to the house of a Jewish orphan to determine whether the child was still of minor age and therefore eligible for conversion. According to Rabbi Kafiḥ, the male was considered a minor so long as his testicles did not reach equal size and were not level with each other. The determining factor for the female's puberty was the protrusion of her breasts and the growth of the pubic hair.[113] Needless to say, in view of the wide range of normal variations in time when puberty begins and the speed and intensity with which it develops, much was left to the arbitrary discretion of the government official who was responsible for the physical examination of the orphan and its results. In many cases abuse of authority was involved.

The evasion of this decree was considered by the Jews of Yemen as a sacred obligation which justified all means. Many of the orphans were smuggled out of Yemen to Aden, which was then ruled by the British. Others were adopted into other families and were introduced as their own children. Still others were quickly married off at a tender age, since married youngsters were considered adults and were therefore exempt from the decree. In many cases, Jews endangered their own lives by serving as accomplices in the circumvention of the ordinance. Indeed, this intriguing and unique chapter in the history of Yemenite Jewry deserves a full study in and of itself.

VI

THE EXILE OF THE YEMENITE JEWS TO MAUZA^c (1679)

1. The Cause of the Exile

Among the many historical forms that religious and racial intolerance is known to have assumed is the expulsion of minorities from some locality. This extreme measure, it should be stressed, was very rare in Yemen. In fact, the only know case of mass expulsion of Jews from the various localities in Yemen is that which transpired in 1679, known among the Yemenite Jews as the Exile to Mauza^c.

It is related that in 1679 the imām of Yemen, Aḥmad ibn al-Ḥasān ibn al-Imām al-Qāsim, known as al-Mahdī (1620–1681),[1] decreed the expulsion of all the Jews of Yemen to the remote and desolate region of Mauza^c in the region of Tihāma. It should be noted that although Yemenite Jewish history is replete with disasters, none had been as radical and devastating in its total import and dimensions as this calamitous expulsion. Galut Mauza^c is considered to be the blackest chapter in the history of Yemenite Jewry.[2]

What prompted this edict of expulsion? According to a popular tradition current among the Jews of Yemen, this unfortunate event was triggered by a promiscuous affair that a Jew by the name of al-Faq^ca had with the daughter of the imām, resulting in her pregnancy. Infuriated by this disgraceful act, the story relates, the imām killed his daughter. He then summoned Suleimān al-Naqash, the leader of the Jews of Sanaa and said to him, "I have decreed that all Jews should choose either Islam or the sword (death)." However, the story goes on to say, the Yemenite Jewish leaders, having failed to obtain the abolishment of this decree, managed to persuade the king to commute the punishment to exile.[3]

It is evident that the al-Faq^ca story is strongly tinged with legendary colors. Though very popular among the Jews of Yemen, no scholar would vouch for its authenticity. It seems to belong to the realm of folktales that are essentially figments of the popular imagination. It also emanates in different versions from later writers far removed in time from the event of the expulsion. We shall concern ourselves with historically credible writings, particularly with contemporaneous records provided by eyewitnesses and victims of the Mauzaᶜ calamity. These writings are relatively ample and they consist mainly of poetic laments written by various poets, mostly in the Arabic vernacular, using Hebrew characters, as was always the case when Jews wrote Arabic. These laments command our interest not only for their literary merits but also as a contemporary source throwing considerable light upon this terrible episode in the history of Yemenite Jewry. Several of these laments were written by Rabbi Shalom Shabazi, the most prominent poet of Yemenite Jewry, who was himself one of those expelled.

The Exile to Mauzaᶜ should be viewed in the context of an extreme situation of heightened religiosity and intolerance, a result of a radical outbreak of religious fanaticism. The Zaydī imām who issued this decree of expulsion (al-Mahdī), is known in the annals of Yemen by the honorary epithet *al-Mujāhid* ("wager of holy wars").[4] Even as a prince, he was referred to as the "Reinforcer of the ordinances and laws of God."[5] Thus we are dealing with a period of extreme religious fanaticism.

Muslim theologians and jurists in the various parts of the Muslim lands had long expressed irritation with the presence of synagogues and churches in their midst, and they were particularly agitated by the sight of magnificent non-Muslim buildings, personal or public. The Pact of ᶜUmar clearly forbids the holding of public religious ceremonies, the displaying of symbols of worship in public places, and the building of houses higher than those of Muslims.[6] It is for this reason that synagogues and churches were often demolished by fanatic rulers or mobs and splendid private houses confiscated.[7] This intolerance of non-Muslim minorities was particularly true of Yemen, which was until recently a sectarian Muslim states ruled by the Zaydī Shīᶜites, who literally believed the Qur'ānic saying that the nonbelievers had "incurred anger from their Lord." Therefore, Muslims believed that for non-believers, "ignominy shall be their portion . . . and wretchedness is laid upon them" (3:112).

It should also be noted that we are dealing with a period following the liberation of Yemen from Ottoman domination, which lasted from 1538 to 1629. The revolt of al-Qāsim and his sons against the Turks (1627–1629) caused the withdrawal of the Turks from Yemen, but it also brought about destruction, famine, and other disasters.[8] Brief chronicles written by Jews who lived in that period recount the tribulations which afflicted the Yemenites in general and the Jews in particular during and after the revolt.[9]

During their reign in Yemen the Turks had introduced various forms of delights and amusements which were totally alien to the spirit of the fanatically religious Muslims in Yemen and were like thorns in their flesh. These pleasures also included the drinking of wine which is strictly forbidden to Muslims.[10] It is natural, then, that with the expulsion of the Turks from Yemen, the Yemenites strove to purge the country of all the "heretical" elements which were introduced by the Turks. It seems that the Jews, who were often accused of collaboration with the Turks, were caught in this cleansing process and its fanaticism. It should be stressed that the land of Yemen has for centuries been regarded by Yemenite Muslim theologians and jurists as a sacred land, an integral part of the region of Mecca. The saying of ᶜUmar, "There should not be two religions in Yemen," was also believed to be applicable to those who espoused those religions in the land of Yemen.[11] It is little wonder that Muslim fanatics would, in outbursts of anti-Jewish agitation, incite their imāms to force conversion upon the Jews, the only non-Muslim minority in Yemen, or expel them, following the example of Muḥammad, who expelled the Jews of the Ḥijāz. The Qur'ān declared the Jews to be rebels and transgressors, and this formed the basis for the often-voiced Muslim contention, "How can this [holy] land tolerate the transgressions of those who rebel against the Qur'ān and God's messenger?"[12]

Sectarian Yemen required but little effort to stir the embers of fanaticism. The Jewish writings relating to the Exile to Mauzaᶜ give us strong indication that the Jews were allegedly accused of polluting the land with their "evil-doings." One of the major accusations voiced by Muslims in Yemen is that the Jews not only manufactured wine for their personal and ritual needs, but also that they sold it to Muslims, thus engendering corruption in the land. Evidently, this accusation is not totally groundless. Fifty years after the expulsion to Mauzaᶜ, Rabbi Ṣaᶜdī, the author of *Dofi ha-Zeman,*[13] the oldest Yemenite Jewish chronicle extant, admonished his brethren, among other things, for selling wine to the Muslims and triggering by their irresponsible action disasters upon the Jewish communities. In his commentary on this admonition of Rabbi Ṣaᶜdī, Kafiḥ noted that the Yemenite Rabbis used to ostracize and excommunicate those Jews who sold wine to Muslims.[14]

The echo of such an accusation is voiced in the Yemenite writings relating to the events that had preceded the expulsion. Thus, for example, Ibn al-'Asbaṭ related that in his efforts to convince the imām to rescind the decree of expulsion, the head of the Jews of

Sanaa (Suleimān al-Naqash) promised the imām: *qad tarakna al-funūn wa'aiḍan al-shurābī,* "we have already abandoned the amusements [literally: arts] and also the drinking [of wine]."[15] This note is also reflected in the writings of the later writer Manṣūra who had the imām rebuke the leader of the Jews in the following words: "You, the shepherd and leader of Israel, why do you allow them [the Jews] to corrupt my people with their wine and evil-doings?"[16] Although the authenticity of Manṣūra's account is very doubtful, it does nevertheless reflect an often recurring voiced accusation.[17]

The various laments written by Jewish exiles also indicate that the expulsion was preceded by a vigorous attempt on the part of imām al-Mahdī to impose forced conversion upon the Jews of Yemen. "*al-Imām,*" complained one poet, "*qad qal nibi*ᶜ *al-dīn*" (The imām said, we should forsake [literally, sell] our faith).[18] Another poet writes that the imam *yashtahī al-dīn yakūn dīn al-'Islām* (desires that religion be [exclusively] that of Islam.)[19] Still another bitterly complains before God: "They have humiliated our faith and told us to apostatize, to sin and desecrate your Torah."[20] The note of forced conversion is repeated in several poems of Shabazi, who himself experienced that turbulent event. Shabazi spoke of continuous and unrelenting pressure exerted on the Jews "tempting them to confuse their faith."[21] In another poem Shabazi bitterly complained:

> The old and evil obstinate [King] covets the [Jewish] remnant's faith;
> He wishes to entice me to abandon the faith of my creator.[22]

The chronicler Ḥabshush tells us that imām al-Mahdī dramatically took the Qur'ān in one hand and the sword in the other hand and commanded the assembled leaders of the Jewish communities to choose one of them—Islam or death.[23] The general picture, which emerges from the various sources at our disposal, is that most of the Jews staunchly kept to their faith and refused to convert to Islam. Some, however, succumbed to the pressures and submitted to the imām's will. Many of these professed Islam outwardly but secretly adhered to their ancestors' faith.

According to Ḥabshush, the edict of expulsion came as a result of the intercession of some prominent Muslims tribal leaders who firmly believed that the shedding of Jewish blood would invoke heavenly retribution, such as drought, famine, and pestilence. These leaders, Ḥabshush said, approached the imām and his ministers, saying, "Why do you seek to inflict a great sin on us and on our land because of the blood of these poor and innocent people, who have done no wrong? How can we witness the slaughter of those who found refuge among us from times immemorial?" The Muslim intercessors also argued that the Jews were known to be stubborn and stiff-necked and would never succumb to pressure of forced conversion. Such attempts, they claimed, had failed in the past, and they were not likely to fare any better then. Having failed to bring about the total abolition of the edict, they convinced the imām to resort to the expulsion of the Jews rather than the shedding of their blood.[24]

This and other references to humane and virtuous manifestations of actions taken by the Muslim personalities and tribal leaders on behalf of the Jews during that unfortunate episode clearly indicate that this phenomenon of mass expulsion was unusual in the known history of Yemen, and that it did not receive the consensus of the Yemenite Muslims. On the other hand, there are also clear indications that Muslim theologians and jurists were strongly behind it and that they ultimately gained the upper hand. Thus, for example, Judge Muḥammad al-Sahūlī dedicated a poem to the imām praising him for the decree of the expulsion of the Jews. He viewed this step as the greatest accomplishment of imām al-Mahdī—the victory of Islam over Judaism. "Had this edict been al-Mahdī's only virtue," wrote al-Sahūlī, "it would have been considered a great accomplishment."[25]

2. Demolition of Synagogues and the Expulsion of the Jews

The expulsion of the Jews to Mauza^c^ was preceded by the demolition of synagogues. According to the Yemenite Muslim chronicler Muḥammad al-Shukānī, the imām ordered the sacred writings to be taken out from the central synagogue of Sanaa, the wine (kept in the synagogues for ritual purposes) poured out, and the synagogue nailed shut. Later, continues al-Shukānī, the imām ordered the destruction of the synagogue and the building of the mosque *Masgid al-Jala* (Mosque of the Expulsion) on its ruins.[26] Indeed, the Jewish poetical laments relating to this episode indicate that in the course of the demolition of the Jewish holy places, scrolls of the laws and others sacred writings were torn up, burned, and trampled upon. A vivid description of the demolition of the synagogue *Kanīsat al-^c^Ulamā'* (Temple of the Sages) is given by Dahoōd bin Sālem Zāhir, an eyewitness to this event. We learn from his and other poems that this was not a case of mere vandalism by unruly mobs, but rather a well-planned destruction initiated by the imām himself and led by him. Thus, we read in Zāhir's poem:

> The Mu^c^allim says: I feel heartsick;
> Anguish seized me because of the demolition of the synagogues.
> My lord Aḥmad himself began the demolition.

How dreadful was the sight of the mob with their axes:
Some were plundering, others were scorning;
They took away the roof-beams, the wood and the doors;
From the stones they erected watchtowers and railings.[27]

With regard to this event, Shabazi poured his heart before God:

. . . They surrounded us like lions
To destroy synagogues,
And my eyes cry with bitter voice
Because of the violence done to treasures of Your arks. . . .
Be zealous [O Lord], for Your holy name and Your gracious Torah,
And for the synagogues which they desecrated. . . .[28]

The laments give us strong indications that the many efforts of the Yemenite Jews to avoid the calamity of mass expulsion or to mitigate its severity had failed. Thus, the poet Abū Sālem complained that the imām had made himself inaccessible to the imploring Jews:

O imām, O Aḥmad, wherefore this great fury?
If we wished to lodge a complaint, and managed to reach the gate [of your palace],
We find [our way to you] blocked by guards and gate-keepers,
And you are in your watchtower behind seven gates.[29]

Ibn al-Asbāṭ complained that fifteen letters addressed to the imām were left unanswered, "although the [the imām] is a great scholar and a reader of the Book," and he surely knows well "that the Jews have been living securely in this land [of Yemen] since the time of the Prophet."[30] In another poem Ibn al-Asbāṭ turned to the Yemenite ruler, imploring:

I said, O Mahdī, have mercy upon us—
Fear God, the God of all created beings,
The Almighty God, omnipotent and enduring
Why do you seek to bring upon us sorrow and anguish
And cause us suffering in the flaming desert?
True, it is in your power to destroy us in a single moment,
But [remember] that we are as if entrusted to your custody.
We always submit to your commands with respect and full obedience. . . .

Convinced, however, that the imām's decree was irrevocable, Ibn al-Asbāṭ turned to his brethren in despair and advised them to submit to the decree of expulsion because "all [implorations] are of no avail."[31]

There are also indications that monetary bribes, which often worked "wonders" in Yemen, failed this time to change the heart of the adamant ruler. A poet by the name of Musallam summed up the desperate situation most succinctly:

'in al-Malik qad ṣar ghaḍbān
walā qābil fī dirhamān
The King [Imām] has become wrathful
And would not even accept [ransom] money.[32]

Shabazi gave us the account of the expulsion in his Arabic poem "*waṣalna hātif al-'Alḥān,*" which reads:

On the second of Rajāb, tidings reached us saying:
Get up and declare the unity of God the Merciful
And read the disastrous edict
Beware and do not be heedless
Because your appointed time is close.
al-Mahdī, the Sulṭān, ordered us to flee,
The Jews of Sanaa were forced to uproot themselves,
heading to the wilderness,
A region abounding with wild beasts and serpents.
And from Mahgam and from Dar^{c}an[33]
The order prevailed over us.
We shall dwell in Mauza^{c}
At the edge of the Arabian peninsula.
All the inhabitants of 'Uzal [Sanaa] obeyed
And they assembled in Damār.
O friend, saddle the camel,
Let it follow the donkey,
We shall go to ^{c}Adīna, ^{c}Amīra and ^{c}Amar.
The young ones and the emaciated—their tears are like showers.
^{c}Adīna, attend to the beloved ones,
Welcome them at the gates,
This is the day of reckoning for [true] friendship.
Comfort the haggard fugitive
So that his fatigue be alleviated.
[Behold] these are the descendants of the tribes [of Jacob],
The pious ones of noble descent.
Ṣafī al-Dīn[34] has already decreed that we not stay in our habitations;
Rich, poor and prominent were expelled.
We shall march according to our capability
At the sign of Saturn—destined to cause destruction.[35]

In another poem written in Hebrew, Shabazi depicted the plight of his brethren:

They are dispersed to the ends of the earth
Awaiting their salvation;
Crushed by the yoke of enemies and oppressors,
They shed their tears—
Forgive, O God, our iniquities
And shed light upon our darkness.[36]

In still another poem written in Aramaic, Shabazi bitterly complained:

> They devise against us false accusations,
> They write and seal;
> They desire to humiliate us.
> They pluck off the hair from our cheeks
> They rip off our clothes—
> We walk in fear, trembling
> In stillness, like a slave . . . [37]

A poignant poem of Shabazi invokes the help of the matriarch Rachel and echoes the cry of a hounded people:

> Weep, Oh Rachel, in our city for [your] wandering sons,
> Awaken our Fathers, let them arise
> To remind (God) of our Covenant. . . . [38]

The imām had chosen Mauzaᶜ in the remote region of Tihāma, close to the Red Sea, as the place to which the Jews were to be exiled. The Jews, some poems imply, were expected to perish under the intolerable conditions there. Shabazi described this region as

> An arid land with deathly simooms
> If wells are there, their water is bloody. . . .
> Happy is the man whose days are fulfilled and dies
> So that he may not see his children scattered in the wasteland.[39]

Ibn al-Asbāṭ, who referred to this region as *Bilād al-Shaiāṭīn* (the Land of the Devils), had this to say about the location:

> They said that the water is salty and the climate hot
> And the weather in Tihāmat is like fire . . .
> O God, save us from the the wild beasts and tigers
> Shelter me from the evil simoons and the heat.[40]

Indeed, this description of the wasteland of Tihāma is far from exaggerated. Travelers and explorers who visited this region complained of its fierceness and of the utter tyranny of the sun there, which blazed like an oven with its piercing rays and blinding glare. Thus, for example, Riḥani, who provided us with an insightful eyewitness account of his visit to Yemen, said of this region:

> Up an azure sky, which is oppressive in its purity, the sun ascends and continues to pour its heat generously until noon, and then—it was 100°F. in the shade, the bottom had fallen out, the land was flooded with fire! . . . Smitten with a stupor that bordered on death. The donkeys in the square looked like statues or stuffed animals; the few trees in the plain were but bits of landscape on canvas; the red bricks of the houses were a brilliant amber in the glare; and the few

people that were out . . . moved about in a listless, shambling gait, a wish-it-were-the-end-of-the-world feeling. Not a breath of air, and not a shred of a cloud. The sun monopolized the sky and earth.
. . . The wind was stirring, and out of the earth, like smoke, rose the dust in circles, in columns. I first saw one whirling circle with a suction of the centre, rising to a height of about 10 feet and moving towards the city, without losing its form; and then another that rose to a column of about 30 feet high and moved in the same manner and direction. . . . The circles and columns met and rose into clouds that filled the horizon all around and swept across the plain, charged against the city . . . The Simoom had silenced the land, overwhelming every sound and voice in its path.[41]

Shalom ^cAshri, who personally experienced this calamity, lamented the fate of the Exiles in the following words:

I shed my tears, like torrents they fall
  Because of the beloved ones who were exiled . . . .
On the day of the Exile of Uzal, and its great misfortune
  The rising sun and moon were snuffed out.
The multitudes of the maidservant's descendants vanquished them
  Fury and wrath, they poured upon them. . . .
Midrash, Talmud and Torah they abolished;
  Leaders and elders were dragged.
The Great Bear, the Pleiades and the moon darkened
  And all the bright luminaries dimmed their lights.[42]

In a penitential prayer composed for *Yom Kippur,* Shabazi bewailed:

I am bent from the multitudes of my enemies;
Bowed down I walk.
Woe to me, I have transgressed
And have rebelled against my Rock.
Rejoice not, O my enemy,
For though I have fallen, I shall rise—

There came the cruel edict by the maidservant's son.[43]
In malice he composed accusations;
He roared with a multitudinous force
And scattered my brethren throughout the land
Woe, when a daughter rises against her mother.
Behold, I was brought forth in iniquity.

Were it not for the help of God,
Who frustrated the schemes of the savage one,
We would have been annihilated
By the one who sought to proselytize us—

God in His mercy shattered their plot
And stirred in them compassion for His people,

And He caused dissension among my enemies
With fury He scattered their bands. . . .
On the day their wrath was kindled
I have remembered the Lord.[44]

One of the most valuable documents pertaining to this event is a letter sent by the Jews of Ẓurān (southwest of Sanaa) to the Jews of Hebron.[45] From this letter, written in the form of a chronicle, we learn that at that very time a "Jewish emissary" (שליח) from Palestine, Rabbi ᶜAmram, was in Yemen for the purpose of collecting money for his community in Hebron. This emissary, about whom we know nothing other than from this letter, preferred to accompany his unfortunate Yemenite coreligionists and share their miserable lot. This letter is of extreme importance, especially as it seems to be the only extant testimony of attempts on the part of Yemenite Jews to communicate with their brethren outside Yemen regarding this unfortunate episode in their history. It is most astonishing that despite this epistle and the probable return of the emissary to Hebron, the story of the exile to Mauzaᶜ was not known outside Yemen, at least not before the nineteenth century.

The letter is written in the form of a *maqāma* (rhymed prose). In it the Yemenites give vent to their great distress:

> . . . When this pious man came to us we were delighted./ We yearned for him./Perchance he came to bring salvation/or perhaps good tidings./But alas! there was the anguish of her that bringeth forth her first child.[46]/And behold, destruction upon destruction.[47]/ Every one sought to dig a grave for himself./ Because of our transgressions God stirred up the spirit of the King of the Land to expel us./We, our women and children/to a desolate wilderness, a place of serpents, scorpions, and consuming fire,/ hunted by fury./ Alas, the verse "I will bring them into the land of their enemies" [Lev. 26:41] was fulfilled upon us/And he demolished our synagogues/And darkened our eyes./And they cried unto us, "Away, you unclean!"[48] And the taskmasters kept driving us on, saying: "Out from there! Purify yourselves.[49]/ . . . But if you abandon your God in Whom you trust and embrace our religion, it will be good for you./[Your God] has cast you away/And delivered you in our hands/so that we may do with you as we wish." And we wandered around to find a place of repose./But lo, we were smitten and wounded,[50]/And we became exposed to disgrace and abuse, to horror, terror and fear; every mouth uttered villany against us.[51]/Messengers of destruction hastened/to plunder our labor,/to take away our houses . . . ./Whoever lagged and was unable to walk, because of his poverty and affliction, they smote him and wounded him, stripped him of his mantle, and plucked off his skin from him.[52]/There was no one to help,/none to intercede for them. All turned aside like a treacher-

> ous bow. . . .[53] And God hid His face from us, and we have all withered like leaves.[54]/We walked with shame and disgrace, hungry and thirsty, naked and impoverished, heading to the place that the king designated for us. He refused to accept ransom/because he sought to exterminate us. . . . And they arrived at a place of aridity,/of robbers and bands of wild beasts,/and in that region the sun comes out of its sheath. . . setting them on fire.[55] And they lifted their voices and wept sore. Many, too many, were those who perished by the scourge before the Lord.[56] And they could not bury them because of the heat. . . . And at night about seventy people escaped, there was no peace for one going out or coming in.[57]/But in the morning the sun shone forth and struck upon their heads. And all of them perished . . . .[58]

Toward the end of the letter Yemenites implored their coreligionists in the Land of Israel to pray for them, for "you are in a holy land, and prayers ascend through the rungs of the ladder stationed [there] upon the earth. There [in Beth 'El] is the Gate of the Heavens."[59]

3. The Annulment of the Decree

The decree of expulsion, as stated previously, did not meet the approval of many of the tribal chiefs. From some of the poems we learn that some of these chiefs displayed acts of piety and acted hospitably to the Jewish exiles who passed through their regions on their way to Mauzaᶜ. Thus, the ruler of Mauzaᶜ, Sayyid Aḥmad, treated the Jews graciously and received them with bread and water.[60] Ḥabshush related that rulers of some regions in Yemen refused to comply with the decree of expulsion and protected the Jews who lived in their midst.[61]

How the Jewish communities fared during this bad time is not fully known. The extant sources do not provide us with conclusive details regarding the duration of the exile or the life that the Jews led in the region of their exile. According to Koraḥ, the exile lasted one year, after which the decree was revoked and the Jews were allowed to return to their cities and villages.[62]

The reasons for the annulment of the expulsion decree by the Yemenite government are shrouded in mystery, and there does not seem to be a clear-cut explanation for this phenomenon. Several conjectures have been posited. According to one source, the expulsion of the Jews was followed by an eruption of black plague among the Muslims and a downpour of hail which destroyed the crops of the land. The Muslims viewed this calamity as an act of vengeance on the part of God and, therefore, exerted pressure upon their rulers to annul the decree.[63] Ratzaby, however, ties the termination of this decree to the death of Imām al-Mahdī in 1681.[64]

Ḥabshush and Koraḥ maintain that the rescission of the decree was occasioned by the economic anarchy that afflicted Yemen after the sudden expulsion of the Jews.[65] The Arabs, they related, suffered from shortages of basic commodities. Koraḥ claimed that tribal chiefs, headed by the high official of ᶜAmran knelt before the imām, kissed his knees according to well-established Arab custom, and pleaded before him, saying, "We came not to intercede for the Jews but for our own benefit and the benefit of all the Muslims [in Yemen]. . . . "[66] Ḥabshush remarked that these officials implored the imām to allow the Jews to return to their habitations because they were "like the salt in the world's food," pointing out that since their deportation, businesses were paralyzed and many Muslims had lost their means of livelihood.[67] Ḥabshush's assumption seems to be the most tenable of the foregoing hypotheses, because it tallies with our knowledge of the general socioeconomic function that the Jews of Yemen fulfilled. As manual workers, masons, and masters in all the local handicrafts in a predominantly agricultural society, the Jews provided all the services which were most indispensable to the farmer, in that they made his ploughs, hoes, spades, and so on. Most of the Jews were artisans: blacksmiths, coppersmiths, silversmiths, goldsmiths, tailors, shoemakers, weavers, leatherworkers, furriers, potters, masons, brickmakers, makers of handmills, and so on. Almost all the arts and crafts were provided by the Jews of Yemen, who were evenly distributed over the country. The Jews indeed owed their continued existence in the midst of intolerant Muslims to the special services that they alone were capable of rendering to their neighbors in peace and war.[68] Without these valuable services, Yemenite society would have suffered; therefore, it stands to reason that the Muslims would have had much to gain from the rescission of this edict.

4. The Effects of the Exile

While much mystery and uncertainty still persist regarding the exact circumstances which brought about the expulsion and its rescission after one year, its consequences are evident enough. The exile had a devastating effect upon Yemenite Jewry in many respects. The intolerable conditions of the exile in the region of Tihāma, the famine and the epidemics—all these wrought havoc among them. Three-fourths of the Jews perished during this year of exile. From the once prosperous Jewish community of Sanaa, which according to Idelsohn counted ten thousand, only one thousand survived.[69] Moreover, the exile caused tremendous social and demographic upheavals. The Jews were not allowed to return to their former residences, which were in the midst of the Muslims, but were consigned to isolated quarters outside the bounds of Muslim habitations. Thus, the Jews of Sanaa had to build a new quarter outside the main city, removed from the vibrant social interaction with Muslims.

Galut Mauzaᶜ had its impact also upon the spiritual domain of the Jews of Yemen. It brought about the decimation of the communities' sages and spiritual leaders and the destruction of much of their sacred writings. According to Rabbi Ṣāliḥ (Mahriṣ), the Jews of Sanaa left behind them a treasury of writings, the fruit of many centuries of productivity, entrusted in the hands of a Muslim in Sanaa. All these manuscripts, Rabbi Ṣāliḥ says, were burned because of Islamic zeal.[70] It is highly plausible that these writings included poems, historical records, and other literary outputs. Thus, the Yemenite Jewish communities emerged from this ordeal decimated, and extremely impoverished materially and spiritually. Furthermore, their legal and social status had declined precipitously. Galut Mauzaᶜ strongly underscored the constant state of anxiety and vulnerability in which the Yemenite Jews lived.

5. Jewish Reaction to Galut Mauzaᶜ

As in all disasters, the Jews of Yemen responded to the Mauzaᶜ calamity with an outpouring of self-flagellation. They saw in their sufferings trials imposed by God. The note of Jeremiah's proclamation, "Your ways and your doings have brought these [disasters] upon you" (5:18) rings through their poems, which call for penitence and repentance. Thus, Shabazi wrote in one of his poems:

> Our glory has been humbled in Yemen during our exile;
> I ponder my condition in its particularity and its totality—
> The Torah calls upon the sages and says:
> Neglect of my study is the reason of their ignorance.
> Let them repent before the Lord and implore Him.
> The day of redemption will come soon,
> And He will gather their exiles . . . .[71]

Mahriṣ's grandfather, who himself experienced the Mauzaᶜ tribulations, addressed his people in terms reminiscent of the sermons of the prophetic fulminations:

God will hand you over [to your enemies]
And will not have mercy upon you.
Strangers would devour your labor
And will multiply your wounds.
They will exile your children
To the land of your seduction,
If you do not return
To your God, your lord.
Harken to my statutes,
Don't harden [your heart] and ignore them.
Hasten to listen to me,
To worship the Holy Rock,
Because you are the pupil of my eye and my beloved.
Then peace will prevail within your walls
And prosperity within thy habitations.[72]

There is no wonder that the Galut theme, namely, lamentation, mourning, and woe, is central in Yemenite Jewish literature. Very often a note of bitter, faint, and distressed hearts permeates the writings of the Yemenite Jews. An awful feeling of frustration and helplessness would sweep their hearts and bring them to the verge of despair: What if they really were cast away from the presence of God, discarded in the nether world, deep in the pit? Maybe they were nothing but "a wretched people forgotten for all generations."[73] This kind of feeling would then elicit a bitter cry:

O you who remember the forgotten, remember me!
Alas, I am forgotten, and my name did not come to mind. . .
I am drowning, the waters have reached my neck;
Yet my Shepherd did not search, did not draw up.
My counsellors are lost, and anguish has seized me like a woman in travail
And rejoicing has vanished.
I have stumbled, the delight of my heart has gone. . .
My foot has slipped, the garland has fallen from my head.[74]

However, these trampled people never lost their confidence in God. They would plead their cause with Him, but the tone was never one of admonition or reproof. Their shadows of doubt would be chased away by their conviction that on account of their sins, God might have hidden His face from them just for a while; but they believed that He was still their rock and refuge and would never deprive them of His saving aid. This thought sustained their confidence in adversity. The more they suffered, the more they clung to God, striving to find shelter in the shadow of His wings:

I sought Him in time of distress,
Time of suffering, misfortune and trouble.
I lifted up to the Rider on clouds

My hands and soul and heart and gall,
And I called with all my power and strength
And cried like a woman in travail.
My times are bad and all my days are woe,
Days of wrath, fury and strife. . . .
Ravaged am I by Philistines and the people of Javan
And by Kedar and Gebal and the sons of Keturah.[75]
I am despised by great and small,
I am repugnant in their eyes.
Plucked are my wings like those of the ostrich,
And I am left without plumage and pinion
They call me "dog" and "ass"
And any loathsome creature without cud and hoofs.[76]
They have prohibited me from wearing white clothing
And from putting a turban on my head. . . . [77]
God, look at their affliction and cease Thy fierce wrath
And forgive our wickedness and trespass and sin.[78]

The Galut theme in Yemenite Hebrew literature is indeed depicted in the most gloomy tones. Yet, though often broken in body, Yemenite Jews refused to be broken in soul. Their pride, which was construed by Muslims as arrogance and defiance of Islam, triggered new waves of persecution aimed at breaking the backs of the Jews. However, the Yemenite Jews, with their enormous spiritual fortitude, defied defeat and degradation.

The Yemenite Jewish poets played a unique and vital role in supplying their dejected people with desperately needed words of inspiration. They created for their people a spiritual world in which they could turn inward and fortify themselves. This world was composed of an absolute faith in God and in His imminent redemption. The poets preached the insignificance of earthly life, and urged their dispirited people to cleave to the Torah and to the commandments. The Torah was in their eyes the fountain of life, the only sure way to salvation and happiness, and the only true guide through the stormy labyrinth of life. In turn, the Torah sustained them and alleviated their agony:

To the graceful doe my soul cleaves,
Forgetful of my distress in the Galut. . . . [79]

They saw in the Torah not only a remedy for their weary souls but also a sure means of hastening the advent of the Messiah and influencing God to effect His promised redemption:

By its [the Torah's] virtue, God will hasten the advent of his Messiah
And will upraise [His people] from the decreed Galut.[80]

VII

YEMENITE JEWRY IN THE EIGHTEENTH AND NINETEENTH CENTURIES

1. Carsten Niebuhr

We became much more knowledgeable about the condition of the Jews of Yemen with the penetration of that country by European travelers, who, within the context of their records about Yemen in general, had something to say about the Yemenite Jews. Thus, in 1763, the Danish explorer Carsten Niebuhr returned from Yemen and gave us the first and heretofore the most detailed account of that country.[1] Niebuhr was followed by other European travelers. Prominent among these were Jacob Saphir—the greatest explorer to visit Yemenite Jewry—in 1859, Joseph Halēvy in 1872 and 1877, E. Glaser in 1882–1894, Wyman G. Bury in 1914, Ameen Riḥani in 1920, and Hugh Scott in 1937–1938.

Niebuhr's records provide us with valuable insights into the state of affairs in Yemen during the last years of al-Mahdī ʿAbbās (reigned 1748–1775).[2] The imamate, as keenly observed by Niebuhr, was then in a state of decline and disintegration. The land of Yemen, remarked our traveler, "was parcelled out among a number of different sovereigns in unequal portions." Many of these sovereigns were nothing but petty sheikhs "who are, however, perfectly independent." The imām's territory was confined to a relatively small area with numerous independent enclaves. These "endless subdivisions of territory, among such a multitude of petty sovereigns," concluded Niebuhr, fatally affected the development of trade and industry, and was the chief cause for the deterioration of that country.[3]

Niebuhr related, among other things, the abject status of the Jews of Yemen and the religious persecutions to which they were subjected by the imāms. The general picture which emerges from his account regarding the community of Sanaa, the largest of the Yemenite Jewish communities, is of a group living in isolation outside the main city and being subjected to religious persecution and extreme measures of humiliation. Niebuhr reported that at the time of his visit,

> the government ordered fourteen synagogues, which the Jews had at Sana, to be demolished. In their village are as handsome houses as the best in Sana. Of those houses likewise all above the height of fourteen fathoms [84 feet] was demolished, and the Jews were forbidden to raise any of their buildings above this height in future. All the stone pitchers in which the inhabitants of the village had used to keep their wines were broken. In short, the poor Jews suffered mortifications of all sorts.[4]

Niebuhr's observations regarding the Jews of Yemen find ample corroboration in Yemenite Jewish records emanating from that period. From these writings we also learn that two Jewish personalities dominated the scene of Yemenite Jewry during the eighteenth century: Rabbi Shalom ben Aharon ha-Kohen ᶜIrāqī and Rabbi Yeḥia Ṣāliḥ.

2. Rabbi Shalom ben Aharon ha-Kohen ᶜIrāqī (d. 1780)

To judge from its name, the origins of the ᶜIrāqī family was most probably ᶜIrāq. This family, which emigrated to Yemen through Egypt,[5] soon assumed a role of leadership through which it exercised a deep and lasting influence upon the Jewish communities in Yemen. Most distinguished among this family were Rabbi Aharon and his son, Rabbi Shalom. The latter, however, attained a remarkable position of reverence among both Jews and Muslims almost unparalleled in the known Yemenite Jewish history. He served as both community leader and royal counsellor. Rabbi Shalom was referred to by the Jews as *Sar Shalom* (chief, Master) and by the Muslims as Sālim *al-ʾUṣṭa* (master craftsman), probably a corruption of *al-ʾUstādh* (Master), which is a form of address to intellectuals.[6]

The date of Rabbi Shalom ᶜIrāqī's birth is not known. He died, however, in 1780. According to Yemenite popular belief, he lived for 120 years, but this has not been substantiated so far.[7]

I should, for the sake of perspective, point out that one of the provisions of the Pact of ᶜUmar is that *dhimmīs* should not hold positions that would enable them to wield power and authority over Muslims. This pact was, however, sometimes ignored by Muslim rulers, and appointment of Jews and Christians to high government positions was not a rare phenomenon. Such appointments were generally motivated by various considerations, particularly by the recognition of the appointees' expertise in the minting of coins, banking transactions, or foreign trade. The extreme vulnerability of the *dhimmīs,* who lacked a power base, and hence their utter dependency on the Muslim rulers, also played an important role in these considerations. The *dhimmī* officials who offered no threat were expected to be very loyal to their masters, and in all but exceptional cases, they were.

In Yemen, appointment of Jews to prominent government positions was very rare. This exceptional phenomenon was noted by Carsten Niebuhr, who reported that ᶜIrāqī was one of the most eminent merchants among the Jews of Yemen, and that he "gained the favour of two successive Imams, and was for thirteen years, in the reign of El Mansor, and for fifteen years under the present Imam [al-Mahdī al-ᶜAbbās], comptroller of the customs and of the royal buildings and gardens; one of the most honourable offices at the court of Sanaa."[8] Thus, according to Niebuhr, ᶜIrāqī served the two imāms of Yemen in the capacity of a high government minister for a period of twenty-eight years.

The Yemenite chronicler Ḥabshush related that ᶜIrāqī's influential position in government of Yemen was a blessing for the Jews. ᶜIrāqī, says Ḥabshush, "raised the prestige of Israel, and in his days the Jews found peace and repose. He sought the welfare of his people and bestowed glory upon them." Ḥabshush lavished praise upon the generosity of Rabbi Shalom ᶜIrāqī who, he says, was kindhearted and righteous. Ḥabshush stressed ᶜIrāqī's charitable nature and the fact that he built many synagogues and bathhouses for his brethren. Ḥabshush's praise concluded with the words, "And there has not arisen [among Yemenite Jewry] a man like the noble Shalom ha-Kohen ᶜIrāqī, none before him or after him."[9]

The respite that ᶜIrāqī's influential position brought upon his brethren did not, however, last for long. Niebuhr reported that the fate of this "venerable old man, of great knowledge" was far from being a happy one, since after about 30 years of service to two imāms he "had fallen into disgrace, and was not only imprisoned, but obliged to pay a fine of 50,000 crowns." The disgrace of ᶜIrāqī, continued Niebuhr, triggered "a degree of persecution upon the rest of the Jews."[10] The fate of ᶜIrāqī is, however, not surprising in view of the extremely precarious position of *dhimmīs* who occasionally gained favor in the eyes of rulers in Muslim countries and often became targets of envy and hostility among Muslim officials and jurists.[11]

ᶜIrāqī was instrumental in the introduction of the Sephardi version of prayer, known in Yemen as *Shāmī*, among the Jewish communities of Yemen. The *Shāmī* version, which was intended to replace the old local version (*Baladī*), became a very controversial issue, greatly opposed by other spiritual leaders, particularly by Rabbi Yeḥia Ṣāliḥ, who was then the chief rabbi of Yemenite Jewry.[12]

3. Rabbi Yeḥia Ṣāliḥ (ca. 1740-ca. 1805)

Rabbi Ṣāliḥ, generally known by his acronym Mahriṣ (*Morenu ha-Rav Yeḥia Ṣāliḥ*), is considered to be the greatest rabbinic personality Yemenite Jewry is known to have produced. He wielded authority over all the Jewish communities of Yemen and was recognized as their highest spiritual and religious authority. Saphir, who visited Yemen in 1859, related that Rabbi Ṣāliḥ had a great knowledge of the Qabbalah, that his name was prominent throughout the land of Yemen, and that the Yemenites still conduct their religious life in light of his *halakhic* decisions and rulings.[13] Other sources reveal that Rabbi Ṣāliḥ earned his living solely from his two occupations: silversmith and scribe of holy writings.

Rabbi Ṣāliḥ was a prolific writer. His literary output included treatises on ritual slaughter and ritual purity (*Zevaḥ Todah, Shaʿare Qedusha, Shaʿare Ṭohora*); a work pertaining to the correct punctuation and reading of the Hebrew Scriptures (*Ḥeleq ha-Diqduq*); an extensive exegesis on the *Tiklal* (Prayer book) (*ʿEṣ Ḥayyim*); responsa and halakhic rulings (*Peʿullat Ṣaddiq*); and a chronicle of the Jews of Yemen (*Megillat Teman*).[14]

It should be noted that Rabbi Ṣāliḥ lived in a time of trials and tribulations. Mention has been made of Niebuhr's report regarding the demolition of fourteen synagogues in Sanaa, an act which was followed by the intensified persecution of the Jews. These distressing events find expression in Rabbi Ṣāliḥ's writings, particularly in his three laments, which echoed the agony and helpless frustration of his brethren. In one of the laments, he depicted the Jewish community of Sanaa as "sitting desolate with fear and trembling" due to the "extreme hostility" which surrounded it. He complained that his community's "comely places and academies of learning are laid waste" and that "Evil people destroyed the Lord's tabernacle and snuffed out the lamps of God's sanctuaries." Rabbi Ṣāliḥ concluded his lament in the following words:

> In the evening, in the black and dark night
> I rise and roam about [the city],
> I set my face to the synagogues—alas, they are in ruin
> And the ark of God was carried away captive.[15]

Most intriguing is the special relationship that Rabbi Ṣāliḥ maintained with the Jews of India, particularly with those of Cochin. To be sure, Jews from Yemen had visited India for various purposes, and some even settled there. Thus, the celebrated sixteenth-century Yemenite writer Zecharia al-Ḍahrī is known to have visited India.[16] Likewise, Jews from India visited their coreligionists in Yemen. A document relates that in 1765, a Jew from Cochin visited Yemen, looking for Yemenite brides for the sons of his master Isaac. The document provides the names of all the personalities involved, as well as the conditions agreed upon. It stipulates that if the bride does not find favor in the eyes of Isaac, she would still, whether married or not, be granted the amount stipulated in her *ketubbah* as well as her travel expenses back to Yemen.[17]

Saphir, who had also visited India, expressed the view that the Jews of Cochin originated from Yemen some 1700 years ago, prompted by persecutions. Saphir stressed what he viewed as the striking similarities between the Jews of Yemen and those of Cochin in their physical appearance and customs.[18] He also related that these "black Jews" of Cochin did not have Cohens and Levites of their own, and they, therefore, hired for ritual purposes Cohens and Levites from the poor Jews who came to them from Yemen and Persia.[19]

The relations between the Jews of India and those of Yemen seem to have been greatly intensified at the time of Rabbi Ṣāliḥ. From the correspondence that Rabbi Ṣāliḥ had with Jews in India, we learn that they consulted him in religious and *halakhic* matters and that he was held in high esteem by them as a spiritual authority. Thus, in a letter sent to Rabbi Ṣāliḥ from Abraham Zakkai, a Jew from Cochin, the former is referred to as a great spiritual leader, "sitting on a lofty chair, to guide the people of God to the way which leads to the dwelling of light. He judges the world with righteousness and delivers the wronged from the wrongdoer." In this letter Zakkai mentioned bills of divorce (*geṭ*) and *ḥaliṣah* that were sent him by Rabbi Ṣāliḥ. He also requested the Rabbi to send him a pair of phylacteries and four *mezuzot.* Furthermore, he informed Rabbi Ṣāliḥ of the death of his wife.[20]

Rabbi Ṣāliḥ's numerous works, particularly his *Peᶜullat Ṣaddiq,* provide us with valuable insights into various aspects of the life and customs of the Yemenite Jews. For example, a question addressed to him relates to the betrothal of a six-year-old girl to a twelve-year-old boy and its dire consequences.[21] Another one deals with the custom prevalent among Yemenite Jews to use old manuscripts for the binding of books and to glue leaves of ancient works one upon another to produce hard covers for the new books. Rabbi Ṣāliḥ rebuked the binders, saying:

> What means the heat of this anger to destroy worn-out sacred writings? I have witnessed such cases and [I am appalled by the fact] that there is none to claim pity and protect the dignity of these writings. Some of these constitute [old] prayer books, others worn-out pages of the Torah that may contain the Ineffable Name; still others, books of Aggadah, Halakha and midrash. On this the mourners mourn. . . . Great is my distress at this disregard for our sacred writings . . . be appalled. . . . Be appalled, O heavens, at this. Clothe yourself with blackness! If I am a Father, where is my honor? And if I am a Master, where is my fear [says the Lord]. . . . [22]

Rabbi Ṣālih left an indelible mark upon many facets in the religious and spiritual life of Yemenite Jewry. His treatises on halakhic matters, grammatical and syntactical readings of the Hebrew scriptures, and on prayer form and ritual are considered most authoritative, and Yemenite Jewry has adhered to them up to this very day.

Rabbi Ṣāliḥ is known to have written a book on the history of the Jews of Yemen. Unfortunately, only a few passages from this book are extant.[23]

4. The Decline of the Qāsimī State

The Yemenite Jewish chronicles relating to the events of the nineteenth century, prior to the second Ottoman occupation of Yemen (1872), read like a catalogue of misfortunes that transpired in rapid succession. The persecution against the Jews intensified; already existing edicts against the Jews, such as those relating to the Jewish orphans and the cleansing of the public latrines, were far more stringently enforced; Jewish life had become less secure and increasingly intolerable.

This state of decline in the social, economic, and political conditions of the Jews should, however, be viewed in the light of the events that befell Yemen during that period. The death of Imām al-Mahdī ᶜAbbās (1748–1775) brought about a further intensification of the process of political disintegration of Yemen. Al-Mahdī's son, al-Manṣūr ᶜAlī (reigned 1775–1809) was, according to both Muslims and Jewish historians, given to lust and the life of leisure, and he entrusted the affairs of the state to three viziers.[24] His reign was punctuated by family disputes and tribal defiance. Acts of robbing and pillage by insubordinate tribes became frequent and lacerated the country. In 1804 the Sulaimānī Sharīf Ḥamūd of Asīr conquered the Tihāma and its coastal region, depriving the Zaydī imamate of a major source of revenue. The territory which Ḥamūd wrested from the imām was itself subject to frequent incursions and pillages by the Wahhābīs[25] and by the Egyptians. Moreover, the general anarchy, which resulted from the country's misrule and from the persistent tribal insurgence, wrought havoc upon the country's economy and considerably diminished the imām's revenues derived from duties on merchandise, export tax, and land-and-poll taxes. As a result of all these, the imām's treasury was depleted to the extent that he was not able to disburse the traditional "customary rights" of the tribes.

In 1808 the powerful Bakīl tribes went to Sanaa to claim their annual "portion" from the imām. When the latter failed to respond to their demand, they laid siege to the capital, causing a scarcity of food and a subsequent sharp rise in the prices of essential commodities. The drought which occurred concomitantly with the siege greatly worsened the dire situation, and the city was struck by famine. Muslim and Jewish chroniclers reported that most of the populace of Sanaa found their death in this famine, which was followed by a plague.[26] In a lament relating to this calamity, the author Yehuda Jasfan bemoaned, "Diverse calamities surrounded me like water." Among these calamities were the three familiar scourges: famine, plague, and the sword. He related that in this severe famine his two sons perished, and he was forced to sell not only his clothes and possessions but also his most precious book, which he himself had written.[27]

Another disastrous event took place in the year 1817. Representatives of some tribes came again to Sanaa to claim their "customary portion" from Imām al-Mahdī ᶜAbdallāh. Ḥabshush related that the imām reacted indignantly toward the tribesmen and ordered the populace of Sanaa to seize them and bring them to prison. One year later (in 1818), the tribes of the Bakīl confederacy, along with other tribal allies, rose against Sanaa and wrought havoc upon the city and its inhabitants. The vulnerable Jewish quarter in Bir al-ᶜAzāb was not spared. Jewish houses were pillaged and destroyed, and Jewish blood was shed. A letter signed by six Yemenite Jews, addressed to the Anglo-Jewish Association in London, related the disastrous effects that the Bakīl invasion had upon the Jews of Sanaa. Their houses were destroyed or burned, all their movable property was looted, and "they were left naked, destitute, famishing from dire want." The letter bemoaned, in particular, the irreparable destruction of Jewish sacred writings during this assault. The "invaders," complained the signatories of the letter,

> robbed us of nearly three hundred Scrolls of the Law, most of which were in the handwriting of our illustrious ancestors. They tore these sacred writings into shreds, and cast them about in all public thor-

> oughfares; and this, too, at the time of the rainy season. Some of the miscreants converted the substance on which the law was written into trappings for their horses, camels, and asses. . . . They also destroyed, beyond the possibility of recovery, many thousands of volumes, both in manuscript and in print, besides destroying books which were thrown down into deep wells.[28]

To judge from the numerous laments relating to this event, the Bakīl assault on the Jews of Sanaa was most unusual in its severity.[29] The extreme bitterness and feelings of bereavement which find expression in these laments are reminiscent of those relating to the Mauza^c calamity (1679). Indeed, the 1818 assault is deeply ingrained in the minds of the Yemenite Jews who refer to it by a special name, "*Ṭam^cat Bakīl*" ("The Pillage of Bakīl").

The Jews lamented that the Bakīl's attack on the Jews of Sanaa occurred on the Eve of Passover. Thus, a night which was designated for singing and rejoicing was transformed into a night of howling and wailing. "Wherefore is this night distinguished from the other [Passover] nights?" sarcastically asked one of the writers. "In other [Passover] nights," he answered, "we drink cups of salvation and blessing. This night," he added, "we drink the poison cup."[30] The laments related the slaughter of young and old, mutilation of bodies, rape of women, and desecration of the holy writings.

The *Ṭam^cah* of Bakīl is surprising not only in its unprecedented dimensions but also in its flagrant violation of the traditional tribal code of conduct, which conferred protection upon the *dhimmīs* and strictly prohibited the shedding of their blood. What then prompted this deadly assault? Several factors seem to have been at work: The general anarchy that prevailed in the country was highly conducive to acts of pillaging, looting, and plundering; the Bakīl assault was directed against the imām and Sanaa, the capital, and the Jewish quarter was an integral part of that city; while the protection accorded to the *dhimmīs* by Islam was generally guarded, this did not preclude occasional outbreaks of fanaticism and spasms of violence against the *dhimmīs*. Yemen was no exception.

Ḥabshush, however, pointed an accusing finger against the Jews of Sanaa and viewed the Bakīl onslaught as a reprisal for manifestations of Jewish hostility toward the Bakīl tribesmen. He related that a year earlier, the Jews, in response to the imām's call, joined the Muslims of Sanaa in attacking the Bakīl representatives who came to claim their "portion." Equipped with rods and sharp tools, the Jews chased the Bakīls and helped to drive them out of the city.[31] This hostile act, which constituted a flagrant violation of the Jewish traditional neutrality, must have kindled the wrath of the tribes and may account for the severity of the retribution. Be this as it may, the advent of the nineteenth century was characterized by a marked deterioration of the economy and the social order in Yemen in general, and of its Jews in particular.

5. The British Occupation of Aden (1839)

In 1839, the British occupied Aden, a small peninsula situated on the south coast of Yemen, ruled at that time by the tribal sultans of Laḥej. For hundreds of years (12th–16th centuries), Aden had served as an international emporium for wide-ranging mercantile activities. This city had then a flourishing Jewish community. From the sixteenth century onward, Aden experienced a rapid decline, which eventually brought about the utter eclipse of its role as a center of commerce; subsequently, its large Jewish community gradually shrank in numbers and significance. In 1839, Captain Haines referred to it as a "little village." This "formerly great city," remarked Haines,

> is now reduced to the most exigent condition of poverty and neglect. In the reign of Constantine this town possessed unrivalled celebrity for its impenetrable fortifications, its flourishing commerce, and the glorious haven it offered to vessels from all quarters of the globe. But how lamentable is the present contrast! With scarce a vestige of its former proud superiority, the traveller sees and values it only for its capabilities, and regrets the barbarous cupidity of that government under whose injudicious management it has fallen low.[32]

Playfair related that the whole population of Aden at the time of the British occupation "did not exceed 600, of which a great portion were Jews."[33] According to reliable estimates, the Jews then numbered about 250, and served as merchants, petty dealers, reed and mat workers, jewelers, bookbinders, masons, and porters.[34]

With the British occupation of Aden, the city experienced great development, which eventually restored it to its former glory. This, together with the peace and security that the British rule bestowed upon the newly acquired colony, made it an attractive haven for immigrants fleeing the turbulence of Yemen. The increasing prosperity of the city, particularly after the opening of the Suez Canal, also attracted immigrants from other parts of the world: Africa, India, Persia, Turkey, Egypt, and Europe. The Jewish population was rapidly augmented and it developed into the most prosperous Jewish community in south Arabia. Saphir, who visited Aden shortly after the British occupation, described with exultation the metamorphosis that Aden and its Jewish community had experienced under

British rule. The British occupation, he exclaimed in almost poetic language, brought light and splendor upon the town; the light penetrated the dwellings of the Jews, and the Arab oppression came to an end. The once desolate desert has been transformed into paradise.[35] The British government immediately accorded equal rights to all the inhabitants of Aden, including the Jews. This development was highly significant; for the first time since the rise of Muḥammad a Jewish community in the Arabian Peninsula could live freely without the stigma of the inferior *dhimmī* status.

Another significant development resulting from the British occupation is the exposure of Aden and its Jewish community to European influence and education. As a result, the Jewish community of Aden gradually developed a culture and customs of its own which sharply distinguished it from the other Jewish communities of Yemen. The influence of the Jewish center of Sanaa upon the Jews of Aden, which was strong before the British occupation, came to an end. The Jewish community of Aden no longer regarded itself as an integral part of Yemenite Jewry.

6. Messianic Expectations: The Two Shukr Kuḥeils

Nineteenth-century Yemen, prior to the Ottoman occupation (1872), was in a state of total anarchy. The proliferation of tribal lawlessness and the utter absence of an efficient centralized authority paralyzed the country.[36] The chaotic conditions of Yemen prior to the Turkish occupation were cogently summed up by ᶜAmram Koraḥ, who wrote:

> The kingdom of the lords of the land utterly collapsed after the death of Imām al-Mahdī ᶜAbdallāh (1834). Its revenues diminished, while its expenses increased. As a result, its treasury was depleted. From 1859, its strength gave out. The inhabitants of the land ceased to pay their dues. Robbers increased in all the roads. Even the streets of Sanaa suffered from lack of security; no one heeded the voice of a policeman. The hoodlums prevailed, for there was no ruler, nor an effective army.[37]

The state of anarchy greatly affected the Jews of Yemen, particularly those of Sanaa. Koraḥ related that the Jewish quarter in Sanaa was repeatedly plundered. Most of the Jews deserted the city and those few who remained lived in an atmosphere of constant fear and trembling.[38]

The pitiful conditions of the Jews of Sanaa were further intensified by a disastrous event which occurred in 1863. In that year, Imām al-

Mutawakkil ordered the execution of Rabbi Shalom Halevi Alsheikh, who was then in charge of the Mint. Moreover, Jewish leaders were imprisoned and tortured, and heavy monetary penalties were imposed upon the whole Jewish community.[39] The decapitation of Alsheikh had a far-reaching impact upon the Jews of Yemen, since it was almost unprecedented in Yemen. The Yemenite Muslims strongly believed that such a mode of killing a condemned Jew triggers a calamity of a seven-year famine. This unusual episode was a result of the general anarchy that prevailed in Yemen at that time, and posed a threat to old-established customs and traditions.

Echoes of the intensified persecution of the Yemenite Jews reached the London committee of Deputies of the British Jews, who responded by soliciting the help of the British government. In a letter dated August 19, 1863, addressed to Lord Earl Russell, the British Foreign Minister, J. M. Montefiore complained that "atrocities of a most fearful description" were being perpetrated against the Jews of Sanaa. These atrocities included the rape of Jewish women, who are "publicly violated in the presence of the husbands." The letter related the intensification of the Latrine Edict, which enjoined even the "aged and honourable members of the community, to collect the excrements of dogs from the streets, amid the jeers and insults of the Mohomedans." The intolerable conditions of degradation and torture to which the Jews were subjected, stressed Montefiore, prompted many desperate Jews to commit acts of suicide.[40]

The British government could do very little to alleviate the situation. The British governor of Aden, who was instructed to exert his influence, responded that "inasmuch as Sanaa was . . . in a state of anarchy, it was impossible for him to carry out the instructions of Her Majesty's Government, and to effect any change in the conditions of the Jews of Yemen."[41]

Mention has been made of the fact that Yemen in general was a fertile ground for messianic aspirations. Indeed, the violent upheavals, which included wars, famine, and plagues, were identified with the series of woes and catastrophic events which were expected to precede the end and to herald the coming of the deliverer. In 1840 a Yemenite Muslim *ṣūfī* by the name of Saᶜīd bin Ṣāliḥ Yasīn al-ᶜAnsī claimed to be the awaited *mahdī* and marched against the imām. He captured Taᶜizz and set up his headquarters near Ibb. He even struck coins of silver; upon one side of the coins he inscribed *al-Mahdī al-Muntaẓar,* and on the other side, *Sulṭān al-Bar wal-Baḥr* (ruler of the land and the ocean). The "*mahdī*" and his followers managed to cause social and political upheavals in Yemen, but he was captured in 1841 by the imām and put to death. His execution brought to an end yet another millenarian Muslim movement in Yemen.[42]

The Yemenite Jews were far more prone to messianic activity than the Muslims. For the Jews, the messianic hope was a safety valve; afflictions and trying experiences nourished and strengthened this hope. Indeed, the atmosphere of the Jewish communities in Yemen during the period before the Ottoman occupation was highly charged with messianic tensions. The messianic expectations were heightened by the appearance of a comet which, according to Wāsiʿī, appeared from the east, and with a terrifying noise fell on a ship which was on its way from Aden to Yemen, setting it on fire.[43] The charged atmosphere among the Jews was ignited in 1859 by Shukr Kuḥeil, a Jew from Sanaa who claimed to be the Messiah of Israel. The various sources referring to this pseudo-messiah depict him as an extremely pious person well-versed in the Bible, Talmud, Qabballah, and even the Qur'ān. His many references to these writings made a strong impression upon Jews and Muslims alike. All the sources agree that Kuḥeil genuinely believed in his messianic mission. He was forty years old, humble, and ascetic in temperament, when the "messianic call" seized him. He divorced his wife in accordance with what he claimed to be Elijah's instructions and wandered throughout Yemen calling for penitence and prayers in preparation for the imminent redemption. He allowed his hair and nails to grow long and strictly refused to accept gifts from his admirers. He captured the hearts of the people because of the many miracles he was believed to have performed. According to Saphir, the imām of Yemen, who was disturbed by the social and religious confusion that Kuḥeil caused among the Jews, ordered his execution.[44] Kuḥeil was shot in 1863 by Muslims and his head was dispatched to Sanaa.

Kuḥeil's death, however, did not diffuse the messianic tension which was strongly felt among the Jews of Yemen. Rumors had it that Kuḥeil's death was transient and that he would soon rise from the dead to bring forth the awaited salvation. Indeed, five years later (in 1868), a Yemenite Jew wandered among the Jewish communities of Yemen, claiming to be the real Shukr Kuḥeil. In a letter that he wrote to the Rabbis of Jerusalem, he said that he had been killed and beheaded because of the sins of Israel, but that Elijah had come and resurrected him. He even summoned the divorcee of the first Shukr Kuḥeil and married her, claiming that Elijah told him to restore his wife. In contradistinction from the first Kuḥeil, who was motivated by a genuine faith and concern for his brethren, the second was a scoundrel and a charlatan who sought to exploit the strained situation of his coreligionists for his own personal gain.[45]

The ample sources that refer to him describe him as a crude ignoramus. To forestall concerns regarding his abysmal ignorance of the Jewish sacred writings, he claimed that he was commanded by

Elijah not to engage in the study of the Torah. "Kuḥeil" was ruthless in his dealings with his Jewish adversaries. His opponent, Suleiman bin Suleiman, who was forced to flee from Sanaa because of threats to his life, related to the Rabbinic court in Jerusalem that the false messiah spread rumors to the effect that he would soon rise with a great army composed mainly of the tribes of Gad and Reuben and accompanied by multitudes from the neighboring regions to lay siege on Sanaa and dethrone the Imam.[46] The many epistles that he wrote to the Jewish communities in Yemen, Aden, Egypt, Jerusalem, India, and Turkey reveal his ultimate goal: money. It was to be incumbent upon all Jews, even the poor and the beggars, to give him a tithe of their income. He signed all his letters with the words, "Mori Shukr Kuḥeil, may his glory be high and his kingdom be exalted."[47]

The story of this Yememite pseudo-messiah emerged from its local confines thanks to the worldwide publicity that Jacob Saphir has given to it. In an article published in *ha-Lebanon,* bearing the presumptuous title, "*The Second Epistle to Yemen,*" Saphir, like Maimonides before him, denounced the false messiah in very stong terms and rebuked him. Saphir's *Epistle* attributed the decline of the Yemenite Jews to this self-declared messiah.[48]

The fate of the second Shukr Kuḥeil is somewhat shrouded in mystery. According to Ṭabib, he was captured by the Turks and sent in chains to Constantinople, where he was executed. Others hold that he returned to Yemen from Turkey and ultimately sank into oblivion.[49] Be that as it may, his messianic venture aggravated the already strained situation of the Jews of Yemen, giving rise to reprisals by the authorities and to the deep frustration that always follows such illusory messianic hopes.

7. The Second Ottoman Occupation of Yemen (1872–1914)

The Jews of Yemen welcomed with jubilation the return of the Turks to Yemen in 1872. According to Karaso, the Jews helped facilitate the Ottoman occupation of Yemen.[50] Thus, for example, they assisted Aḥmad Mukhtar Pasha, the commander of the Turkish forces, find his way through Yemen. At the risk of their lives, they supplied the Turkish soldiers with food and water; they even sheltered and fed in their houses Turkish soldiers who were wounded in battles.

The expectations of the Jews for a significant amelioration of their pitiful conditions were high. They looked at the Ottomans as redeemers who were about to extricate them from what the *Jewish*

Chronicle termed as an "unpretending tale of perpetual woe."[51] They referred to the Sublime Porte as a luminary which would illuminate the darkness of Yemen with all its splendor. This "government of grace and mercy" would certainly cast off from their shoulders the yoke of oppression.[52]

It should be noted that these expectations for the Turkish occupation were nourished by the idealized example of other Jewish communities throughout the Ottoman empire, who by virtue of Sultan Abdülmecid's *islahat fermani* (reform decree)[53] enjoyed a great deal of freedom. This Ottoman decree, generally referred to by Westerners as *hatti hümayun* (imperial rescript) reaffirmed the equality of all the Ottoman subjects "without distinction of class or of religion" and guaranteed "the security of their persons and property and the preservation of their honor." The decree further promised entire freedom in the exercise of all religions and declared that "every distinction or designation pending to make any class whatever of the subjects of my empire inferior to another class, on account of their religion, language, or race, shall be forever effaced from administrative protocol."[54]

The Yemenite Jewish writings relating to the Ottoman occupation lavish praise upon Mukhtar Pasha, the first Ottoman governor of Yemen. In his endeavor to enforce the *islahat* in Yemen, the governor summoned Rabbi Suleimān al-Qare, the Chief Rabbi of Sanaa, received him "most gravely and graciously," encouraged him to voice all the Jewish concerns and grievances, and promised him that he would treat the Jews on the same basis of equality as other subjects of the Sublime Porte.[55] Mukhtar Pasha immediately freed the Jews from the yoke of the "Latrine Decree," which the Jews viewed as the most loathsome and disgraceful servile labor. He is even said to have threatened to cut off the hand of any Jew who engaged in this contemptible task.[56] Indeed, in a letter signed by six Yemenite Jews, addressed to the Anglo-Jewish Association in London, the signatories related that with the Ottoman occupation, "a glimpse of cheerful life dawned upon us . . . we passed from the sway of heartless masters to the merciful rule of the humane Sultan."[57]

Rabbi Yeḥia Koraḥ wrote in the same vein:

> Know that in the past and until last year (1872), the Jews of Yemen, particularly those of Sanaa . . . were viewed by the Muslims as the lowest in social status. And I (a Jew from Sanaa) tasted their cup of wrath. The great calamities which passed over our heads stagger belief. Our life was constantly threatened by the sword, captivity and pillage. We used to flee from one corner to the other to the extent that we preferred death over life. But now God . . . has delivered us from darkness and brought us to light under the kingdom of our lord Sulṭān ᶜAbd al-ᶜAzīz, may his glory be exalted . . . .[58]

It did not, however, take long for these hopes to be shattered. The Yemenite Jews were soon reminded that "the rose is surrounded by thorns."[59] The Turkish occupation, like all past foreign regimes, was met with violent opposition on the part of the Zaydīs, who united under a new line of Qāsimī imāms, the Ḥamīd al-Dīn. The Turks found themselves confronted with relentless guerrilla attacks by the tribes and had to expend most of their energy and resources in attempting to suppress the revolt against their rule.[60] Thus, the general atmosphere in Yemen was not conducive to social and religious reform. The Ottomans' attempt to better the conditions of the Jews were particularly met with much opposition on the part of the Muslims. The sudden deliverance from oppression, the Yemenite Jews complained in their letter to the Anglo-Jewish Association, "aroused the indignation of all who were accustomed to trample us under foot, they gnashed their teeth at us. . . . "[61] To undermine the Jews' newly acquired liberty, the Muslims, remarked the Jews in their writings, used the weapon of calumny and slander. The Turkish officials were constantly incited against the Jews. Whenever Jewish notables approached the Turkish rulers, their words were distorted by the Muslim dragoman. Thus, in a letter written by a Yemenite Jew to his friend in Egypt, the former said that "although [the Muslims] ceased to strike the Jews with their rods, since there is now a government to avenge their blood, they did not cease to hit them with their tongues; they constantly speak evil of them before the Turkish governor. . . . "[62] The Turks, who desired to maintain good relations with the Muslims, found themselves forced to yield to this stong opposition. From the many letters sent by Yemenite Jews to their coreligionists in London, Paris, Turkey, Egypt, and elsewhere, there emerges a gloomy picture of utter frustration with the Turkish rule in Yemen.[63] One of the letters addressed to the Alliance Israélite Universelle in Paris complains of a heavy poll tax (*jizya*) that was imposed by the Turkish government upon the Jews of Yemen.[64] This tax, which was collected by force, diminished their resources and impoverished the Jewish community of Sanaa. This and other grievances were also brought to the attention of the Anglo-Jewish Association, which responded by soliciting the help of the British government.

In a letter dated December 16, 1873, addressed to the British Foreign Minister, the president of the Anglo-Jewish Association conceded that the Ottoman rule had indeed affected some improvements in the life of the Yemenite Jews: Direct acts of oppression were stopped; the Jews "were relieved of the disgraceful and degrading labours which they had previously been compelled to perform." He complained, however, that the Yemenite Jews "were subjected instead to a special impost, which was levied against them by way of commutation for those labors. . . . "[65] In another letter addressed to the Turkish Ambassador in London, the Association reminded His Excellency that the Jews of Yemen "have hailed with delight the change of Government . . . and congratulate themselves on being now placed under the protection of the laws of humanity." The letter enjoined the Turkish Ambassador to urge his government "to grant the Jews of Yemen the same protection, which it extends to all its other subjects."[66]

The heavy pressures which were brought to bear on the Turkish rulers by the Yemenite Muslims resulted in the rescindment of most of the social privileges which had been conferred upon the Yemenite Jews by the Ottoman rulers. The discriminatory edicts, including the one pertaining to the cleansing of the public latrines, were again enforced.[67] Furthermore, in his effort to centralize his rule, the Turkish governor of Yemen, Ayyūb Pasha, issued a decree that deprived the Jewish courts in Yemen of their long-established authority to resolve monetary and civil affairs within the confines of the Jewish communities. Their jurisdiction was strictly limited to the religious and the matrimonial spheres. Moshe Ḥanokh summed up the bitter Jewish response most succinctly: "From the days when our forefathers were exiled to Yemen and until now, such a decree had never been issued nor heard of."[68] This annulment of *din torah* had a far-reaching implication. It imposed Islamic law, the Ottoman *qanūn,* upon the Jews.[69]

Complaints relating to incidents of flagrant abuse of Jews by Turkish officials were also voiced in letters that the Yemenite Jews sent to their coreligionists abroad. Most disturbing, however, was the kidnapping of eighty Jews from the Jewish quarter in Sanaa by Turkish soldiers, who forced them to desecrate their Sabbath and Sukkoth holiday to serve as stretcher-bearers, carrying on their shoulders wounded soldiers from Sanaa to Ḥudeida, an extremely difficult mountainous terrain. This episode, which took place in October 1875, had such a devastating effect upon the Jews that they referred to the year 1875 as *Sanat al-Qaʿāʾid* (the year of the stretchers).[70]

The Yemenite Jewish experience of Ottoman rule, which began with high hopes, ended in deep frustration. The Ottoman government did not effect significant and lasting change in the social status of the Jews of Yemen. The stigma of inferior status and the discriminatory enactments associated with such a status were not wiped out. It should be noted, however, that despite the shattering of many expectations, the conditions of Jews in Yemen were relatively improved. The Ottomans put an end to the anarchy and lawlessness that preceded their occupation and which allowed the pillage of Jews and the shedding of their blood with utter impunity. The Ottoman rule brought about a considerable improvement in the economic conditions of the Jews of Yemen, resulting in the restoration, repopulation, and extension of the Jewish quarter in Sanaa, which was almost deserted before the advent of the Turks. The Turks allowed the building of new houses and new synagogues, a privilege which was deemed inconceivable prior to their occupation. The Turkish government even allowed the appointment of a *Ḥakham Bashi* for the Jews of Yemen, conferring upon him all the honors and privileges which are usually associated with such an office.[71] The Turkish rule also opened new horizons for the Jews of Yemen: It exposed them to a far more advanced civilization and considerably enhanced their contacts with Jewish communities in the Ottoman Empire and Europe. But by the same token, the sudden exposure of the Yemenite Jews to the relatively free and liberal way of the Ottoman soldiers brought about some relaxation of the otherwise very stringent religious and moral conduct of many Jews. Yemenite rabbis and chroniclers bitterly complained that Jews befriended the Turkish soldiers, supplied them with alcoholic drinks, and even provided them with Jewish women. Prostitution, casting off of the yoke of Torah, desecration of the Sabbath and holidays, and neglect of religious obligations were among the many such manifestations that the Yemenite writings emanating from the Ottoman period bemoan.[72]

8. Yosef ᶜAbdallāh: A Yemenite Pseudo-Messiah

The last two decades of the nineteenth century witnessed the rise of the last messianic Jewish movement in Yemen. In 1888, a Jew by the name of Yosef ᶜAbdallāh claimed to be the messiah of Israel and declared that the redemption was very imminent, just around the corner. The two chronicles referring to this episode (Ḥabshush's and Koraḥ's), their tone of scorn and hostility toward ᶜAbdallāh notwithstanding, stress that the "impostor" managed to attract multitudes of followers who provided him with material and moral support.[73] Moreover, from a letter written in 1888 and addressed to Rabbi Yeḥia Kafiḥ, the author, who disparagingly described ᶜAbdallạh as "boorish and wicked," conceded that this impostor managed with his "deceptive visions" and supposedly miraculous healing powers to make a strong impression upon his audience, to penetrate Yemenite Jewish communities, and to "strike roots bearing poisonous and bitter fruit." This "false messiah," grieved the author of the letter, even managed to exert a strong influence upon many rabbis, including

Mori Suleimān.[74] The reference, one may reasonably assume, is to Mori Suleimān al-Qare, the chief Rabbi and Hakham Bashi of Yemenite Jewry.

Several factors seem to have converged to confer credence upon the new messianic claimant: The frustrating experience that the Yemenite Jews had had with the Ottoman occupation infused the ever-present messianic longings with new vitality; the drought and subsequent famine, which afflicted Yemen in 1888, were interpreted as the "birth pangs" of the messiah; and the strong popular belief that the messiah would appear in 1888, a year designated in the Hebrew calendar by the letters תרמ"ח, which were read by the Yemenites as תרח"ם (to have pity), evoking the biblical verse, "Thou will rise and have pity on Zion, it is the time to favor her" (Ps. 102:13).[75] These and other factors provided an expedient background for the rise of ᶜAbdallāh.

The above-mentioned letter provides us with very valuable insights into the impact that ᶜAbdallāh had on Yemenite Jewry. Central to this letter is a detailed description of a religious ceremony that ᶜAbdallāh and his disciples held at the Jewish cemetery in Sanaa for the purpose of calling upon the heavens to bring forth rain and relieve the country of its consuming famine. ᶜAbdallāh and his followers, relates the letter, marched toward the cemetery, carrying the Ark wrapped in a black sheet and incessantly blowing seven roebuck *shofars* (horns).[76] The sun and the moon, sarcastically noted the author, were split by the thundering sounds. The ceremony consisted of the display and shaking of withered *lulavs* and *ethrogs* and the recitation of the whole compendium of *hoshaᶜana* prayers.[77] These ceremonial rituals which, the author noted scornfully, belong exclusively to the Feast of Tabernacles were performed on a day of Tammuz.[78] One wonders, he continued derisively, why they did not also bring with them bitter herbs, *ḥaroseth* and *maṣṣa*.[79]

Be that as it may, the heavens did open up their gates and showered their rain upon the parched land. The letter writer claimed that the proximity of this relieving blessing to the ceremony was coincidental. The multitudes, however, attributed it to ᶜAbdallāh's intercession, resulting in the strengthening of their faith in his proclaimed messianic mission. That these messianic expectations failed to materialize, however, greatly undermined the credibility of ᶜAbdallāh. A crusade against him, led by Ḥabshush, the celebrated Yemenite Jewish chronicler, strove to drive the impostor out of Sanaa and even to bring about his incarceration.[80] Koraḥ related that Ḥabshush managed to convince the Ottoman authorities that ᶜAbdallāh's activities were causing unrest among the Jews of Yemen, drawing their attention to previous messianic movements and their dire consequences. Koraḥ went on to say that Ḥabshush contended before the authorities that ᶜAbdallāh and his disciples were committing abominations and acts of debauchery. This unruly conduct, Ḥabshush cautioned, was liable to kindle the wrath of God and bring about disasters upon the country. As a result of these arguments, so Koraḥ said, ᶜAbdallāh was expelled from Sanaa. Thus, Ḥabshush was able, Koraḥ concluded, to "expunge the evil spirit" from Sanaa.[81]

ᶜAbdallāh was the last link in the long chain of false messiahs that the Yemenite Jewry produced.

9. Endeavors for Reform: The *Dor-Deᶜah*

The longtime seclusion of Yemenite Jewry and its remoteness from the mainstreams of Jewish culture in Europe and elsewhere kept its traditional social structures intact without any meaningful alterations. Thus, the tides of the *Haskalah* (Enlightenment)—which swept the Jewish communities in Europe and elsewhere during the eighteenth and nineteenth centuries and brought about a radical transformation of their cultural, social, religious, and economic life—did not affect the Jews of Yemen.

The Turkish occupation, however, opened the gates of Yemen to foreign influence. Tourism in Yemen by Europeans and Ottomans developed, and these visitors included many Jews who came to Yemen for commercial, scientific, and other purposes. Yemenite Jews were able to correspond freely with their coreligionists abroad and develop strong relationships with Jewish personalities in various countries in Europe and the Ottoman Empire. The exposure of Yemenite Jewry to foreign influence spurred among some Yemenite Jews a strong desire for enlightenment and fostered a critique of some traditional notions and customs. The chief protagonists of these reform trends were Ḥayyim Ḥabshush (died in 1899–1900) and Rabbi Yeḥia ben Solomon Kafiḥ (1850–1932). Both were very well versed in Jewish lore and possessed a sound knowledge of medieval philosophy and Arabic literature as well. Moreover, their personal contacts with European Jewish scholars, particularly with Joseph Halévy and Edward Glaser,[82] who visited Yemen for scientific purposes, exposed them to the literature of the *Haskalah.*

It was, however, Joseph Halévy, who unwittingly played a unique role in the molding of the thoughts of Ḥabshush and Kafiḥ and, consequently, in the precipitation of the reform movement. This French scholar, who was an orientalist and Hebrew writer, was commissioned by the Académie des Inscriptions et Belles-Lettres to visit

Yemen in 1870–1871. In his search for Sabaean inscriptions, he was accompanied and assisted by Ḥayyim Ḥabshush, who copied many of the inscriptions for him.[83] Although Halévy strove to focus almost exclusively upon his scientific mission and to refrain from any involvement in the internal affairs of the Yemenite Jews, he nevertheless exerted an immense influence upon Ḥabshush, instilling in him the germs of scientific curiosity and inquisitiveness. Ḥabshush, who refers to Halévy as "my venerable teacher," described the impact of his encounter with his "master" as follows:

> He [Halévy] immersed me in the *mikveh* ["pool"] of the soul-saving Enlightenment, and I have washed my mind of the filth of the demons [superstitions] that dwelt in me. . . . Since then I became attached to him with love-bonds. And how can a slave find favor in the eyes of his master except by fulfilling his master's wish?[84]

Ḥabshush and Rabbi Kafiḥ were the chief spokesmen for the cause of reform and progress in Yemen. They and their followers established a movement which bore the name *Dor-De^cah* (A Generation of Reason).[85] The aspirations of these more advanced persons, derisively nicknamed *Darade^cah*[86] by their opponents, were rather modest. They mainly wished to develop a relatively modern system of education which would provide Jewish students with some rudiments of secular knowledge (arithmetic, science, geography, grammar, composition, Hebrew, Arabic, and Turkish); to foster an intellectual and critical approach to the study of the Bible and the Targums and to do away with the mechanical sing-song recitation which then prevailed; to provide students with professional education and instruction in the crafts in order to promote their prospects for employment; to strive for more spacious and sanitary facilities that would be far more conducive to learning, replacing the dark and dilapidated rooms in which students sat huddled together; to put more emphasis on a modern pedagogical and methodological approach in education; and to eliminate the cruel use of the rod for which the Yemenite Jewish *mu^callims* (instructors) were notorious.[87]

Rabbi Yeḥia Kafiḥ was instrumental in the establishment of such a Jewish school in Sanaa, which was financially supported by the Turkish government. The school was opened in 1910 and directed by Rabbi Kafiḥ himself. The new institution aroused great enthusiasm among a segment of the Jews of Sanaa, but it also triggered a bitter and ferocious opposition on the part of the Orthodox rabbis, who viewed these modern trends as a threat to Jewish tradition. Rabbi Kafiḥ soon realized that it was exceedingly difficult to swim against the prevailing conservative tides; the school was shut in 1915, five years after its establishment. Thus, the hopes of the *Dor-De^cah* for educational reform were thwarted, and their efforts were abortive.[88]

It should be noted that the activities of the *Dor-de^cahs* were not confined to the educational sphere. In their endeavors to purge Yemenite Jewry of its pervasive belief in superstitions, demons, charms, saints, quacks and witch doctors, they voiced strong opposition to the Qaballah. This literature, Kafiḥ claimed, sprang from sources alien to the spirit of authentic Judaism and are inimical to progress and enlightenment. The Zohar, contended Kafiḥ, fosters ignorance in that it feeds the minds with superstition and prejudice.[89] He advocated focusing upon the study of the Talmud, the works of Sa^cadia Gaon, Yehudah Halevi, Maimonides, and the ancient Yemenite writings. This rejection of the Qabbalah only served to heighten the intense antagonism of the Orthodox rabbis to the new reform movement, an antagonism characterized by harsh and ugly manifestations, unprecedented in the known Yemenite Jewish history. The conservatives, scornfully referred to by *Dor-de^cahs* by the name *^cIqshim* (crooked), did not restrict themselves to insults, calumnies, and excommunications, but also denounced their opponents to the government authorities, accusing them of undermining the foundation of the Jewish faith. Their complaints triggered the intervention of government officials in Jewish internal affairs and led to arrests and the humiliation of rabbis and other Jewish leaders. The rivalry reached its climax in 1913–1914.

The *Dor-de^cah* movement in Yemen was short-lived and its achievements were far from being significant. Their aspirations for reform were strongly curtailed by ungovernable social circumstances. Thus, instead of yielding sweet grapes, it yielded the wild grapes of bitter conflict and discord, which far outweighed, even nullified, its limited achievements.[90] Divested of its aspirations for reform, but not of its utter rejection of the Qabbalah, the *Dor-de^cah* schism continued its distinctive existence as a dissenting Jewish faction in Sanaa until the mass exodus of Yemenite Jewry to Israel.

10. The End of the Ottoman Occupation

The Ottoman occupation of Yemen, although initially welcomed and even encouraged by the notables of Sanaa,[91] who were disturbed by the then prevailing state of anarchy and lawlessness, was nevertheless met with opposition from the outset on the part of the Zaydī tribes. The short-lived Ottoman period of reign (1872–1914) over parts of Yemen (with fluctuating fortunes) was punctuated by acts of violence, and the Ottoman rulers had to contend with a series of revolts, which they attempted to suppress. The revolt against the Turks was greatly intensified with the accession to the imamate of Imām al-Mutawakkil Yaḥia who, in 1904, succeeded his father al-Manṣūr Billāh.

In 1905 Imām Yaḥia and his army of tribesman laid siege to Sanaa for six months. The siege had a disastrous effect, not only on the Turks who were entrapped there, but also on the inhabitants of the entire city. It greatly aggravated the desperate conditions caused by the drought that year. The subsequent famine, reported Wāsiᶜī, consumed more than half the inhabitants of Sanaa. Because of the devastating scarcity of food, he added, the hearts became impenitent: Some fathers slaughtered their daughters for food; parents abandoned their children in the streets; people were totally indifferent to the deaths of their beloved.[92]

The toll which this famine took upon the Jews of Sanaa was very heavy. According to Shalom Koraḥ, ninety percent of the Jews of Sanaa perished. Death, he mourned, "honed its scythe and reaped from end to end: man and woman, infant and suckling . . . synagogues and houses of study were deserted."[93]

The revolt of 1904–1905 was not confined to the capital; it raged throughout the land and paralyzed it. Its economic consequences were similarly disastrous. Anarchy reigned supreme.

A few months later, the Turks recaptured Sanaa, and Imām Yaḥia had to flee to his stronghold in Shahara. The struggle, however, continued, and the Ottomans embarked upon a series of negotiations in order to establish a framework for peaceful coexistence with the imām. The pressures of the Ottoman wars in the Balkans and in North Africa, along with the defeats in Yemen, forced the Ottomans to make concessions to the principal demands of the imām. In a treaty concluded in 1911, known as the Treaty of Daᶜan, the Ottomans recognized the imām as the spiritual and temporal leader of the Zaydī community, and granted him the authority to appoint governors and judges in the districts under his rule. The treaty also recognized the supremacy of the *Sharīᶜa* in those areas. The Porte was allowed to preserve nominal sovereignty in Yemen.[94]

At the end of World War I, the Turks evacuated Yemen, and the country became an independent state under the theocratic rule of Imām Yaḥia whose long reign (1904–1948) brought peace and stability to the country. This shrewd and astute monarch managed to unite the country under his absolute leadership and to forge the conflicting factions into one nation.[95] In 1905, following his capture of Sanaa, Imām Yaḥia issued a decree, "intended to remind them [the Jews] of what the governors of the State, the Ottoman governors, abolished."[96] The decree imposed upon the Jews the payment of "half of a tithe" (five percent) of their commerce in addition to the *jizya* (poll tax). Relating to the social and religious status of the Jews, the decree states:

> It is also forbidden to them to help each other against a Muslim, and they shall not raise their houses above the Muslim houses [a Jew's house may not be higher than a Muslim's] and they shall not disturb Muslims in their path and shall not encroach on their occupations, and shall not slight the religion of Islam, and shall not curse any prophet, and shall not irritate a Muslim in his belief, and shall not sit on saddles, but sideways [both feet at the side], and shall not wink, and shall not point to a Muslim's nakedness, and not display their Torah outside their synagogue, and not raise their voices while reading, and not sound the shofar loudly—a low voice is sufficient for them. They are also forbidden to engage in shameful things which bring a curse from Heaven. It is their duty to exalt the Muslim and honour him.[97]

Despite the fact that Imām Yaḥia reinstated all the anti-Jewish discriminatory measures that were prevalent in Yemen before the Ottoman occupation, Jewish chroniclers lavish praise upon him and depict him as the champion of justice and compassion. This is, however, not surprising. Imām Yaḥia managed to put an end to the state of anarchy, lawlessness, and violence which had lacerated the country and inflicted immense suffering upon its inhabitants, including the Jews. During his long reign, the Jews enjoyed almost unprecedentedly favorable conditions of peace and tranquility.[98]

Epilogue

IN THE LAND OF ISRAEL

Yemenite Jewish immigrants are known to have come to Israel during the past few centuries on a sporadic, occasional, and individual basis. One of these was Rabbi Shelmo ʿAdani, who emigrated to Israel aroung 1571 and composed there an extensive commentary on the Mishna, known as *Melekhet Shelomo*.[1] The year 1882 (תרמ"ב), however, is considered a landmark in the history of Yemenite Jewish emigration to Eretz Israel. In that year, the first group of more than two hundred Yemenite Jews came to Israel.

Several factors converged to trigger this first wave of emigration. Most prominent among these factors were: the distressful political, economic, and moral conditions that prevailed in Yemen; with the Ottoman Occupation in 1872, Yemen became an integral part of the Ottoman Empire, a fact which facilitated the movement of Jews to Palestine, also a part of this empire; the opening of the Suez Canal in 1869 made the land of Israel far more accessible; rumors that Rothschild, whom the Yemenites thought to be the King of the Jews, had bought extensive stretches of land in Palestine and was giving them away, free of charge, to poor Jewish immigrants; rumors that the Sulṭān of the Ottoman Empire had issued a declaration, permitting Jews from all over the world to settle in Palestine.[2]

The foremost catalyst for this influx into Israel, however, was the strong conviction then prevalent among the Yemenite Jews that the messianic expectations would be fulfilled in that particular year, 1882. Indeed, a Yemenite messianic apocalypse attributed to Rabbi Shalom Shabazi reads:

> In the year תרמ"ב (1882) the scriptural verse "I say I will climb the palm tree [תמר]," [3] will be fulfilled. The star Venus will appear with its tail, and a voice will emanate from Heaven saying: "Today, if you hearken unto His voice." And the voice was heard throughout the land of Yemen, enjoining the Jews to embark on ships and enter the Holy Land. . . . They will encounter many hardships, and this is the esoteric meaning of 'Blessed is the man who thou chastenest.' But later on they will live in tranquility."[4]

Charged with messianic fervor and great hopes, the first group of Yemenites arrived in Jerusalem only to encounter a harsh and frustrating reality. The Jews of Jerusalem, Ashkenazim and Sephardim alike, were organized in tight communities known as *kolelim,* sustained by a charity system called *ḥaluqqah.*[5] These organizations, generally based on the countries of origin, were supported by their respective Jewish communities in the Diaspora and by funds collected by their special *sheliḥim* (emissaries), who traveled for this particular purpose even to the most remote places in the Jewish world. The new Yemenite arrivals found themselves "outside the walls" of this long-existing social structure. And they could not form a *kolel* of their own, since they could not expect financial support from their poor brethren in Yemen. Moreover, they soon realized that their traditional occupations and specializations—artisans, craftsmen—were almost totally useless in their new environment. The most distressing condition, however, was the lack of housing facilities for these Yemenites, whose number was augmented with the subsequent waves of new immigrants from their country. Many of the Yemenite Jews were forced to dwell in tents and booths. Some found shelter in caves and crevices in the Valley of Kidron and elsewhere. The "promised" Rothschild lands were not waiting for them. Instead, they were visited with hunger, disease, and frustration.[6] A poignant expression of this grim reality is to be found in a letter written by Rabbi A. Alsheikh, one of the 1882 Yemenite immigrants, two months after his arrival in Jerusalem. In that letter addressed to his family in Sanaa, Rabbi Alsheikh warned his relatives not to leave Yemen. He wrote that the rumors regarding the building of houses for the poor were certainly true but the rose had a canker:

> Every person is concerned with his own kin: the Ashkenazi for the Ashkenazim and the Sephardi for the Sephardim. . . . And here is how it works: Money is collected from the rich in their city of origin and sent to Jerusalem in order to build houses for the poor, who emigrate to Jerusalem from their midst. [This they do] for their own virtue. But the Yemenites—there is no one to be concerned for [them]. . . . Therefore, do not believe in the rumors which you have heard. The place which every one of you now has is surely a thousand times better. [Let us wait] until God wishes to redeem us.

Rabbi Alsheikh concluded his letter by informing his family that the sorrowful conditions in Palestine (unemployment and lack of dwellings) forced him and some of his friends to leave the country, and that he had left for Egypt, heading back to Yemen.[7]

Some of the leaders of the Jewish community in Jerusalem viewed with grave concern the arrival of these immigrants from Yemen and tried to discourage further immigration of Yemenite Jews to Israel. Thus, for example, Israel Frumkin, the editor of the weekly *Ḥavaṣelet,* reacted with consternation to the news that a new wave of Yemenite immigrants was on its way to the Land of Israel. "It is difficult to believe," wrote Frumkin, "that these people would come here and would not learn a lesson from the frightful conditions of their brethren, who are already here."[8]

A moving chapter in the history of the early Yemenite Jewish immigrants to Palestine is the uniquely warm relationship which developed between them and the Christian colony of Americans and Swedes (later known as the American colony), who had come to Palestine motivated by a spiritual urge and religious fervor. The encounter of these Christians with the Yemenite Jews was electrifying. These American-Swedish colonists were greatly impressed by the exotic distinctiveness of the Yemenites, so different from other Jews. These Yemenites, remarked Bertha Vester, the daughter of the spiritual leader of the colony, were characterized by "classical purity and semitic features." They had, she adds, "dark skin with dark hair and dark eyes. They wore side curls. . . their dress was Arabic. They had poise, and their movements were graceful, like those of the Bedouins. They were slender and somewhat undersized."[9] The Christian colonists referred to the Yemenites by the name Gaddites, believing that the Yemenite Jews are descendants of the tribe Gad.

On the other hand, the Christian colonists were extremely moved by the pathetic sight of these "ragged and half-starved people." "These Yemenites," reminisced Lind, who was then a little boy in the American colony, "had been three months on their way to Jerusalem and now they had neither food nor shelter." Further, he remarked that the Gaddites complained of the attitude of rejection, even ridicule, that they had encountered from the other Jewish communities in Jerusalem. Some Jews had even cast doubt upon the Jewishness of these Yemenites, or at least questioned its authenticity.[10]

These romantic Gaddites, Lind added, created intense interest and excitement among the American colonists, who took it upon themselves to support them with food and tried to ameliorate their pitiful living conditions. A special bond of mutual admiration and respect had developed between both communities, and the Yemenites, Lind went on to say, looked at the Christian community as "heaven-sent benefactors."[11]

That the gloomy picture is essentially true, emerges from these remarks, from the ample documents referring to the frightful conditions of the early Yemenite immigrants in Jerusalem, and from the cool reception that they were accorded by other Jewish communities.

These facts, however, should be viewed within the larger and general context of the social, religious, and economic situation of the Jews in Palestine at that particular time. The Jewish communities in Jerusalem, Ashkenazim and Sephardim alike, lived on very meager resources, received chiefly from the *ḥaluqqah,* the financial support of their coreligionists in the Diaspora. It should be remembered that the 1881–1882 Yemenite emigration to Palestine preceded by a few months that of *Bilu,* the first group of pioneers from Europe. Jewish agricultural settlements were not yet available. Indeed, in that very year (1882), the settlements Rishon le-Zion and Zichron Yaᶜakov were established, and shortly afterwards—Rosh Pinah. The settlement of Petaḥ Tikvah, which was founded in 1878, was later abandoned. The first group of Yemenite immigrants preceded by fifteen years the first Zionist Congress (1897), namely, the establishment of the Zionist movement by Herzl; it coincided with the publication of Pinsker's *Autoemancipation* (1882), which did not consider Palestine as the most suitable territory for the Jewish state.

The very small Jewish communities in Jerusalem were dedicated to religion, and generally were opposed to the establishment of Jewish agricultural settlements, fearing secularization. These Jewish communities were concentrated within the narrow confines of the walled Old City of Jerusalem. Housing facilities were extremely limited and mostly owned by Arab landlords who demanded exorbitant rental fees. The narrow streets of the Jewish quarter in Jerusalem were then full of Jewish destitutes and beggars.

The Yemenites who came to Jerusalem without resources and prospects for financial support aggravated the already existing wretched conditions, and their burden was, therefore, heavily felt. The financial help which was accorded to them by various donors was like a scrap which could not and did not satisfy the lion.

The predicament that the arrival of the Yemenites had created finds, indeed, a poignant expression in the poem, "The Yemenites," composed by none other than the celebrated poet Naftali Hertz Imber, the author of *ha-Tikvah,* which later became the Israeli national anthem. In this poem, which is charged with a range of emotions—sympathy, bitterness, indignation, and frustration—the author proclaimed:

> Not for you, my dear Yemenite brethren,
> Not for you, have we waited with searching eyes.
> Why have you come, O faithful brothers,
> Have you come to increase poverty?

Imber, like other Jews who thought of the Arabian Jews in terms of the legends regarding the glorious and invincible Ten Tribes, vividly expressed his frustration at the marked contrast between expectations and reality:

For them we yearn, for the Ten Tribes
Swift horsemen carrying armored shields
For them we long, for the sons of the Rechabites
The cavaliers, the gallant ones.

Mighty warriors with fiery faces
Carrying shields, spears and lances
For the sons of Moses—Sambation is their boundary—
Terror they spread, glory dwells in their habitation.

Imber refused to part with those exotic and colorful legends with which Jews were nourished for so many generations. Despite his deep frustration at the sight of the Yemenite Jews, he exclaimed:

On my watch, on the summit of Moriah I will stand
Anxiously hoping for their arrival
To see the glimmer of the glorious sunshine
The glare and blaze of their flaming swords
When I see them, my soul will find repose. . . . [12]

Mention has been made above of Israel Frumkin, who had expressed in his weekly *Ḥavaṣelet* genuine concern for the Yemenites and the problems resulting from their uncontrolled influx into Palestine. Frumkin, however, did not remain idle; in his periodical, he wrote several articles to draw the attention of the Jewish communities in Europe, the United States, and elsewhere to the deplorable conditions of the Yemenite Jews. As a result of his intercession, donations were made from various sources and a special fund, "*ᶜEzrat Niddaḥim,*" was established in 1883 to help alleviate some of the Yemenite Jews' suffering and to promote their absorption into their new environment. With the help of this fund, Frumkin founded the first Yemenite suburb, Kefar ha-Shiloaḥ, on the slope of the Mount of Olives. Two years later, houses were built for the Yemenite Jews in Mishkenot Yisra'el, financed by the "Yemen Refugee Fund," and established by Jews in England. In 1887, the number of Yemenite Jews in Jerusalem was about five hundred.[13]

In spite of the many social and economic hardships, which the early small community of Yemenite immigrants encountered in Palestine, they revealed remarkable tenacity, easing the process of their adaptation. They soon acquired a reputation for being industrious laborers who were able to integrate with astonishing rapidity into the general economic and cultural fabric of the developing Jewish homeland. They learned new trades, particularly those associated with building and construction: stonecutters, masons, plasterers, and tile-layers. At the end of World War I, there were 4,500 Yemenite Jews in Palestine integrated into every craft where work was available, including goldsmithery, embroidery, and other artistic crafts.[14] Their adjustment was greatly facilitated by their willingness to engage in service and utility works thought repugnant by others. The Yemenite, it was soon learned, did not like to sit with folded arms; he would rather do any manual work, even for relatively low wages.

The Yemenites, it should be stressed, were motivated by a strong inner faith and a sense of messianic fulfillment. In fact, they saw in their difficulties an essential component of the process of redemption. Thus, in a letter written in Arabic, dated Tevet 1888, a Yemenite Jew urged his relatives to ignore all the rumors which spoke ill of the Land of Israel and to join him in Jerusalem. The love for Jerusalem, he remarked, compensates for all the adverse conditions, and "happy is the one who attains the merit of eating even from the dust of Jerusalem." Jerusalem, he added, is "like a paradise, and he who dwells in Jerusalem is like the one who enters Paradise in his own lifetime."[15]

With the founding of the Zionist Organization and the subsequent establishment of Jewish agricultural settlements in Palestine, the Yemenite Jews were as if discovered anew and recognized as a very valuable element for the development and enhancement of Jewish agricultural colonization of Palestine. This goal, which was central to the Zionist pioneering ideology, was greatly hampered by the lack of an adequate number of Jewish skilled laborers capable of competing with the ample, cheap, and experienced Arab workers. The Jewish Ashkenazi pioneers were accustomed to a relatively high standard of living; they lacked experience and found it difficult to adjust to heavy physical labor under the blazing sun of Palestine. As a result, Jewish villagers preferred the highly competitive, docile, and efficient Arab laborers, a fact which threatened to undermine the Zionist ideology of creating a Jewish land-working force.

It should be noted that the first encounter of the Yemenite Jews with Jewish villagers was far from a happy one. The Yemenite writer Abraham Ṭabib told us that the committee members of the Jewish settlement Rishon le-Ṣion, who were looking for laborers, inspected the Yemenite candidates but were extremely disappointed with the "merchandise": "Their very pale and emaciated looks, their thin hands and lean thighs indicated that they were unfit for the task." These frustrated committee members, added Ṭabib, looked with fury on those who dared to introduce these "human skeletons" as workers. With bitterness they murmured something to the effect, "Have you come to make fun of us?"[16]

These "human skeletons," however, soon earned the reputation of being hard workers, capable of adjusting to the most rigorous conditions and competing even with the strong-muscled Arab workers. Little wonder, the attention of Zionist leaders in Palestine was drawn to them. "The Yemenites," observed Arthur Ruppin, the head of the Palestine Office of the Zionist Organization in Jaffa, "made few demands on life and—thanks to their contentedness, industry and intelligence—had firmly established themselves in Palestine." Dr. Ruppin went on to say that his observation of the Yemenites convinced him that this community had "a better chance of holding its own in the *moshavot* against the competition from the Arabs."[17] Dr. Ruppin saw in the Yemenites the ideal solution for the labor problem.

The urgent need for a Jewish labor force prompted Ruppin to encourage Yemenite emigration to Palestine. To underscore this urgency and to expedite Yemenite *ᶜaliyyah,* in 1911 he sent a young worker, Shmuel Yavnieli, as an emissary to Yemen, "in order to tell them [the Yemenite jews] that they could earn their living as workers in the agricultural colonies in Palestine." The Jews of Yemen, remarked Ruppin, received Yavnieli with enthusiasm and the mission, which lasted one year, proved to be "extremely successful." Dr. Ruppin conlcuded that "until the Great War, 2,000 Yemenites Jews emigrated to Palestine and found work in the *moshavot.* By 1940, their number had risen to 15,000."[18]

Ruppin's plan, which called for utilizing the Yemenites as a labor force, while hailed by the leadership of the Zionist Organization, aroused some serious moral and ethical questions. The so-called solution does not, it should be remembered, envision the Yemenites as owning their own lands and cultivating them, but rather as hired workers for the East European settlers. Ruppin wrote that the Yemenites "spoke Arabic . . . had the lifelong habits of the Arabs" and, like the Arabs, they "made few demands on life."[19] They could, therefore, effectively replace the Arab workers. Some Zionist ideologists, however, claimed that this approach was ethically wrong, because it reduced the Yemenites to the status of second-class citizens, "hewers of wood and drawers of water" for the Ashkenazi settlements. Moreover, Ruppin's plan raised high expectations with respect to the Yemenites, ignoring the fact that these people, although very industrious and conscientious workers, had no experience in farming; agricultural work in Yemen was done almost exclusively by the Arabs.

It should be borne in mind that Ruppin's attitude toward the Yemenites reflected that of the Zionist Organization and of the Jewish settlers who were then almost all Ashkenazi. The Yemenites, to judge from the ample literature pertaining to this particular topic, were treated like inferiors and were exploited by their own coreligionists. Indeed, the Yemenites' complaints and grievances read like a scroll of agony. They include stories of discrimination, ridicule, harsh treatment, and exploitations. In 1920, the Council of Yemenite Laborers issued a resolution which gave vent to their bitterness:

> The situation of hundreds of Yemenite families in the settlements, who immigrated to Palestine with devotion of soul and out of love for the country and desire to work its land and to take root in it, has become worse from year to year. The yoke of oppression was put on our necks, on our women and children, degrading our honor, suppressing our spirit and filling us with bitterness. The uncertainty and unemployment increased. The health of the immigrants has deteriorated. And the bad and oppressive conditions—no adequate housing, insufficient wages, no permanent work—with which we had to put up ever since we immigrated, have shown their effect: the generation which in the days of its immigration was in its best strength, has grown old and weak before its time, after ten years of work and suffering. The angel of death reaps his frightening harvest among our children who were born in this country, the number of our infants whom we buried in the ancestral soil has reached hundreds; the young generation which immigrated and grew up in this country has lost the pride of liberty and the power of resoluteness which beat in the hearts of the Yemenite Jews in their exile-birthplace. Our daughters and wives, whose necks never had to bear the yoke of earning a livelihood, have been compelled here, on account of impatience and great poverty, to leave their children and their houses and to go to the houses of the farmers. Our young generation has grown up without Tora and without education, and our numbers in all the settlements has diminished instead of growing. The *moshava,* in the shadow of which we wanted to live, has become for us a bitter disappointment.[20]

The above resolution—or rather, a cry of agony—pointed an accusing finger at both the Zionist leadership and the Jewish agricultural settlements. A warning should, however, be given against sweeping generalizations and hasty conclusions. The literature, emanating from both Yemenite and Ashkenazi sources, clearly shows that many Zionist ideologists and farmers of European origin expressed their indignation, even revulsion, at the discrimination, mistreatment, and exploitation of the Yemenite Jews.[21] Their intervention on behalf of the Yemenites not only contributed to a more equitable attitude toward the latter, but also helped to provide them with opportunities for their own development. In the course of time, the Yemenites founded villages and established settlements of their own. In 1948, the number of Yemenites in the newly established State of Israel numbered approximately forty thousand. Operation

"On Eagles' Wings" (popularly known as "Magic Carpet") brought 55,000 new Yemenite immigrants to Israel.

The attitude of uncertainty, suspicion, and at times even contempt displayed by the Jewish communities toward the early Yemenite immigrants gradually gave way to that of respect and admiration. Thus, for example, the celebrated Israeli poet Nathan Alterman welcomed the post-1948 Yemenite Jews (of the "Operation Magic Carpet") with effusive excitement. In his poem entitled "*Bo'i Teman*" (Come Thou, South), he ecstatically spoke about this ancient community, "This hard core which shattered the tooth of times," but which was not consumed itself. Alterman exclaimed that these Yemenites were indeed thin and emaciated, but they were so rich in spiritual virtues that the Jewish people were truly fortunate to have these Yemenites share these lofty virtues with them. Referring to the Operation "On Eagles' Wings," Alterman said:

> In short, as they descend from Heavens to Lod [Airport]
> Let us receive them with salute and awe.[22]

Despite their relatively small numbers in the general Jewish population of Palestine, the Yemenites have made significant contributions to contemporary Israeli culture. They brought with them from Yemen a rich repertory of dance, music, and folklore which was outstanding for its originality and distinctive features. Their age-old folklore, which seems to reflect ancient Hebrew culture, was soon recognized and became an object of emulation and a source of inspiration for the newly developing Israeli culture. Thus, the uniqueness of Yemenite music, which is totally different from that of Middle Eastern Jewish music, was recognized and researched, particularly by Idelsohn, who integrated many of the Yemenite melodies into the developing music culture of Eretz Israel.[23] As for the Yemenite Jewish dance, Gurit Kadman noted that its steps and other aspects appealed to the *ṣabras* (Israeli-born) and subsequently became a dominant element in modern Israeli folk dance. She added that the Yemenite dances are characterized by outstanding richness and originality. Like most ancient dances, the Yemenite dances "were never meant for mere entertainment. They were always a vital factor in individual and community life, with magical, religious, and social meaning."[24]

The Yemenite dancers, as I myself have observed, progress from elegant to violent movements. With the intensification of emotions, the pace quickens and the agility strengthens with ever-increasing speed. The dancers bounce rigorously up and down, while their souls soar aloft to heights of religious fervor. They gradually cast off the corporeal garments of their wretched existence and yearn for a mystic union of their souls with the divine, as if proclaiming: "All my bones shall say, Lord, who is like unto thee?" (Ps. 35:10). The excitement becomes contagious, spirits rise, and an intense feeling of ecstasy permeates the whole congregation.

Such an occasion is described in the following passage taken from the Hebrew novel *Y*ᶜ*ish* by Ḥayyim Hazaz. This excerpt, although from a novel, provides an authentic and apt characterization of the distinctive mood and significance of Yemenite Jewish dance.

> He [Yᶜish] saw and perceived that permission to act in a frivolous manner in a ceremonial rejoicing had not been granted from Heaven, and that he would not be allowed to treat the dances as something profane, nor to use the poems of Rabbi Shalom Shabazi as a violin to be played by jesters. . . . And through the course of his dancing, he was gradually awakened and attracted to heights with yearning and with attachment to the extent of annihilation of consciousness. It seemed as if he were uplifted from earthly matters and exalted over everything and, as it were, he hovered high above the earth between thunder and lightning, between clouds and winds. At the moment the song came to an end and he stopped dancing, all the partakers of the ceremony were like dreamers. . . . And when they awakened and regained consciousness. . . . they kissed him and embraced him . . . and one of them said to him: "Your dance is like a Rabbi in a synagogue expounding the *halakha*. . . . " and one of the elders who was versed in mystical teachings, shook his old beard and whispered to him: "Several deep secrets, combinations and *gematria* were revealed to me (through your dance), as if you were an angel from heaven."[25]

It is no wonder that the developing contemporary Israeli culture, desperately searching for roots and ancient tradition, welcomed the Yemenite culture and drew heavily from it. Thus, in the blending of the diverse cultural influences and the creation of a modern Israeli culture, the Yemenite participation is certainly one of the most salient.

The Yemenite community, noted Saul Lieberman, is different from all other Jewish communities in that its books, customs, and culture form an archive of documents from lost or forgotten sources. They have preserved for us a treasury of old manuscripts and provided us with ancient spiritual works otherwise not know to us.[26]

Scholars of Judaica have also recognized that, in addition to an Arabic tradition related to the reading of Saᶜadya Gaon's translation of the Bible, the Yemenite community preserved several traditions of Hebrew and Aramaic. Thus, Shelomo Morag expressed the opinion that the Yemenite reading tradition of Babylonian Aramaic "reflects the structure of a living dialect—an Aramaic dialect used by the Jewish community of Babylonia in the Gaonic period. . . ." Morag also noted that the Yemenites "are the only Jewish community that used for generations and have preserved to the present the Babylonian vocalization of Targum Aramaic [Onquelos and Jonathan], the only reliable vocalization of these Targumim."[27]

Yemenite Jewry left us a legacy of spiritual heroism and passionate affirmation of the human spirit determined to overcome defeat and degradation. Despite the interminable suffering, it never lost hope in redemption. Faith in salvation was an integral part of its spiritual saga, and the Messiah always loomed upon its horizon. Its literature captures the hopes and dreams of its people; it is also an extremely powerful and magnificent part of human literature as a whole.

NOTES

Introduction

1. See Shlomo Barer, *The Magic Carpet,* 1952.
2. November 8, 1949, p. 1.
3. *Magic Carpet,* p. IX.
4. *Palestine Post,* November 8, 1949, p. 1.
5. Jacob Saphir (1822–1885) visited Yemen in 1859, and recorded his travels and experiences in a book entitled *'Even Sappir* (2 vols, 1866 and 1874; reprinted, 1969); condensed by A. Ya^cari and published as *Sefer Massa^c Teman* (Hebrew). Saphir is considered to be the discoverer of Yemenite Jewry. He was the first outsider who lifted the veil from this long-secluded Jewish community. In his book he provided us with most significant details about the life and customs of the Jews of Yemen. This included valuable information regarding their innermost life, livelihood, traditions, folklore, and literature.
6. *'Even Sappir,* vol. 1, pp. 60–61.
7. *Bilu* (בילו״ן); Hebrew initials of *Bet Ya^cakov Lekhu ve-Nelkha,* "House of Jacob, come ye and let us go." (Isa. 2:5). This was a small group of Russian Jews who pioneered the return to Israel in 1882. See N. Sokolow, *Ḥibbath Zion,* pp. 169–175 et passim; idem, *History of Zionism,* vol. I (1919). On the early Yemenite immigrations to Palestine, see Yehudah Nini, *Teman ve-Ṣiyyon* (1982); Druyan Nitza, *be-'En Marvad Qesamim* (Hebrew; Jerusalem, 1981); Ya^cari Abraham, "*^cAliyyat Yehude Teman,*" *Shevut Teman,* pp. 37–54.
8. See A. Epstein, ed., *Eldad ha-Dani;* E. N. Adler, *Jewish Travellers.*

Rabbi Benjamin ben Jonah of Tudela was the most famous of the medieval Jewish travelers. *The Itinerary of Benjamin of Tudela* was first published at Constantinople in 1543. The standard editions are those edited by A. Asher (London 1840–1841; reprinted New York, 1927), and by M. N. Adler (New York, 1907), with critical Hebrew text and English translation. See the article "Benjamin (Ben Jonah) of Tudela" in *Encyclopedia Judaica,* vol. 4 (1972), pp. 535–538.

Obadiah ben Abraham of Bertinoro was one of the most distinguished Italian rabbis of his time. His commentary on the Mishna known as "The Bertinoro" remains a standard work. See "The Letters of Obadiah Jare de Bertinoro" in E. N. Adler, *Jewish Travellers,* pp. 209–250. See also A. Ya^cari, ed., *Iggerot 'Eretz Yisra'el,* pp. 98–144; S. Sachs in *Jahrbuch für die Geschichte,* vol. 3, pp. 193–270.

9. Adler, *Jewish Travellers,* p. 239; see also Ben-Zvi, *The Exiled and the Redeemed,* p. 180.
10. This legendary river is also called Sanbatyon and Sabbatyon. It is mentioned in the Targum Pseudo-Jonathan (Exod. 34:10). See also Lam. R. 2:9; Gen. R. 73:6. Eldad depicted the river as follows: "The children of Moses are surrounded by a river resembling a fortress, which contains no water but rather rolls sand stones with great force. If it encountered a mountain of iron it could undoubtedly grind it into powder. On Friday at sunset, a cloud surrounds the river so that no man is able to cross it. At the close of the Sabbath the River resumes its normal torrent of stones. . . ."

The mythical Sambation, remarked Friedlaender, "finds its parallel, if not its prototype, in the 'sand river' of the Greek Pseudo-Callisthenes" ("The Jews of Arabia and the Rechabites," p. 254; see also pp. 255–257). See Epstein, *Eldad ha-Dani,* pp. 5–6. See also the article "Sambation" in *Encyclopedia Judaica,* vol. 14, pp. 762–764.

11. According to a *midrash* (*Yalqut Shir ha-Shirim*), the exiles of Judah and Benjamin are destined to go to these tribes, which dwell in exile across the Sambation River, and bring them to Palestine. See Abraham Ya^cari, "*Shelihim me-Erets Yisra'el la-^cAseret ha-Shevatim,*" pp. 163–178; 344–356; 474–482. See also idem, "*Shelihim me-Erets Yisra'el le-Teman,*" pp. 392–430.

12. For a discussion of the various aspects of this incident, see Ratzaby, "*^cEzra ha-Sofer ve-ha-Temanim,*" pp. 108–111; Ratzaby, "*Nosafot le-^cEzra ha-Sofer,*" p. 382.

13. Rabbi Shelomo ^cAdani was born in Sanaa. Around 1571 he emigrated to Eretz Israel, and settled in Safed. His extensive commentary on the Mishna is considered by all Jewish circles as one of the best.

14. "*Mishnayot Zera^cim,*" in *Melekhet Shelomo* (Vilna, 1939).

15. Rabbi Yeḥia Ṣaliḥ, known among the Yemenite Jews by the abbreviation מהרי"ץ "*Mahriṣ,*" is considered among the few most prominent personalities in the history of Yemenite Jewry. He composed several books dealing with religious matters. He died in the year 1859. See Koraḥ, *Sa^carat Teman,* p. 31. See also Ratzaby, "*Mahriṣ ve-Sifro Pe^cullat Ṣaddiq,*" pp. 100–117.

16. "*Megillat Teman,*" published by David Sassoon in *ha-Ṣofeh le-Ḥokhmat Yisra'el,* vol. 7 (1923).

17. *'Even Sappir,* vol. 1, p. 99a.

18. *Ginze Qedem,* vol. 3, pp. 16–17.

19. See Ratzaby, "*^cEzra ha-Sofer,*" pp. 110–111; Kafiḥ, "*Qeshareha Shel Yahadut Teman,*" p. 30; Yeshay^cahu, "*Shevile ha-^cAliyya mi-Teman,*" pp. 39–40.

20. See, for example, Ratzaby, "*^cEzra ha-Sofer,*" p. 110.

21. "*Qeshareha Shel Yahadut Teman,*" p. 30. The Qur'ān (9:30) claims that the Jews of Arabia referred to Ezra as "the son of God." While the Qur'anic contention is probably exaggerated, it may reflect the Arabian Jewish reverence for Ezra.

22. *'Even Sappir,* vol. 1, p. 99a.

23. "*^cEzra ha-Sofer,*" p. 110.

24. "*Shevile ha-^cAliyya mi-Teman,*" p. 39.

25. "*Sefer She'erit Yisra'el*" constitutes the second part of *Yosipon* (Amsterdam, n.d.), pp. 15–16. For a version of this story relating to the Jews of Worms, see Rabbi David Kimhi (Radak) in *Qol Mevasser* (Jerusalem, 1923).

26. *Book of Kuzari,* trans. by H. Hirschfeld (1969), pp. 100–101.

27. *Travels in Arabia* (1811).

28. Philby, *The Heart of Arabia,* vol. I, p. xv.

29. See the article "Yemen" in EI^1, pp. 1155–1158; Wenner, *Modern Yemen,* pp. 23–24.

30. See the article "Yemen" in *Encyclopedia Britannica,* vol. 19 (1984), pp. 1084–1089.

31. See ibid., and "Yemen" EI^1, pp. 1155–1158.

32. See, for example, Wāsi^cī, *Ta'rīkh al-Yaman,* p. 30 et passim.

33. Based on Jer. 9:12.

34. Based on Isa. 66:16.

35. Based on Lam. 4:8.

36. *Sefer Dofi ha-Zeman,* pp. 195–196. See also Koraḥ, *Sa^carat Teman,* p. 27.

37. Tritton, *The Rise of the Imams,* p. 119.
38. *ʿOlelot,* p. 63.
39. Koraḥ, *Saʿarat Teman,* p. 94. See also Kafiḥ, *Halikhot Teman,* pp. 218–221.
40. See Donaldson, *The Shīʿite Religion* (London, 1933); see the article "al-Zaidiya," *EI*[1], vol. 4, pp. 1196–1198; Serjeant, "The Zaydis," pp. 285–301.
41. The titles *sayyid* (pl. *sāda*) or *sharīf* (pl. *ashrāf*), which are used before the name of a Muslim, are common to both Sunnīs and Shīʿites.
42. See Serjeant, "The Saiyids of Ḥadramawt," pp. 3–29; Brown, "The Yemeni Dilemma," pp. 349–367.
43. *Arabian Peak and Desert,* pp. 196–197.
44. Niebuhr, vol. 2, pp. 103–104.
45. *Al-Yemen,* pp. 32–33. For a list of the tribes in Yemen, see Wāsiʿī, *Taʾrīkh,* pp. 219–220. See also, Stookey, *Yemen,* pp. 149–155.
46. See Serjeant, "South Arabia," p. 228.
47. *Masʿot Ḥabshush,* pp. 51–52.
48. *Arabian Peak,* pp. 71–72.
49. *The Yemen,* p. 36.
50. Ibid., p. 184.
51. *Arabian Peak,* p. 65.
52. *Ḥafeṣ Ḥayyim,* p. 589.
53. Ishmaelite refers to the Arabs, who according to their tradition are descendants of Ishmael, the son of Hagar, the maidservant of Sarah (see Genesis 16:1; 15; 21:10). "Savage" (Hebrews: *pereh*) refers to Ishmael, based on Genesis 16:12).
54. *Ḥafeṣ Ḥayyim,* p. 142.
55. Seri and Tobi, *Shirim Ḥadashim,* pp. 135–136.
56. "*ʿOlelot,*" pp. 62–64.
57. *Al-Yemen,* p. 9.
58. *ʾEven Sappir,* vol. 2, p. 68b. Goitein (*Jews and Arabs,* p. 49), also characterized the Yemenites as "the most Jewish of all Jews."
59. "*Hilkhot Teman,*" pp. 349–355.
60. See ch. III, below.

I
Antiquity of Jewish Settlement in Arabia

1. See Pritchard, *ANET* (1955), pp. 278–279. See also Hitti, *History of the Arabs,* p. 37.
2. Yosef Kafiḥ, ed., "*Qorot Yisraʾel be-Teman le-Rabbi Ḥayyim Ḥabshush,*" pp. 246–286; reproduced in Tobi, *Toledot Yehude Teman: mi-Kitvehem,* pp. 1–41.

Ḥayyim Ḥabshush (1833–1899) is best known for serving as the Yemenite guide of the celebrated French traveler Joseph Halévy, who explored Yemen in 1870 in search of Sabaean inscriptions. Ḥabshush, who copied many of the inscriptions for Halévy, wrote an account of Halévy's travels from Sanaa to the Jauf to Najrān, and the return through Marib. The original Arabic text was edited and published with an English summary by S. D. Goitein as *Ḥezion Teman* (Jerusalem, 1941). In the English summary (p. 3) Goitein remarked that Ḥabshush's book "is in many respects a very valuable contribution to our knowledge of one of the most important and least known parts of South-Arabia." Goitein also translated the book into Hebrew and published it under the title, *Mas^c ot Habshush* (The Travels of Ḥabshush) (Tel-Aviv, 1939). See also Goitein's "*Ḥayyim Ḥabshush ve-Sifro Ḥezion Teman,*" pp. 89–96; E. Brauer, *Ethnologie der Jemenitischen Juden,* pp. 11–13.

3. The founder of the Zaydī dynasty of the Yemen.

4. "*Qorot Yisra'el be-Teman,*" p. 249.

5. See his book *Arabian Peak and Desert: Travels in Al-Yaman,* pp. 224–225. The Yemenite Jewish writer Ḥubara remarked that because of the scarcity of paper, Jews used smoothed and burnished cows' bones as surfaces upon which to write the Hebrew alphabet or verses from the Torah. These bones were then considered as sacred as regular scrolls, and when they got worn out they would be deposited in a *Genizah.* Ḥubara added that it was customary for a Yemenite Jew who owned a book to inscribe the following words in it: "This book is for me and for my descendants until the end of times." The inscription would end with a vigorous curse for whoever steals the book (*Bi-Tela'ot Teman,* pp. 295–296).

6. Because of the scarcity of paper, old manuscripts were generally not discarded by the Yemenite Jews, but rather used for the bindings of books. Manuscripts were pasted one upon another and aligned properly to form thick covers for books. Many valuable works were and are still being discovered by the careful separation of these leaves.

7. These fragments were published by David Sassoon under the title *Megillat Teman* (The Scroll of Yemen), in *ha-Ṣofe le-Ḥokhmat Yisra'el,* 7 (1923), 1–14.

8. Edited and published by Josef Kafiḥ in *Ṣefunot,* vol. I (1956), pp. 185–242; Reproduced in *Toledot Yehude Teman: mi-Kitvehem,* ed. by Yosef Tobi, pp. 59–116.

9. The oldest historical composition which has come to us from the Jews of Yemen is an abridged version of Joseph bin Guryon's *Yosippon* (*History of the Jews during the Second Temple*), which was done by Zechariah ben Sa^c id al-Yamani who lived in the tenth century C.E. See A. Neubauer, "Pseudo-Josephus, Joseph Ben Gorion," *JQR,* XI (1899), 351–361; M. Steinschneider, *Die Arabische Literature der Juden,* p. 114.

10. Ṣa^c dī, p. 191.

11. Ibid., p. 188.

12. Ibid., p. 200.

13. For a discussion of the book *Dofi ha-Zeman* and the identity of its author, see S. D. Goitein, "*Ketav-Yad ^c Ivri-^c Aravi,*" *Kiryat-Sefer,* 14 (1938), 256–270.

14. This most tragic chapter in Yemenite Jewish history will be fully discussed in chapter VI, below.

15. See discussion following and section 4, below.

16. Cp. I Sam. 15.

17. This seems to be a confusion with Absalom. See II Sam. 15–18.

18. See the extensive study of Hirschberg, "*ha-Meqorot ha-^c Araviyyim,*" *Zion,* 10 (1945), 81–101; *Zion* 11 (1946), 17–37. See also Goitein, "*Isra'iliyat,*" in *Tarbiz,* 6 (1935), 89–101, 510–522.

19. These four kinds of plants are used in the Jewish ritual of the Feast of Tabernacles. Their names in Hebrew are: *'ethrog, lulav, hadas,* and *^c arava.*

20. See Saphir, *'Even Sappir,* vol. 1, p. 99. Saphir also remarks that he heard the Yemenite Jews referring to the land as "The Paradise of Yemen" (ibid.). On Mount Nuqūm which towers over the city of Sanaa lies the ruins

of a city which, according to a Yemenite Jewish tradition, was built by the first Jewish immigrants to Yemen. But when the Yemenite Arabs embraced Islam, so the tradition says, the Jews were driven away in accordance with Islamic law, which prohibits non-Muslims from dwelling in quarters or houses higher than those of Muslims. See Koraḥ, *Sa^{c}arat Teman,* p. 4.

21. Until recently Yemenite Jews believed that their forefathers entered Yemen through a miraculous cave which passes through Mount Nuqūm. This mysterious cave, they held, will be revealed with the coming of the Messiah, and through it the return of the Yemenite Jews to Zion will be effected. Yemenite Jews, now living in Israel, relate that a Jew by the name of Alnaddaf was obsessed with finding the opening of this cave, and because of that he was nicknamed *al-Khuzqī,* "The Tunnel Man." See Yisra'el Yesha^{c}yahu, "*Shevile ha-^{c}Aliyya,*" pp. 37–38.

22. כי בעוונותינו ובעוונות אבותינו אנו מונים לחרבן בית אלהינו ולפיזור עם ה׳ אלה מעל אדמת קדשנו, היום לחרבן בית שני אשר בנה עזרא אדוננו (כך וכך שנים) שני יגונותינו. ולחרבן בית ראשון ולפיזור אנשי גלותנו אנחנו הגולים פה בארצות מונינו היום(כך וכך שנים) על רוב עוונותינו.
See Koraḥ, *Sa^{c}arat Teman,* p. 3.

23. "*Qeshareha shel Yahadut Teman,*" pp. 29–30.

24. Mahalal Ha^{c}adani, *Ben ^{c}Aden ve-Teman,* pp. 83–84.

25. *'Even Sappir,* vol. 1, p. 101. See also Goitein, *From the Land of Sheba,* p. 93. Benjamin of Tudela remarked about the Jews of Arabia: "At this place lives Salmon the Nasi, the brother of Hanan the Nasi . . . who are the seed of David, for they have their pedigree in writing" (Adler, *Itinerary,* p. 48).

26. Saphir, who examined the epitaphs in the old Jewish cemetery in Aden, related that they were dated in accordance with the "Era of the Contracts" (i.e., Seleucid). The earliest epitaph observed by him is dated "20 of the Era of the Contracts." This and other factors led him to believe that Jews must have already been in Aden in the time of Simeon the Righteous, in whose time the "Era of the Contracts" began (35 years after Ezra's departure to Jerusalem), *'Even Sappir,* vol. 2, pp. 13–28. A. Neubauer, however, expressed skepticism regarding Saphir's conclusions, which were based on the epitaphs. "It is evident," contended Neubauer, "that the thousand is omitted, and that the full date is 1020 Sel., equal to 709 of the Christian era," "The Literature of the Jews of Yemen," *JQR,* 3 (1891), 608. Neubauer, however, failed to explain how the alleged "thousand" was omitted, but see also Goitein, "The Age of the Hebrew Tombstones," pp. 81–84.

27. See, for example, I Chron. 5:9.

28. Herodotus III, 107, 113. For the role of Arabia in ancient and pre-Islam's times, see O'Leary, *Arabia Before Mohammed* (New York, 1927). F. Altheim and R. Stiehl, *Die Araber in der Alten Welt* (5 vols.; Berlin, 1964–1968).

29. See Ezek. 27:22–23 and the discussion below on Solomon and the Queen of Sheba.

30. See *EI*^{2}, vol. 3, p. 525.

31. Herodotus III, 97. See also the extensive study by Groom, *Frankincense and Myrrh* (1981).

32. See Lev. 2:15, 16; 24:7.

33. Song of Solomon 1:3–4; 3:6. See also Esther 2:17; Prov. 7:17. For the importance and usage of these commodities in the ancient world, see Van Beek, "Frankincense and Myrrh," pp. 82–86; idem, "Prolegomenon," pp. XXVI–XXVII.

34. *Die Israeliten zu Mekka* (1864).

35. Torrey (*The Jewish Foundation of Islam,* p. 15) dismissed Dozy's theory as "a fanciful essay." See also Graff's criticism of Dozy's assertions in *ZDMG* 19 (1865), 330–351.

36. It is the consensus of biblical scholars that this passage comes from an old tradition; or, as Curtis (The *Book of Chronicles,* pp. 116–117) has it, the passage is "an annotated paragraph taken from some old source." See also *Encyclopedia Biblica,* vol. IV, cols. 4527–4528.

37. See I Kings 10:1–13 and its parallel in 2 Chron. 9:1–12.

38. See the discussion of this aspect in Pritchard, ed., *Solomon and Sheba,* pp. 11–12; Groom, *Frankincense and Myrrh,* London (1981), pp. 38–51; Scott, "Solomon and the Beginning of Wisdom in Israel," pp. 262–279; Van Beek, "Prolegomenon" pp. IX–XXXI.

39. The existence of these four kingdoms was first related to us by Strabo (*Geographica,* ed. by A. Meineke 16 768), which he bases on the now lost work of Eratostenes (Third Century B.C.E.). For the opinions regarding the dates and chronology of the southern Arabian kingdoms, see Müller, *Die Burgen und Schlösser Südarabiens nach dem Iklil des Hamdânî,* vol. II, pp. 29ff.; 60ff.; Glaser, *Skizze der Geschichte und Geographie Arabiens* (New York, 1976), pp. 357–470. Albright, "The Chronology of Ancient South Arabia . . . ," in *BASOR,* 119 (1950), 5–15. See also the article "Arabia" in EI^2, vol. I, pp. 204–209.

40. See Della Vida, "Pre-Islamic Arabia," pp. 30–35; Albright, "A Note on Early Sabaean Chronology," *BASOR,* 143 (1956), 9–10; Van Beek and A. Jamme, "An Inscribed South Arabian Clay Stamp from Bethel," in *BASOR,* 151 (1958), 9–16; A. Jamme and Van Beek, "The South-Arabian Clay Stamp from Bethel Again," in *BASOR,* 163 (1961), 15–18; Gray, *I and II Kings; A Commentary,* p. 157. Actually, all we really know about the Queen of Sheba is found in the Bible. So far none of the numerous inscriptions found in southern Arabia (including Marib) refers to any Sabaean ruler earlier than about 800 B.C.E. See Phillips, *Qataban and Sheba,* 106–107.

41. See Musil, *Arabia Deserta,* p. 477.

42. Ibid., p. 477. See also Luckenbill, *Ancient Records of Assyria and Babylonia,* vol. I, pp. 279, 293; vol. 2, pp. 7–8, 27; EI^2, vol. I, pp. 524–525; Abbot, "Pre-Islamic Arab Queens" in *AJSLL,* 58 (1941), 1–22. The Assyrian records also mention other Arab queens: Iat^{c}e, who in 703 B.C.E. helped the Babylonian king against Sannacherib, King of Assyria (705–681 B.C.E.); also Tabûa, Adiâ, Te^{c}elhunu. See Luckenbill, vol. 2, pp. 130, 158, 364–366, 214, 400. See also EI^2, p. 525.

43. See also Ps. 72:10; Isa. 60:6; Ezek. 27:22–23.

44. *Frankincense and Myrrh,* p. 54.

45. Della Vida, "Pre-Islamic Arabia," pp. 30–35.

46. Van Beek's historical and archaeological study of southern Arabia, "The Land of Sheba," p. 40.

47. *I and II Kings: A Commentary,* pp. 257 and 259.

48. *A History of Israel,* p. 215.

49. *Solomon and Sheba,* p. 37.

50. Quoted by Pritchard, ibid., p. 12. No reference is given.

51. See I Kings 9:26–28; 10:14–29. Excavations during 1938–40 at Ezi-ongeber revealed traces of shipbuilding there. See Hourani, *Arab Seafaring in the Indian Ocean,* p. 9.

52. See Van Beek, "Frankincense and Myrrh," pp. 70–95; idem, "Prolegomenon," pp. XXVI–XXVII.

53. *Arabia and the Bible,* p. 106.

54. I Kings 10:10. See also Van Beek, "Prolegomenon," pp. XXVII–XXVIII.

55. See Alois Musil, *The Northern Hegâz,* p. 274.

56. See, for example, Gray, *I and II Kings,* p. 257.

57. *Antiquities,* VIII, 5:3.

58. Scott, *In the High Yemen,* p. 198. The story of the Queen of Sheba captured the oriental imagination and became in extra-canonical writings and commentaries the subject of extensive elaborations and embellishments. According to the Qur'ān (27:22–44), Solomon was informed about the Queen (her name is not quoted in the Qur'ān) and her people, and their worship of the sun by the hoopoe (*hudhūd*). King Solomon sent a letter to her with the hoopoe, and the Queen responded by sending him gifts. But when these presents were rejected by Solomon, she went to Jerusalem herself to see him. It is further related that King Solomon employed a ruse in order to cause the Queen to uncover her legs: She was asked to enter a smooth hall made of glass which she mistook for a pool of water, and so lifted her skirt and revealed her legs. Eventually the Queen, according to the Qur'ān, surrendered to Allah. Muslim commentators (Ṭabarī, Zamakhsharī, Baiḍāwī) elaborate on this story and give the name Bilqis to the Queen. They also provide the motivation for Solomon's ruse to cause the Queen to uncover her legs: The demons at Solomon's Court, who were concerned with the possibility that Solomon would marry the Queen, spread a rumor that the Queen had hairy legs and the foot of an ass. Hence, the need for the ruse. (Watt, "The Queen of Sheba in Islamic Tradition," pp. 85–103.) In Persian art Bilqis may often be seen standing in water before Solomon. The same scene is depicted on a window in King's College Chapel, Cambridge.

Such embellishments are also prevalent in Jewish sources such as *Targum Sheni* to Esther. See Lou H. Silberman, "The Queen of Sheba in Judaic Tradition," pp. 65–84. Embellished versions of the legend appears in the *Kebra Nagast* (Glory of the Kings), the Ethiopian national saga, which traces the Ethiopian dynasty back to Solomon and Makeda, the Ethiopian name of the Queen of Sheba. See Edward Ullendorrf, "The Queen of Sheba in Ethiopic Tradition," pp. 104–114. For the reflection of this topic in Christian tradition, see Paul Watson, "The Queen of Sheba in Christian Tradition," pp. 115–145. See also Andre Chastel, "*La légende de la Reine de Saba,*" *RHR,* 119 (1939), 204–205; 120 (1939) 27–44; and Philby's succinct notes on the various traditions in his *Sheba's Daughters,* pp. 10–13.

59. The main Assyrian inscriptions pertaining to the topic of discussion here are: (A) the so-called "Nabonidus Chronicle," first published by T. G. Pinches, in *Transactions of the Society of Biblical Archaeology,* vol. VII (1882), pp. 139ff.; then by Sidney Smith, in *Babylonian Historical Texts, Relating to the Downfall of Babylon* (henceforth *BHT*) (London, 1924), Pls. XI–XIV, pp. 110ff.; republished in James B. Pritchard, ed., *Ancient Near Eastern Texts Relating to the Old Testament* (henceforth *ANET*), pp. 305–307. This inscription depicts the main events of the reign of Nabonidus year by year and describes the fall of Babylon. (B) "Verse Account of Nabonidus," published by Sidney Smith (*BHT,* Pls. V–X, pp. 83ff.; see also *ANET,* pp. 312–315. Passages in this inscription narrate Nabonidus's conquest of Teima and the state of affairs in Babylonia. For a thorough discussion of these documents, see Raymond P. Dougherty, *Nabonidus and Belshazzar* (New Haven, 1929). In

1956 more inscriptions were discovered by D. S. Rice at Harran, and were published by C. J. Gadd, "The Harran Inscriptions of Nabonidus," in *Anatolian Studies,* VIII (1958), 35–92.

60. The word *ᶜerev* generally means "mingled people." Here it may refer to the Arabs. Indeed, 2 Chron. 9:14 substitutes the word *ᶜArav* for the *ᶜErev* of 1 Kings 10:15.

61. The Septuagint version of this verse in Genesis reads: "Saban, Taiman and Dedan."

62. *Nabonidus and Belshazzar,* p. 160.

63. "The Harran Inscriptions of Nabonidus," p. 88. The text of inscription H_2 is provided by Gadd, pp. 57–65.

64. For a comprehensive discussion of this topic, see Dougherty, *Nabonidus and Belshazzar,* pp. 138–160.

65. See *ANET,* p. 313; Dougherty, *Nabonidus and Belshazzar,* pp. 142–143.

66. Torrey, *The Jewish Foundation of Islam,* pp. 10–12.

67. See Gadd, "The Harran Inscriptions," col. III: 14–16, pp. 64–65.

68. *ANET,* p. 313–314.

69. *The Jewish Foundation of Islam,* p. 12.

70. Gadd, "The Harran Inscriptions," pp. 86 and 87.

71. For "Prayer of Nabonidus," see J. T. Milik, "*Priere de Nabonide,*" in *Revue biblique,* 63 (1956), 407ff. A part of the fourth line, as translated by Milik, reads: ". . . *(Dieu) m'accorda un devin; C'etait un homme Juif*". See also Gadd, "Harran Inscriptions" pp. 87–88; Bickerman, *Four Strange Books of the Bible,* p. 76.

72. "The Harran Inscriptions," p. 88.

II
Post-Biblical and Pre-Islamic Times

1. *History of the Arabs* (1970), p. 3. For a general treatment of Arabia in pre-Islamic times, see F. Altheim and R. Stiehl, *Die Araber in der Alten Welt* (5 vols.; Berlin, 1964–1968); A. P. Caussin de Perceval, *Essai sur l'histoire des Arabes avant l'islamisme. . .* " (3 vols.; Paris, 1847–1848); Philip Hitti, *History of the Arabs,* (1970[10]), pp. 3–108. See also Sydney Smith, "Events in Arabia in the 6th Century A.D.," in *BSOAS,* 16 (1959), 425–468; M. Höfner, *Beiträge zur historischen geographie des vorislamischen Südarabien* (1952). Other works will be mentioned in the course of this study.

2. *Antiquities,* XV, IX. 3.

3. See Strabo, *Geographica,* 16:4, 22. See also O'Leary, *Arabia Before Mohammed,* pp. 75–78. For a detailed description of Gallus's venture, see E. Glaser, *Skizze der Geschichte und Geographie Arabiens,* pp. 43–56.

4. *A Social and Religious History of the Jews,* vol. 3, p. 64.

5. This topic has been extensively discussed by Arab historians and by many scholars. See, for example, Montgomery Watt, *Muhammad at Medina,* pp. 192–220.

6. Strabo, *Geographica,* 16:4, 22.

7. Philostorgius, *Historica ecclesiastica,* III. 4, 5 (Patrologiae . . . series graeca, Migne, Paris, LXV, cols. 481–486). See also Baron, *A Social and Religious History of the Jews,* vol. 3, pp. 63–64; Z. W. Hirschberg, *Yisra'el ba-ᶜArav* (Hebrew), pp. 58–59; Kenneth Scott Latourette, *A History of the Expansion of Christianity,* vol. I, pp. 231–238.

8. See Hirschberg, *Yisra'el ba-ᶜArav,* pp. 53–57.

9. For a study of *Qawl,* see G. Ryckmas, "*Le qayl en Arabie meridionale préislamique,*" pp. 144–155.
10. See the article "Arabia" in *Encyclopedia Judaica,* vol. III, pp. 235–236. See also Hirschberg, *Yisra'el ba-ᶜArav,* pp. 53–57; Izhak Ben-Zvi, *The Exiled and the Redeemed,* pp. 54–55.
11. *Yisra'el ba-ᶜArav,* pp. 54–55.
12. See *Tal. Yerush., Kil'a'im,* ch. 9:4.
13. *Yisra'el baᶜArav,* pp. 54–55.
14. See note 1, above, and also L. Cheikho, *Le Christianisme et la littérature chrétienne en Arabie avant l'Islam* (Beirut, 1912); Ifran Shahîd, *The Martyrs of Najrân* (Bruxelles, 1971).
15. *ha-Soṣiologia shel ha-yehudim,* vol. 1, p. 17.
16. See, for example, Hitti, *History of the Arabs,* p. 61. See also the discussion of this aspect and the references in Y. Ben-Ze'ev, *ha-Yehudim ba-ᶜArav,* pp. 29–30. Izhak Ben-Zvi, contended that multitudes of Judaized Ḥimyarites were assimilated into the Jewish communities (*Nidḥe Yisra'el,* p. 59).
17. See Sidney Smith, "Events in Arabia in the 6th Century A.D.," in *BSOAS* 16 (1959), 462.
18. These sources, remarked Georgio Della Vida, are "copious, perhaps even too copious; we suffer from an overabundance rather than from a scarcity" ("Pre-Islamic Arabia," p. 41).
19. See Della Vida, pp. 41–42; D. S. Margoliouth, *The Relations between Arabs and Israelites prior to the Rise of Islam,* p. 59.
20. See the detailed study of Hirschberg, "*ha-Meqorot haᶜAraviyyim le-Qorot Yehude ᶜArav,*" in *Zion* 10, 83–84, 98–101.
21. This Ḥimyarite king is referred to in the various sources relating to him by a wide variety of names. In Arab tradition he is generally known by the name Zurᶜa ibn Tibbān Asᶜad. The Arab sources claim that he assumed the name Yusuf following his conversion to Judaism (see Baron, *A Social and Religious History of the Jews,* vol. 2, pp. 243–245). Inscription Ja 1028 gives his full name as Yūsuf As'ar Yath'ar (see A. Jamme, *Sabaean and Hasaean Inscriptions from Saudi Arabia,* pp. 39–42. In Arabic he is also referred to as Dhū Nuwās (in Greek Dounaas). Dinawārī gives him another name Zur'a ibn Zayd. In addition to these names, Dhū Nuwās is referred to in Christian sources by a host of pejorative nicknames (see note 25, below).
22. The main sources are: *The Book of the Himyarites,* ed. by A. Moberg, in *Acta regiae Societatis humaniorum litteratum Lundensis,* vol. 7 (Syriac Text; Lund, 1924, pp. 1–61); Jacob of Sarûj, *Letter to the Ḥimyarite Christians,* ed. R. Schröter, *Trostschreiben Jacob's von Sarug an die himjaritischen Christen,* in *ZDMG,* 31 (1877), 360–405 (Syriac Text, pp. 369–385); *Martyrium Arethae,* the standard edition is that of Ed. Carpentier in *Acta Sanctorum,* Octobris tomus X (1861), 721–759; John of Ephesus, *Life of Simeon of Bêth Arshâm,* ed. E. W. Brooks, *John of Ephesus, Lives of the Eastern Saints,* X, *The History of Mar Simeon the bishop, the Persian debater,* in *Patrologia Orientalis,* vol. 17, fasc. 1 (1923), pp. 137–158. For an exhaustive bibliography, see Shahîd, *The Martyrs of Najrân,* pp. 277–286. For a helpful survey of the sources, see A. A. Vasiliev, *Justin the First* (Cambridge, Mass., 1950), pp. 9–42 et passim.
23. *The Martyrs of Najrân,* pp. 266–267.
24. Thus, for example, J. Halevy denied the authenticity of the letter of Simeon Bêth Arsham. See his "*Examen critique des sources relatives à la persécution des chrétiens de Nedjran par le roi juif des Himyarites, REJ* 17 (1889), 16–42; 161–178. See also Baron, *A Social and Religious History,* vol. 3, p. 67.

25. See the discussion of the pejoratives applied to Dhū Nuwās ("Masrūq," "Dimîon," "Judas," "butcher," "killer," "executioner," etc.) in Shahîd, *The Martyrs of Najrân,* pp. 260–266.
26. See, for example, Hitti, *History of the Arabs,* p. 61; A. A. Vasiliev, *Justin the First,* pp. 289–291.
27. *The Origins of Islam in its Christian Environment,* pp. 35, 61.
28. *History of the Arabs,* p. 62. See also Obermann, "Islamic Origins," p. 61.
29. *Arabia Before Mohammed,* p. 145.
30. Shahîd, *The Martyrs of Najrân,* p. 7.
31. See, however, Hirschberg, "*Mar Zuṭra Rosh ha-Sanhedrin bi-Tveria,* pp. 147–153; idem, "*Yosef Melekh Ḥimyar ve-ʿAliyyato shel Mar Zuṭra,* pp. 139–146.
32. I. Guidi, ed., *La lettera di Simeone vescovo di Bêth Arsam,* pp. 471–515.
33. Quoted by Baron, *A Social and Religious History,* vol. 3, p. 67, and Hirschberg, *Yisraʾel ba-ʿArav,* p. 90. See also Shahîd, *The Martyrs of Najrân,* p. 119. On the ties between the Jews of Arabia (particularly those of northern Arabia) and Eretz Israel in pre-Islamic times, see M. J. and Menachem Kister, "On the Jews of Arabia" (1979), pp. 231–247.
34. "*Qeshareha shel Yahadut Teman,*" p. 31. See the article, "Judaizers," in *Encyclopedia Judaica,* vol. 10 (1972), pp. 397–401.
35. See Hirschberg, "*ha-Meqorot haʿAraviyyim le-Qorot Yehude ʿArav,*" p. 23.
36. D. S. Margoliouth, *The Relations between Arabs and Israelites prior to the Rise of Islam,* p. 64; this is also the view of Sweetman, *Islam and Christian Theology,* vol. I, p. 1; Baron, *A Social and Religious History,* vol. 3, p. 67.
37. "*Gilluyim Ḥadashim ʿal Bet ha-Melukha be-Teman,*" in *Haʾareẓ* (March 25, 1955), *Tarbut ve-Sifrut,* p. 1. Elsewhere ("The Jews of Yemen," p. 228), Goitein says that he does not share the widely held belief that the Yemenites are mainly or largely the descendants of pre-Islamic Ḥimyarite proselytes. The type of religion developed by a foreign population won over to Judaism may best be studied in the Falashas, the so-called Jews of Ethiopia. Their beliefs and practices have very little to do with Judaism. On the other hand, the Yemenites may be called the most Jewish of all Jews, so that it is rather unlikely that all or even most of them should be the offspring of Ḥimyarites, for Judaism used to be essentially the religion of a people, not one adopted by conversion.
38. Baron, *A Social and Religious History,* vol. 3, p. 66. For an extensive bibliography relating to these inscriptions, see ibid., p. 258, n. 81. See also Ryckman's series of "*Inscriptions sud-arabes,*" in *Le Muséon,* vols. 40–69.
39. See *Corpus Inscriptionum Semiticarum,* n. 543.
40. *The Relations between Arabs and Israelites,* p. 70.
41. See the article "Khazars" in *Encyclopedia Judaica,* vol. 10, pp. 944–953. See also D. M. Dunlop, *History of the Jewish Khazars* (1954), and the extensive bibliography therein.
42. *Encyclopedia Judaica,* vol. 10, p. 948.
43. A comparison between these two Jewish kingdoms, the Ḥimyarite and the Khazar, deserves a full treatment. However, it is not within the scope of this study.
44. See J. A. Montgomery, *Arabia and the Bible,* pp. 105–113.
45. See G. W. van Beek, "Prolegomenon," pp. XXVI–XXVII. See also idem, "The Land of Sheba," pp. 40–63.
46. *Arabia and the Bible,* p. 123.

III
Yemenite Jewry in the Early and High Medieval Ages

1. *Saḥīḥ Muslim,* trans. by Siddīqī, vol. 3, pp. 963–964; see also al-Balādhurī, *Futūḥ al-Buldān,* trans. by Philip K. Hitti as *The Origins of the Islamic State* (New York, 1916), pp. 40–41; H. Lammens, *L'Arabie occidentale avant l'hégire* (1928), pp. 51–99. For a translation of various Muslim sources, see N. Stillman, *The Jews of Arab Lands,* pp. 119–151.

2. See the article "Khaybar" in *EI*[2] vol. IV, pp. 1137–1143; Watt, *Muḥammad at Medina,* pp. 217–219 et passim; Rodinson, *Mohammed,* trans. by Anne Carter (New York, 1971), pp. 252–254; Ibn Isḥāq, *Sīrat Rasūl Allāh,* trans. by A. Guillaume under the title *The Life of Muḥammad* (1968), pp. 510–518. *Saḥīḥ Muslim,* vol. III, pp. 992–996. See also the references to the Ḥadīth sources in Wensinck, *A Handbook of Early Muhammadan Tradition* (1960), pp. 122–123; Hirschberg, *Yisra'el ba-ʿArav,* pp. 138–158; Izhak Ben-Zvi, *Nidḥe Yisra'el* (Jerusalem, 1966), pp. 63–92.

3. This tradition is also handed out in a wider meaning: لا تصلح قبلتان بارض (There cannot be two *qiblas* in one country). See Ibn Hishām, *al-Sīra,* p. 779; al-Tabarī, *Ta'rīkh,* vol. I, p. 1590; Ibn al-Athīr, *al-Kāmil,* vol. II, p. 171. Another tradition is reported from the prophet: "Expel the Jews from the Ḥijāz and the people of Najrān [the Christians] from the Arabian peninsula" (al-Ramlī, *Nihāyat al-Muḥtāj,* VII, p. 223). This tradition, however, is not supported by an *Isnād.* See also al-Balādhurī, *Futūḥ al-Buldān,* p. 28 (Eng. trans., *The Origins of the Islamic State,* p. 48); for a discussion of the various traditions in this respect, see R. Gottheil, "Dhimmis and Moslems in Egypt," pp. 353–358.

4. *Saḥīḥ Muslim,* p. 963. See also Hirschberg, *Yisr'el ba-ʿArav,* pp. 155–166.

5. *Saḥīḥ Muslim,* p. 963.

6. Ibid., p. 965. See also Friedlander, "The Jews of Arabia and the Gaonate," *JQR,* n.s. I (1910–1911), 249–250.

7. See, for example, Siddīqī's comment in *Saḥīḥ Muslim,* pp. 964–965, notes 2240–2241. Despite the related expulsion of the Jews from northern Arabia, there are repeated references to their continued existence in that region, particularly in Wādī-'l-Qura, Taymaʿ, and Khaybar. These reports, which persisted during the tenth and eleventh centuries, were attested by Arab authors. Thus, in describing the blessed and well-cultivated lands of Wādī-'l-Qura, the Arab historian Muqaddasī (died 990 A.D.) remarks that most of the inhabitants there were Jews (*Aḥsan al-Taqāsīm fī Maʿrifāt al-'Aqālīm,* pp. 83–84. See also Ben-Ze'ev *ha-Yehudim ba-ʿArav,* p. 227). Further testimony of the existence of Jews in that area comes from writings as late as the beginning of the eleventh century A.D. Questions from the Jews of Wādī-'l-Qura were addressed to Rabbi Sherira Gaon and his son Rav Hai Gaon regarding matters of land inheritance and the growing of palm trees (see the discussion and references in Ben-Zvi, *Nidḥe Yisra'el,* pp. 63–92). Moreover, two letters from the eleventh century sent from Tyre and addressed to the Jews of Wādī-'l-Qura are extant (Mann, *The Jews in Egypt,* vol. 2, p. 130). Reports regarding the Jews of Arabia come to us from the celebrated twelfth-century Jewish traveler Benjamin of Tudela (see Adler, *The Itinerary of Benjamin of Tudela,* pp. 46–49). See also al-Balādhurī, *The Origins of the Islamic State,* p. 57. "The existence of Jews on the Arabian peninsula," Friedlander remarked ("The Jews of Arabia," p. 252), "many

centuries after their supposed total expulsion from that country—cannot be doubted."

8. See Hirschberg, *Yisra'el ba-ᶜArav,* pp. 60–61.

9. With the proclamation of Muᶜāwiya as caliph (660 C.E.), Damascus became the capital of the Muslim empire. See Hitti, *History of the Arabs,* p. 189.

10. See al-Balādhurī, *Futūḥ al-Buldān,* p. 71 (Eng. trans., *The Origins of the Islamic State,* p. 109). Goitein ("The Jews of Yemen," p. 227) provided a reasonable explanation for the survival of the Jews in contradistinction to the Christians. The Christians, he said, "were a predominantly urban population whose wholesale expulsion constituted no grave administrative problem once it had been decided to realize the dictum ascribed to Muhammad that in Arabia there should be no religion other than Islam (the Muslim sources speak only about the expulsion of the Christians from Najrān, the seat of the Bishop)." The Jews on the other hand, continued Goitein, were probably then as later "widely dispersed all over the country, less conspicuous and . . . difficult to replace, because they formed a large section of the country's caste of artisans and craftsmen."

11. Three edited versions of this document have been published to date: S. D. Goitein, *Kitāb Dhimmat al-Nabī,* in *Kiryat Sefer,* 9 (1932–33), 507–521; Yosef Rivlin, *Ṣava'at Muḥammad le-ᶜAlī ben Abī-Ṭāleb,* pp. 139–156; Nissim B. Gamli'eli, "*Waṣāiat al-Dhimma,*" in his *Ḥadre Teman,* pp. 135–141. The references to this document as well as the quotations are from Goitein's edition as translated in Stillman, *The Jews of Arab Lands,* pp. 255–258.

12. The three editions of the document differ in many respects. With regard to the time of the Jewish raid against the heathen, both Goitein's and Rivlin's editions maintain that it took place on the eve of the Sabbath. But according to Gamli'eli's edition, the Jews refrained from desecrating the Sabbath and, therefore, waited for the evening following the Sabbath to launch their assault against Muḥammad's opponents. The divergencies in the versions of this document, which in itself is a sheer fabrication, are most probably due to elaborations and embellishments. Compare the document with Hirschfeld's "Arabic Portion of the Cairo Geniza at Cambridge," *JQR,* o.s. 15 (1903), 167–179. See in particular the second division of Hirschfeld's fragment, which consists of a letter "from Muḥammad," addressed to "Hanina and the people of Kheibar and Maqna and their progeny. . . " (p. 170). See Goitein's observations on this fragment in his edition of the document, pp. 514–521.

13. *Ḥadre Teman,* p. 141, n. 5.

14. Ibid.

15. See, for example, the views of Goitein, Rivlin, and Gamli'eli expressed in their editions of the documents (See n. 11, above).

16. "Dhimmi and Moslems," p. 356. See also Steinschneider, *Polemische und Apologetische Literatur,* p. 186.

17. See *Asiatic Quarterly Review,* 19 (1905), 156, 158.

18. See Arendonk, *Les Débuts,* p. 134; Stookey, *Yemen,* pp. 79–82.

19. Al-ᶜAlawi, *Sīrat,* pp. 51–52. See also Arendonk, *Les Débuts,* pp. 127–130.

20. *Sīrat,* pp. 51–52.

21. See Stookey, *Yemen,* p. 92. See also Wāsiᶜī, *Ta'rīkh al-Yaman,* pp. 21–23.

22. Wāsiᶜī, *Ta'rīkh al-Yaman,* p. 21.

23. *Qorot,* pp. 284–285.

24. See the relevant Arabic text in Arendonk, *Les Débuts,* pp. 322–329.

25. This book was edited and translated from Arabic into English by David Levine (New York, 1908; reprinted, New York, 1966); it was edited and translated into Hebrew by Yosef Kafiḥ, *Gan ha-Sekhalim* (Jerusalem, 1954).

26. See Pines, "Nathanël ben al-Fayyūmī," pp. 5–22. Ibn Paquda lived in the second half of the eleventh century in Muslim Spain, probably at Saragossa (see *EJ*, vol. 4, col. 106–108). In ch. 3, Ibn Fayyūmī mentioned Ibn Paquda's work and claimed that the purpose of his book is to remedy some deficiencies in Ibn Paquda's work, and to put some views in a more accurate perspective.

27. Fifty-two of these epistles are extant. See *EI*[2], vol. 3, pp. 1071–1076.

28. "The Medieval Polemics," p. 121–122.

29. See the collection of polemics and disputations between Jews and Christians in J. D. Eisenstein, *Oṣar Wikuḥim* (A Collection of Polemics and Disputations, Hebrew, 1969). The attitude of the Christians toward the "Old Testament" is succinctly stated in the well-known principle later enunciated by St. Augustine: "In the Old Testament the New Testament is concealed; in the New Testament the Old Testament is revealed." See also David Berger, *The Jewish-Christian Debate* (1979); Jeremy Cohen, *The Friars and the Jews* (1982).

30. The *Sunna,* as manifested in *Ḥadīth,* is the secondary source from which the teachings of Islam are drawn. While the Qur'ān deals with the broad principles of Islam, the *Ḥadīth* supply the details in religious matters. See Gätje, *The Qur'ān and its Exegesis,* pp. 16–17; Guillaume, *The Traditions of Islam* (1924). Islamic orthodoxy believes that the Qur'ān is literally the word of God, eternal and uncreated, transmitted in Arabic to Muḥammad by the Archangel Gabriel. See Arberry, *The Holy Koran,* p. 20. The Qur'ān itself claims that it is an inimitable miracle, a gift of God, who Himself "Hath made known the Qur'ān" (Qur'ān 55:2; see also 10:38, 12:88). The evidence for the divine origin of the Qur'ān, claim the Muslims, is in itself, in its beauty, elegance, majesty, and perfection. On the miraculous nature of the Qur'ān, see al-Baqillāni, *Iᶜjāz al-Qur'ān* (1930), and the English translation of pp. 13, 36–38 of this book in Jeffery, *Islam, Muḥammad and His Religion* (New York, 1958), pp. 54–57. See also Ibn Khaldūn, *The Muqaddimah* (New York, 1958), pp. 191–194; for divergent opinions expressed on the literary merits of the Qur'ān, see Arberry, *The Holy Koran,* pp. 14–16.

31. See the article "*Ahl al-Kitāb*" *EI*[2], vol. I, p. 265. See also Qur'ān 98:2–3.

32. The Qur'ān names about twenty-five prophets who preceded Muḥammad. Several of these, such as Hūd, Ṣāliḥ, Luqmān, Dhū-'l-Qarnain, are not mentioned in the Bible. It is stated in a *Ḥadīth* that 124,000 national prophets appeared before the advent of Muḥammad. It is incumbent upon a Muslim to believe in all the prophets of the world. See Ali, *The Religion of Islam,* pp. 221–223. The faith of Islam may be summed up in two brief principles of faith: "There is no god but Allāh and Muḥammad is His messenger." These two components of the accepted Islamic creed are known as the *Shahāda* (testimony).

33. "Koran and Agada," pp. 23–24. One example of these gross corruptions, frequently cited by Jews, is found in Qur'ān 28:38, according to which Pharaoh commanded Haman, "Kindle for me (a fire) . . . to bake the mud; and set up for me a lofty tower in order that I may survey the god of Moses."

34. In Qur'ān 62:5 Muḥammad likened the Jews "who are entrusted with the Law of Moses, yet apply it not," to "the ass carrying books." See also Qur'ān 2:42, 3:71, 6:91, 5:15.

35. Abraham S. Halkin, ed., trans. into English by Boaz Cohen (New York, 1952); also edited and trans. into Hebrew by Yosef Kafiḥ, *Rabbenu Moshe ben Maimon,* Igrot (Jerusalem, 1972).

36. The numerical value of במאד מאד is 92, the same as that of מחמד . See Zuker, "*Berurim be-Toledot ha-Vikkuḥim shebben ha-Yahadut ve-ha-Islam,*" pp. 3–35. Extensive use of *gematria* purporting to prove that Muḥammad figures in many biblical verses is to be found in the anti-Jewish pamphlet of the Jewish convert to Islam, "Abd al-Hakk al-Islami," trans. by Perlmann, *JQR,* n.s. 31 (1940–41), 181–189. See also Steinschneider, *Polemische,* pp. 320–322.

37. P. VIII.

38. See, for example, Qur'ān 4:171.

39. See his letter to Obadiah the Proselyte, in *Igrot ha-Rambam,* ed. by Y. Angel, pp. 39–40.

40. However, it should be noted that while Islam categorically rejects the divinity of Jesus, it does recognize him as the last of the Hebrew prophets through whom God revealed the *Injīl* (Gospels). The Qur'ān confers several honorable titles upon Jesus. Both Mary, after whom an entire *sūra* (XIX) was named, and Jesus are spoken of with reverence. Nevertheless, the Qur'ān emphatically states that Jesus "was no other than a messenger, messengers (the like of whom) had passed away before him" (5:75). The Qur'ān unequivocably stresses the Oneness of God, 'He begetteth not nor was begotten, and there is none comparable unto Him" (Qur'ān 112:3–4). It is no wonder that Islam has been characterized by certain scholars as "a Judaism with universalistic tendencies" and as "a recast of the Jewish religion on Arab soil. . . ." See Goitein, *Jews and Arabs,* pp. 35 and 53.

41. In the Barcelona disputation (1263), Nahmanides, according to his testimony, argued that the basic Christian dogmas and doctrines could not be accepted by reason and that nature could not admit them. See his full argument in *Ramban (Nachmanides) Writings and Discourses,* vol. II, trans. and annotated by Charles B. Chavel (New York, 1978), p. 673.

42. See Berger, *The Jewish-Christian Debate* (1979).

43. Kafiḥ, *Igrot ha-Rambam,* p. 11.

44. Edited by G. R. Smith, "*The Ayyūbids,*" vol. I (1974).

45. "They were utterly divided, each tribe had its own Commander of the Faithful and a pulpit." See al-Hamdānī, *Kitāb al-Simṭ,* p. 16; Smith, *The Ayyūbids,* vol. 1, p. 52).

46. See Smith, *The Ayyūbids,* vol. 1.

47. Halkin, *Epistle,* p. II.

48. Maimonides's midrashic interpretation of these three names seems to be based on Targum Pseudo-Jonathan, *ad locum,* which reads: וצאיתא וסוברא ושתוקא .

49. Halkin, *Epistle to Yemen,* p. XVIII. It should be noted that Maimonides's *Epistle* is characterized by a strong anti-Muslim polemical thrust, the purpose of which is to vindicate the humbled and ridiculed Jewish faith and to uplift the downcast spirits of his Yemenite brethren.

50. *The Book of Beliefs and Opinions* (1948).

51. *Book of Kuzari,* p. 28.

52. The wide range of religious disputations between Muslims and Jews

revolves around several topics. Most prominent, however, are: abrogation (*naskh*), distortion or forgery in Scriptures (*taḥrīf*), and anthropomorphism (*tajsīm*).

53. *Bustān al-'Uqūl,* pp. 114–115.

54. (Cairo, 1903). See also Perlmann, "Polemics between Islam and Judaism," pp. 109–114.

55. See his "*Ifḥām al-Yahūd*" (Silencing the Jews), *PAAJR,* vol. 32 (1964).

56. *Bustān al-'Uqūl,* p. 105.

57. See Perlmann, "The Medieval Polemics," pp. 110–112.

58. *Bustān al-'Uqūl,* p. 106.

59. Of all the many prophets named in the Qur'ān only six were dignified with special titles: Adam *Ṣafīy Allāh* (the Chosen of God); Noah *Nabī Allāh* (the Prophet of God); Abraham *Khalīl Allāh* (the Friend of God); Moses *Kalīm Allāh* (the Converser with God); and Jesus *Rūḥ Allāh* (the Spirit of God).

60. *Bustān al-ᶜUqūl* pp. 108–109. The origin of the doctrine of abrogation known as *naskh* is in Qur'ān 2:106 which reads, "such of Our revelations as We abrogate or cause to be forgotten, We bring (in place) one better or the like thereof." (See also 16:101.) This doctrine, according to which later divine messages or revelations may abrogate earlier ones, is unique to the Qur'ān and is not to be found in other sacred Scriptures. In its narrower sense, this theory refers to the abrogation of all previous sacred Scriptures, claiming that the "Qur'ān is a divine revelation which took the place of previous revelations" (Ali, *The Religion of Islam,* p. 34, n. 8). An extensive theology has developed around the concept of *naskh* both in Islam and in Judaism. See Jeffery, *Islam,* pp. 66–68; Gätje, *The Qur'ān,* pp. 57–59; Saᶜadia Gaon, *The Book of Beliefs,* pp. 157–173; Zuker, *Berurim,* pp. 33–34.

61. *Bustān al-ᶜUqūl,* p. 105.

62. Ibid., p. 105.

63. For example, Maimonides asserted that the teachings of both Christ and Muḥammad "only served to clear the way for king Messiah, to prepare the whole world to worship God with one accord. . . ." See the non-censored version of *Hilkhot Melakhim,* ch. XI:4, in Mossad Harav Kook edition. See also Isadore Twersky, *A Maimonides Reader,* pp. 226–227.Rabbi Yehuda Halevi wrote in a similar vein: *Kuzari,* pp. 226–227. It should be stressed that this notion, according to which prophets were sent by God to all nations and in every age in order to direct human progress to a predestined goal, is very fundamental to Islam. However, whereas Jewish thinkers conceived the culmination of this process in the advent of the Messiah, Islam saw the grand aim of the divine scheme culminating in the advent of one universal prophet, Muḥammad, whose coming has been prepared by the national prophets. Thus Muḥammad is viewed as the final prophet, to all peoples, sent by Allāh for the regeneration of all humanity. See Qur'ān 7:158, 68:52; 81:27; 38:87; 21:107. See also 3:80–84. The origin of this notion, its interreligious development, and its reflection in medieval theological and philosophical works is undoubtedly deserving of a thorough study of its own.

64. See his introduction to *Epistle to Yemen,* p. VIII.

65. *Bustān al-ᶜUqūl,* p. 108.

66. *Epistle to Yemen,* pp. VIII–IX.

67. See Boaz's translation of Halkin's *Epistle to Yemen,* p. 11.

68. *Gan ha-Sekhalim,* pp. 7–10.

69. See Guttman, *Philosophies of Judaism,* p. 50.

70. See above, n. 14.
71. On the overall nature and significance of the Cairo Geniza, see Goitein, *A Mediterranean Society,* vol. 1 (1967), pp. 1–28.
72. B. Lewin, "*'Igrot Ga'on mi-Bavel le'Ereṣ Yaman ve-Yamama,*" *Ginze Qedem,* 3, 14–23.
73. Jacob Mann, *The Jews in Egypt and in Palestine Under the Fātimid Caliphs,* vol. II (1979), pp. 366–367.
74. Goitein, "*Temikhatam shel Yehude Teman,*" *Tarbiz,* 31 (1966), 357–370. See also Goitein, "*Yahadut Teman ben Ge'onut Misra'im,*" *Sinai,* 33 (1953), 225–237.
75. *Epistle to Yemen,* p. 1.
76. See W. Heyd, *Histoire du Commerce du Levant au Moyen Age,* vol. I (Leipzig, 1885–1886), pp. 378–379 et passim; David Neustadt, "*Qavvim le-Toledot ha-Kalkalah shel ha-Yehudim,*" *Sinai,* 2 (1937), 216–255; J. Gavin, *Aden Under British Rule,* pp. 1–38; R. B. Serjeant, *The Portuguese Off the South Arabian Coast,* (1974)[2]; Abir Mordechai, "*ha-Saḥar ha-Benle'ummi ve-ha-Yehudim be-Teman,*" in *Pe^c amim,* 5 (1980), 5–28.
77. See Ingrams, *The Yemen,* London (1963), p. 5.
78. See Goitein, "*Temanim bi-Rushala'im u-ve-Miṣra'im,*" *Har'ael,* pp. 133–148.
79. Goitein, *Letters of Medieval Jewish Traders,* p. 186. For the participation of Jews of Aden in the Indian trade, see Eli Strauss, *Massa^c le-Hodu, Zion,* 4 (1939), 217–231.
80. See Adler, *Jewish Travellers,* pp. 100–101. The fragment was previously published with a facsimile in Adler's *Von Ghetto zu Ghetto,* pp. 197–200, and is preserved in the Jewish Theological Library in New York.
81. See Goitein, *Letters of Medieval Jewish Traders,* p. 14; see also Kafiḥ, "*Qehillat San^c a she-be-Teman,*" *Maḥana'im* 119 (1968), 38.
82. See Goitein, *Mediterranean Society,* vol. 1, pp. 42–59.
83. Ibid., p. 57. See also Goitein, "*Temanim bi-Rushala'im u-ve-Miṣra'im,*" *Har'ael,* pp. 133–148.
84. The so-called "Pact of ^c Umar" stipulated the conditions under which *dhimmīs* (non-Muslims) were allowed to live in Muslim countries. The pact imposed serious humiliating social and religious restrictions upon non-Muslims. However, while many of these restrictions were generally ignored by Muslim rulers, they were resurrected in times of fanatical outbursts of anti-Jewish or anti-Christian feelings. Occasionally, such outbursts found expression also in violent religious persecutions, and these triggered mass emigrations. See Goitein, *Jews and Arabs,* pp. 62–88. See also chapter IV, below.
85. See n. 78, above. The prominence of Madmun is borne out by the fact that the famous Spanish Jewish writer al-Ḥarizi dedicated his book *Taḥkemoni* or a copy of it to Madmun. See Mann, *The Jews in Egypt,* vol. 2, p. 338; also Goitein, *Letters of Medieval Jewish Traders,* p. 216, n. 2; Goitein, "*Yahadut Teman ve-Saḥar Hodu ha-Yehudi,*" *Yahadut Teman,* pp. 47–69. Of special interest is the existence of the office of *nagid,* "exilarch" in Yemen, a fact attested to by other Geniza documents. See Eli Strauss, "*Massa^c le-Hodu,*" *Zion,* 4 (1939), 217–231.
86. See Y. Kafiḥ, "Qehillat San^c a she-be-Teman," *Maḥana'im* 119 (1968), 38; Y. Nini, "*Te^c uddot Mishpaḥtiyyot mi-Tokh ha-Musawwada',*" *Moreshet Yehude Teman* (1977), pp. 118–131.
87. One of the most prominent Yemenite rabbis. He died in 1881.

88. *Levavi Yaḥsheqa ᶜOfra*" (My Heart Desires the Gazelle), *Ḥafeṣ Ḥayyim,* pp. 416–419.

89. Regions on the river of Gozan. According to 2 Kings 17:6, Shalmaneser, the king of Assyria, carried away the exiles of Samaria to these regions (722 B.C.E.).

90. *Ḥafeṣ Ḥayyim,* p. 417. See also Ratzaby, "*Teᶜuddot le-Toledot Yehude-Teman,*" *Sefunot,* vol. 2 (1958), pp. 288–289.

91. See Goitein, *Letters of Medieval Jewish Traders,* pp. 212–214. See also D. Z. Baneth, "*Mikhtav mi-Teman mi-Shenat 1202,*" *Tarbiz* 20 (1950), 205–214.

92. See Wāsiᶜī, *Ta'rīkh al-Yaman,* p. 182; Stookey, *Yemen,* p. 295.

93. Goitein, *Letters of Medieval Jewish Traders,* p. 213.

94. Ibid. pp. 216–217, 218.

95. See Mirsky, *Piyyuṭe Yosse ben Yosse* (Jerusalem, 1977).

96. Such, for example, are the poems published by Ratzaby in *Maḥan'im* (Hebrew) 39 (1959), 93–96.

97. See, for example, Abraham Epstein in his introduction to the book *Eldad ha-Dani,* pp. XVII–XIX. Reprinted in Haberman's *Kitve Avraham Epstein,* vol. 1, pp. 10–12. As early as the end of the fifteenth century, the famous Jewish traveler Obadiah da Bertinoro wrote, "The Jews [of Yemen] do not possess the books of the Talmud; all that they have are the works of R. Isaac Alfasi, together with commentaries on them, and the works of Maimonides" (See Adler, *Jewish Travellers,* p. 246).

98. "*Daf mi-Shas Teman,*" in *Sinai,* 37 (1955), 368–372. See also Yosef Tobi, *ᶜAl ha-Talmud be-Teman* (1973); A. Neubauer, "Eldad the Danite," *JQR,* 3 (1891), 541–544; Yosef Kafiḥ, "*Shas Teman,*" *Sinai,* 28 (1951), 19–23; Yehuda Ratzaby, "*Heᶜara le-Daf mi-Shas Teman,*" *Sinai,* 40 (1957), 186; Ratzaby, "*ha-Talmud Vihude Teman,*" *Maḥana'im,* 57 (1961), 124–129.

99. *'Even Sappir,* vol. 1, p. 53a.

100. See, for example, Tobi, *ᶜAl ha-Talmud be-Teman,* 1973.

101. Ibid., pp. 23–25.

102. The greatest scholar and author of the gaonic period. See the article "Saadiah Gaon" in *EJ,* 14, 543–555.

103. See Sion Maḍmoni, "*ha-Rambam ve-Noseh ha-Tefilla shel Yehude Teman,*" pp. 373–394. See also Kafiḥ, "*Qeshareha shel Yahadut Teman,*" pp. 37–41.

104. *Kitve ha-Ramban,* p. 341.

105. *'Even Sappir,* vol. 1., p. 53a.

106. See R. Degen, "*Ktovet mi-Temanᶜal 24 Mishmarot-ha-Kohanim,*" *Tarbiz,* 42 (1973), 302–303. See also E. Urbach, "*Mishmarot u-Maᶜmadot*" in ibid., 304–305.

107. *Mishmarot u-Maᶜmadot,*" 307, 308.

108. Yaᶜqūb al-Qirqisānī, *Kitāb al-'Anwār wal-Marāqib,* edited by Leon Nemoy, vol. 1, p. 135.

109. A. Neubauer, "The Literature of the Jews of Yemen," *JQR* 3 (1891), 612. Reprinted by Ktav Publishing House, 1966. See also S. Morag, "*Masorot shel Yehude Teman,*" *Yahadut Teman,* pp. 357–366; Morag, *ha-ᶜIvrit she-be-Fi Yehude Teman* (1963); idem, "*Masorot ha-Darot Bikhfifa Aḥat,*" *Har'el* (1962), pp. 157–149; idem, "*Ktav-Yad Bavli-Temani shel Massekhet Kippurim,*" pp. 11–18; Yisra'el Yevin, "*Qitᶜe Miqra mi-Teman she-Masortam Bavlit,*" in Y. Naḥum, *Ḥasifat Genuzim mi-Teman,* pp. 2–10.

110. Saphir, *'Even Sappir,* vol. 2, pp. 11–28.

111. Ibid., vol. 1, p. 53b.

112. See Kafiḥ, "*Qeshareha shel Yahadut Teman,*" pp. 29–46.
113. Halkin, *Epistle to Yemen,* p. 1.
114. Adler, *The Itinerary of Benjamin of Tudela,* p. 46. See n. 7, above.
115. Ibid., pp. 47–48.
116. Ibid., pp. 44 and 45.
117. *The Social and Religious History of the Jews,* vol. 6, p. 224.
118. *The Itinerary of Benjamin of Tudela,* p. 67.

IV
Jewish Literary Creativity in Yemen in the Thirteenth and Fourteenth Centuries

1. See G. R. Smith, "The Ayyūbids and Rasūlids—The Transfer of Power," *Islamic Culture* 43 (1969), 175–188.

2. For major works relating to the Rasulid period in Yemen, see al-Khazrajī, *al-ᶜUqūd al-Lu'lu'iya fī Ta'rīkh al-Dawla al-Rasūliya* (2 vols.); al-Hamdānī, *Kitāb al-Simṭ,* pp. 201–567. See also Stookey, *Yemen,* pp. 101–126.

3. Cf., e.g., the poetical introductions to the *Midrash ha-Gadol,* ed. by M. Margaliot (Jerusalem, 1967), pp. 17–18. Although the lines in these poems rhyme, they lack metric structure, and their style is fundamentally biblical.

4. For the linguistic, literary, and cultural impact of the Arabs on the Jews following the conquest of Islam, see Abraham Halkin, "The Judeo-Islamic Age," pp. 215–263. See also S. D. Goitein, *Jews and Arabs,* pp. 154–167.

5. Goitein, *Jews and Arabs,* p. 167.

6. Yemenite Hebrew literature consists mainly of poetry; prose writings are scant. The term "Spanish school of Hebrew literature" denotes not only the literature composed in Spain but also its offshoots in Italy and elsewhere.

7. See Kafiḥ, *Gan ha-Sekhalim* (Introduction), p. 12. See also Yosef Tobi, "*Piyyuṭ Reviᶜi,*" *Afiqim* (February 1983), 13; "*Ḥiqqui u-Maqor be-Shiratam shel Yehude Teman,*" pp. 29–38.

8. See Yehuda Ratzaby, "*mi-Sifrutam shel Yehude Teman.*", pp. 153–155. The poem *ᶜAl ha-Sheḥiṭa* is essentially a didactic poem dealing with rules of Jewish ritual slaughtering. The Yemenites were excessively devoted to the topic of *sheḥiṭa,* more so than any other Jewish community. Yemenite Hebrew literature abounds with poems, books, and treatises pertaining to this topic, written by various authors throughout the past eight centuries. Goitein remarked that he was "often astounded and put to shame" by "knowledge of the anatomy of animals and the countless questions of ritual connected with it, possessed by ordinary Yemenites" ("*The Jews of Yemen,*" p. 231).

9. See Tobi, "*Yaᶜavor ᶜAlai Reṣonkha le-Rihal ba-Piyyuṭ ha-Temani,*" *Afiqim* (March 1970), 4 and 10.

10. *Sefer ha-Musar,* ed. by Ratzaby, p. 84.

11. "*She'erit min Diwan Abraham ben Ḥalfon,*" pp. 58–81. Five other poems were edited by Ish Shalom (*Tarbiz* 18 (1949), 187–193). An additional poem on *sheḥiṭa* was edited by Tobi, "*Shir ᶜal Hilkhot Sheḥiṭa,*" pp. 6–7.

12. See Lieberman, *Midreshe Teman* (Jerusalem, 1940); Rabinowitz, "*ha-Yeṣira ha-Midrashit shel Yehude Teman,*" *Yahadut Teman,* pp. 367–372; idem, "*Midrash Ḥadash,*" *Ḥasifat Genuzim mi-Teman,* pp. 30–37. *Midrash ha-Gadol,* edited by M. Margaliot, Genesis-Exodus (Jerusalem, 1947); S. Rabinowitz, Numbers (Jerusalem, 1967); S. Fish, Deuteronomy (Jerusalem, 1973); A. Steinsalz, Leviticus (Jerusalem, 1976).

13. See Ratzaby, *ᶜAl Meḥabbero shel Midrash ha-Gadol, Tarbiz,* 34 (1965), 263–271.

14. See A. Steinsalz, "*Darkhe ha-Ḥariza ba-Midrash ha-Gadol,*" ibid., 94–97; S. Morag, "*Darkhe ha-Ḥariza shel Meshorere Teman,*" ibid., 257–262.

15. Edited and translated into Hebrew by Yosef Kafiḥ, *Sefer Me'or ha-'Afela* (Jerusalem, 1957).

16. ha-Rofe is known by his initials Haraza (הרז"ה). For a list of his works, see *Afiqim* (February 1968), 11–12. See in particular his *Midrash ha-Ḥefeṣ,* ed. by M. Havaselet. See also Y. Naḥum's extensive article, "*Le-Toledot ha-Raza,*" pp. 180–237.

17. Edited, translated, and annotated by David Blumenthal, *The Commentary of R. Ḥōṭer ben Shelōmō to the Thirteen Principles of Maimonides* (Leiden, 1974). See Y. Naḥum, "*Le-Toledot R. Ḥoṭer be-Rav Shelomo ben al Muᶜallim,*" *Ḥasifat Genuzim mi-Teman,* pp. 238–243.

18. For a succinct presentation on the intellectual creativity in Yemen, see Blumenthal's introduction to his *Commentary of R. Ḥōṭer ben Shelōmō,* pp. 5–26.

19. See R. Kerr, *General History and Collections of Voyages and Travels,* vol. 6, p. 265.

20. See Abir, "*ha-Saḥar ha-Benle'ummi,*" *Peᶜamim,* vol. 5, pp. 5–28.

21. W. Foster, *England's Quest of Eastern Trade,* p. 194. The most significant illustration of the decline of Aden and its disappearance from the commercial map is provided by Sir Robert Grant, the Governor of Bombay, who in 1837 reported: "The harbour of Aden is excellent, and ruins of great extent prove that it was once a mart of great importance. It might again, under good management, be made the port of export of coffee, gums, and spices of Arabia, and the channel through which the produce of England and India might be spread through the rich provinces of Yemen and Hadhar-el-Mout. The trade with the African coast would also be through into the Aden market" (L. Hoskins, *British Routes to India,* p. 199).

22. The Turkish occupation of Yemen began in 1538, with the capture of Aden, Zabīd, and southern Tihāma by Sulaimān Pasha al-Khadim, the Ottoman governor of Egypt.

23. For a comprehensive list of al-Ḍahrī's works, see Ratzaby's introduction to al-Ḍahrī's *Sefer ha-Musar,* pp. 44–45.

24. *Sefer ha-Musar,* ed. by Ratzaby (Jerusalem, 1965), p. 51.

25. Ibid., p. 52. The Hebrew term *musar* has a wide range of meanings, among them being ethics, morals, chastisement, castigation, instruction, etc. Al-Ḍahrī must have had in mind the Arabic concept "'*adab*" with its wide range of humanistic connotations: belles lettres, anecdotal writings, ethical and social norms of behavior, etc. (See the article "'*Adab*" in *EI*², 1, 174.

26. Al-Ḥarīrī's *maqāmāt* were extremely popular and gave rise to countless imitations in various languages, including Hebrew. See "al-Ḥarīrī," *EI*², vol. 3, pp. 221–222.

27. See Ratzaby, "*Hashpaᶜat al-Ḥarīrī ᶜal al-Ḍahrī,*" *Biqqoret u-Farshanut,* 11–12 (1978), 55–83. Yehuda al-Ḥarīzī rendered into Hebrew the *maqāmāt* of the Arabic poet al-Ḥarīrī in a book, which he entitled *Maḥbarot Iti'el* (ed. by Y. Peretz, 1951). Al-Ḥarīzī's major work, however, is his *Sefer Taḥkemoni* (ed. by Y. Toporowsky, 1952), trans. into English by Victor E. Reichert (*The Tahkemoni of Judah al-Harizi* (Jerusalem, 1965), which consists of fifty *maqāmāt.* Most intriguing is the fact that al-Ḥarīzī's *Taḥkemoni* provides us

with the only written evidence of a direct personal contact between a Spanish Hebrew poet and Jews in Yemen. On p. 350 of his book (ed. by Toporowsky), al-Ḥarīzī mentioned "Rabbi Seʿadia of Yemen, 'who is intelligent, delightful, and of immeasurable wisdom.' " Moreover, al-Ḥarīzī dedicated a copy of his book to Shemaria ben David of Yemen (Introduction, ed. by Kaminka, 1889, pp. XXXVI).

28. *Sefer ha-Musar,* p. 53.

29. Ibid., ch. 5, p. 112.

30. Ibid., Introduction, pp. 51–52. The details provided by al-Ḍahrī with respect to this event are vague and it is difficult to determine whether the decree affected all the Jews of Yemen or only those of Sanaa. It should be stressed that the narrative is written in rhymes, a fact which imposed considerable limitations upon the author. Moreover, writing history was not the primary concern of the book.

31. Ibid., ch. 2, pp. 68, 69.

32. Ibid., ch. 12, p. 169.

33. *al-Barq al-Yamanī fī al-Fatḥ al-ʿUthmānī,* pp. 95–99. See also Musṭafā Sālim, *al-Fatḥ al-ʿUthmānī al-ʾAwwāl lil-Yaman,* pp. 165–192; Stookey, *Yemen,* p. 134.

34. See al-Nahrawālī, *al-Barq al-Yamanī,* pp. 128–129; Stookey, *Yemen,* pp. 137–148.

35. See ch. 6, pp. 116–123; ch. 23, pp. 261–266; ch. 10, pp. 146–157, respectively.

36. Ch. 3, pp. 78, 81, 82–83.

37. See, for example, ibid., ch. 19, pp. 224–226.

38. *Qoveṣ ʿal-Yad,* vol. 5 (1984), pp. 9–14. Other passages and chapters from the book were published later on by others in various periodicals. The complete and annotated text of the book was published in 1965 by Ratzaby, based on four manuscripts. See Ratzaby's introduction to *Sefer ha-Musar,* pp. 23–25.

39. See Wāsiʿī, *Taʾrīkh,* p. 52.

40. See A. al-Madaḥ, *al-ʿUthmānīyūn wal-ʾImām al-Qāsim* (1982); M. al-Ḥaddad, *Taʾrīkh al-Yaman al-Siyāsi,* pp. 315–332; and F. Abaẓa, *al-Ḥukm al-ʿUthmānī fī al-Yaman* (Cairo, 1975).

41. See Ratzaby, "Mered al-Qāsim," *Zion* 20 (1955), 32–46.

42. Based on Prov. 10:7.

43. *Ḥemdat Yamim,* vol. 2, p. 208.

44. See Ms. Or. 3329 and Tritton, *The Rise of the Imams of Sanaa,* pp. 2 and 117.

45. Two of these laments were published by Ratzaby, "Mered al-Qāsim," pp. 32–46. A third one was published by Tobi in *Afiqim* (1977), pp. 13–14.

46. See Ratzaby, "Mered al-Qāsim," p. 41.

47. Ibid., p. 44.

48. The major part of his extant poems has been published; see Mekiton, *Ḥafeṣ Ḥayyim;* Ratzaby, *Yalqut Shire Teman;* Seri and Tobi, *Shirim Ḥadashim le-Rabbi Shalom Shabazi.* The salient feature of his commentary *Ḥemdat Yamim* (2 volumes) is the mystical approach.

49. See the collections of legends in Seʿadia Ḥoze, *Sefer Toledot ha-Rav Shalom Shabazi,* pp. 24–45.

50. Gen. 49:10.

51. Seven years before the birth of Sabbatai Ṣevi (1626–1678).

52. Confusion of two verses: Gen. 7:7 and Gen. 41:46.

53. *Ḥemdat Yamim,* vol. 2, p. 208. See also R. Yisra'el Hakkohen, *Sefer Segullat Yisra'el,* vol. 2, p. 172.
54. *EI*[1], vol. 1, p. 497.
55. *al-Barq al-Yamanī,* p. 171.
56. See *Ḥemdat Yamim,* vol. 2, p. 208.
57. See Ratzaby, "*Appoqalipsot ve-Ḥishuve Qeṣ,*" p. 313.
58. Refers to Lev. 25:13, "In this year of Jubilee each of you shall return to his property."
59. Ephraim is a reference to Messiah ben-Yosef. According to Jewish tradition, Messiah ben-Yosef (also named ben-Ephraim) is a belligerent Messiah distinguished from the spiritual Messiah ben-David. See Klausner, *The Messianic Idea,* pp. 402–403. Yinnon is a reference to Messiah ben-David (see Ps. 72:17).
60. See the poem in Ratzaby, "*Teᶜuddot le-Toledot Yehude Teman,*" pp. 295–296.
61. *Taᶜrīkh al-Yaman,* p. 56. His full name was al-Ḥasīn ibn al-Ḥusain ibn al-Qāsim. In the body of the poem, Shabazi referred to him by the name Ḥasīn ibn Shams al-Dīn.
62. See chapter VI on *Galut Mauzaᶜ*, below.
63. *Ḥafeṣ Ḥayyim,* p. 8.
64. Ibid., p. 70. The expression, "thirsting like a hind," is based on Ps. 42:2,6.
65. H. Brody, *Selected Poems on Jehudah Halevi,* p. 2; see also pp. 3–7.
66. *Ḥafeṣ Ḥayyim,* p. 241.
67. Ibid, p. 171.
68. See Erwin I. J. Rosenthal, *Judaism and Islam,* p. 7. On the status of the Jews in Muslim lands, see Jacob R. Marcus, *The Jew in the Medieval World,* pp. 13–19.
69. Israel Zinberg, *A History of Jewish Literature,* vol. 1, trans. and ed. by Bernard Martin, pp. 65–69, 85.
70. Moses Maimonides, *The Commentary to Mishnah Aboth,* trans. by Arthur David (New York, 1968), pp. 19–23; see also Neal Kozodoy, "Reading Medieval Hebrew Love Poetry," *AJS Review,* 2, (1977), 111–113; Ḥayyim Schirmann, "*ha-Rambam ve-Hashira ha-ᶜIvirt,*" pp. 433–436.
71. On the *qaṣīda,* see the entry "*Kaṣida*" in *EI*[2], vol. IV, pp. 713–714; H. A. R. Gibb, *Arabic Literature,* London, pp. 13–31; Régis Blachère, *Histoire de la littérature Arab,* 3 vols. (Paris, 1952–1966), and see his exhaustive index and bibliography; Mary Catherine Bateson, *Structural Continuity in Poetry: A Linguistic Study of Five Pre-Islamic Arab Odes* (Paris, 1970), pp. 23–39; Renate Jacobi, *Studien zur Poetik der alterabischen Qaside* (Wiesbaden, 1971); Reynold A. Nicholson, *A Literary History of the Arabs* (Cambridge, England, 1966), pp. 76–78; Linda F. Compton, *Andalusian Lyrical Poetry and Old Spanish Love Songs: The Muwashshaḥ and its Kharja* (New York, 1976); Michael Zwettler, *The Oral Tradition of Classical Arabic Poetry* (Columbus, 1978), pp. 28–29, 42–43, 61–62, et passim.
72. This artistic shift from the erotic introduction to the subject proper is known in Spanish Hebrew poetry as יפי הפתיחה (the beauty of extrication or release). See D. Yelin, *Torat ha-Shira ha-Sefaradit,* pp. 73–88.
73. See the poem, "'*Emuna 'Eslo 'Amana*" in M. Bet-Aryeh, "*Emunah,*" pp. 37–50.
74. *Ḥafeṣ Ḥayyim,* p. 8.
75. Ibid., p. 9. The bridegroom is God, and the bride is Kneset Israel.

76. Ibid., p. 151. For the qabbalist, *shekhina* serves as a technical term for the tenth *sefirah.* The *shekhina,* or "bride," is now separated and exiled from her husband (God), but with the advent of messianic times, she will be restored to perpetual union with her husband. See Scholem, *Sabbatai Sevi,* p. 17.

77. *Ḥafeẓ Ḥayyim,* p. 5.

78. Goitein, *From the Land of Sheba,* p. 21.

79. Joseph Klausner, *The Messianic Idea in Israel,* p. 400.

80. Zohar, Leviticus 194:2.

81. *Ḥafeẓ Ḥayyim,* p. 141.

82. See Ratzaby, "*Gevurat Bene Dan u-Vene Rekhav,*" pp. 130–137.

83. *Ḥafeẓ Ḥayyim,* p. 3.

84. *Taḥkemoni* (Warsaw, 1889), pp. 40–41.

85. *In the High Yemen,* p. 92.

86. It was too close to the Sabbath eve, and they did not wish to desecrate the holy day.

87. Ḥoze, *Sefer Toledot ha-Rav Shalom Shabazi,* p. 32. See also Dov Noy, "*Peṭirat R. Shalom Shabazi,*" pp. 132–149; *idem,* "*R. Shalem Shabazi be-Aggadat ha-ᶜAm,*" pp. 106–133.

V
The Impact of the Sabbatean Movement on the Jews of Yemen

1. See, for example, Qur'ān 9:29, which enjoins the Muslims to "fight against such of those who have been given the Scripture . . . , and follow not the religion of truth, until they pay the tribute readily, being brought low."

2. The Pact of ᶜUmar was probably initiated about 637 C.E. by ᶜUmar I, after the conquest of Christian Syria and Palestine. There are many variants of the text, and scholars deny that the text as it now stands could have come from the pen of ᶜUmar I. It is generally assumed that the Pact was expanded by accretions, and that its present form dates from about the ninth century. Although this Pact was originally concluded by ᶜUmar and the conquered Christians, its regulations were binding upon all non-Muslims. Thus, the limitations directed against the Christians and their churches applied also to the Jews and their synagogues. For extensive studies of this Pact, see Antoine Fattal, *Le statut légal des non-musulmans en pays d'Islam* (Beirut, 1958); A. S. Trilton, *The Caliphs and their Non-Muslim Subjects,* London, 1930. See also Norman A. Stillman, *The Jews of Arab Lands,* pp. 157–161; Jane S. Gerber, "The Pact of ᶜUmar in Morocco," *Proceedings of the Seminar on Muslim-Jewish Relations in North Africa,* pp. 40–50. J. R. Marcus, "*The Jew in the Medieval World: A Source Book,* pp. 13–15. For the Mamluk's version of the Pact of ᶜUmar, see al-Qalqashandī, *Subḥ al-Aᶜsha,* vol. 13 (Cairo, 1293/1918), pp. 378–379. See the translation of these pages in Stillman, *The Jews of the Arab Lands,* pp. 273–274. See also L. A. Mayer, "ᶜ*Emdat ha-Yehudim Bime ha-Mamlukim,*" *Sefer Magnes* (Jerusalem, 1938), pp. 161–167.

3. E. Strauss, "The Social Isolation of *Ahl Adh-Dhimma,*" *Études orientales à la mémoire de Paul Hirschler,* p. 76.

4. See Jacob Mann, *The Jews in Egypt and in Palestine Under the Fāṭimid Caliphs,* vol. I, pp. 32–33.

5. Strauss, "The Social Isolation," p. 81.

6. See Philipp K. Hitti, *History of the Arabs,* pp. 620–621.

7. Strauss, "The Social Isolation," p. 77.

8. See Jacob R. Marcus, *The Jews in the Medieval World,* pp. 13–19.

9. Compare this position of the Jew as the *dhimmī par excellence* with that of Morocco, where "there have been no native Maghrebi Christians since at least the time of Almohads (1147–1269)." N. Stillman, "Muslims and Jews in Morocco: Perceptions, Images, Stereotypes," *Proceedings of the Seminar on Muslim-Jewish Relations in North Africa,* pp. 13–27.

10. On the attitude of the Zaydīs in Yemen toward the Jews, see Goitein, *Jews and Arabs,* pp. 35 and 53; M. Sadoq, "*ha-Yeḥasim ben ha-Yehudim ve-ha-^{c}Aravim be-Teman,*" *Yahadut Teman,* pp. 147–163. See also the article "al-Zaidiya" in EI^1, vol. 4, pp. 1196–1198.

11. See Goitein, *Jews and Arabs,* pp. 73–74; Ṣadoq, "*ha-Yeḥasim,*" p. 153.

12. See G. Scholem, *Sabbatai Ṣevi* (1973); S. Sharot, *Messianism, Mysticism and Magic* (1982), pp. 86–87.

13. *Ḥemdat Yamim,* vol. 2, p. 208.

14. *Qorot Yisra'el be-Teman,* pp. 257–258. See also ibid, pp. 252–255; M. Kehati, "*ha-Tenu^{c}a ha-Shavta'it be-Teman,*" *Zion* 5 (1933), 78–88.

15. See A. Z. Idelsohn, "*ha-Meshorer ha-Temani R. Shalom ben Yosef Shabazi ve-Shirato ha^{c}ivrit,*" in *Mizraḥ u-Ma^{c}arav,* vol. I (1920), p. 13.

16. Based on Isa. 24:16. Shabazi substituted *ṣevi ṣaddiq,* "the righteous Ṣevi" (reference to Sabbatai Ṣevi) for the biblical *Ṣevi le-Ṣaddiq,* "glory for the righteous."

17. *Ḥafeṣ Ḥayyim,* p. 585. See also Shabazi's poem *Mesos Ḥatan,* ibid, p. 643.

18. The full title of this work as designated by Gershom Scholem is "*Ge Ḥizzayon: A Sabbatian Apocalypse from Yemen,*" in *Qoveṣ ^{c}al-Yad,* n.s. 4 (Jerusalem, 1966), 103–141. Ḥabshush remarked that this book is full of "allusions and secrets," referring to Sabbatai Ṣevi ("*Qorot Yisra'el be-Teman,*" p. 252).

19. Isa. 25:9.

20. Jer. 23:6. An esoteric reference to *ṣevi ṣaddiq,* "the righteous Ṣevi" (Isa. 24:16). See n. 16, above.

21. *Ge Ḥizayyon,* p. 116.

22. See Sharot, *Messianism,* p. 89.

23. Published by Yosef Tobi under the name "*ha-Kronika ^{c}al Gzerat ha-^{c}Aṭarot: Me'ora^{c}ot ha-Shavta'ut be-Teman (1667) le-Rabbi Se^{c}adia Halevi,*" in Tobi, *Toledot Yehude Teman: mi-Kitvehem,* pp. 51–52.

24. Ibid., p. 51. As an illustration of the heightened messianic expectations, Ḥabshush (*Qorot Yisra'el be-Teman,* pp. 258–259), provided us with an intriguing story regarding an old and lonely Jewish woman, who was greatly concerned lest the Messiah would come in the middle of the night and she, being hard of hearing, might not hear his call. She, therefore, bought a donkey, tied her leg with a rope to the donkey's neck, hoping that the messianic excitement in the Jewish quarter would cause the donkey to bray and thus wake her up. See the English translation of the story in Goitein, *From the Land of Sheba,* pp. 121–122.

25. *Toledot Yehude Teman,* p. 52.

26. "*Te^{c}uddot le-Toledot Yehude Teman,*" *Sefunot,* vol. 2 (1958), pp. 292–293.

27. See Num. 17:11.

28. See Lam. 2:3.

29. See Mic. 5:7.

30. See Lam. 3:5.

31. *Zed,* which in Hebrew means evildoer, is a play on the word Zaydī, and thus a covert reference to the governing Shī^{c}ite Muslim sect in Yemen.

32. See Isa. 10:34.
33. See Zech. 12:12.
34. See Jer. 13:16.
35. See Isa. 49:22.
36. Isa. 60:22.
37. Referring to the redemption as prophesied by Dan. 12:12.
38. "*Qorot Yisra'el be-Teman,*" pp. 252–253.
39. These sources consist mainly of memoirs and notes by Yemenite writers in colophons and flyleaves of the bindings of manuscripts, Yemenite Muslim chronicles, and oral traditions.
40. This imām was called al-Mutawakkil, not Mahdī (1607–1659). See al-Wāsiʿī, *Ta'rīkh al-Yaman,* p. 53. See also Kafiḥ, *Qorot Yisra'el be-Teman,* p. 252, n. 47.
41. A city northwest of Sanaa.
42. This is a pejorative used by the Muslims of Yemen for the Jewish Messiah. Kafiḥ remarked that the Yemenite Muslims refer to the Messiah also by the pejorative *al-dajjāl,* which carries the connotations of "quack," "impostor," "deceiver." For reference to this topic in the *Ḥadīth,* see Wensinck, *A Handbook of Early Muḥammadan Tradition,* pp. 50–51.
43. *Khātam al-nabīyyīn* (Qur'ān 33:40), namely, the apex of prophethood, the last and ultimate channel whereby the will of God was revealed to mankind. See Ahroni, "From *Bustān al-ʿUqūl* to *Quiṣṣat al-Batūl*" (1981), pp. 312–314.
44. Based on Amos 5:2.
45. The reference is to the maidens of Paradise, described in various passages in the Qur'ān (2:25; 3:15; 4:57; 55:56). When the Muslim enters Paradise he is welcomed by one of these beings; a large number of them are placed at his disposal, and he can cohabit with each of them as often as he has fasted in Ramaḍan and in accordance with his good deeds (56:36). See *EI*[1], vol. 2, p. 337.
46. The irony is borne out by the parodical use of Biblical verses. See, for example, Isa. 1:19–20.
47. "*Qorot Yisra'el be-Teman,*" p. 252.
48. Thus, for example, Shabazi related that some time after 1619, the year he was born, the Yemenite decreed that all Jews should convert to Islam. Many Jews, said Shabazi, converted to Islam, while others preferred death to apostasy. He said that his own father was tortured "until his clothes were stained with blood." This was because he refused to abandon his faith. *Ḥemdat Yamim,* vol. 2, p. 208.
49. The first cousin of Muḥammad and the husband of Muḥammad's daughter Fāṭima (ruled 656–661). See Hitti, *History of the Arabs,* pp. 179–182.
50. See I Kings 14:15.
51. See I Chron. 5:26. The references seem to be to the Jews of Khaybar and Ḥijāz, who were crushed and expelled by Muḥammad. See above, Ch. 4.
52. The formula *la Ilāh illā Allāh wa-Muḥammad Rasūl Allāh,* "there is no God but God and Muḥammad is the messenger of God," is the most frequently repeated Islamic saying. It briefly sums up the central notions of Islam, namely, the unity of God (*tawḥīd*) and the status of Muḥammad as the seal of the prophets (*khātam al-nabīyyīn*).
53. Ezek. 18:23.
54. *Qorot Yisra'el be-Teman,* pp. 253–254.

55. See Ahroni, "*From Bustān al-ᶜUqūl to Qiṣṣat al-Batūl,* pp. 311–360.
56. Ps. 116:15.
57. Deut. 13:4.
58. See the discussion of this concept in Ahroni, "From Bustān al-ᶜUqūl to Qiṣṣat al-Batūl," pp. 327–330.
59. Reference to the "Writ of Protection" discussed in Ch. 4, above.
60. *Qorot Yisra'el be-Teman,* p. 254.
61. Ibid., pp. 254–255.
62. Ibid., p. 249.
63. For a discussion and evaluation of the various traditions, see Ibn Khaldun, *The Muqaddimah,* vol. 2, pp. 156–186. See also the references in Wensinck, *The Oral Traditions of Islam,* p. 139.
64. Ibn Khaldūn, *The Muqaddimah,* p. 160.
65. Ibid., pp. 156–186. See also the article "Mahdī" in *EI*[1], vol. 3, pp. 111–115. Some traditions identify the Mahdī with ᶜIsa (Jesus), saying "There is no Mahdī except Jesus, the son of Mary" (Ibn Khaldun, *The Muqaddimah,* p. 185). It should be noted that the term *mahdī* ("the divinely guided one") has also been used by certain individuals as an honorific title. In Islamic eschatology, however, it refers exclusively to the future deliverer. See *EI*[1], vol. 3, pp. 111–115.
66. See *EI*[1], vol. 1, pp. 406–412; D. Donaldson, *The Shīᶜite Religion,* pp. 226–241.
67. *Ta'rīkh al-Yaman,* pp. 22–23. See also pp. 55, 114, 252.
68. *al-Muqtataf min Ta'rīkh al-Yamān,* pp. 185–186. See also Stookey, *Yemen.* p. 154.
69. See Ḥabshush, *Qorot Yisra'el be-Teman,* p. 249; Goitein, "*ha-Mashiaḥ mi-Beiḥan,*" *Ha'areṣ* (November 17, 1950), p. 5.
70. See Ḥabshush, *Qorot Yisra'el be-Teman,* pp. 260–262.
71. Many of these decrees were no different from those enacted against Jews and Christians by various Muslim rulers in the vast Muslim empire during various phases of history.
72. See n. 2, above, *Toledot Yehude Teman,* p. 52.
73. This date is given by Rabbi Sāliḥ, "*Megillat Teman,*" p. 11. Ḥabshush, however, dated this enactment in 1673 (*Qorot Yisra'el be-Teman,* p. 257).
74. See Ḥabshush, *Qorot Yisra'el be-Teman,* p. 257.
75. *Ḥafeṣ Ḥayyim,* p. 142. The *ᶜatara* in Hebrew has the connotation of crown, diadem, glory. Thus, the poet views the prohibition of wearing headgear as depriving the Jews of their glory.
76. See Seri and Tobi, eds., *Shirim Ḥadashim le-Rabbi Shalom Shabazi,* pp. 135–136. The *ᶜAtarot* decree was referred to by two other contemporary Jewish poets: Dahood ibn Salem wrote, "*walʼimām 'alqadīm qad shāl 'alᶜamā'em*" (and the previous Imam has taken away the headgear) (see Ratzaby, "*Galut Mauzaᶜ,*" *Sefunot,* vol. 5 (1961), p. 370). Mussalam complained, "*min yaum zāl minna alᶜamā'em . . .* ," "from the day our headgears were removed. . . " (ibid., p. 376). It should be noted that similar humiliating edicts were imposed by the Almohades upon the Jews of the Maghreb. Thus, the historiographer of the Almohades, Abdo-'l Wāḥid al-Marrekoshī, related that the Almohad ruler Abu Yūsuf (1184–1192) decreed that the Jews of the Maghrib should wear ugly blue clothes and, instead of turbans, long veils "of the ugliest form that reach under their ears." ("*The History of the Almohades,* ed. by Dozy, p. 223.) See also E. Strauss, "The Social Isolation of *Ahl adh-dhimma,*" *Études Orientales,* p. 77.

77. *Sa^c^arat Teman,* p. 8.

78. Ibid. The Yemenite Yosef Madmoni related an intriguing incident which befell a group of Yemenite Jewish immigrants, who in 1882 were on their way from Yemen to Palestine aboard an Italian ship. A severe storm forced all the passengers of the ship to spend some time in the port of Jedda (Saudi Arabia). The dangling earlocks aroused curiosity among the Muslims of Jedda, who had never seen a Jew with earlocks before. Concerned with the safety of his Jewish passengers, who were forced to land in a hostile environment, the captain of the Italian ship took scissors and clipped the earlocks of all the male children, saying, "When you arrive in Palestine, you can allow your earlocks to grow as freely as you wish." The children, said Madmoni, burst into tears at the loss of their most treasured "possessions," and they felt utterly disgraced without them (see Y. Nini, *Teman ve-Ṣion,* p. 201).

A humorous but revealing story relating to the earlocks was told by Rabbi Kafiḥ (*Gan ha-Sekhalim,* p. 8, n. 1): A sharp and witty Jew, who passed through one of the Muslim streets, saw a group of Muslim boys gathered around an emaciated dog. The boys were cruelly beating the dog for biting one of the boys, who had provoked it. Seeing the Jew, one of the Muslim boys cried toward him, "Come and see, they are beating your brother." The Jew "earnestly" approached the dog and examined it and summarily dismissed the whole thing, saying, "This is not my brother. Can't you see that he has no earlocks?" The Jew, continued Kafiḥ, was later incarcerated for hinting that the dog was Muslim.

79. *Sefer Sheveṭ Yehuda le-Rabbi Shelomo ben Virga,* p. 207, n. 25.

80. *The History of the Turkish Empire,* p. 212.

81. *Sabbatai Sevi: The Mystical Messiah 1626–1676,* pp. 457, 458, and 458, n. 305. See also the article "Juden" in *Lexikon der christlischen Ikonographie,* vol. 2 (1970), pp. 449–454.

82. The Yemenite Muslims called the earlocks *zanānīr.*

83. The similarities between the Jews of Yemen and those of the Maghrib are indeed very striking. This is certainly a most interesting domain which requires a full-fledged and detailed investigation, which, it is hoped, will be undertaken in the near future. See H. Z. Hirschberg, *A History of the Jews in North Africa,* vol. I (Leiden, 1974; vol. 2 is available only in Hebrew). See also Norman Stillman, "Muslims and Jews in Morroco: Perceptions, Images, Stereotypes," in *Proceedings of the Seminar on Muslim-Jewish Relations in North Africa* (New York, 1974), pp. 13–27.

84. *Jews and Arabs,* p. 75.

85. "Iggeret Mahriṣ," in *Tiklal Shivat Ṣiyyon,* ed. by Yosef Kafiḥ (Jerusalem, 1952; the pages of the epistle are not numbered).

86. *Sa^c^arat Teman,* p. 26.

87. See Ḥabshush, *Qorot Yisra'el be-Teman,* pp. 274–275; Koraḥ, *Sa^c^arat Teman,* pp. 26–27. It should be noted that this degrading edict was not unique to Yemen.

88. al-Mutawakkil Muḥammad ibn Yaḥia ibn al-Manṣūr. See al-Wāsi^c^ī, *Ta'rīikh al-Yaman,* p. 72.

89. *Qorot Yisra'el be-Teman,* pp. 274–275.

90. *Ibid.,* p. 275.

91. The epistle was discovered by Ratzaby in a flyleaf which was used for the binding of a book, and published by him in his article "*Gerush Mauza^c^,*" pp. 203–207. Ḍuran is a village in Yemen, southwest of Sanaa.

92. Written by Se^c^adia ben-Yosef. See Ratzaby, *Yalquṭ,* p. 85.

93. See Ibn al-Fūṭī, *al-Ḥawādeth al-jāmiᶜa,* pp. 64–68. See also A. Ben-Jacob, *Meqorot Ḥadashim,* p. 64.

94. The letter was published in the *Jewish Chronicle,* September 18, 1863, p. 5. In this letter Montefiore implored the British Foreign Minister to intervene on behalf of the Jews of Yemen, "to direct the interposition of the British Consular Agent at Sanaa, or at Aden," so that he may use his influence with the authorities of Sanaa to take steps to alleviate the suffering of the Yemenite Jews. From another letter, dated December 16, 1873, written by the President of the Anglo-Jewish Association and addressed to Earl Granville, the British Foreign Minister, we learn that British intercession on behalf of the Yemenite Jews was deemed impossible. The British Governor of Aden stated that: "inasmuch as Sanaa was at that moment in a state of anarchy, it was impossible for him to carry out the instructions of Her Majesty's Government, and to effect any change in the conditions of the Jews of Yemen."

95. *Arabian Peak and Desert* (New York, 1930), pp. 82, 83.

96. *Ḥafeṣ Ḥayyim,* p. 142.

97. Ibid., p. 151.

98. Ibid., p. 69.

99. *Dhimmīs* in Yemen referred exclusively to Jews, who were the only non-Muslim minority there.

100. In Seri and Tobi, eds, *Shirim Ḥadashim,* p. 174.

101. Ibid., p. 135–136.

102. *Qorot Yisra'el be-Teman,* p. 248.

103. See Lybyer, *The Government of the Ottoman Empire in the Time of Suleiman the Magnificent* (1913), pp. 90–113. See also *EI*², vol. 2, pp. 210–212.

104. See Palmer, "The Origin of the Janissaries," *BJRL,* 35 (1952–53), 448–481; *EI*², vol. 2, p. 210.

105. See *EI*², vol. 2, p. 211; Palmer, "The Origin," p. 467; Lybyer, *The Government,* p. 51.

106. *EI*², vol. 2, p. 211.

107. Lybyer, *The Government,* pp. 51, 53, 54.

108. Children whose *father* died before they reached puberty.

109. See, for example, *Saḥīḥ Muslim,* vol. IV, pp. 1398–1399. Referring to this *ḥadīth,* al-Ghazālī said, "I heard, too, the tradition related to the Prophet of God according to which he said 'Everyone who is born is born with a sound nature; it is his parents who make him a Jew or a Christian or a Magian.' " See W. Montgomery Watt, *The Faith and practice of al-Ghazali* (reprint; Lahore, 1963), p. 21.

110. See Goitein, *Jews and Arabs,* pp. 77–78; *EI*², vol. 2, p. 932.

111. Kafiḥ, *Halikhot Teman,* p. 107.

112. See A. S. Halkin, "*le-Toledot ha-Shemad bime ha-'Almuwaḥḥidīn,*" *The Joshua Starr Memorial Volume,* pp. 101–110. Halkin in "*le-Toledot*" quoted extensively from Ibn ᶜAqnin's manuscript. See also D. Corcos, "*le-'Ofi Yaḥasam shel Shalliṭe ha'almuwaḥḥidun la-Yehudim,*" *Zion,* 32 (1967), 137–160.

113. *Halikhot Teman,* p. 107.

VI
The Exile of the Yemenite Jews to Mauzaᶜ (1679)

1. Al-Mahdī ascended the throne in 1676, following the death of his uncle al-Mutawakkil. He ruled Yemen for five years (1676–1681), considered the most turbulent years in the known history of Yemenite Jewry.

2. For a comprehensive study of this topic, see Y. Ratzaby, "*Galut Mauza*^{c}, *Zion*, 37 (1972), 197–215; idem, "*Gerush Mauza*^{c}," *Sefunot*, vol. 5 (1961), pp. 339–395.
3. The story is related in Abraham ^{c}Arusi's *Qore ha-Dorot* and published by Ratzaby in his "*Galut Mauza*^{c}," pp. 391–395. Another version of the story is related by Manṣura. See ibid., pp. 383–390.
4. See Muḥammad al-Shukānī, *al-Badr al-Tāle*^{c}, vol. I, pp. 43–44.
5. See Ḥabshush, *Qorot Yisra'el be-Teman*, p. 248.
6. See ch. IV, n. 2, above.
7. See Gottheil, "Dhimmis and Moslems in Egypt," pp. 353–414.
8. See al-Wāsi^{c}ī, *Ta'rīkh al-Yaman*, p. 52; Playfair, *A History of Arabia Felix or Yemen*, pp. 111–112.
9. See Ratzaby, "*Mered al-Qāsim*," pp. 32–46.
10. See Qur'ān 2:219, 4:43; 5:90. See also the article "Khamr" in EI^2, vol. 4, p. 994.
11. See Idelsohn, "*ha-Meshorer ha-Temani R. Shalom Shabazi*," p. 11.
12. Ḥabshush, *Qorot Yisra'el be-Teman*, p. 262.
13. See ch. II, n. 9, above.
14. *Dofi ha-Zeman*, pp. 213–214.
15. Ratzaby, "*Gerush Mauza*^{c}," p. 213.
16. Ibid., pp. 384–385.
17. See Ahroni, "From Bustān al-^{c}Uqūl," p. 342. It should be noted that although the Hebrew Scriptures and the Rabbis deprecate drunkenness and look upon it as a serious evil (see Prov. 20:1, 21:17; 23:19–21; 29:35; see also B. Ned. 10a and Erub. 64a), the drinking of wine in moderation is rather encouraged and even considered a blessing (see Judg. 9;13; Prov. 31:6–7; Ps. 104:15; Eccl. 10:19 See also BB 58b, Gen. R. 15:7).
18. Ratzaby, "*Galut Mauza*^{c}," p. 382.
19. Ibid., p. 366.
20. Ibid., p. 380.
21. Ibid., p. 352.
22. *Ḥafeṣ Ḥayyim*, p. 137.
23. *Qorot Yisra'el be-Teman*, p. 262.
24. Ibid., pp. 262, 262–263.
25. *Al-Badr al Tāle*^{c}, vol. I, p. 46.
26. Ibid., p. 45. See also Ratzaby, "*Galut Mauza*^{c}," pp. 340–341.
27. Ratzaby, "*Galut Mauza*^{c}," p. 370.
28. Ratzaby, "*Gerush Mauza*^{c}," p. 207.
29. Ratzaby, "*Galut Mauza*^{c}," p. 372.
30. Ibid., p. 366.
31. Ibid., p. 360.
32. Ibid., p. 376.
33. of Dar^{c}an and al-Baqar.
34. Reference to the imām, literally, "pure of faith." See Ḥabshush, *Qorot Yisra'el be-Teman*, p. 255.
35. *Ḥafeṣ Ḥayyim*, pp. 313–315.
36. Ratzaby, "*Galut Mauza*^{c}," p. 342.
37. Ibid., p. 353.
38. *Ḥafeṣ Ḥayyim*, p. 314.
39. Ratzaby, "*Galut Mauza*^{c}," pp. 354–356.
40. Ibid., p. 358.
41. *Arabian Peak and Desert*, pp. 267–277.

42. *Ḥafeṣ Ḥayyim,* p. 14.
43. Referring to the Arabs, who according to their tradition are descendants of Ishmael, the son of Hagar. Hagar, according to Genesis (16:1; 15; 21:10), was the maidservant of Sarah.
44. See Ratzaby, "*Galut Mauza*ᶜ," p. 351.
45. The letter was discovered by Ratzaby in a flyleaf which served as the binding of a book, and was published by him in his article "*Gerush Mauza*ᶜ," pp. 203–207.
46. See Jer. 4:31.
47. Jer. 4:20.
48. See Lam. 4:15.
49. See Exod. 5:13 and Isa. 52:11.
50. See I Kings 20:37.
51. See Isa. 9:16.
52. See Mic. 3:2.
53. See Ps. 78:57.
54. See Isa. 64:5.
55. See Mal. 3:19.
56. See Num. 14:37.
57. See 2 Chron. 15:5.
58. Ratzaby, "*Gerush Mauza*ᶜ," pp. 203–205.
59. Ibid., p. 206. See also Gen. 28:17.
60. See the poem of Ibn al-Asbaṭ in Ratzaby, "*Galut Mauza*ᶜ," p. 350.
61. *Qorot Yisra'el be-Teman,* p. 263.
62. *Saᶜarat Teman,* p. 12.
63. See Idelsohn, "*ha-Meshorer ha-Temani,*" p. 11.
64. "*Galut Mauza*ᶜ," pp. 346–347.
65. "*Qorot Yisra'el be-Teman,*" p. 23; *Saᶜarat Teman,* p. 11.
66. *Saᶜarat Teman,* pp. 11–12.
67. "*Qorot Yisra'el be-Teman,*" p. 263.
68. See Eric Brauer, *Ethnologie der Jemenitischen Juden,* pp. 231–263. See also H. Scott, *In the High Yemen,* pp. 51 and 135.
69. Idelsohn, *ha-Meshorer ha-Temani,* p. 11.
70. *Megillat Teman,* p. 12.
71. "*Waṣalna Hātef al-Alḥān,*" *Ḥafeṣ Ḥayyim,* p. 314.
72. *ᶜEṣ Ḥayyim,* vol. 3, p. 159.
73. Ratzaby, *Yalquṭ,* p. 128.
74. Ibid., p. 79.
75. The poet cryptically uses names of well-known biblical nations which were hostile to Israel. The reference is, of course, to the Arabs in Yemen.
76. This refers to unclean animals according to Lev. 11:13.
77. Allusion to the *ᶜAtarot* ("headgear") decree. See above, Ch. 5.
78. Ratzaby, *Yalquṭ,* pp. 89–90.
79. *Ḥafeṣ Ḥayyim,* p. 43. The "graceful doe" is an appellative both for the Torah and Keneset Israel.
80. Ibid.

VII
Yemenite Jewry in the Eighteenth and Nineteenth Centuries

1. *Travels Through Arabia,* 2 vols. (Edinburgh, 1792); also, *Travels in Arabia* in J. Pinkerton, *A General Collection of the Best and Most Interesting Voyages,*

vol. 10 (London, 1811). Niebuhr's expedition was sponsored by King Frederick V of Denmark. Its purpose was the exploration of Arabia, particularly Yemen.

2. al-ᶜAbbās ibn al-imām al-Manṣūr Ḥasīn ibn al-Qāsim. See Wāsiᶜī, *Ta'rīkh al-Yaman,* pp. 58–59; al-Ḥaddad, *Ta'rīkh al-Yaman al-Siyāsī,* pp. 338–339; Playfair, *A History of Arabia Felix,* pp. 116–122.

3. *Travels Through Arabia,* vol. 2, pp. 45, 46, 47.

4. Ibid., vol. 1, p. 379.

5. See Ḥabshush, *Qorot Yisra'el be-Teman,* p. 267. Another branch of this family emigrated to India, where it established the Hebrew press in Calcutta. For the genealogy of this family, see Y. Nini, *Teᶜuddot Mishpaḥtiyyot,* pp. 119–123.

6. See *'Even Sappir,* vol. 1, p. 100b.

7. See Koraḥ, *Saᶜarat Teman,* p. 19.

8. *Travels Through Arabia,* vol. 1, p. 378.

9. *Qorot Yisra'el be-Teman,* p. 267. ᶜIrāqī built the most magnificent synagogue in Sanaa, named after him, *Kanīsat al-'Uṣṭā.*

10. *Travels Through Arabia,* vol. 1, pp. 378–379.

11. See W. Fischel, *The Jews in the Economic and Political Life of Medieval Islam,* 1969.

12. See Koraḥ, *Saᶜarat Teman.* pp. 16–17; Ḥabshush, *Qorot Yisra'el be-Teman,* p. 267.

13. *'Even Sappir,* vol. 1, p. 101b.

14. For references to Rabbi Ṣāliḥ's works, see Ratzaby's bibliography, *Ḥeqer Yahadut Teman.* see also idem, "*Mahriṣ ve-Sifro Peᶜullat Ṣaddiq,*" *Shevut Teman,* pp. 101–102.

15. Published in Koraḥ, *Saᶜarat Teman,* pp. 150–152.

16. See his *Sefer ha-Musar,* ch. 8, pp. 130–137.

17. Published by Ratzaby, "*Yehude Cochin vihude Teman,*" *Sinai,* 89 (1981), 85–86.

18. *'Even Sappir,* vol. 1, pp. 43a–43b.

19. Ibid, vol. 2, p. 69.

20. See Ratzaby, "*Teᶜuddot u-Meqorot,*" *Bo'i Teman,* pp. 252–254.

21. Ibid., vol. 2, question 184.

22. Ibid., question 143.

23. Published by David Sassoon, "*Megillat Teman,*" *ha-Ṣofe le-Ḥokhmat Yisra'el,* 7 (1923), 1–14.

24. See Wāsiᶜī, *Ta'rīkh al-Yaman,* pp. 59–60.

25. On the religious movement of the Wahhābīs, which then convulsed the whole Arabian Peninsula, see Playfair, *A History of Arabia Felix,* pp. 127–130.

26. See Ḥabshush, *Qorot Yisra'el be-Teman,* p. 271.

27. See S. ᶜArusi, "*Meṣuqot Teman,*" *Sefunot,* vol. 5 (1961), pp. 399–413.

28. Published in English translation in the *Jewish Chronicle,* August 29, 1873, p. 367, and continued September 5, 1873, p. 379.

29. Eight laments relating to this event were published by Ratzaby, "*Gzera ᶜal Yehude Sanᶜa,*" *Minḥa Lihuda,* pp. 267–283. Of a later pillage of Sanaa by the Hashid-Bakil confederacy in 1851, Wāsiᶜī, (*Ta'rīkh al-Yaman,* p. 83) said that 6,000 men of those tribes "entered Bir al-ᶜAzab and plundered everything in it, leaving only the stones." See also Hubeira, *Bitla'ot Teman,* pp. 371–376.

30. See Ratzaby, "*Gzera ᶜal Yehude Sanᶜa,* p. 268.

31. *Qorot Yisra'el be-Teman,* pp. 271–272.
32. Quoted from F. Hunter, *An Account of the British Settlement of Aden,* p. 165. For the events that took place in Aden from 1728 to 1839, see Playfair, *A History of Arabia Felix,* pp. 159–163.
33. *Ibid,* p. 163.
34. See Hunter, *An Account of the British Settlement of Aden,* p. 28.
35. *'Even Sappir,* vol. 2, pp. 1–6. See also Mahalal ᶜAdani, *Ben ᶜAden ve-Teman,* pp. 1–17; A. Klein-Franke, *"ha-Yehudim be-ᶜAden ba-Me'ah ha-19,"* *Peᶜamim,* vol. 10 (1981), pp. 37–59.
36. See Stookey, *Yemen,* p. 159.
37. *Saᶜarat Teman,* p. 32.
38. Ibid. On the conditions of the Jews in Yemen prior to the Ottoman occupation, see Tobi, *Yehude Teman ba-Me'ah ha-19,* pp. 48–70.
39. See Saphir, *'Even Sappir,* vol. 2, pp. 146–149. The execution of Alsheikh was widely published by Saphir in *ha-Lebanon,* 1 (1863) 27–28, and then in his own book, *'Even Sappir,* vol. 2, pp. 141–149. The *Jewish Chronicle,* August 7, 1863, p. 2, published the story under the title "A Martyr of Sana."
40. Published by the *Jewish Chronicle* September 18, 1863, p. 8.
41. See the report of the Anglo-Jewish Association (1873–1874), pp. 32–33.
42. See al-Jarāfī, *al-Muqtaṭaf,* p. 197.
43. *Ta'rīkh al-Yaman,* p. 91.
44. *'Even Sappir,* vol. 2, p. 151.
45. See Koraḥ, *Saᶜarat Teman,* pp. 36–37. For the many sources relating to Shukr Kuḥeil, see Yaᶜari, "Shukr Kuḥeil," *Shevut Teman,* pp. 124–148.
46. Yaᶜari, "Shukr Kuḥeil," p. 136.
47. See D. Sassoon, "An Autograph Letter of A Pseudo-Messiah," *JQR,* 19 (1907), 162–167.
48. See Yaᶜari, "Shukr Kuheil," pp. 146–148, for an extensive bibliography.
49. Koraḥ (*Saᶜarat Teman,* p. 38) claimed that he himself witnessed the funeral of Kuḥeil, accompanied by "about ten people."
50. *"Zikhron Teman,"* in *Yehude Teman,* ed. by Y. Tobi, p. 157.
51. *Jewish Chronicle,* August 29, 1973.
52. See Ḥabshush, *Masᶜot Ḥabshush,* pp. 87, 90, 172. See also Yosef Saᶜid's letter, published by Tobi in his *Yehude Teman,* p. 248. For the Muslims' reaction to the Turkish occupation, see Wāsiᶜī, *Ta'rīkh al-Yaman,* pp. 109–113.
53. For the full text of this decree, which was issued on February 18, 1856, see J. C. Hurewitz, *Diplomacy in the Near and Middle East* (1956), pp. 149–153. See also R. Davison, *Reform in the Ottoman Empire,* pp. 52–80.
54. Hurewitz, *Diplomacy,* pp. 150, 151.
55. See *Jewish Chronicle,* August 29, 1873.
56. See J. Feinstein's letter in Tobi, ed., *Yehude Teman,* p. 262.
57. The letter with slight changes was published in English translation by the *Jewish Chronicle* in two parts, August 29 and September 5, 1873. A photocopy of this letter is available in the Central Archives for the History of the Jewish People, microfilm HM 2/631.
58. In his commentary to Shabazi's poem *Ayyuma, Ḥafeṣ Ḥayyim,* p. 142.
59. *Jewish Chronicle,* September 5, 1873, p. 379.
60. See F. 'Abaẓa, *al-Ḥukm al-ᶜUthmānī fī al-Yaman.*
61. *Jewish Chronicle,* September 5, 1873, p. 379.

62. Yosef ᶜArusi, published in *ha-Lebanon* 9/1 (1872), pp. 7–8.

63. Three of these letters were published by Ratzaby, "*Yehude Teman Taḥat Shilṭon ha-Turkim,*" *Sinai,* 64 (1969), 53–77. Others were published in various periodicals. For extensive discussion of the various sources relating to the Jews in Yemen during the Ottoman rule (1872–1904), see Tobi, *Yehude Teman ba-Meah ha-19;* Y. Nini, *Teman ve-Ṣiyyon,* pp. 69–99 et passim.

64. Published by Ratzaby (n. 45, above), pp. 61–64.

65. Published in the report to the Anglo-Jewish Association for 1873–1874, pp. 32–33.

66. Ibid, pp. 33–34.

67. See a letter published by Ratzaby (n. 63, above), pp. 68–71.

68. Published in *ha-Lebanon* 12/28 (1876), p. 218. See also Ratzaby (n. 63, above), pp. 73–74.

69. It should be noted that the Ottoman *qanūn* was also imposed upon the Muslims. The treaty of Daᶜan (1911), however, which restored much of the authority of the imām, made the *Sharīᶜa* the official legal code for the Zaydī districts. See Wāsiᶜī, *Ta'rīkh al-Yaman,* p. 111; Wenner, *Modern Yemen,* p. 47. See Ḥabshush, *Masᶜot,* pp. 49–50; Karaso, *Zikhron Teman,* p. 160. See also Nini, *Teman ve-Ṣiyyon,* pp. 131–141.

70. See Ratzaby (n. 63, above), pp. 74–77; Koraḥ, *Saᶜarat Teman,* p. 42.

71. Such an office was conferred upon Rabbi Suleiman al-Qare and then on Rabbi Yisḥak Shaul, who was "imported" from Turkey.

72. See relevant documents in Tobi, *Yehude Teman,* pp. 191–214.

73. Ḥabshush ("*Qorot Yisra'el be-Teman,*" pp. 278–280) dates the messianic appearance of ᶜAbdallāh to the year 1893, while Koraḥ (*Saᶜarat Teman,* pp. 53–55) locates it in 1895. However, according to a reliable document (published by Ratzaby in *Bo'i Teman,* pp. 207–209), ᶜAbdallāh began his "messianic" activity in 1888.

74. Published by Ratzaby, "*Teᶜuddot u-Meqorot,*" *Bo'i Teman,* pp. 207–209. The letter was found mutilated, particularly toward the end, making it impossible to detect the name of the author.

75. In a letter dated 1888 written by Shalom Gamal (who was later appointed *Ḥakham Bashi* of Sanaa) and addressed to his father in Jerusalem, the former wrote: "And I have heard from our reckoners [of the end of days] that in this year all the people [Jews] of Yemen will return to Sanaa, and then the Redemption would come, in accordance with the prophecy of our master Salem Shabazi" (see Naḥum, *mi-Ṣefunot Yehude Teman,* pp. 29–30). The document itself is in Naḥum's archives, *Mifᶜal Ḥasifat Genuzim mi-Teman,* Holon. For other messianic speculations, variously designating other years for redemption, see Ratzaby, *Appoqalipsot,* pp. 295–322.

76. Ratzaby, "*Teᶜuddot*", pp. 207–208.

77. *Lulavs* (palm branches) and *ethrogs* (citrons) are two of the four species of plants used in the ritual of the Feast of Tabernacles. The prayers begin with "Save, I pray," appealing to God for deliverance. These prayers are recited in the Feast of Tabernacles.

78. Four months before the Feast of Tabernacles.

79. *Ḥaroseth:* a mixture of ground nuts, fruit, spices, and wine used to sweeten the bitter herbs, eaten on Passover; *maṣṣa:* unleavened bread.

80. See his *Qorot Yisra'el be-Teman,* pp. 278–280.

81. See his *Saᶜarat Teman,* pp. 53–55.

82. See Goitein, "*Mi Haya Edward Glaser,*" *Shevut Teman,* pp. 149–154.

83. For an account of Halévy's travels and adventures in Yemen, see

Ḥabshush, *Travels in Yemen,* ed. by Goitein (Jerusalem, 1941). Habshush composed this account in 1893–1894 (more than twenty years after the events), at the request and encouragement of Edward Glaser, who visited Yemen four times. Like Halévy before him, Glaser hired Ḥabshush for the purpose of copying Sabaean inscriptions for him.

84. Goitein, *Mas^c ot Ḥabshush,* p. 6. See also Koraḥ, *Sa^c arat Teman,* pp. 40, 51–53.

85. The name also calls to mind Darda^c, whom the Bible (1 Kings 5:11) mentions as one of the celebrated wise men, whose wisdom was surpassed only by King Solomon.

86. Arabicized plural of the Hebrew word *Dor-de^c ah,* producing a meaningless "Arabic" word which blurs and distorts the connotation of the Hebrew name.

87. See the articles on *Dor-de^c ah* published in *Shevut Teman,* pp. 166–211.

88. See Ḥayyim Shar^c abi, "*Peraqim,*" *Shevut Teman,* pp. 200–201.

89. see Ratzaby, "*Darda^c im,*" *^c Edot* I/3 (1946), pp. 165–180. See also the correspondence between Rabbi Kuk and Rabbi Kafiḥ in *Shevut Teman,* pp. 212–226. On the life and activities of Rabbi Kafiḥ, see S. Koraḥ, *'Iggeret Bokhim* (1963).

90. See Shar^c abi (n. 93, above), p. 201.

91. *Ta'rīkh al-Yaman,* pp. 204–205.

92. Ibid., p. 200. See also Wenner, *Modern Yemen,*pp. 45–47.

93. "*'Iggeret Bokhim,*" in Tobi, *Toledot Yehude Teman,* p. 189. For documents relating to the devastating effects of the siege on the Jews, see also Ratzaby, "*ba-Maṣor uva-Maṣoq,*" pp. 73–102.

94. See the text of the Treaty in Wāsi^c ī, *Ta'rīkh al-Yaman,* pp. 236–239; see also the detailed discussion on the negotiations in 'Abāẓa, *al-Ḥukm al-^c Uthmānī,* pp. 229–283.

95. See Wāsi^c ī, *Ta'rīkh al-Yaman,* pp. 261–275; 'Abāẓa, *al-Ḥukm,* pp. 345–414; Wenner, *Modern Yemen,* pp. 438–481.

96. See S. Ḥabshush, *Sefer Ashkelot Merorot,* pp. 26–27. For an English translation of the decree, see H. Cohen, *The Jews of the Middle East,* pp. 62–63.

97. H. Cohen, *The Jews of the Middle East,* pp. 62–63.

98. See S. Koraḥ, "*'Iggeret Bokhim,*" pp. 193–195; S. Gamli'el, *Pequde Teman* (1982).

Epilogue
In the Land of Israel

1. For an exhaustive survey of Yemenite Jewish emigration to Palestine during the previous centuries, see Ya^c ari, "*^c Aliyyat Yedude Teman,*" *Shevut Teman,* pp. 11–36.

2. See Ya^c ari, "*Mas^c ot Ereṣ Yisra'el,*" pp. 644–645; Nini, *Teman ve-Ṣiyyon,* pp. 179–195. All these rumors, however, were totally groundless.

3. Song of Solomon 7:9. The Yemenites understood the phrase אמרתי אעלה בתמר as "I shall go to Israel in the year תרמ״ב (interchange of the letters contained in the word בתמר), namely, in 1882.

4. See Yosef Ḥubara, *bi-Tela'ot Teman,* p. 362.

5. The charity system *ḥaluqqah* is based on the strong religious and emotional attachment of the Jewish people to the Land of Israel. The Jewish communities in the Diaspora considered it an obligation and a virtue to support their brethren who chose to dwell in the land of their forefathers. See M. Rothschild, *ha-Ḥaluqqah* (1969).

6. See Druyan, *be-'En Marvad Qesamim,* pp. 19–34; Nini, *Teman ve-Ṣiyyon,* pp. 237–275.

7. See Ratzaby, "*Rishone ^{c}Ole Teman,*" p. 73.

8. *Ḥavaṣelet* 15/8 (1886), p. 239.

9. *Our Jerusalem* (New York, 1977^{2}).

10. See N. Lind, "The Return of the Gaddites," pp. 151–160, especially pp. 153, 154.

11. Ibid., p. 153.

12. *Kol Shire Naftali Herẓ Imber* (Tel-Aviv, 1950), pp. 221–223. See I. Friedlaender, "The Jews of Arabia and the Rechabites," *JQR,* n.s. I, 252–257.

13. See Druyan, *Be-'En Marvad Qesamim,* pp. 22–34, and the extensive relevant bibliography therein.

14. See the article "Yemen," in *EJ,* vol. 16, p. 752.

15. Published in Naḥum, *mi-Ṣefunot Teman,* pp. 267–268.

16. "*le-Toledot Yishuv 'Eḥad,*" *Shevut Teman,* p. 60.

17. *Memoires, Diaries, Letters,* p. 110.

18. Ibid. Yavnieli's mission to Yemen is described in detail in his book, *Massa^{c} le-Teman* (1952).

19. *Memoires,* p. 110.

20. See the pamphlet *Aḥdut ha-^{c}Avoda* (1920); see also *Shevut Teman,* p. 48. The English translation is taken from Patai, *Israel Between East and West,* p. 198.

21. For selections of writings pertaining to this topic, see Yosef Tobi, ed. *'E^{c}ele be-Tamar: Meqorot* (1982).

22. Nathan Alterman, *ha-Tur ha-Shevi^{c}i,* vol. 2, pp. 117–118.

23. See Abraham Z. Idelsohn, "*Yehude Teman: Shiratam u-Manginatam,*" *Reshumot,* I (1925), 3–66; *idem, Jewish Music in its Historical Development,* pp. 23, 367–376; Joanna Spector, "Bridal Songs and Ceremonies from Sanaa, Yemen," in *Studies in Biblical and Jewish Folklore,* pp. 255–284; M. Geshuri, "*be-^{c}Olam ha-Shir veha-Niggun shel Yehude Teman,*" in *Har'el* (1962), pp. 170–176. See also Paul F. Marks, *Bibliography of Literature Concerning Yemenite-Jewish Music* (Detroit, 1973).

24. Gurit Kadman, "Yemenite Dance," in *The Jews of Yemen,* pp. 6–8. See also *idem,* "Yemen Dances and their Influence on the New Israeli Folk Dances," in *Journal of the International Folk Music Council,* 4 (1952), 27–30.

25. See Ḥayyim Hazaz, *Ya^{c}ish* (Tel-Aviv, 1968), vol. 1, pp. 46–48.

26. "*Hilkhot Teman,*" in *Yahadut Teman,* pp. 349–355.

27. "Oral Traditions and Dialects," in *Proceedings of the International Conference on Semitic Studies,* p. 182. See also Morag, *ha^{c}Ivrit she-be-Fi Yehude Teman;* "*ha-'Arammit ha-Bavlit be-Masortam shel Yehude Teman* in *Tarbiz,* 30 (1961), 120–129; "*Masorot ha-Darot bi-Khfifa 'Aḥat*" in *Har'el* (1962), pp. 149–157.

SELECTED BIBLIOGRAPHY

List of Abbreviations of Journals, Hebrew Volumes, and Encyclopedias

Afiqim	*A Yemenite Jewish Periodical* (Hebrew).
AJS Review	*Association for Jewish Studies Review.*
AJSLL	*American Journal of Semitic Languages and Literatures.*
ANET	*Ancient Near Eastern Texts Relating to the Old Testament,* ed. by J. B. Pritchard. Princeton, 1955.
BA	*Biblical Archaeology.*
BASOR	*Bulletin of the American School for Oriental Research.*
Bo'i Teman	*Bo'i Teman: Studies in Documents Concerning the Culture of the Yemenite Jews,* ed. by Yehuda Ratzaby. Tel-Aviv, 1967 (Hebrew).
BJRL	*Bulletin of the John Rylands Library.*
BSOAS	*Bulletin of the School of Oriental and African Studies of the University of London.*
EI^1	*Encyclopaedia of Islam,* first edition.
EI^2	*Encyclopaedia of Islam,* new edition.
EJ	*Encyclopaedia Judaica,* new English edition.
Ginze Qedem	*A Geonitic Scientific Periodical.* Haifa (Hebrew).
Ḥafeṣ Ḥayyim	*An Anthology of Yemenite Jewish Poems,* Brothers Mekiton. Jerusalem, 1966 (Hebrew).
HAR	*Hebrew Annual Review.*
Har'el	*Rabbi R. Alsheikh Memorial Volume,* ed. by Yehuda Ratzaby and Iṣḥaq Shivṭi'el. Tel-Aviv, 1962 (Hebrew).
HUCA	*Hebrew Union College Annual.*
JA	*Journal Asiatique.*
JNES	*Journal of Near Eastern Studies.*
JQR	*Jewish Quarterly Review,* old series.
JQR, n.s.	*Jewish Quarterly Review,* new series.
JRAS	*Journal of the Royal Asiatic Society.*
JSSt	*Journal of Semitic Studies.*
Kiryat Sefer	*Bibliographical Quarterly of the Jewish National and University Library.* Jerusalem (Hebrew).
Moreshet	*Moreshet Yehude Teman: Studies and Researches,* ed. by Yosef Tobi. Jerusalem, 1977 (Hebrew).
PAAJR	*Proceedings of the American Academy for Jewish Research.*
Pe^{c}amim	*Studies in the Cultural Heritage of Oriental Jewry.* Ben-Zvi Institute for the Study of Jewish Communities in the East, Jerusalem (Hebrew).
REJ	*Revue des Etudes Juives.*
RHR	*Revue de l'Histoire de Religions.*
Sefunot	*Sefunot. Annual for Research on the Jewish Communities in the East* (Hebrew).
Shevut Teman	ed. by Yisra'el Yesha^{c}yahu and Aharon Ṣadoq. Tel-Aviv, 1944 (Hebrew).

Sinai	*A Periodical for Torah Science and Literature,* published by Mossad Harav Kook. Jerusalem (Hebrew).
Tarbiz	*Tarbiz. A Quarterly for Jewish Studies* (Hebrew).
VT	*Vetus Testamentum.*
Yahadut Teman	*Yahadut Teman: Studies and Researches,* ed. by Yisra'el Yeshaᶜyahu and Yosef Tobi. Jerusalem, 1975 (Hebrew).
ZDMG	*Zeitschrift des Deutschen Morgenlandischen Gesellschaft.*
Zion	*Zion: A Quarterly for Research in Jewish History* (Hebrew).
Zion, o.s.	*Zion,* old series (Hebrew).

Abāẓa, Farūq ᶜUthmān. *al-Ḥukm al-ᶜUthmānī fī al-Yaman (1872–1918).* Cairo, 1975.
Abir Mordechai. "*ha-Saḥar ha-Benle'umi ve-ha-Yehudim be-Teman ba-Me'ot 15–19.*" In *Peᶜamim,* vol. 5 (1980), pp. 5–28 (Hebrew).
Abbot, Nabia. "Pre-Islamic Arab Queens." *AJSLL,* 58 (1941), 1–22.
Abraham Halkin, ed. *Moses Maimonides' Epistle to Yemen,* trans. by Boaz Cohen. New York, 1952.
ha-ᶜAdani, Mahalal. *Ben ᶜAden ve-Teman.* Tel-Aviv, 1947.
Adler, Elkan Nathan, ed. *Jewish Travellers: A Treasury of Travelogues from 9 Centuries.* Second ed., with a preface by Cecil Roth. New York, 1966 (first ed., 1930).
Adler, Marcus Nathan. *The Itinerary of Benjamin of Tudela.* New York, 1907.
Ahroni, Reuben. "From Bustān al-ᶜUqūl to Qiṣṣat al-Batūl: Some Aspects of Jewish-Muslim Religious Polemics in Yemen." In *HUCA,* vol. 52 (1981), pp. 311–360.
———. "The Theme of Love in Yemenite Hebrew Literature." In *HAR,* vol. 4 (1980), pp. 1–13.
———. "*Tribulations and Aspirations in Yemenite Hebrew Literature.*" *HUCA,* vol. 49 (1978), pp. 267–294.
al-ᶜAlawī, ᶜAlī ibn Muḥammad alᶜAbbāsī. *Sīrat al-Hādī ila'l-Ḥaqq Yaḥia ibn al-Ḥusain,* ed. by Suhayl Zakkār. Beirut, 1972.
Albright, W. F. "The Chronology of Ancient South Arabia in the Light of the First Campaign of Excavation in Qataban." *BASOR,* 119(1950), 5–15.
Albright, W. F. "A Note on Early Sabaean Chronology." *BASOR,* 143 (1956), 9–10.
ᶜAlī, Muḥammad. *The Religion of Islam.* Lahore, Pakistan, 1950.
Alter, Robert. "From the Echo Chamber." *The Times Literary Supplement,* October 29, 19 .
Alterman, Nathan. *ha-Ṭur ha-Shevīᶜī,* vol. 2. Tel-Aviv, 1962.
Altheim, F., and R. Stiehl. *Die Araber in der alten Welt.* Vols. I–V/1, Berlin, 1964–1968.
Andrae, Tor. *Der Ursprung des Islams und das Christentum.* Uppsala, Stockholm, 1926.
Angel, Y., ed. *Igrot ha-Rambam.* Tel-Aviv, 1953.
Arberry, A. J. *The Holy Koran: An Introduction with Selections.* London, 1953.
van Arendonk, Cornelis. *Les Débuts de l'imamat Zaïdite au Yémen,* trans. Jacques Ryckmans. Leyden, 1960.
ᶜArusi, Saᶜid. "*Meṣuqot Teman,*" ed. by Yosef Kafiḥ. In *Sefunot,* vol. 5 (1961), pp. 399–413.
Asaf, Simḥa. *mi-Miṣra'im veᶜAden le-Hodu. Zion,* IV (1939), 232–236.

Bacher, W. "Der Südarabische Siddur und Jahjâ Sâlih's Commentar zu Demselben." *JQR,* o.s. 14 (1901–1902), 581–621.

al-Balādhurī, Aḥmad ibn-Jābir. *Kitāb Futūḥ al-Buldān,* ed. by M. J. de Goeje. Leiden, 1968^2 (first ed., 1866). English trans. by Philip K. Hitti as "*The Origins of the Islamic State.* New York, 1916.

Baneth, D. Z. "*Mikhtav mi-Teman mi-Shenat 1202.*" *Tarbiz,* 19 (1950), 205–214.

Barer, Shlomo. *The Magic Carpet.* New York, 1952.

Baron, Salo Wittmayer. *A Social and Religious History of the Jews,* vols. 3–9. New York, 1957–1965.

Bateson, Catherine. *Structural Continuity in Poetry: A Linguistic Study of Five Pre-Islamic Arab Odes.* Paris, 1970.

Beek, Gus W. van. "Frankincense and Myrrh." *BA,* 23 (1960), 70–95.

———. "The Land of Sheba." In *Solomon and Sheba,* ed. by J. B. Pritchard, London, pp. 40–63, 1974.

———. "Prologomenon" to James Montgomery's *Arabia and the Bible.* pp. IX–XXXI. New York, 1969.

———. "A Radio-Carbon Data for Early South Arabia." *BASOR,* 143 (1956), 6–9.

Beek, Gus W. van, and A. Jamme. "An Inscribed South Arabia Clay Stamp from Bethel." *BASOR,* 151 (1958), 9–16.

Bell, Richard. *The Origin of Islam in its Christian Environment.* London, 1926.

Ben Jacob, A. *Meqorot Ḥadashim le-Toledot Yehude Bavel ba-Me'ot ha-12-13. Zion,* n.s. 15 (1950), 56–69.

Benjamin of Tudela. *The Itinerary of Benjamin of Tudela,* ed. and trans. by M. N. Adler. London, 1907.

Ben Yehsaᶜia, Netan'el. *Nur al-Ẓalām,* ed. and trans. into Hebrew by Yosef Kafiḥ. *Me'or ha-'Afela.* Jerusalem, 1957.

Ben-Ze'ev, Yisra'el. *ha-Yehudim ba-ᶜArav.* Jerusalem, 1957^2 (Hebrew).

Ben-Zvi, Izḥak. *Nidḥe Yisra'el.* Jerusalem, 1969 (Hebrew).

———. *The Exiled and the Redeemed,* trans. from Hebrew by Isaac A. Abbady. Philadelphia, 1957.

Berreby, Jean-Jacques, "*De l'intégration des juifs Yéménites en Israël.*" *L'Année sociologique.* Ser. 3 (1953–1954), pp. 69–163.

Berger, David. *The Jewish-Christian Debate in the High Middle Ages: A Critical Edition of the Nizzahon Vetus.* Philadelphia, 1979.

Bet-Arie Malachi. "'*Emuna Yoṣrah 'Eṣlo 'Amana.*" In *Shai le-Heman: A. M. Habermann Jubilee Volume,* ed. by Zvi Malachi, pp. 37–50. Jerusalem, 1977.

Bialik, H. N. *Kol Kitve H. N. Bialik.* Tel-Aviv, 1962.

Bickerman, Elias. *Four Strange Books of the Bible.* New York, 1967.

Blachère, Régis. *Histoire de la littérature Arab.* Paris, 1952–1966. 3 vols.

Blumenkranz, Bernhard. *Le Juif Médiéval au Miroir de l'Art Chrétien.* Paris, 1966.

Blumenthal, David, ed., trans., and annot. *The Commentary of R. Ḥōṭer Ben Shelōmō to the Thirteen Principles of Maimonides.* Leiden, 1974.

Brauer, Erich. *Ethnologie de Jemenitischen Juden.* Heidelberg, 1934.

Bright, John. *A History of Israel.* Philadelphia, 1981^3.

Brockelmann, C. "Makama." *EI,* vol. 3 (1936), pp. 161–164.

Brody, Heinrich., ed. *Selected Poems of Jehudah Halevi.* English trans. by Nina Salaman. Philadelphia, 1924.

Brown, William R. "The Yemeni Dilemma." *The Middle East Journal,* 17 (1963), 349–367.

Buhl, Frants. *Das Leben Muhammeds,* German trans. by H. H. Schaeder. Heidelberg, 1930.
al-Bukhārī. *al-Jāmi*ᶜ *al-Ṣaḥīḥ,* ed. by M. Ludolf Krehl and completed by Th. W. Juynboll. 4 vols. Leiden, 1862–1908.
Bury, Wyman G. *Arabia Infelix of the Turks in Yamen.* London, 1915.
Cahen, Claude. "Dhimma." *EI*^{2}, vol. 2.
Caspi, Mishael M. "*Beginnat ᶜEden Besamav.*" *Afiqim,* 13 (1978), 10–11, 19.
———. *Piyyuṭe ha-Maranot.* Tel-Aviv, 1982.
———. "*Shemesh Kemo Dama ᶜEt Raṣ be-Maᶜalotav (ᶜAl Shir ve-Tarbut ha-Shir ba-Shira ha-ᶜIvrit).*" In *Yahadut Teman,* ed. by Yisra'el Yeshaᶜyahu and Yosef Tobi, pp. 333–346. Jerusalem, 1975.
Caussin de Perceval, A. P. *Essai sur l'histoire des Arabes avant l'Islamisme, pendant l'époque de Mohamet et jusqu'à la réduction de toutes les tribus sous la loi musulmane.* 3 vols. Paris, 1847–1848.
Chastel, André. "*La Légende de la Reine de Saba.*" *Revue de l'Histoire de Religions,* 119 (1939), 204–205; 120 (1940), 27–44.
Chavel, Charles B., ed. and trans. *Ramban [Nachmanides]: Writings and Discourses.* New York, 1978.
Chieko, L. *Le christianisme et la littérature chrétienne en Arabie avant l'Islam,* Vol. I. *L'histoire du christianisme dans l'Arabie préislamique.* Beirut, 1912.
Cohen, Boaz, Eng. trans. *Moses Maimonides' Epistle to Yemen,* ed. by Abraham S. Halkin. New York, 1952.
Cohen, Hayyim. *The Jews of the Middle East, 1860–1872.* New York, Toronto and Jerusalem, 1973.
Cohen, Jeremy. *The Friars and the Jews: The Evolution of Medieval Anti-Judaism.* Ithaca and London, 1982.
Corcos-Abulafia, David. "*Le-'Ofi Yaḥasam Shel Shalliṭe ha-al-Muwaḥḥidūn la-Yehudim.*" *Zion,* 32 (1967), 137–160.
Costa, Paolo M. *The Pre-Islamic Antiquities at the Yemen National Museum.* Rome, 1978.
Curtis, Edward. *Critical Book of Chronicles (I.C.C.).* New York, 1910.
al-Ḍahrī, Zecharia. *Sefer ha-Musar,* ed. by Yehuda Ratzaby. Jerusalem, 1965.
Davidson, Yisra'el. "*She'erit min Diwan Abraham ben Ḥalfon.*" In *Ṣiyyunim: Qoveṣ le-Zikhrono shel Simḥoni,* pp. 58–81. Berlin, 1929.
Davison, Roderic H. *Reform in the Ottoman Empire 1856–1876.* New York, 1973.
Degen, R. "*Ketovet mi-Teman ᶜal ᶜEsrim ve-Arbaᶜa Mishmerot ha-Kohanim.*" *Tarbiz,* 42 (1973), 302–303.
Donaldson, Dwight M. *The Shīᶜite Religion.* London, 1933.
Dozy, Reinhart. *Dictionnaire détaillé des noms des vêtements chez les Arabes.* Amsterdam, 1845.
———, ed. *The History of Almohades* by Abdo-'l Wahid al-Marrekoshi. Amsterdam, 1968.
———. *Die Israeliten zu Mekka von Davids Zeit bis ins fünfte Jahrhundert unserer Zeitrechnung.* Leipzig, 1864.
———. "American Zionist Efforts on Behalf of Yemenite Jews in Eretz Israel, 1912–1914." *American Jewish History,* 69 (1979), 92–98.
Dougherty, Raymond Philip. *Nabonidus and Belshazzar: A Study of the Closing Events of the Neo-Babylonian Empire.* New Haven, 1929.
Druryan, Nitza. *be-'En Marvad Qesamim: ᶜOle Teman be-Ereṣ Yisra'el 1882–1914.* Jerusalem, 1981 (Hebrew).
Epstein, A., ed. *Eldad ha-Dani.* Pressburg, 1891 (Hebrew).

Faris, Nabih Amin, ed. *The Arab Heritage.* New Jersey, 1944.
Fattal, Antoine. *Le Statut Légal des non-musulmans en pays d'Islam.* Beirut, 1958.
al-Fayyūmī, Nathanael Ibn. *The Bustan al-Ukul,* ed. by David Levine. New York, 1966 (first ed., 1908).
Fischel, Walter J. *Jews in the Economic and Political Life of Mediaeval Islam.* New York, 1969 (first published by the Royal Asiatic Society of Great Britain and Ireland, London, 1937).
Foster, William. *England's Quest for Eastern Trade.* London, 1933.
Friedlaender, Israel. "The Jews of Arabia and the Gaonate." *JQR,* n.s. 1 (1910–1911), 249–252.
———. "*The Jews of Arabia and the Rechabites.*" *JQR,* n.s. I (1910–1911), 252–257.
Gadd, C. J. "The Harran Inscriptions." *Anatolian Studies,* 8 (1958), 35–92.
Gamal-Eddine, Heyworth Dunne. *Al-Yemen: A General Social, Political and Economic Survey.* Cairo, 1952.
Gamli'el, Shalom. *Pequde Teman: Mas he-Ḥasut be-Teman.* Jerusalem, 1982.
Gamli'eli, Nissim Binyamin. "*ha-ᶜAravim shebe-Qirvam Ḥayu Yehude Teman.*" In *Yahadut Teman,* ed. by Yisra'el Yesaᶜyahu and Yosef Tobi, pp. 165–192. Jerusalem, 1975.
———. *Ḥadre Teman: Sippurim ve-Aggadot.* Tel-Aviv, 1978.
Gavin, R. J. *Aden Under British Rule,* 1839–1967. New York, 1975.
Gaon, Saᶜadia. *The Book of Beliefs and Opinions,* trans. by Samuel Rosenblatt. New Haven, Conn., 1948.
Gätje, Helmut. *The Qur'ān and its Exegesis,* trans. by Alford T. Welch. Berkeley, 1976.
Gerber, Jane S. "The Pact of ᶜUmar in Morocco: A Reappraisal of Muslim-Jewish Relations." In *Proceedings of the Seminar on Muslim-Jewish Relations in North Africa,* pp. 40–50. New York, 1974.
Gibb, H. A. R. *Arabic Literature: An Introduction.* London, 1966.
Glaser, Eduard. *Skizze der Geschichte und Geographie Arabiens von den ältesten Zeiten bis zum Propheten Muhammad.* New York, 1976.
Goitein, S. D. "The Age of the Hebrew Tombstones from Aden." *JSSt.,* 7 (1962), 81–84.
———, ed. *From the Land of Sheba: Tales of the Jews of Yemen,* trans. by Christopher Fremantle. New York, 1947.
———. "*Gilluyim Ḥadashim ᶜAl Bet ha-Melukha ha-Yehudi be-Teman.*" *Ha'areṣ, Tarbut ve-Sifrut,* March 25, 1855, p. 1.
———. "*Ḥayyim Ḥabshush ve-Sifro Ḥezion Teman.*" In *Sefer Magnes: Magnes Anniversary Book,* pp. 89–96. Jerusalem, 1938 (Hebrew).
———. "*Isra'iliyat.*" *Tarbiz,* 6 (1935), 89–101; 410–522.
———. *Jews and Arabs: Their Contacts Through the Ages.* Third revised edition. New York, 1974.
———. "The Jews of Yemen." In *Religion in the Middle East.* ed. by A. J. Arberry. Vol. 1, pp. 226–235. Cambridge, England, 1969.
———. "*Ketav-yad ᶜIvri-ᶜAravi ᶜal Qorot ha-Yehudim be-Teman.*" *Kiryat Sefer,* 14 (1937), 256–270.
———. "*Ketovet du-Leshonit Ḥimyarit-ᶜIvrit.*" *Tarbiz,* 41 (1972), 151–156.
———. "*Kitab Dhimmat al-Nabi. Kiryat Sefer,* 9 (1932–33), 507–521.
———. *Letters of Medieval Jewish Traders,* trans. from the Arabic, with Introductions and Notes by Goitein. Princeton, 1974.
———. "*ha-Mashiᶜaḥ mi-Beiḥan.*" *Haᶜareṣ,* Nov. 17, 1950, p. 5.

———. *A Mediterranean Society.* 3 vols. Berkeley-Los Angeles, 1967.
———. *Mas^c ot Ḥabshush,* ed. and trans. from Arabic into Hebrew by S. D. Goitein. Tel-Aviv, 1939.
———. *"Negide 'Ereṣ Teman."* In *Bo'i Teman,* ed. by Y. Ratzaby, pp. 15–25. Tel-Aviv, 1967.
———, ed. *Religion in a Religious Age: Proceedings of Regional Conferences Held at the University of California, Los Angeles, and Brandeis University in April, 1973.* Cambridge, Mass., 1974.
———. "The Social Structure of Jewish Education in Yemen." In *Jewish Societies in the Middle East: Community, Culture and Authority,* ed. by Shlomo Deshen and Walter P. Zenner, pp. 211–233. Washington, 1982.
———. *Studies in Islamic History and Institutions.* Leiden, 1966.
———. *"Temanim bi-Rushala'im uv-Miṣra'im be-Tequfatam Shel ha-Rambam ve-Shel Beno R. Avraham."* In *Har'el,* ed. by Y. Ratzaby and I. Shivṭi'el, pp. 133–148. Tel-Aviv, 1962.
———. *"Temikhatam Shel Yehude Teman bi-Shivot Bavel ve-'Ereṣ Yisra'el u-Vishivat ha-Rambam." Tarbiz,* 31 (1966), 357–370.
———. *"Yahadut Teman ben Ge'onut Miṣra'im leven Rashut ha-Gola Shel Bavel." Sinai,* 33 (1953), 225–237.
———. *"Yahadut Teman ve-Saḥar Hodu ha-Yehudi."* In *Yahadut Teman,* ed. by Yisra'el Yesa^c yahu and Yosef Tobi, pp. 47–69. Jerusalem, 1976.
Gordis, Robert. *The Book of God and Man.* Chicago, 1965.
Gottheil, Richard J. H. "Dhimmis and Moslems in Egypt." In *Old Testament and Semitic Studies in Memory of William Rainey Harper,* ed. by Robert Francis Harper et al. Vol. 2, pp. 353–414. Chicago, 1908.
Graham, Gerald S. *A Concise History of the British Empire.* New York, 1970.
Gray, John. *I and II Kings: A Commentary.* Second, fully revised edition. Philadelphia, 1970.
Groom, Nigel. *Frankincense and Myrrh: A Study of the Arabian Incense Trade.* London and New York: Longman, 1981.
Grossman, G. C., ed. *The Jews of Yemen.* Chicago, 1976.
Guidi, I., ed. *La Lettera de Simeone vescovo di Bêth Arśâm. Atti della R. Accademia dei Lincei,* serie III, vol. VII, pp. 471–515. Rome, 1881. Reprinted in I. Guidi, Raccolta di Scritti, vol. I, pp. 1–60. Rome, 1945.
Guillaume, Alfred. *The Life of Muhammad,* a trans. of Ibn Ishaq's, *Sirat Rsaul Allah.* Pakistan, 1968.
———. *The Traditions of Islam.* Oxford, England, 1924.
Guttman, Julius. *Philosophies of Judaism,* trans. by David W. Silverman. London, 1964.
Haberman, A. M. *Kitve Avraham Epstein.* Jerusalem, 1950.
Haberman, A. M. *Maḥbarot ^c Immanu'el ha-Romi.* Tel-Aviv, 1946.
Ḥabshush, Ḥayyim. *Ḥezion Teman,* published by S. D. Goitein with a summary in English. Jerusalem, 1941. Also trans. into Hebrew by S. D. Goitein under the title, *Mas^c ot Habshush.* Tel-Aviv, 1939.
———. *"Qorot Yisra'el be-Teman,"* published by Yosef Kafiḥ. In *Sefunot: Annual for Research on the Jewish Communities in the East.* Vol. 2, pp. 246–286. Jerusalem, 1958.
Ḥabshush, Suleiman ben Yehia. *"Sefer Ashkelot Merorot va-Halikhot Sheva,"* ed. by S. D. Goitein. In *Qoveṣ ^c al-Yad.* Vol. 2 (1937), pp. 1–34.
al-Ḥaddad, Muḥammad Yaḥia. Ta'rīkh al-Yaman al-Siyāsī. Cairo, 1977.
Hakkohen, Yisra'el. *Sefer Segullat Yisra'el.* 2 vols. Tel Aviv, 1972.
Hakkohen, Mordechai. "Daf mi-Shas Teman." *Sinai,* 37 (1955), 368–372.

Halevi, Judah. *Book of Kuzari,* trans. from the Arabic with an Introduction by Hartwig Hirschfeld. New York, 1969.

Halevi, Seᶜadia. "*ha-Kronika ᶜal-Gzerat haᶜAtarot; Me'oraᶜot ha-Shavta'ut be-Teman (1667).*" In *Toledot Yehude Teman: mi-Kitvehem,* ed. by Yosef Tobi, pp. 51–52. Jerusalem, 1979 (Hebrew).

Halévy, J. "Examen critique des sources relatives à la persécution des chrétiens de Nedjran par le roi juif des Himyarites." *REJ,* 18 (1889), 16–42, 161–178.

———. "Rapport sur une Mission archéologique dans le Yemen." *JA,* 19 (Paris, 1872).

———. "Remarque sur un point contesté touchant ta persécution de Nedjran." *REJ,* 21 (1890), 73–77.

Halkin, A. S. "Ibn ᶜAknin's Commentary on the Song of Songs." In *Alexander Marx Jubilee Volume,* pp. 389–424. New York, 1950.

———. "*Le-toledot ha-Shemad Bime ha'Almuwaḥḥidīn.*" In *The Joshua Starr Memorial Volume,* pp. 101–110. New York, 1953.

———. "The Judeo-Islamic Age: The Great Fusion." In *Great Ages and Ideas of the Jewish People,* ed. by Leo W. Schwarz, pp. 215–263. New York, 1956.

———, ed. *Moses Maimonides' Epistle to Yemen: The Arabic Original and the Three Hebrew Versions,* and an English trans. by Boaz Cohen. New York, 1952.

al-Hamdānī, Badr al-Dīn Muḥammad ibn Hātim al-Yāmī. *Kitāb al-Simṭ al-Ghālī al-Thaman fī Akhbār al-Mulūk min al-Ghuzz bi'l-Yaman,* ed. by G. R. Smith, *The Ayyūbids and Early Rasūlids in the Yemen.* London, 1974.

Harris, W. B. *A Journey Through the Yemen.* Edinburgh, 1893.

Ḥavaṣelet, Me'ir, ed. *Midrash ha-Ḥefeṣ ᶜal-Ḥamisha Ḥumshe Torah: Ḥibbro R. Zecharia ben Shelomo ha-Rofe, Sefer Bereshit.* Jerusalem, 1981.

Hazaz, Ḥayyim. *Yaᶜish.* Tel-Aviv, 1968 (Hebrew).

Heyd, W. *Histoire Du Commerce Du Levant au Moyen Age.* 2 vols. Leipzig, 1885–1886 (second edition, Amsterdam, 1959).

Hirschberg, H. Z. *ha-Meqorot ha-ᶜAraviyyim le-Qorot Yehude ᶜArav. Zion,* 10 (1945), 81–101; 11 (1946), 17–37.

———. "Arabic Portion of the Cairo Genizah at Cambridge." *JQR,* o.s. 14 (1903), 167–179.

———. *A History of the Jews in North Africa.* 2 vols. Vol. 1, Leiden, 1974. Vol. 2 is available only in the Hebrew edition, *Toledot ha-Yehudim be-'Afriqa ha-Ṣefonit,* Jerusalem, 1965.

———. "*Mar Zuṭra Rosh ha-Sanhedrin bi-Ṭveria.*" In *Kol 'Ereṣ Naftali,* ed. by H. Z. Hirschberg, pp. 147–153. Jerusalem, 1967.

———. *Yisra'el ba-ᶜArav,* Tel-Aviv, 1946.

———. "*Yosef Melekh Ḥimyar veᶜAliyyato Shel Mar Zuṭra li-Ṭveria.*" In *Kol 'Eres Naftali,* pp. 139–146. Jerusalem, 1967.

Hirschfeld, Hartwig. "The Arabic Portion of the Cairo Geniza at Cambridge." *JQR,* 15 (1903), 167–179.

———, ed. *Book of Kuzari* by Rabbi Judah Halevi, trans. from the Arabic with an Introduction. New York, 1969.

Hitti, Philip K. *History of the Arabs*^{10}, (tenth ed.). London, 1970 (first ed., 1937).

Höfner, M. *Beiträge zur historischen Geographie des vorislamischen Südarabien: Abhandlungen der Akademie der Wissenschaften und der Literatur.* Geistes- und sozialwissenschaftliche Klasse, ann. 1952, Heft 4, Weisbaden, 1952.

Hogarth, David George. *The Penetration of Arabia.* New York, 1904.

Hommel, Fritz. *Ethnologie und Geographie des Alten Orients.* Munich, 1926.
Hoskins, Halford Lancaster. *British Routes to India.* New York, 1928.
Hourani, George F. *Arab Seafaring in the Indian Ocean in Ancient and Early Medieval Times.* Princeton, N.J., 1951 (reprint, Beirut, 1963).
Ḥoze, Seᶜ Adia, *Sefer Toledot ha-Rav Shalom Shabazi.* Jerusalem, 1973.
Ḥubara, Yosef. *Bi-Tela'ot Teman vi-Rushala'im.* Jerusalem, 1970.
Hurewitz, J. C. *Diplomacy in the Near and Middle East: A Documentary Record: 1553–1914.* Vol. 1, Princeton, N.J., 1956.
Ibn al-Athīr, *al-Kāmil fī al-Taᶜrīkh,* ed. C. J. Tornberg. 13 vols. Leiden, 1867–1879.
Ibn Fayyūmī, Saᶜadia. *The Book of Beliefs and Opinions,* trans. by Samuel Rosenblatt. New Haven, 1968.
Ibn al-Fūṭi. *al-Ḥawādeṭ al-jāmiᶜa.* Baghdad, 1932.
Ibn Ḥazm. *Kitāb al-Fiṣāl.* Cairo, 1903.
Ibn Hishām. *al-Sīra al-Nabawīyya.* 2 vols. Cairo, 1955.
Ibn Isḥāq. *Sīrat Rasūl Allāh,* trans. with an Introduction and Notes by Alfred Guillaume under the name *The Life of Muhammad.* Lahore, 1968.
Ibn Khaldūn. *The Muqaddimah,* trans. by Franz Rosenthal. 3 vols. New York, 1958.
Idelsohn, A. Z. "*Ha-Meshorer ha-Temani R. Shalom Shabazi ve-shirato ha-ᶜIvrit.*" In *Mizraḥ U-Maᶜarav,* vol. 1 (1920), pp. 8–16, 228–237.
———. *Jewish Music in its Historical Development.* New York, 1929.
———. *Shire Teman.* Cincinnati, 1931.
———. "*Yehude Teman, Shiratam umanginatam.*" In *Reshumot.* Vol. I (1925), pp. 3–66 (Hebrew).
Imber, Naftali. *Kol Shire Naftali Herẓ Imber.* Tel-Aviv, 1950 (Hebrew).
Ingrams, Harold. *The Yemen: Imams, Rulers and Revolutions.* London, 1963.
Ish-Shalom, Michael. "*Ḥammisha Piyyuṭim le-Rabbi Abraham ben-Ḥalfon.*" *Tarbiz,* 18 (1949), 187–193.
Jamme, A. *Sabaean and Hasaean Inscriptions from Saudi Arabia.* Rome, 1966.
al-Jarāfī, Qāḍī ᶜAbdullāh ibn ᶜAbd al-Karīm. *al-Muqtaṭaf min Ta'rīkh al-Yaman.* Cairo, 1951.
Jeffery, Arthur, ed. *Islam: Muhammad and His Religion.* New York, 1958.
Kadman, Gurit. "Yemen Dances and their Influence on the New Israeli Folk Dances." *Journal of the International Folk Music Council,* 4 (1952), 27–30.
———. "Yemenite Dance," in *The Jews of Yemen,* ed. by Grace Cohen Grossman. Chicago, 1976.
Kafiḥ, Yosef, ed. *Gan Ha-Sekhalim,* translation into Hebrew with commentary of al-Fayyūmī's *Bustān al-ᶜUqūl.* Jerusalem, 1954.
———. *Halikhot Teman.* Jerusalem, 1961.
———, ed. "*'Iggeret Mahriṣ.*" In *Tiklal Shivat Ṣiyyon.* Jerusalem, 1952.
———. *'Iggeret Teman,* translation into Hebrew of Maimonides' *Epistle to Yemen.* In *'Igrot ha-Rambam,* pp. 15–60. Jerusalem, 1972.
———. "*Qehillat Sanᶜa she-be-Teman.*" *Maḥana'im,* 119 (1968), 38.
———. "*Qeshareha shel Yahadut Teman ᶜim Merkeze ha-Yahadut.*" In *Yahadut Teman,* ed. by Yisra'el Yesaᶜyahu and Yosef Tobi, Jerusalem (1976), pp. 29–46.
———, ed. "*Qorot Yisra'el be-Teman le-Rabbi Ḥayyim Ḥabshush.*" In *Sefunot: Annual for Research on the Jewish Communities in the East,* vol. 2, Jerusalem (1958), pp. 246–286.
———. "*Shas Teman: Daf mi-Masekhet Makkot.*" *Sinai,* 28 (1951), 19–23.
———, ed. "*Sefer Dofi ha-Zeman le-Rabbi Saᶜid Saᶜdi: Qorot Yehude Teman bishnot 1717–1726.*" In *Sefunot,* 1, (1956), pp. 185–242.

———. *Sefer Me'or ha-'Afela* (trans. of Netan'el ben Yesha^{c}ia's *Nūr al-Ẓalām*). Jerusalem, 1957.

Karaso, David. "*Zikhron Teman,*" ed. by Yosef Tobi. In *Yehude Teman ba-Me'ah ha-19,* pp. 121–190. Tel-Aviv, 1976.

Kassar, Shalom. "*Reshit ^{c}Aliyyatam shel Yehude Teman.*" In *Har'el,* ed. by Y. Ratzaby and I. Shivti'el, pp. 236. Tel-Aviv, 1962

Katsh, Abraham. *Judaism in Islam.* New York, 1954.

Kehati, Moshe. "*ha-Tenu^{c}a ha-Shavta'it be-Teman.*" *Zion,* 5 (1933), 78–88.

Kerr, Robert. General History and Collections of Voyages and Travels. Vol. 6. Edinburgh, 1812.

al-Khazrajī, ^{c}Alī ibn al-Ḥasān. *al-^{c}Uqūd al-Lu'lu'īyya fī Ta'rīkh al-Dawla al-Rasūlīyya.* 2 vols. Cairo, 1911 and 1914. Trans. by J. W. Redhouse as *The Pearl-Strings: A History of the Resūlī Dynasty of Yemen.* 2 vols. London, 1906 and 1907.

Kister, M. J. and Menachim. "On the Jews of Arabia—Some Notes." *Tarbiz,* 48 (1979), 231–249 (Hebrew).

Klausner, Joseph. *The Messianic Idea in Israel,* trans. by W. F. Stinespring. New York, 1955.

Klein-Franke, Avivah. "*ha-Yehudim be-^{c}Aden ba-Me'ah ha-19.*" In *Pe^{c}amim,* vol. 10 (1981), pp. 37–59.

ha-Kohen, Rabbi Yisra'el ben Shelomo. *Sefer Segullat Yisra'el.* Vol. 1 (Genesis–Exodus). Rosh ha-^{c}Ayin, 1975.

Koraḥ, ^{c}Amram. *Sa^{c}arat Teman: Qorot ha-Yehudim be-Teman.* Jerusalem, 1956.

Koraḥ, Shalom. *Iggeret Bokhim.* Bet-Shemesh, 1963. Reprinted in Tobi, ed., *Toledot Yehude Teman,* pp. 182–196. Jerusalem, 1979.

———. "'^{c}Olelot." In *Bo'i Teman,* ed. by Yehuda Ratzaby, pp. 58–66. Tel-Aviv, 1967.

Kozodoy, Neal. "Reading in Medieval Hebrew," *AJS Review,* 2 (1977).

Lammens, Henry. *L'Arabie Occidentale Avant l'Hégire.* Beirut, 1928.

Lancaster, Halford. *British Routes to India.* New York, London, 1928.

Lane-Pool, Stanley. *A History of Egypt in the Middle Ages.* London, 1914.

Latourette, Kenneth Scott. *A History of the Expansion of Christianity.* Vol. I. New York and London, 1937, pp. 231–238.

Levanon, Yosef. *The Jewish Travellers in the Twelfth Century.* Lanham, Md., 1980.

Levine, David, ed. *The Bustan al-Ukul by Nathanael Ibn al-Fayyumi.* New York, 1966.

Lewin, Benjamin M. "'*Igrot Ga'on mi-Bavel le-Ereṣ Yaman ve-Yamama.*" *Ginze Qedem: A Geonitic Scientific Periodical,* 3 (1925), 14–23 (Hebrew).

Lieberman, Saul. "*Hilkhot Teman.*" In *Yahadut Teman,* ed. by Yisra'el Yesha^{c}yahu and Yosef Tobi, pp. 349–355. Jerusalem, 1976.

———. *Midreshe Teman.* Jerusalem, 1940 (Hebrew).

Lind, Nils E. "The Return of the Gaddites: Reminiscences of the American Colony and of the Yemenite Jews in Jerusalem." *Palestine Exploration Quarterly* (1973), pp. 151–160.

Luckenbill, Daniel David. *Ancient Records of Assyria and Babylonia.* 2 vols. Chicago, 1926–1927.

Lybyer, Albert Howe. *The Government of the Ottoman Empire in the Time of Suleiman the Magnificent.* Cambridge, Mass., 1913.

Macdonald, D. B. "*Fiṭra.*" EI^{2}, vol. II, pp. 931–932.

Macro, Eric. *Yeman and the Western World, since 1571.* New York and Washington, 1968.

al-Madaḥ, Amīrat ᶜAli. *al-ᶜUthmāniyūn wal-'Imām al-Qāsim bin ᶜAlī fī al-Yaman: 1598–1620.* Jidda, 1982.

Madmoni, Ṣiyyon. "*ha-Rambam ve-Nosaḥ ha-Tefilla shel Yehude Teman.*" In *Yahadut Teman,* ed. by Yisra'el Yeshaᶜyahu and Yosef Tobi, pp. 373–394. Jerusalem, 1975.

Maḥmūd, Ḥasan Sulaimān. *Ta'rīkh al-Yaman al-Siyāsī fī al-ᶜAṣr al-Islāmī.* Baghdad, 1969.

Mann, Jacob. "A Second Supplement to 'The Jews in Egypt and in Palestine under the Fāṭimid Caliphs.' " *HUCA,* vol. III (1926), 301–303.

———. *The Jews in Egypt and in Palestine under the Fatimid Caliphs.* 2 Vols. New York, 1970 (first published, 1920).

Marcus, Jacob R. *The Jew in the Medieval World: A Source Book, 315–1791.* New York, 1969.

Margaliot, Mordekhai, ed. *Midrash ha-Gadol.* Jerusalem, 1947.

Margoliouth, D. S. *The Relations between Arabs and Israelites Prior to the Rise of Islam.* London, 1924.

Marks, Paul F. *Bibliography of Literature Concerning Yemenite-Jewish Music.* Detroit, 1973.

Martyrium Arethae (BHG 166). The Standard edition is that of Ed. Carpentier in *Acta Sanctorum,* Octobris tomus X (1861), pp. 721–759. First ed., Boissonade, *Anecdota graeca,* vol. V, pp. 1–62. Paris, 1833 (photocopy reprint, Hildesheim, 1962).

al-Masᶜūdī. *Kitāb al-Tanbīb wa'l-Ishrāf,* ed. by M. J. de Goeje. Vol. 8. Leiden, 1894.

Mayer, L. A. "*ᶜEmdat ha-Yehudim Bime ha-Mamlukim.*" In *Sefer Magnes,* pp. 161–167. Jerusalem, 1938 (Hebrew).

Middleton, Sir Henry. *The Last East-Indian Voyage.* Amsterdam, 1971.

Milik, J. T. "Priere de Nabonide." *Revue Biblique,* 63 (1956), 407.

Mirsky, Aharon. *Piyyuṭe Yosse ben Yosse.* Jerusalem, 1977 (Hebrew).

Moberg, A., ed. "The Book of the Himyarites," In *Acta regiae Societatis humaniorum litteratum Lundensis.* Vol. 7 (Syriac Text), pp. 1–61. Lund, 1924.

Montgomery, James. *Arabia and the Bible.* New York, 1969.

Morag, Shelomo. "*ha-Arammit ha-Bavlit be-Masortam shel Yehude Teman.*" *Tarbiz,* 30 (1961), 120–129.

———. "*Darkhe ha-Ḥariza shel Meshorere Teman u-She'elot Yiḥuso shel Midrash ha-Gadol le-Rabbi David al-ᶜAdani.*" *Tarbiz,* 34 (1965), 257–262.

———. *ha-ᶜIvrit she-be-Fi Yehude Teman.* Jerusalem, 1963.

———. "*Ketiv u-Qeri ba-Sifrut shelle-'Ahar ha-Miqra be-Masortam shel ᶜEdot.*" In *Bo'i Teman,* ed. by Y. Ratzaby, pp. 26–45. Tel-Aviv, 1967.

———. *Ktav-Yad Bavli-Temani shel Massekhet Kippurim.* In *Ḥasifat Genuzim mi-Teman,* ed. by Yehuda Levi Naḥum, pp. 11–18. Ḥolon, 1971.

———. "*Masorot ha-Darot bi-Khfifa 'Aḥat.*" In *Har'el, Raphael Alsheikh Memorial Volume,* ed. by Y. Ratzaby and Yiṣḥaq Shivṭi'el, pp. 157–169. Tel-Aviv, 1962.

———. "*Masorot ha-Lashon shel Yehude Teman.*" In *Yahadut Teman: Studies and Researches,* ed. by Yisra'el Yeshaᶜyahu and Yosef Tobi, pp. 357–366. Jerusalem, 1975.

———. "Oral Traditions and Dialects." In *Proceedings of the International Conference on Semitic Studies,* pp. 180–189. Jerusalem, 1965.

Müller, D. H. *Die Burgen und Schlösser Südarabiens, nach dem Iklil des Hamdânî.* 2 pts., Vienne, 1879; II Wien, 1881.

al-Muqaddasī (or al-Maqdīsī). *Aḥsan al-Taqāsīm fī Maᶜrifat al-Aqālīm.* 2 Vols., Leiden, 1938–1939.

Musil, Alois. *Arabia Deserta: A Topographical Itinerary.* New York: American Geographical Society, 1927 (reprint, New York, 1978).

———. *The Northern Ḥegâz: A Topographical Itinerary.* New York: American Geographical Society, 1926 (reprint, New York, 1978).

———. *Northern Negd: A Topographical Itinerary.* New York: American Geographical Society of America, 1927 (reprint, New York, 1978).

Naḥum, Yehuda Levi. *Ḥasifat Genuzim mi-Teman.* Ḥolon, 1971.

———. "*Le-Toledot ha-Rav Zecharia ha-Rofe (Yeḥia ben Suleiman al-Ṭabīb).*" In *Hasifat Genuzim mi-Teman,* pp. 180–237. Ḥolon, 1971. (The article deals with various works of ha-Rofe and includes his midrash on Esther and Song of Solomon.)

———. "*Le-Toledot R. Ḥoter be-Rav Shelomo ben al-Muᶜallim.*" In *Ḥasifat Genuzim mi-Teman,* pp. 238–243. Ḥolon, 1971.

———. *mi-Ṣefunot Yehude Teman.* Tel-Aviv, 1962.

Nemoy, Leon, ed. *Kitāb al-'Anwār wal-Marāqib* by Yaᶜqūb al-Qirqisānī. New York, 1939.

Neubauer, A. "Eldad the Danite," Review of Abraham Epstein's monograph *Eldad ha-Dani. . . . JQR,* III (1891), 541–544.

———. "The Literature of the Jews of Yemen." *JQR,* III (1891), 604–621 (reprint, Ktab Publishing House, 1966).

———. "Pseudo-Josephus, Joseph Ben Burion." *JQR,* XI (1899), 351–361.

Neustadt, David. "*Kavvim le-Toledot ha-Kalkala shel ha-Yehudim ve-Yishuvam be-Miṣra'im.*" *Sinai,* 2 (1937), 216–255.

Nicholson, Reynold A. *A Literary History of the Arabs.* Cambridge, England, 1966.

Niebuhr, M. *Travels Through Arabia and Other Countries in the East,* English trans. by Robert Heron. 2 vols. Edinburgh, 1792.

Niebuhr, Carsten. *Travels in Arabia.* In *A General Collection of the Best and Most Interesting Voyages and Travels in All Parts of the World,* abr. and trans. by J. Pinkerton. Vol. 10. London, 1811.

Nini, Yehuda. *Teman ve-Ṣiyyon: ha-Reqaᶜ ha-Medini, ha-Ḥevrati ve-Haruḥani laᶜAliyyot ha-Rishonot mi-Teman, 1800–1914.* Jerusalem, 1982 (Hebrew).

———. "*Teᶜuddot Mishpaḥtiyyot mi-Tokh "ha-Musawwada.*" In *Moreshet Yehude Teman: ᶜIyyunim u-Meḥqarim,* ed. by Yosef Tobi. Jerusalem, 1977 (Hebrew).

Noy, Dov. "*Peṭirat R. Shalem Shabazi be-Aggadat haᶜAm ha-Temanit.*" In *Moreshet Yehude Teman: ᶜIyyunim u-Meḥqarim,* pp. 132–149. Jerusalem, 1977.

———. "*R. Shalem Shabazi be'Aggadat ha-ᶜAm shel Yehude Teman.*" In *Bo'i Teman,* ed. by Y. Ratzaby, pp. 106–133. Tel-Aviv, 1967.

Obermann, Julian. "Islamic Origins: A Study in Background and Foundation." In *The Arab Heritage,* ed. by Nabih Amin Faris, pp. 58–120. Princeton, N.J., 1944.

———. "Koran and Agada." *AJSLL,* 58 (1941), 23–48.

O'Leary, De Lacy. *Arabia Before Mohammed.* New York, 1927.

Owen, W. F. W. *Narrative of Voyages.* 2 Vols. London, 1833.

Palmer, J. A. B. "The Origins of the Janissaries." *BJRL,* 35 (1952–53), 448–481.

Patai, Raphael. *Israel Between East and West: A Study in Human Relations.* Philadelphia, 1953.

Perlmann, Moseh. "A Legendary Story of Kaᶜb al-Aḥbar's Conversion to

Islam." In *The Joshua Starr Memorial Volume,* pp. 85–99. New York, 1953.
———. "The Medieval Polemics Between Islam and Judaism." In *Religion in a Religious Age,* ed. by S. D. Goitein, pp. 103–138. Cambridge, Mass., 1974.
Philby, J. B. *The Heart of Arabia.* 2. vols. New York, 1923.
———. *Sheba's Daughters.* London, 1939.
Phillips, Wendell. *Qataban and Sheba.* New York, 1955.
Philostorgius, "*Historia ecclesiastica.*" In *Philostorgius Kirchengeschichte: Die Griechischen Christlichen Schriftsteller,* ed. by J. Bidez. Vol. 21. Leipzig, 1913.
Pines, S., "Nathanël ben al-Fayyumi et la théologie ismaeliënne." *Review de l'Histoire Juive en Egypte,* 1 (1947), 5–22.
Playfair, Robert L. *A History of Arabia Felix of Yemen.* Amsterdam, 1970 (first published in Bombay in 1859).
Poole, Stanley Lane. *A History of Egypt in the Middle Ages.* London, 1938.
Prestage, Edgar. *The Portuguese Pioneers.* London, 1933.
Pritchard, James B. "The Age of Solomon." In *Solomon and Sheba,* ed. by Pritchard, pp. 17–39. London, 1974.
———, ed. *Ancient Near Eastern Texts Relating to the Old Testament.* , 1955.
———, ed. *Solomon and Sheba.* London, 1974.
al-Qalqashandī. *Subḥ al-Aᶜshā.* Vol. 13, pp. 378–379. Cairo,
al-Qirqisānī, Yaᶜqub. *Kitāb al-'Anwār wal-Marāqib,* ed. by Leon Nemoy, Vol. 1. New York, 1939.
Rabinowitz, Z. M. "*ha-Yeṣira ha-Midrashit shel Yehude Teman.*" In *Yahadut Teman,* ed. by Yisra'el Yeshaᶜyahu and Yosef Tobi, pp. 367–372. Jerusalem, 1975.
———. "*Midrash Ḥadash ᶜal Parashat Shemini.*" In *Ḥasifat Genuzim mi-Teman,* ed. by Yehuda Levi Nahum, pp. 30–37. Holon, 1971.
———. '*Qetaᶜ shel Mishna vi-Rushalmi Sheviᶜit.*" In *Ḥasifat Genuzim mi-Teman,* ed. by Yehuda Levi Nahum, pp. 19–29. Holon, 1971.
al-Ramlī, *Nihāyat al-Muḥtāj ila Sharḥ al-Minhāj.* Cairo, 1886.
Ratzaby, Yehuda. "ᶜ*Al Meḥabro shel Midrash 'Ḥemdat Yamim'.*" *Taggim,* 3–4 (1972), 73–74.
———. "*Appoqalipsot ve-Ḥishuve Qeṣ be-Yahadut Teman.*" *Meḥqere ha-Merkaz le-Ḥeqer ha-Folklore,* 1 (1970), 295–322.
———, ed. *Bo'i Teman: Meḥqarim u-Teᶜuddot be-Tarbut Yehude Teman.* Tel-Aviv, 1967 (Hebrew).
———. "*Dardaᶜim: Kat Mitnaggede ha-Qabbalah ben Yehude Teman.*" *ᶜEdot* 1/3 (1946), 165–180.
———. "ᶜ*Ezra ha-Sofer ve-ha-Temanim.*" *Sinai,* 15 (1945), 108–111.
———. "*Galut Mauzaᶜ* (1679–1680)." *Zion,* 37 (1972), 339–395.
———. "*Gerush Mauzaᶜ le'-Or Meqorot Ḥadashim.*" *Sefunot,* Vol. 5 (1961), pp. 197–215.
———. "*Gevurat bene Dan u-Vne Rekhav be-Masoret Yehude Teman.*" *Maḥana'im,* 87 (1964), 130–137.
———. "*Gzerah ᶜal Yehude Sanᶜa be-Fesaḥ 1818,*" In *Minḥa Lihuda,* ed. by S. Asaf et al., pp. 258–283. Jerusalem, 1950.
———, ed. *Har'el: Rabbi Alsheikh Memorial Volume.* Tel-Aviv, 1962.
———. "*Hashpaᶜat al-Ḥarīrī ᶜal al-Ḍahrī.*" *Biqoret 'u-Farshanut,* 11–12 (1978), 55–83.
———. "*ba-Maṣor uva-Maṣoq.*" In *Bo'i Teman,* pp. 73–102.

———. "*ha-Rambam be-Aggada ha-Temanit.*" *ha-Boker,* April 24, 1939.
———. "*Rishone ᶜOle Teman ba-ᶜAliyyat 1882.*" *Maḥana'im,* 72 (1963), 70–75.
———. "*ha-Ṣippiyya li-Ge'ulla be-Teman bi-Shnot 1560–1648.*" *Maḥana'im,* 38 (1959), 75–78.
———. "*ha-Talmud vihude Teman.*" *Maḥana'im,* 57 (1961), 124–129.
———. "*Heᶜara le "Daf mi-Shas Teman.*" *Sinai,* 40 (1957), 186.
———. "*Mahriṣ ve-Sifro Peᶜullat Ṣaddiq.*" In *Shevut Teman,* pp. 100–117.
———. "*Mered al-Qasim.*" *Zion,* 20 (1955), 32–46.
———. "*mi-Sifrutam shel Yehude Teman.*" *Areshet,* 5 (1972), 153–155.
———. "*Nosafot le-ᶜEzra ha-Sofer ve-ha-Temanim.*" *Sinai,* 18 (1946), 382.
———. "*Piyyuṭe Bavel be-Maḥazor Teman.*" *Ha'areṣ, Tarbut ve-Sifrut,* Oct. 1, 1968.
———. "*Rabbi Shalem Shabazi ve-Shirato.*" In *Sefer Zikkaron le-Izḥak ben-Ṣevi,* ed. by Meir Benayahu, Vol. II (1964), pp. 135–136. Republished in *Sefunot,* vol. 9 (1965), pp. 135–166.
———, ed. *Sefer ha-Musar: Maḥbarot R. Zecharia al-Ḍahrī.* Jerusalem, 1965.
———. "*Shir Sofrim Qadum la-Torah.*" *ᶜAlle-Sefer,* vol. 3 (1977), pp. 54–62.
———. "*Teᶜuddot le-Toledot Yehude Teman.*" *Sefunot,* vol. 2 (1958), pp. 287–302.
———. *Yalqut Shire Teman.* Jerusalem, 1968.
Rihani, Ameen. *Arabian Peak and Desert: Travels in Al-Yaman.* Boston and New York, 1930.
Rivlin, Yosef. "*Ṣava'at Muḥammad leᶜAli ben abi Ṭaleb.*" In *Minḥa le-David: David Yelin Jubilee Volume,* pp. 139–156. Jerusalem, 1935.
Rodinson, Maxime. *Mohammed,* trans. by Anne Carter. New York, 1971.
Rosenthal, Erwin I. J. *Judaism and Islam.* London, 1961.
Rothschild, M. *ha-Ḥaluqqa ke-Biṭṭui le-Yaḥasah shel Yahadut ha-Golah la-Yishuv ha-Yehudi be-Ereṣ Yisra'el ba-Shanim 1810–1860.* Jerusalem, 1969.
Ruppin, A. *ha-Soṣiologia shel ha-Yehudim.* 4 Vols. Tel-Aviv, 1934.
———. *Memoirs, Diaries, Letters.* Jerusalem, 1971.
Rycaut, Paul. *The History of the Turkish Empire from 1623–1677.* London, 1680.
Ryckmans, G. *Inscriptions sud-arabes (dixième série). Le Muséon,* 66 (1953), 267–317.
———. "Le *qayl* en Arabie méridionale préislamique." In *Hebrew and Semitic Studies Presented to Godfrey Rolles Driver,* ed. by Winton Thomas and W. D. McHardy, pp. 144–155. Oxford, England, 1963.
Ryckmans, Jacques. "*Inscriptions historiques sabéennes de l'Arabie Centrale.*" *Le Muséon,* 66 (1953), 319–342.
Sachs, S., ed. *Jahrbuch für die Geschichte der Juden und des Judenthums.* Vol. 3 (1863).
Ṣaᶜdi, Saᶜid. "*Sefer Dofi ha-Zeman': Qorot Yehude Teman bi-Shnot 1717–1726.*" ed. by Yosef Kafiḥ. *Sefunot,* vol. 1 (1957), pp. 185–242.
Ṣadoq, Aharon, ed. *Shevut Teman.* Jerusalem, 1945 (Hebrew).
Ṣadoq, Moshe. "*ha-Yeḥasim ben ha-Yehudim ve-ha-ᶜAravim be-Teman.*" In *Yahadut Teman,* ed. by Yisra'el Yeshaᶜyahu and Yosef Tobi, pp. 147–163. Jerusalem, 1976.
———. *Yehude Teman, Toledotehem ve-'Orḥot Ḥayyehem.* Tel-Aviv, 1967.
Ṣāliḥ, Yeḥia (Mahriṣ). "*Megillat Teman,*" ed. by David Sassoon. *ha-Ṣofe le-Hokhmat Yisra'el,* 7 (1923), 1–14.
Sālim, al-Sayyid Musṭafa. *al-Fatḥ al-ᶜUthmānī al-Awwāl lil-Yaman.* Cairo, 1969.

Samau'al, al-Maghrībī. *Ifḥam al-Yahūd* (Silencing the Jews), ed. and trans. by M. Perlmann. *PAAJR,* Vol. 32.C (1964).
Saphir, Ya[c]akov. *'Even Sappir.* 2 Vols. Vol. 1, Lyck, 1866. Vol. 2, Mainz, 1874 (Hebrew). Reprinted, 1969; abridged by A. Ya[c]ari and published as *Sefer Massa[c] Teman,* Tel-Aviv, 1944 (Hebrew).
Sassoon, David S. "An Autograph Letter of a Pseudo-Messiah." *JQR,* 19 (1907), 162–167.
———. "*Megillat Teman.*" *ha-Ṣofeh le-Ḥokhmat Yisra'el,* 7 (1923), 1–14.
Schechtman, Joseph. "The End of Galut Yemen." *Jewish Affairs,* 4 (1950), 3–33.
Schechter, M. A. *Studies in Judaism.* Philadelphia, 1911.
Schirmann, Hayyim. "*Yehuda al-Ḥarizi ha-Meshorer ve-ha-Mesapper.*" *Mozna'im,* 2 (1934), 101–115.
———. "*ha-Rambam ve-Hashira ha-[c]Ivrit.*" *Mozna'im,* 3 (1935), 433–436.
Scholem, Gershom, ed. "*Ge Ḥizayyon.*" *Qoveṣ [c]al-Yad,* n.s. 4, Jerusalem (1966), 103–141.
———. *Sabbatai Sevi.* Princeton, 1973.
Schröter, R. *Trostschreiben Jacob's von Saruj an die Himjaritischen Christen.* *ZDMG,* 31 (1877), 360–405 (Syriac Text, 369–385).
Scott, Hugh. *In the High Yemen.* London, 1942.
Scott, R. B. Y. "Solomon and the Beginning of Wisdom in Israel." Supplement to *Vetus Testamentum,* 3 (1955), 262–279.
Serjeant, R. B. *The Portuguese off the South Arabian Coast: Ḥadrami Chronicles.* Beirut, 1974.
———. "The Zaydīs." In *Religion in the Middle East,* ed. by A. J. Arberry, vol. 2, pp. 285–301. Cambridge, England, 1969.
Seri, Shalom, and Yosef Tobi, eds. *Shirim Ḥadashim le-Rabbi Shalom Shabazi.* Jerusalem, 1976 (Hebrew).
Shabazi, Shalom. *Ḥemdat Yamim: A Commentary on the Pentateuch.* 2 vols. Jerusalem, 1977 (Hebrew).
al-Shahārī, Muhammad [c]Alī. *Ṭarīq al-thawrāt al-Yamanīyah.* Cairo, 1966.
Shahîd, Irfan. *The Martyrs of Najrân: New Documents.* Bruxelles, 1971.
Shar[c]abi, Hayyim. "*Peraqim mi-Parashat Dor-De[c]ah be-Teman.*" In *Shevut Teman,* pp. 198–211.
Sharot, Stephen. *Messianism, Mysticism, and Magic: A Sociological Analysis of Jewish Religious Movements.* Chapel Hill, N.C., 1902.
Shemen, Yosef. "*Qontreṣ Ḥayye ha-Temanim,*" ed. by Y. L. Naḥum and Yosef Tobi. In *Yahadut Teman,* ed. by Yisra'el Yesa[c]yahu and Yosef Tobi, pp. 115–143. Jerusalem, 1976.
al-Shukanī, Muḥammad [c]Alī. *al-Badr al-Ṭāle[c].* Cairo, 1944.
Ṣiddiqi, [c]Abdul Ḥamid. English translation and commentary of *Ṣaḥīḥ Muslim.* Lahore, 1973.
Silberman, Lou H. "The Queen of Sheba in Judaic Tradition." In *Solomon and Sheba,* ed. by J. B. Pritchard, pp. 65–84. London, 1974.
Simeon of Bêth-Arshâm, *Letter* (S) to Simeon Abbot of Gabbula (BHO 99–101), ed. by I. Guidi, *La lettera di Simeone vescovo di Bêth-Arśâm sopra i martiri omeriti,* in *Atti della R. Accademia dei Lincei,* serie III, vol. VII, pp. 471–515 (Syriac Text, pp. 501–515). Roma, 1881 Reprinted in I. Guidi, *Raccolta di scritti,* vol. I, pp. 1–60. Rome, 1945.
Smith, G. R., ed. *The Ayyūbids and Early Rasūlids in the Yemen,* vol. 1 (a critical edition of Ibn Hātim al-Hamdānī's *Kitāb al-Simṭ*). London, 1974.

———. *The Ayyūbids and Early Rasūlids in the Yemen* (567–594/1173–1295), Vol. 2. London, 1978.
———. "The Ayyūbids and Rasūlids—The Transfer of Power in the 7th/13th Century Yemen." *Islamic Culture,* 43 (1969), 175–188.
Smith, Sidney. *Babylonian Historical Texts, Relating to the Downfall of Babylon.* London, 1924. The Nabonidus Chronicle in Pls. XI–XIV, pp. 110 ff.
———. "Events in Arabia in the 6th Century A.D." *BSOAS* 16 (1959), 425–468.
———. *Isaiah Chapters XL–LV: Literary Criticism and History.* London, 1944.
Smith, Wilfred Cantwell. "Some Similarities and Differences Between Christianity and Islam: An Essay in Comparative Religion." In *The World of Islam: Studies in Honor of Philip K. Hitti,* ed. by James Kritzeck and R. Bayly Winder, pp. 47–59. London, 1960.
Sokolow, Nahum. *Hibbath Zion (The Love for Zion).* Jerusalem, 1961.
———. *History of Zionism (1600–1918).* 2 vols. London, 1919.
Starr, Joshua. *The Jews in the Byzantine Empire, 641–1204.* New York, 1939.
———. *The Joshua Starr Memorial Volume.* New York, 1953.
Steinsalz, A. "*Darkhe haḥariza ba-Midrash ha-Gadol.*" *Tarbiz,* 34 (1964), 94–97.
Steinschneider, M. *Die Arabische Literature der Juden.* Stuttgart, 1902.
———. *Polemische und apologetische Literatur in arabischer Sprache.* Leipzig, 1877.
Stillman, Norman A. *The Jews of Arab Lands: A History and Source Book.* Philadelphia, 1979.
———. "Muslims and Jews in Morocco: Perceptions, Images, Stereotypes." In *Proceedings of the Seminar on Muslim-Jewish Relations in North Africa,* pp. 13–27. New York, 1974.
Stookey, Robert W. *Yemen: The Politics of the Yemen Arab Republic.* Boulder, Colorado, 1978.
Strabo. *Geographica,* ed. by A. Meineke. Lipsiae, 1866.
Strauss, Eli. "*Massaᶜ le-Hodu: Mikhtav meᶜAden le-Miṣra'im bi-Shenat, 1153* C.E.." *Zion,* 4 (1930), 217–231.
———. "Social Isolation of Ahl Adh-dhimma." In *Études Orientales a la Mémoire de Paul Hirschler,* ed. by O. Komlos, pp, 73–94. Budapest, 1950.
———. "*Teᶜuddot le-Ḥeker ha-Historia ha-kalkalit ve-ha-Ḥevratit shel ha-Yehudim ba-Mizraḥ ha-Karov.*" *Zion,* 7 (1942), 140–155.
Sweetman, J. Windrow. *Islam and Christian Theology.* London and Redhill, 1945.
Tabari, Ali. *The Book of Religion and Empire,* trans. and ed. by A. Mingana. Manchester Univ. Press, 1922.
al-Ṭabarī. *Ta'rīkh al-Rusūl wa'l-Mulūk* (Annales), ed. by M. J. de Goeje et al. 15 vols. Leiden 1879–1901 (reprint, Leiden, 1964).
Ṭabib, Abraham. "*Le-Toledot Yishuv 'Eḥad.*" In *Shevut Teman,* ed. by Yisra'el Yesaᶜyahu and Aharon Ṣadoq, pp. 59–74. Tel-Aviv, 1945.
Tobi, Yosef. "The Authority of the Community of Sanᶜa in Yemenite Jewry." In *Jewish Societies in the Middle East: Community, Culture, and Authority,* ed. by Shlomo Deshen and Walter P. Zenner, pp. 235–250. Washington, D.C., 1982.
——. "*Ben Shirat Teman le-Shirat Sefarad.*" In *Yahadut Teman,* ed. by Yisra'el Yeshaᶜyahu and Yosef Tobi, pp. 303–332. Jerusalem, 1975.
———. *ᶜAl ha-Talmud be-Teman.* Tel-Aviv, 1973 (Hebrew).
———. "*ha-Keronika ᶜal Gzerat haᶜAṭarot: Me'oraᶜot ha-Shavta'ut be-Teman (1667) le-Rabbi Seᶜadia Halevi.*" In *Toledot Yehude Teman: mi-Kitvehem,* ed. by Yosef Tobi, pp. 51–52. Jerusalem, 1979.

———. "*Ḥiqqui u-Makqor be-Shiratam shel Yehude Teman.*" In *Peᶜamim,* pp. 29–38. Jerusalem, 1979.
———. "*Piyyut Reviᶜi le-Rabbi Daniel be-Rabbi Fayyūmi.*" *Afiqim,* February 1983, 13 and 24.
———. "*Shir ᶜAl Hilkhot Sheḥita le-Rabbi Abraham ben Ḥalfon.*" *Afiqim,* May 1976, pp. 6–7.
———. *Toledot Yehude Teman: mi-Kitvehem.* Jerusalem, 1979.
———. " *'Yaᶜavor ᶜAlai Reṣonkha' le-Rihal ba-Piyyut ha-Temani.*" *Afiqim,* 34 (March 1970), 4 and 10.
———, ed. *Yahadut Teman: Studies and Researches.* Jerusalem, 1975.
———. *Yehude Teman ba-Me'ah ha-19: Toledot u-Meqorot.* Tel-Aviv, 1976.
———. "*le-Zihui Meḥabro shel Midrash Ḥemdat Yamim ha-Temani.*" *Taggim,* 3–4 (1972), 63–72.
Torrey, Charles Cutler. *The Jewish Foundation of Islam.* New York, 1967.
Tritton, A. S. *The Caliphs and Their Non-Muslim Subjects: A Critical Study of the Covenant of ᶜUmar.* Reprint. London, 1970.
Tritton, A. S. *The Rise of the Imamas of Sanaa.* London, 1925. (Reprint, 1981).
Twersky, Isadore. *A Maimonides Reader.* New York, 1972.
Ullendorff, Edward. *Ethiopia and the Bible.* London, 1968.
———. "The Queen of Sheba in Ethiopian Tradition." Ch. V of *Solomon and Sheba,* ed. by J. B. Pritchard, pp. 104–114. London, 1974.
Urbach, E. E. "*Mishmarot u-Maᶜmadot.*" *Tarbiz,* 42 (1973), 304–327.
Vasiliev, A. A. *Justin the First: An Introduction to the Epoch of Justinian the Great.* Cambridge, Mass., 1950.
Vester, Bertha Spafford. *Our Jerusalem: An American Family in the Holy City, 1881–1949.* New York, 1977.
Vida, Giorgio Levi della. "Pre-Islamic Arabia." In *The Arab Heritage,* ed. by Nabih Amin Faris, pp. 24–57. Princeton, N.J., 1944.
al-Wāsiᶜī, Abd al-Wāsiᶜ ibn Yaḥia. *Ta'rīkh al-Yaman.* Cairo, 1928.
Watson, Paul F. "The Queen of Sheba in Christian Tradition." Ch. VI of *Solomon and Sheba,* ed. by J. B. Pritchard, pp. 115–145. London, 1974.
Watt, W. Montgomery. *The Faith and Practice of al-Ghazali.* Lahore, 1963.
———. *Muhammad at Medina.* Oxford, 1956.
———. "The Queen of Sheba in Islamic Tradition." Ch. IV of *Solomon and Sheba,* ed. by J. B. Pritchard, pp. 85–103. London, 1974.
Weinryb, Bernard D. "The Khazars, An Annotated Bibliography." In *Studies in Bibliography and Booklore,* vol. 6 (1963), pp. 111–129.
Wensinck, A. J. *A Handbook of Early Muhammadan Tradition.* Leiden, 1960.
Wissman, H. von. "Ḥimyar, Ancient History." *Le Muséon,* 77 (1964), 429–497.
Wright, Ernest G. *Biblical Archaeology.* London, 1957.
Yaᶜari, Abraham. "*Aliyyat Yehude Teman le-Ereṣ Yisra'el.*" In *Shevut Teman,* ed. by Yisra'el Yeshaᶜyahu and Aharon Ṣadoq, pp. 37–54. Tel-Aviv, 1945.
———. 'Iggerot 'Ereṣ Yisra'el. Tel-Aviv, 1943.
———. *Masᶜot Ereṣ Yisra'el.* Ramat-Gan, 1976.
———. *Sefer Massaᶜ Teman Me'et Yaᶜkov Saphir.* Abridgment of Saphir's *'Even Sappir.* Jerusalem, 1944 and 1951.
———. "*Sheliḥim me-Ereṣ Yisra'el la-ᶜAseret ha-Shevaṭim.*" *Sinai,* 6 (1940), 163–178; 344–356; 474–482.
———. "*Sheliḥim me-Ereṣ Yisra'el le-Teman.*" *Sinai,* 4 (1930), 392–430.
———. "Shukr Kuḥeil." In *Shevut Teman,* pp. 182–196. Tel-Aviv, 1945.

Yarmolinsky, Abraham. "The Khazars, A Bibliography." *Bulletin of the New York Public Library,* 42 (1938), 695–710.

———. "The Khazars: A Bibliography (1940–1958)." *Bulletin of the New York Public Library,* 63 (1959), 237–41.

Yavni'eli, S. *Massa*ᶜ *le-Teman.* Tel-Aviv, 1952.

Yelin, D. *Torat ha-Shira ha-Sefaradit.* Jerusalem, 1972.

Yeshaᶜyahu, Yisra'el. "*Shevile ha*ᶜ*Aliyyah mi-Teman le-Ṣiyyon.*" In *Shevut Teman,* ed. by Yisra'el Yeshaᶜyahu and Aharon Ṣadoq, pp. 39–40. Tel-Aviv, 1944.

———, ed. *Shevut Teman.* Tel-Aviv, 1945.

———, ed. *Yahadut Teman: Studies and Researches.* Jerusalem, 1976.

Yevin, Yisra'el. "*Qit*ᶜ*e miqra mi-Teman she-Masortam Bavlit.*" In *Ḥasifat Genuzim mi-Teman* ed. by Yehuda Levi Naḥum, pp. 2–10. Ḥolon, 1971.

Zinberg, Israel. *A History of Jewish Literature.* Vol. 1, trans. and ed. by Bernard Martin. Cleveland, 1972.

Zwemer, Samuel M. *Arabia: The Cradle of Islam (1900).* New York, 1900–1912.

Zwettler, Michael. *The Oral Tradition of Classical Arabic Poetry: Its Character and Implications.* Columbus, 1978.

Zuker, Moshe. "*Berurim be-Toledot ha-Vikuḥim shebben ha-Yahadut ve-ha-Islam.*" *Festschrift Armand Kaminka.* Wien, 1937.

INDEX

ᶜAbbās, al-Mahdī, Imām, 141
ᶜAbbāsids: intertribal hostilities, 53
ᶜAbdallāh, Yosef (false messiah), 152–54
Abdülmecid, Sultan, reform decree of, 149
Abyssinia: occupation of Ḥimyar, 45, 48
Academie des Inscriptions et Belles Lettres, 154
Academies, Babylonian Jewish, 74
ᶜAdani, David ben ᶜAmram ha-, 80–81
ᶜAdani, Shelomo, Rabbi: on Jews' rejection of Ezra's call, 4–5; on Ezra legend, examined, 6; emigration to Israel, 159
Aden: commerce and culture, 68–69, 70, 79, 82, 144; Ottoman Turks in, 82; decline of port, 82; British occupation of, 144–45; and persecution of Jews of Sanaa, 146
Aden, Jews of: and Gaonic academies, 67; and *yeshivot* in Egypt, 68; and forced conversion, 71
Africa: commerce, 68; emigration from, 144
Agriculture: Arabs in, 44, 164, 165; in southern Arabia, 50–51; in Palestine, 164; Yemenite Jews in, 164–65
Aḥmad Mukhtar Pasha, 148, 149
Aḥmad, Sayyid (Ruler of Mauzaᶜ), 131
Allegory: and Shalom Shabazi, 93, 96
Alsheikh, A., Rabbi, 160
Alsheikh, Shalom Halevi, Rabbi, 146
Amalekites: Moses' attack on, 24–25
Anglo-Jewish Association, 142–43, 149, 150, 151
al-ᶜAnsī, Saᶜīd bin Ṣāliḥ Yasīn: as Mahdī, 146
Answer, reply (poetic form), 80
Arabia: Jewish migration to, 39–40; as center of Islam, 50
Arabia, northern: and southern Arabia compared, 50. *See also* Ḥijāz
Arabia, southern: Abyssinian occupation of, 48; agriculture, 48; conversion to Islam, 48; economy, 48. *See also* Yemen
Arabian Peninsula: domain of ten lost tribes, 3–4; in Hebrew scriptures, 27; commerce, 27–29; in inscriptions, 28; strategic role of, 28; kingdoms in, 30; decline of, 51
Arabic literature: discussed, 42; medieval, 79; metrics, 79
Arethas: martyrdom of, 45
Asᶜad, Abū Kārib, King, 50
al-Asbāṭ, Ibn: and exile to Mauzaᶜ, 126
Ashkenazim, 114, 160, 162
ᶜAshri, Shalom: on exile to Mauzaᶜ, 129
Assyrian records: on origins of Arabs, 20
Astrology: and Shalom Shabazi, 89–90; role in society, 90; and messianism, 102
Ayyūbids: conquest of Yemen, 60–61; in Yemen, 71
Ayyūb Pasha, 151

Babylonia: Jewish academies in, 67; and Yemenite Jews, 67–75 *passim;* liturgical poetry, 72; biblical texts, 74; spiritual centers, 75
Baghdad: as ᶜAbbāsid capital, 53; and Benjamin of Tudela, 76
Bakīl: Muslims, 13–14; confederacy, 142; invasion, 142–44
Banking: and dhimmīs, 138
Barer, Shlomo, 1–2
Benjamin of Tudela, 76–77
Bet-Sheᶜarim, 40–41
Betrothal customs, 140
Biblical texts: Babylonian, 74
Bilu: emigration from, 3
Bookbinding: old manuscripts in, 140–41
British: in Aden, 144–45
Bundar, Ḥasan (Japheth) bin, 69, 70
Burial customs: Jewish, 38, 40–41
Bury, Wyman G. (traveler), 136
Bustān al-ᶜUqūl (Garden of the Intellects), 56, 60, 62, 66

Cairo: commerce, 69
Cairo Geniza Documents. *See* Geniza Documents
Cassia trade, 28
Ceylon: commerce, 69
Christian churches: and Hebrew scriptures, 57; demolition of, 101
Christianity: and Ḥimyar, 46; Jewish po-

lemics against, 59; and moral perfection, 65
Christians: expulsion from Yemen, 21; and southern Arabia, 40; persecution of, 44–45, 49; conversion to Islam, 50; conscription of children, 118–19; colonists, 161
Chronicles, Book of, 29
Chronicles, Yemenite: and Ḥayyim Ḥabshush, 20; as history, 21; didactic purpose of, 22, 24
Cinnamon trade, 28
Cochin (India). *See* India, Jews of
Comet: and messianism, 147
Commentaries, Yemenite Hebrew: on Hebrew scriptures, 81; and Maimonides, 81; of Rabbi Zecharia al-Ḍahrī, 83
Commerce: Arabian Peninsula, 27–28; and Solomon, 32; Queen of Sheba, 32–33; and Jehoshaphat, 32–33; and Hiram, King of Tyre, 33; Teima, 34, 45; and immigration of Jews, 37; international, 50–51; India, 68; Yemen, 68, 136; Aden, 68–69, 70, 79, 82, 144; and Zaydīs, 78; and Rasūlids, 79; and Arabs, 82; and dhimmīs, 137–38. *See also* commodity names
Communications: among Jewish communities, 68–69
Constantine, Emperor, 40
Conversion, forced: and exile to Mauza[c], 121; in Jewish writings, 124
Cosmology: and Shalom Shabazi, 93
Courts, Jewish: restrictions on, 151
Culture, Yemenite Jewish, 18; effect on Israeli culture, 167–69

Da[c]an, Treaty of, 157
al-Ḍahrī, Zecharia, Rabbi: commentaries of, 83; and Zohar, 86; contributions of, 87. *See also Sefer ha-Musar*
Dan (tribe): and Seraia, 97
Dance: Yemenite Jewish, 167–68
Darin, Sa[c]id, Rabbi: on Sanaa, 89
Dating system: era of the contracts, 75
David, King, 25
David, Madmun bin: letter of, 71
Dead Sea Scrolls, 36
Dedan (tribe), 30, 34
dhimmī: and Yemenite Jews, 15; regulations on, 16–17; advantages, 18; and forged documents, 53; taxation of, 55; and Pact of [c]Umar, 100; and dress code, 101; Zaydīs' persecution of, 101–02; and latrines, 116; and Orphans Edict, 117–18; as officials, 137–38; and Bakīl invasion, 143; in Aden, 145
Diaspora, 160, 162
Dīn, Ḥamīd al-: and Ottoman Turks, 150
al-Dīn, Nūr (Yemenite ruler), 78
Divine unity: in Islam, 58
Dofi ha-Zeman (*Faults of the Times*): didactic purpose of, 22, 24
Dor-De[c]ah (*Generation of Reason*): and Ḥayyim Ḥabshush and Yosef Kafiḥ, 154–56; reform goals of, 155; and orthodoxy, 155–56; reviewed, 156
Drought, 18, 53, 89, 110, 142, 153

Earlocks Edict, 112–14
Economy: Yemenite Jews, 6, 67, 152; Yemen, 14, 70, 142, 144–46; Arabia, 48; Zaydīs, 78; Rasūlids, 79; Sanaa, 157; Palestine, 162
Egypt: Jewish academies in, 67, 68; commerce, 68–69; Jewish migration to, 69; immigration to Aden, 144
Eilat (harbor), 33
Eldad the Danite (explorer), 3–4
Election, divine, 97
Elijah, Prophet, 133, 147, 148
England, Jews in, 163
Enlightenment, 154
Epistle to Yemen, 58, 61, 67–68, 70–75 *passim*
Eroticism: and works of Shalom Shabazi, 93–96 *passim*
Ethiopians: Christianization of, 46
Europe: immigration to Aden, 144; influence on Aden, 145
Excavation: Arabia, 33; Bet-She[c]arim, 40
Exodus, new, 97
Ezra the Scribe: curse of, 4–6; Jews' grudge against, examined, 6–7; and Spanish Jews, 7; and Torah, 63

Faddak (Jewish colony), 49–50
Fadlī Pasha, 88
Famine: effect on Yemenites, 3; in Jewish writings, 10–11; and Yemenite economy, 14; and mobility, 18; and anarchy, 53; in Sanaa, 89, 142, 157; and messianism, 104–05, 153; frequency of, 110; and Turks in Yemen, 122
al-Faq[c]a: and exile to Mauza[c], 121
Fayyūmī, Daniel, Rabbi, 80
Fayyūmī, Ibn: polemics against Islam, 60; on Jews as chosen, 62, 63; and

Qur' ān, 64; and Muḥammad, 65–66; and *Bustān al ᶜUqūl, 71*
Fayyūmī, Jacob Natan'el, 70
Fire: worship of, 46
Folktales, Yemenite Jewish: rural life in, 17–18; Muslims and Jews in, 18; and Israel, 167
Frankincense: use of, 28; trade, 28, 32, 48
Frumkin, Israel, 161, 163

Gad (tribe), 28, 148
Gallus, Aelius (Prefect of Egypt), 39, 40
Gamli'eli, Nissim B., 52
Gedor: Simeonites' raid of, examined, 29
Ge Ḥizzayon: and Sabbatai Ṣevi, 103–04
Generation of Reason. See Dor-Deᶜah
Geniza Documents, 67–72 *passim*
Glaser, E. (traveler), 136, 154
Gold trade, 28, 32

Ḥabshush, Ḥayyim (chronicler): and *History of the Jews in Yemen,* 20–21; on al-Hādī, 55; and Sabbatai Ṣevi, 103, 105–09; and Seᶜadia Halevi, 105–06; historicity of, 106, 107; on Latrines or Scrapers Edict, 115; and forced conversion, 124; on exile to Mauzaᶜ, 131–32; on Shalom ᶜIrāqī, 138; and Bakīl invasion, 142, 143; and Yosef ᶜAbdallāh, 152, 153; and reform, 154–55
al-Hādī, Yaḥya: and Rassīd dynasty, 54; against non-Muslims, 54–55; and Najrān dhimmīs, 55–56. *See also* al-Rāssī, Yaḥya
al-Ḥākim, Caliph: and dress code, 101; demolition of Christian churches, 101
Hakkalir, Elᶜazar (poet), 72
Halevi, Seᶜadia, Rabbi: and messianism, 104; and Ḥayyim Ḥabshush, 105–06; and Headgear Edict, 111
Halevi, Yehuda, Rabbi: influence on Shalom Shabazi, 92
Halévy, Joseph (French scholar): and *Haskalah,* 154–55; and Ḥayyim Ḥabshush, 155
Ḥalfon, Abraham ben (poet), 80
Ḥamūd, Sharīf: and Tihāma, 141–42
al-Ḥarīrī (Muslim poet), 83
al-Ḥarīzī: rhymed-prose of, 83
Ḥashīd Muslims, 13–14
Ḥazm, Ibn: and Hebrew scriptures, 63
Headgear Edict, 111
Hebrew scriptures: Christian churches' view of, 57; and Islam, 57; distortion of, 63, 64; commentaries on, 81
Hebron, Epistle to Jews of, 115
Hebron, Jews of: and letter from Jews of Ẓurān, 130–31
Herod, King, 39–40
Ḥijāz: Jews in, 36, 49; Jews' expulsion from, 50, 51. *See also* Arabia, northern
Ḥimyar, 38, 45, 50–51
Ḥimyarites: Judaization of, 42–46 *passim;* as forebears of Yemenite Jews, discussed, 47–48
Hiram, King of Tyre: and Solomon, discussed, 31–32; commerce, 33
Historians, Arab: on wars between Muḥammad and Jews, 49
History of the Jews in Yemen, 20–21

ibn Muḥammad, Qāsim, 87
Imber, Naftali Hertz (poet), 162–63
Immigration: and Jews in Arabia, 33–34; to Aden, 144; to Israel, 159–60
Incense trade, 39
India: commerce, 68; Jews of, 140; immigration to Aden, 144
Inscriptions: Yemenite, 30; Assyrian, 30, 36; on Nabonidus, 34–35, 36; and Judaization, 47; Hebrew, 74
ᶜIrāqī, Shalom, Rabbi: and Sanaa, 16, 27; and Yemenite Jews, 27; biography, 137; disgrace of, 138; and prayer, 139
Islam: conversion to, 50; Arabia as center of, 50; expansion of, 51; and al-Hādī, 55; view of Hebrew scriptures, 57; and monotheism, 58–59; and moral perfection, 65; and Jews of Aden, 71; messianism in, 109–11; Mahdī in, 110
Islamic polemics, 59, 63, 68
Ismāᶜīl, al-Mālik al-Muᶜizz (Ayyūbid ruler of Yemen), 71
Israel: Yemenite migration to, 1–2; and kingdom of Sheba, 29–30; burial of Jews in, 38; Jewish immigration to, 159–60; Yemenite Jewish contributions to, 166–69

Jehoshaphat, King: commerce, 32–33
Jeremiah, Prophet: on Jews' return to homeland, 1; warning to Jerusalem, 25; in penitential poetry, 133
Jerusalem: and Jeremiah, 25; conditions in, 160; Jewish communities in, 162; as "paradise," 164
Jerusalem, Jews of: and Yemenite immigration, 160–61; economic aid to, 163; and messianism, 164

Jewish polemics: and Christianity, 56, 59; and Islam, 56, 59–60; and *Bustān al-ᶜUqūl,* 62; and Ḥayyim Ḥabshush, 106
Jews: Qur'ān on, 123; in Aden, 144–45
Jews, British: and Jews of Sanaa, 146
Jews, orthodox: and *Dor-Deᶜah,* 155–56
Jews, Yemenite: social standing, 4–5, 93, 102, 133, 136, 144, 149, 151, 158, 160, 162, 165–66; origins discussed, 19; conversion to Islam, 50, 55; survival of, 51–52; isolation discussed, 72, 75; social degradation of, 108–20 *passim;* and custom of earlocks, 113–14; and wine, 123; as artisans, 132; economy, 132; and exile to Mauzaᶜ, 132–33; and destruction of writings, 133; and Rabbi Yeḥia Ṣāliḥ, 139, 141; betrothal customs, 140; and Jews of India, 140; and Ottoman Turks, 148, 151–52; moral conduct, 152; immigration to Israel, 159–60; and Christian colonists, 161; as laborers, 164–65; in Israel, 166–67; contributions of, 167–69
Josephus, 39–40

Kabbalism, 93
Kafiḥ, Yeḥia, Rabbi: and reform, 154–56
Kafiḥ, Yosef, Rabbi, 46
Kārib, Abū, King of Ḥimyar, 43
al-Khaṭṭāb, ᶜUmaribn, Caliph, 50, 51
Khaybar (Jewish settlement), 49
Khazars: conversion examined, 47
Kidron, Valley of, 160
Kings, Book of, 29–30
Kitāb al-Simṭ, 60
Koraḥ, ᶜAmram, Rabbi; and Yemen, 70; and Earlocks Edict, 112
Koraḥ, Shalom, Rabbi: writings of, 17
Kuḥeil, Shukr (false messiah), 147–48

Lamentation (theme): as literary convention, 16–17; in Yemenite Jewish literature, 133–35, 139
Land of the Devils. *See* Tihāma
Latrines or Scrapers Edict: Ḥayyim Ḥabshush on, 115; persistence of, 116; intensification of, 144, 146; abolished, 149; and Ottoman Turks, 151
Law, Islamic: imposed on Jews, 151
Law, Jewish: and locusts, 11; and Ḥimyar, 47
Law, Ottoman: and forced conversion, 118
Legend: Arabian Jews in, 3–8
Locusts: and Jewish law, 11; as food source, 11–12; and economy, 14

al-Mahdī (Divinely Guided One): defined, 109; in Muslim sects, 110; in Christianity, 110
al-Mahdī, Ismāᶜīl (Imām of Yemen): persecution of Jews, 106–09; and enforced conversion, 106–09, 124; and exile to Mauzaᶜ, 121–22; and religious fanaticism, 122; and expulsion of Jews, 125; death of, 132
Mahriṣ. *See* Ṣāliḥ, Yeḥia, Rabbi
Maimonides, Moses: on locusts, 11; *Epistle to Yemen,* 58, 61, 67–68, 70, 71, 75; influence of, 73–74; commentaries, 81; on Hebrew language, 94
Malabar, commerce, 69
Manasseh (tribe), 28
al-Manṣūr, ᶜAlī, (Yemenite ruler), 141
Manṣūra (Jewish writer), 124
Manuscripts: used in bookbinding, 140–41
Maranot (poetic form), 72
Marib (capital of Sheba), 31
Marriage customs: Yemenite, 3
Martyrdom, 21, 55
Mauzaᶜ, exile to: location, 121; in legend, 121–22; in Jewish writings,123, 126–32; in Muslim writings, 125; discussed, 130–32; effects of, 132–33
Medīna, 50, 51
Mediterranean region: migration of Jews in, 69; Portugese in, 82
Messiah: in works of Shalom Shabazi, 95; and vengeance, 97–98
Messiah, false: effect of, 61. *See also* ᶜAbdallāh, Yosef
Messianic age: and Ibn Fayyūmī, 63
Messianism: and Sabbatai Ṣevi, 102–04; Muslim reactions to, 104–19 *passim;* in Islam, 109–111; Muslim, 146; Yemenite Jews, 147–48; Jewish, 152–53; and immigration to Israel, 159–60; and Jews in Jerusalem, 164
Metrics, Arabic, 79
Midrash ha-Gadol, 80–81
Migration: of Jews to Arabia, discussed, 36–37; of exiles from Israel, 39; and religious persecution, 69–70; of Jews to Yemen, 69–70
Miracles, 147, 152
Mishne Torah: and Talmud, 73
Monotheism: and Islam, 58–59
Montefiore, J. M. (British Foreign Minister): and Jews in Sanaa, 146
Moses: against Amalekites, 24–25; Israelites' rebellion against, 25; law of, 64; and Muḥammad, 66
Muḥammad, Prophet: and Sayyids, 12; and Israelites, 25; and south Arabians,

48; destruction of Jewish communities, 49; and north Arabian Jews, 50; Yemenite Jews' support of, 51–52; tithes on Muslims, 55; in Qur'ān, 57; and Torah, 58; and Ibn Fayyūmī, 65; as prophet, 65–66; and messianism, 109
Mukhtar Pasha, 149, 152–53
al-Muntaẓar (Expected One), 110
Musallam (Yemenite Jewish poet), 126–27
Music: Yemenite Jewish, 167
Muslims: and protection of Yemenite Jews, 13, 124–25; in Yemenite folktales, 18; and Writ of Protection, 52–53; taxation, 100; religious persecution, 100–02; and wine, 123; enforced conversion, 123–25; and decree of Imām Yaḥia, 158
Muslims, Yemenite: and Ottoman Turks, 123, 150; economy, 132; and end of Jewish privilege, 151
Muṭahhar (Yemenite ruler), 85, 90
al-Mutawakkil, Caliph: and dhimmīs, 101; and Shalom Halevi, 145–46
Myrrh: use of, 28; trade, 28, 32, 48
Mysticism: and Talmud: 74; and works of Shalom Shabazi, 94

Nabonidus (Chaldean King), 34–36 *passim*
Nabonidus, prayer of, 36
Naḍīr, Banū (tribe): in Arabia, 39–40; battle with Muḥammad, 49
Najrān, 51, 55
al-Naqash, Suleiman, 121, 124
Nathan of Gaza, 102
Niebuhr, Carsten (Danish explorer): on Yemen, 136; on Shalom ᶜIrāqī, 138
Ninth of Av, 24–25, 26
Nuqūm, Mount, 26
Nuwās, Dhū, King of Ḥimyar: Judaization of, 43–46; historicity of sources, 44, 45–46; persecution of Christians, 44, 45, 49; mentioned, 42

Obadiah da Bertinora (Jewish explorer), 4
Operation Magic Carpet, 1, 166–67
Oral traditions, Yemenite Jewish, 21, 25–26
Orphans Edict, 117–20, 141
Ottoman Empire, 159
Ottoman Turks: and Zaydīs, 14, 87, 150–51, 156–57; occupation of Aden, 82; and Muṭahhar, 85; and Yemen, 85–86, 87, 122–23; 148–49, 156–57; in Jewish writing, 87–88; and Muslims' intolerance, 123; taxation, 150; rescind social reforms, 151; and Sanaa, 151, 157; effect on Yemenite Jews, examined, 151–52; effect on Jewish messianism, 153; and Yosef ᶜAbdallāh, 153–54; Treaty of Daᶜan, 157

Pact of ᶜUmar. *See* ᶜUmar, Pact of
Palestine: Jewish academies in, 67; poetic form, 72; conditions in, 160–61; economy, 162; and Yemenite Jews, 163–64; agriculture, 164
Paper: scarcity of, 21–22
Passover: and Bakīl invasion, 143
Pentateuch: in Qur'ān, 57–58
Persia: commerce, 68; immigration to Aden, 144
Persian Empire: rivalry with Rome, 44
Persian Gulf: commerce, 68
Philostorgius (historian), 40
Piyyuṭ (poetic form), 72
Poetry: Eretz Israelite, 79; Hebrew medieval, 86; Jewish Babylonian, 79; liturgical, 72
Poetry, Arabic, 86–87, 94–95
Poetry, Spanish Hebrew: influence on Yemenite Hebrew poetry, 79–80, 81; answer, reply form, 80; influence on *midrashim,* 80–81; influence on Shalom Shabazi, 92; eroticism in, 93; *qaṣīda,* 94–95
Poetry, Yemenite Hebrew: sources, 79–80; and Spanish Hebrew poetry, 79–80, 81
Poetry, Yemenite Jewish: and messianism, 103; inspirational role of, 135
Poll tax, 100, 150
Polygamy, 3
Prayer: and Babylon, 75; and Shalom ᶜIrāqī, 139
Printing facilities: scarcity of, 21
Punishment, divine, 22, 24

Qabbalah: and Yemenite Jews, 74; and al-Ḍahrī, 86; and Shalom Shabazi, 94; and opposition of *Dor-Deᶜah,* 156
al-Qare, Suleimān, Rabbi, 149
Qarqar, Battle of, 20
Qaṣīda (Arabic ode), 94–95
al-Qāsim, Imām, 88–89; 122–23
Qaynuqā' (tribe), 40, 49
Qur'ān: and al-Hādī, 54; Islamic view of, 57; Pentateuch in, 57–58; and Torah, 58; and Ibn Fayyūmī, 65; and discrimination by Muslims, 100, 102; intolerance of Jews in, 123
Qurayẓa (tribe), 40, 49

al-Rāssī, Yaḥia, Imām: biography, 53–54; and Treaty of Da^can, 157; and taxation of Jews, 157–58; examined, 158. *See also* al-Hādī, Yahya
Rāssid Dynasty, 54
Rasūlids, 78, 79
Red Sea: commerce, 68, 79
Redemption theme: and Shalom Shabazi, 96–98
Reform: and foreign influence, 154; and Ḥayyim Ḥabshush, 154–55; and Rabbi Kafiḥ, 154–56. *See also Dor-De^cah*
Religious persecution: of Christians, 44–45; and migration of Jews, 69–70; and Talmud, 73; in *Sefer ha Musar,* 84–86; by Fadlī Pasha, 88; and Shalom Shabazi, 93; by Muslims, 100–02; and Sabbatai Ṣevi, 104; in literature, 104–06; and Jewish messianism, 105–20 *passim;* and Pact of ᶜUmar, 122; and Zaydī Shīᶜites, 122; of Sanaa, 136–37; and Shalom ᶜIraqī, 138; and Rabbi Yeḥia Ṣāliḥ, 139; and Imām Yaḥia, 158. *See also* Bakīl, invasion; Conversion, forced; edict names; Mauzaᶜ, exile to
Reuben (tribe), 28, 148
Rhymed-prose, Hebrew, 83
Roman Empire: 44–45; expedition to Arabia, 39–40
Ruppin, Arthur, Dr. (Zionist Organization head), 165

Sabaeans, 30
Ṣaᶜdī, Saᶜīd, Rabbi: on Yemenite famine, 10–11; and *Faults of the Times,* 22, 24, 123
al-Sahūlī, Muḥammad, Judge, 115
Saᶜadia Gaon, Rabbi, 72, 75
Sālem, Abū (poet), 126
Ṣāliḥ, Yeḥia, Rabbi: and Sanaa, 16; and history of Yemenite Jews, 22; on destruction of sacred writings, 139–41; as spiritual authority, 140
Sālim, Jacob bin: letter of, 67
Sambation River, 4
Sanaa: as spiritual center, 16; political upheavals on, 16; in Yemenite writings, 17; social standing of Jews in, 27; and Rabbi Shalom ᶜIrāqī, 27, 138; internecine warfare, 85–86; turbulence in, 88–89; in poetry of Saᶜid Darin, 89; effects of exile to Mauzaᶜ on, 133; religious persecution in, 137; destruction of synagogues, 139; Bakīl attack, 142; and Jews in Aden, 145; anarchy in, 149; Yosef ᶜAbdallāh in, 153–54; and reformed Jewish school, 155–56; economy, 157
Sanaa, Jews of: persecution of, 145–46; and Turks, 151; revival of, 152
Saphir, Jacob (explorer): in Yemen, 139; on Rabbi Yeḥia Ṣāliḥ, 139; "Second Epistle to Yemen," 148
Saudi Arabia, 8, 10
Sayyid Muslims, 12–13
Scholarship: and migration, 69
Scott, Hugh (traveler), 136
Seᶜadia, Zecharia ben, Rabbi, 80
Sefer ha-Musar: didactic purpose of, 83; described, 83–84; religious persecution in, 84–86; examined, 87
Sephardim, 160, 162
Ṣevi, Sabbatai: as messiah, 102–03; literary reactions to, 102–05; and religious persecution, 105–20 *passim;* and custom of earlocks, 114
Shabazi, Shalom, Rabbi: and Sanaa, 16, 91; lamentation theme in, 17, 133; and Qabbalah, 86; on Fadlī Pasha, 88; *Ḥemdat Yamim* of, 88; contributions of, 89, 90–92, 98; literary themes, 91, 93, 133; and eroticism, 93–96 *passim;* and mysticism, 94; and messiah, 95, 97–98; sainthood of, 98–99; and Sabbatai Ṣevi, 103; and Headgear Edict, 111; on Jews as chosen, 117; and exile to Mauzaᶜ, 122, 127–30 *passim;* and forced conversion, 124; on destruction of synagogues, 126; and messianic expectations, 159
Shāfiᶜī Muslims, 12–13
Shalmaneser III, 20
Sheba, kingdom of, 29–30
Sheba, Queen of: and Solomon, 29–33 *passim;* origins discussed, 30–31; commerce, 32
Shelomo, Ḥoṭer ben, Rabbi, 81
Shipping, commercial, 48
Shīᶜites: Zaydī, 12–13; religious restrictions of, 93–94
al-Shukānī, Muḥammad (writer), 125
Sicily: commerce, 68
Simeonites, 29
Spain: commerce, 68; Hebrew literature in, 79
Spice trade, 32, 38
Social structure: of Zaydīs, 15; of Yemenite Jews, 15–18
Solomon, King: use of frankincense and myrrh, 28; and Queen of Sheba, 29–30; and Hiram, King of Tyre, discussed, 31–32; commerce, 32; wisdom, discussed, 33
Stretchers, year of the, 151
Sublime Porte, 149, 157
Suez Canal, 144, 159

Suleiman, Suleiman bin, 148
Sunnī: 12; Rasūlids, 78
Superlinear punctuation: Babylonian System, 76
Syllaeus (Nabatean commissioner), 40
Synagogue: in Jewish life, 16; destruction of, 24, 122, 125–26, 137, 139; construction of, 138, 152

Tabernacles, Feast of, 25, 153
Tālib, ᶜAli ibn Abī, 52
Talmud: Babylonian version, 72; Yemenite version, 72; study of, 73; and *Mishne Torah,* 73; and mysticism, 74; Yemenite pronunciation of, 74
Taxation, 100, 142, 150, 157–58
Teima: commercial importance of, 34; Jews in, 35–36
Temple, first: destruction of, 25, 26, 34, 37; and Jewish migration, 37
Temple, second: destruction of, 4, 5, 6, 26
Ten Lost Tribes: and Arabian Peninsula, 3–4; messianic implications, 4; in Arabia, 25; migration to Yemen, 42–43, 70; as forebears of Yemenite Jews, 48; in poetry of Naftali Hertz Imber, 162–63
Tiglat Pileser IV, 30
Tihāma: as place of exile, 128; in Jewish writings, 128–29; conquest of, 141–42
Torah: and Muḥammad, 58; falsification of, 63; familiarity with, 73; and Yemenite Jews, 95; in works of Shalom Shabazi, 95; inspirational role of, 135; destruction of, 142–43; and Kuḥeil Shukr, 148; and decree of Imām Yaḥia, 158
Tourism: effect on Yemenite Jews, 154
Travel literature: and *Sefer ha-Musar,* 83–84
Trinity: denounced by Islam, 58–59
Turkey: immigration to Aden, 144
Turks, Ottoman. *See* Ottoman Turks

ᶜUmar, Caliph. *See* al-Khaṭṭāb, ᶜUmar
ᶜUmar, Pact of: terms of, 100; and destruction of synagogues, 122; enforcement of, 137–38
al-ᶜUzairi, Shelomo ben Ḥoṭer, 104–05

Wāsiᶜī (Yemenite Muslim chronicler): on false Mahdīs, 110–11
Wine: and persecution of Jews, 123
Writ of Protection, 52, 53, 66, 70

Yaḥia, Imām. *See* al-Hādī, Yaḥya; al-Rāssī, Yaḥia
Yanai (poet), 72
Yemen: exploration of, 8; physical features, 8, 10; and Saudi Arabia, 8, 10; "Arabic" nature of, 18; settlement of Jews in, 51; internal conflict, 53, 60–61, 141–42, 145; conquest by Ayyūbids, 60–61; Jewish migration to, 69–70; economy, 70, 132, 142, 144–46; religious atmosphere of, 94; as sacred land, 123; and exile to Mauzaᶜ, 132; commerce, 136; taxation, 142; and Imām Yaḥia, 157–58; in Ottoman Empire, 159. *See also* Arabia, southern
Yemenite Laborers, Council of, 166
Yemen Refugee Fund, 163
Yeshaᶜya, Netan'el ben, Rabbi, 81
Yeshivot (Jewish academies), 68
Yosse, Yosse ben, 72

Zāhir, Dahoōd bin Sālem (poet), 125–26
Zaranīq Muslims, 13–14
Zayd, Imām, 12
Zaydī Muslims: identified, 12; tribal autonomy, 13; social segregation of, 15; commerce, 78; and Rasūlids, 78; internecine hostility, 78, 82; and Ottoman Turks, 87, 150; and Yemenite Jews, 88; fanaticism of, 101–02; and Treaty of Daᶜan, 161; Shīᶜites, 122
Zionist Organization, 164, 165
Zohar: and al-Ḍahrī, 86
Ẓurān, Jews of: letter to Jews of Hebron, 130–31